Europe's Cold War Relations

New Approaches to International History

Series Editor:

Thomas Zeiler, Professor of American Diplomatic History, University of Colorado Boulder, USA

New Approaches to International History covers international history during the modern period and across the globe. The series incorporates new developments in the field, such as the cultural turn and transnationalism, as well as the classical high politics of state-centric policymaking and diplomatic relations. Written with upper level undergraduate and postgraduate students in mind, texts in the series provide an accessible overview of international, global and transnational issues, events and actors.

Published:

Decolonization and the Cold War, edited by Leslie James and Elisabeth Leake (2015)

Cold War Summits, Chris Tudda (2015)

The United Nations in International History, Amy Sayward (2017)

Latin American Nationalism, James F. Siekmeier (2017)

The History of United States Cultural Diplomacy, Michael L. Krenn (2017)

International Cooperation in the Early Twentieth Century, Daniel Gorman (2017)

Women and Gender in International History, Karen Garner (2018)

International Development, Corinna Unger (2018)

The Environment and International History, Scott Kaufman (2018)

Forthcoming:

The International LGBT Rights Movement, Laura Belmonte

Canada and the World since 1867, Asa McKercher

Reconstructing the Postwar World, Francine McKenzie

The History of Oil Diplomacy, Christopher R. W. Dietrich

The First Age of Industrial Globalization, Maartje Abbenhuis and Gordon Morrell

Global War, Global Catastrophe, Maartje Abbenhuis and Ismee Tames

Europe's Cold War Relations

The EC Towards a Global Role

Edited by
Ulrich Krotz, Kiran Klaus Patel and Federico Romero

BLOOMSBURY ACADEMIC
LONDON • NEW YORK • OXFORD • NEW DELHI • SYDNEY

BLOOMSBURY ACADEMIC
Bloomsbury Publishing Plc
50 Bedford Square, London, WC1B 3DP, UK
1385 Broadway, New York, NY 10018, USA

BLOOMSBURY, BLOOMSBURY ACADEMIC and the Diana logo
are trademarks of Bloomsbury Publishing Plc

First published in Great Britain 2020

Series design: Catherine Wood
Cover image: Aerial view of the marble mosaic with the compass rose
at the foot of the Monument to the Discoveries, Lisbon, Portugal (2018)
(© Peek Creative Collective/Alamy Stock Photo)

A catalogue record for this book is available from the British Library.

A catalog record for this book is available from the Library of Congress.

ISBN: HB: 978-1-3501-0451-8
        ePDF: 978-1-3501-0452-5
        eBook: 978-1-3501-0453-2

Series: New Approaches to International History

Typeset by Integra Software Services Pvt. Ltd.
Printed and bound in Great Britain

Contents

Part Three Reflections and Conclusions

Illustrations

Figures

Tables

Contributors

Elena Calandri is Associate Professor at the University of Padua. Her recent publications include "Understanding the EEC Mediterranean Policy: Trade, Security, Development and the Redrafting of Mediterranean Boundaries", in *European Integration in a Globalizing World 1970–1985*, ed. Claudie Hiepel (Baden-Baden: Nomos Verlag, 2014), 165–184; *Prima della globalizzazione, L'Italia, la cooperazione allo sviluppo e la Guerra* fredda (Padova: CEDAM, 2013); *Détente in Cold War Europe. Politics and Diplomacy in the Mediterranean and the Middle East* (London, I. B. Tauris, 2012) (ed. with Daniele Caviglia and Antonio Varsori).

Lucia Coppolaro is Rita Levi Montalcini tenured researcher at the Department of Political and Juridical Sciences and International Studies of the University of Padova (Italy). She holds a Ph.D. in History from the European University Institute, Florence (2006). She was a post-doctoral researcher at the Institute of Social Sciences of the University of Lisbon and a visiting professor at the Department of Economy and Business of the Universitat Pomepu Fabra (Barcelona). She has written widely on GATT and the European Union's trade policy, and she has published articles in journals including *Contemporary European History* and *International History Review*. Her recent publications on the topic include: "In search of power. The European Commission in the Kennedy Round negotiations (1963–1967)", in *Contemporary European History*, Vol. 23:1, (2014), 23–41; *The Making of a World Trading Power. The European Economic Community (EEC) in the GATT Kennedy Round Negotiations (1963–1967)* (Farnham, UK; Aldershot, Burlington, VT: Ashgate, 2013); "U.S. policy on European integration during the GATT Kennedy Round negotiations (1962–1967): the last Hurrah of America's Europeanists," in *International History Review*, Vol. 33:3, (2011), 409–429.

Enrico Fardella is Tenured Associate Professor at the History Department of Peking University (PKU) and Director of PKU's Center for Mediterranean Area Studies (CMAS, 北京大学地中海区域研究中心). In this capacity he jointly works with TOChina Hub as director of the ChinaMed Project and Area Director of the ChinaMed Business Program. He is Global Fellow of Woodrow Wilson International Center for Scholars in Washington D.C., Research Scholar at the Machiavelli Center for Cold War Studies, member of the Academic Committee at Pangoal Institution in Beijing and Fellow of the Science & Technology China Program of the European Commission. Enrico is also managing editor of OrizzonteCina monthly review focusing on China's relations with Europe and the greater Mediterranean region. His fields of interests are: Chinese foreign policy; Sino-European relations; China's role in the Mediterranean; the Belt and Road Initiative; History of international relations; History of contemporary China.

Giuliano Garavini is currently Senior Research Fellow in the Humanities at New York University Abu Dhabi. He has mainly written about European integration, decolonization and the Global South, and the history of energy and petroleum. He is the author among others of "After Empires. European Integration, Decolonization and the Challenge from the Global South, 1957–1986" (OUP, 2012), and has recently co-edited "Oil Shock. The 1973 Crisis and its Economic Legacy" (IB Tauris, 2016), and "Counter-Shock. The Oil Counter-Revolution of the 1980s" (IB Tauris, 2018). His latest book "Petrostates. The Rise and Fall of OPEC in the 20th Century", will come out in 2019 with Oxford University Press.

Konrad H. Jarausch is the Lurcy Professor of European Civilization at the University of North Carolina at Chapel Hill and a former director of the Centre for Contemporary History in Potsdam. He has written or edited about fifty books in modern German and European history and has held some forty-five grants. His most important publications include *Out of Ashes: A New History of Europe in the Twentieth Century* (Princeton: Princeton University Press, 2015); Broken Lives: How Ordinary Germans Experienced the Twentieth Century (Princeton: Princeton University Press, 2018); *Shattered Past: Reconstructing German Histories* (Princeton: Princeton University Press, 2002).

Eirini Karamouzi is Lecturer in Contemporary History, University of Sheffield, and author of *Greece, the EEC and the Cold War, 1974–1979: The Second Enlargement* (Basingstoke: Palgrave Macmillan, 2014).

Ulrich Krotz is Professor at the European University Institute, where he holds the Chair in International Relations in the Political Science Department and the Robert Schuman Centre for Advanced Studies, and serves as Director of the programme on Europe in the World in the Global Governance Programme at the Schuman Centre. His publications include *Shaping Europe: France, Germany, and Embedded Bilateralism from the Elysée Treaty to Twenty-First Century Politics* (with Joachim Schild) (Oxford: Oxford University Press, 2013; paperback edition 2015); *History and Foreign Policy in France and Germany* (Basingstoke: Palgrave Macmillan, 2015); and *Flying Tiger: International Relations Theory and the Politics of Advanced Weapons* (Oxford: Oxford University Press, 2011).

Wilfried Loth is Professor Emeritus of Modern and Contemporary History at the University of Duisburg-Essen. His most recent publications include *Building Europe: A History of European Unification* (Berlin: De Gruyter, 2015; paperback edition 2017); *Disintegration and Integration in East-Central Europe, 1919–post-1989* (Baden-Baden: Nomos, 2014) (ed. with Nicolae Paun); *Global Interdependence: The World after 1945 (A History of the World, Vol. 6)*, with Akira Iriye et al. (Cambridge, MA: Harvard University Press, 2014); Die Rettung der Welt. Entspannungspolitik im Kalten Krieg 1950–1991 (Frankfurt, New York: Campus, 2016).

N. Piers Ludlow is Associate Professor in International History at the London School of Economics. His most recent publications include "Safeguarding British Identity or

Betraying It? The Role of British 'Tradition' in the Parliamentary Great Debate on EC Membership, October 1971," *Journal of Common Market Studies,* 53 (2015), 18–34; "The Real Years of Europe?: U.S. West European Relations during the Ford Administration," *Journal of Cold War Studies,* 15 (2013), 136–161; *The European Community and the Crises of the 1960s: Negotiating the Gaullist Challenge* (London: Routledge, 2006).

Charles S. Maier is the Leverett Saltonstall Research Professor of History at Harvard University. His most recent publications include *Once within Borders: Territories of Power, Wealth, and Belonging since 1500* (Cambridge, MA: Harvard University Press, 2016); *Recasting Bourgeois Europe: Stabilization in France, Germany, and Italy in the Decade after World War I* (Princeton: Princeton University Press, 1975; reprinted 1988 and for a 40th anniversary edition in 2015, and translated into Italian and Spanish); *Leviathan 2.0: Inventing Modern Statehood* (Cambridge, MA: Harvard University Press, 2014).

Kiran Klaus Patel is Professor of European history at Ludwig Maximilians University in Munich after professorial appointments in Maastricht and at the EUI in Florence. In 2014–2015, he was the Gerda Henkel Visiting Professor at the London School of Economics and the German Historical Institute London. His most recent publications include *European Integration and the Atlantic Community in the 1980s* (New York: Cambridge University Press, 2013) (ed. with Kenneth Weisbrode); *The Historical Foundations of EU Competition Law* (Oxford: Oxford University Press, 2013) (ed. with Heike Schweitzer); and *The New Deal: A Global History* (Princeton: Princeton University Press, 2016).

Angela Romano is a Senior Research Fellow at the European University Institute and invited Lecturer at the Faculty of Economics, University of Rome Tor Vergata. Her publications include *From Détente in Europe to European Détente. How the West Shaped the Helsinki CSCE* (Brussels: Peter Lang, 2009); "Untying Cold War Knots: The European Community and Eastern Europe in the long 1970s," *Cold War History,* 14 (2014), 153–173. She is currently working on her second monograph, which analyzes the broad Ostpolitik of the European Community in the 1970s–1980s (London: Routledge, *forthcoming*), and 'Re-designing Military Security in Europe: Cooperation and Competition between the European Community and NATO during the early 1980s', European Review of History 24:3 (2017), 445–471.

Federico Romero is Professor of History of Post-War European Cooperation and Integration at the European University Institute in Florence In addition, he is one of two directors of the "A. De Gasperi Research Center of the History of European Integration" at EUI. His most recent publications include "Cold War Historiography at the Crossroads", *Cold War History,* 14 (2014), 685–703; *International Summitry and Global Governance: The Rise of the G7 and the European Council, 1974–1991* (London: Routledge, 2014) (ed. with Emmanuel Mourlon-Druol); "European Socialist regimes facing globalisation and European co-operation: dilemmas and responses", special issue of the "*European Review of History*", 21:2 (2014) (ed. with Angela Romano); *Storia guerra fredda: l'ultimo conflitto per l'Europa* (Turin: Einaudi, 2009).

Albrecht Rothacher is a Principal Administrator in the Russia division of the European External Action Service in Brussels. During 2011–2015 he served as a Minister Counsellor at the Delegation of the European Union to Japan. He has written several books on Japan. His doctoral thesis at the London School of Economics was on *Economic Diplomacy between the European Community and Japan 1959–1981*. For a number of years he was the editor-in-chief of the *Asia–Europe Journal* of the Asia–Europe Foundation in Singapore.

Katja Seidel is Senior Lecturer in History at the University of Westminster. Among her recent publications are "Contested Fields: The Common Agricultural Policy and the Common Fisheries Policy," *The European Commission 1973–1986: History and Memory of an Institution*, ed. Eric Bussière et al. (Luxembourg: Office for Official Publications of the European Communities, 2014), 313–336; *The Process of Politics in Europe: The Rise of European Elites and Supranational Institutions* (London: IB Tauris, 2010); "The Challenges of Enlargement and GATT Trade Negotiations: Explaining the Resilience of the European Community's Common Agricultural Policy in the 1970s," The International History Review (February 2019).

Kenneth Weisbrode is Assistant Professor of History at Bilkent University in Ankara. His recent publications include *Old Diplomacy Revisited: A Study in the Modern History of Diplomatic Transformations* (New York: Palgrave Macmillan, 2014); *European Integration and the Atlantic Community in the 1980s* (New York: Cambridge University Press, 2013) (ed. with Kiran Klaus Patel); *A Brief History of Americanism* (Washington, DC: American Historical Association, 2013).

Acknowledgments

We wish to thank all of the institutions and individuals who helped to realize the project that led to this book. First, we express our appreciation to the Research Council of the European University Institute (EUI) for its generous support. Kiran Klaus Patel would also like to thank the European Union's Erasmus+ program for awarding him a Jean Monnet Chair (Decision n. 2014–2974/001–001), which complemented the funds provided by the EUI. These two funding sources allowed us to host two workshops to discuss preliminary drafts of the various chapters of this book. The first, planned to take place at Maastricht University's Brussels Campus in November 2015, was made impossible by the city's lockdown after a series of terrorist attacks and had to be relocated to Maastricht on short notice. We are grateful for our contributors' flexibility and perseverance, which made the meeting a success despite the difficult circumstances. The second workshop, hosted in Florence by the EUI's Robert Schuman Centre for Advanced Studies in June 2016, went smoothly and allowed us to make further progress with this project.

For administrative support of the workshop in Brussels/Maastricht, we thank Anja Servais; for the one in San Domenico, we recognize the Schuman Centre's conference unit, in particular Monique Cavallari and Elisabetta Spagnoli. We are grateful to Lindsay Aqui, Meredith Dale, Masha Hedberg, Richard Maher and Sarah Tarrow for their superb editorial work. Eva Durlinger and Ismay Milford helped us enormously in polishing the book's various chapters.

At Bloomsbury, it was a great pleasure to work with Maddie Holder and Dan Hutchins.

List of Abbreviations

ACP	African Caribbean and Pacific Group
CAP	Common Agricultural Policy
CCP	Chinese Communist Party
CCP	Common Commercial Policy
CET	Common External Tariff
CMEA	Council for Mutual Economic Assistance
CoCom	Coordinating Committee for Multilateral Export Controls
COMECON	Council for Mutual Economic Assistance
COREPER	Committee of Permanent Representatives
CSCE	Conference on Security and Cooperation in Europe
DAC	Development Assistance Committee
DG	Directorate General
EAD	Euro-Arab Dialogue
EBRD	European Bank for Reconstruction and Development
EC	European Community
ECSC	European Coal and Steel Community
EDC	European Defence Community
EDF	European Development Fund
EEC	European Economic Community
EFTA	European Free Trade Association
EPC	European Political Cooperation
ESA	European Space Agency
EU	European Union
EUR	Bureau of European Affairs
EURATOM	European Atomic Energy Community
FAO	Food and Agriculture Organisation

FDI	Foreign Direct Investment
FIDES	*Fonds d'investissement pour le développement économique et social*
FLN	National Liberation Front
FTA	Free Trade Area
GATS	General Agreement on Trade in Services
GATT	General Agreement on Tariffs and Trade
GMP	Global Mediterranean Policy
GSP	Generalized Scheme of Preferences
IPALMO	Institute for the Relations between Italy and Countries from Africa, Latin America, Middle and Far East
IR	International Relations
ISA	International Sugar Agreement
LDP	Liberal Democratic Party
MENA	Middle East and North Africa Region
MFN	Most Favoured Nation
MITI	Ministry of International Trade and Industry
NATO	North Atlantic Treaty Organization
NTBs	Non-Tariff Barriers
OAU	Organisation of African Unity
OCT	Overseas Countries and Territories
ODA	Official Development Assistance
OECD	Organisation for Economic Co-operation and Development
OEEC	Organization for European Economic Cooperation
OPEC	Organization of Petroleum Exporting Countries
PASOK	Panhellenic Socialist Movement
PLA	People's Liberation Army
PLO	Palestine Liberation Organization
POM	Pays d'Outre-Mer
PRC	People's Republic of China
PSE	Producer Support Estimate

RA	Regional Affairs
SACEUR	Supreme Allied Commander Europe
SEA	Single European Act
SEM	Single European Market
START	Strategic Arms Reduction Treaty
TEA	Trade Expansion Act
TEC	Agreement on Trade and Economic Cooperation
TMC	Third Mediterranean Countries
TRIMs	Trade-Related Investment Measures
TRIPs	Agreement of Trade-Related Aspects of Intellectual Property Rights
TTIP	Transatlantic Trade and Investment Partnership
UNCTAD	United Nations Conference on Trade and Development
UNESCO	United Nations Education, Scientific and Cultural Organization
UNRWA	United Nations Relief and Works Agency for Palestine Refugees in the Near East
UoA	Units of Account
WEU	Western European Union
WTO	World Trade Organisation

Introduction:
EC External Relations—Towards a Global Role

Kiran Klaus Patel and Federico Romero

A Nation Writ Large

In 1973, Jean Monnet's close collaborators Max Kohnstamm and Wolfgang Hager published *A Nation Writ Large? Foreign-Policy Problems before the European Community*. It came out at a time when many long-held assumptions about Europe's international relations and its place in the world had come to seem outdated. When Kohnstamm concluded its preface in December 1972, the Bretton Woods system—as the set of rules defining monetary management and financial relations among North American and Western Europen nations—was showing serious cracks. It collapsed completely just a few months later. Quite generally, transatlantic relations were in distress, with the Nixon administration (1969–1974) more critical of supranational integration in Western Europe than any of its predecessors. Superpower *détente*, the end of the thirty-year post-war economic boom, war in the Middle East and the first oil crisis: all these events and processes demonstrated that Europeans needed to rethink their role in world affairs. Against this backdrop, *A Nation Writ Large* aimed at outlining the main problems ahead. Ahead of whom? Kohnstamm chose his words carefully when he referred to the "main problems in the realm of foreign policy which confront the nations now forming the European Community." He quickly added that the book's "authors hope that within the present decade it will be possible to speak of the foreign policy of the European Community," while "they are under no illusion concerning the difficulties that have to be overcome before this can be the case."[1]

We now know that in 1980, the European Community (EC) still had no foreign policy to speak of, at least when compared to the instruments and impact of national foreign policies.[2] It was not until the Maastricht Treaty of 1992, building on small inroads in this policy domain, that the Common Foreign and Security Policy was created, with many other steps to follow. Even today, the precise role and nature of the European Union's international relations remain contested. The European Union (EU) has become one of the globe's economic superpowers, but on other dimensions, such as security, it has remained a dwarf. Moreover, the very nature of the beast remains unclear—sometimes identified as a power, a center of gravity, a model, a regime or merely an arena, or a combination of some of these factors.[3] It certainly has not replaced traditional national foreign policies, and in many other ways too, the EC and then the EU have failed to turn into a nation writ large.

Having said this, a book with the title Kohnstamm and Hager chose would have been improbable or at least highly presumptuous just a decade earlier, some five years after the Treaties of Rome and more than a decade after the Schuman Declaration. The nascent European Community of the 1950s and 1960s had a rather technical focus and restricted powers, mainly in the fields of coal, steel, nuclear energy and the common market. In the area of external relations, the Treaties of Rome left the European Community's overall authority vague and only spelled out powers for specific policy domains such as trade.[4] After failed attempts to venture into security, first under supranational auspices in the early 1950s and again during the early 1960s in an intergovernmental framework, the daily work of the EC remained largely outside the realm of high politics. European integration commenced with a strong focus on relations between its member states, much less than as an international actor positioning itself vis-à-vis the wider world. By the early 1970s, however, this had changed notably. By now, some Europeans felt that a more visible role for the Community in international relations was desirable, and that it was also realistic. Another twenty years later, the Maastricht Treaty aimed at creating a legal and administrative platform for the EU to fulfill the role of an international actor. In doing so, it did not just create a springboard to give the EU a more robust and visible global role, but also systematized and summarized developments that had unfolded incrementally over the preceding decades. While not replacing national foreign policies, integration under the banner of the EC/EU did fundamentally change Europe's international relations and its place in the world.

The essays in this volume offer a comprehensive review and analysis of the EC's external relations during the Cold War from the 1950s to the Maastricht Treaty, and in particular their broader impact and significance, tracing the multifaceted and often discrete ways in which the EC became an actor in world affairs. While it is true that the EC did not develop a clear-cut foreign policy during the Cold War, it did deploy a long list of other means to interact with the world.

This book pursues three main goals. First, to bring together in a single volume the analysis of foreign relations over the entire EC period and across all relevant policy domains. Second, to systematically relate the EC external projections to the broader international context, and particularly to the Cold War system and its dynamics. Finally, to connect and compare historical analysis with the categories and concepts used by International Relations (IR) scholars, in an interdisciplinary conversation on the matter that is long overdue.

Why EC External Relations Matter

The analysis of the history of these external relations is important for three reasons. First, because this early trajectory has had a massive impact on more recent developments. Anyone seeking to understand the external and foreign policies of today's EU, including their rationales, capabilities, and future potentials, ought to be aware of their preconfiguration during the Cold War. What almost sounds like a truism is not reflected in the state of the art. Scholarly attention focuses mostly on the period since the 1990s, on the aspirations for a bigger EU role nourished by the Maastricht Treaty, the failed attempts to manage the violent disintegration of Yugoslavia and the post-Maastricht approaches to develop autonomous EU capabilities in the foreign policy, security, and defense realms. It was also only in the 1990s that research on the EU's external and foreign relations turned into a visible research field. Still, the developments, discussion, and drama of the EU's interaction with the wider world since the 1990s can only be understood against the backdrop of the earlier history of the EC's external relations.

Second, and more important from a historical vantage point, each of our empirical-historical chapters covers the entire period from 1957 to 1992. They thus bring together strands of historical research on the EC's international projection and role that have been understudied or addressed only in isolation. So far, historical analyses of sectoral, policy-specific or single-country relations have progressed unevenly and mostly focused on rather short spans of time (often less than a decade). Above all, they have not been unified in a coherent and cohesive analysis that covers the whole Cold War period. In identifying and explaining overarching trends, key decisions, historical conjunctions and inflection points—as well as the role of specific actors and institutions and how they evolved during this period—each chapter offers a comprehensive analysis of the individual subject it investigates, including the main scholarly literature, debates, and findings relevant to the topic. Together, the chapters help to reconceptualize the long arc of the EC's international role from its inception in the 1950s to the end of the Cold War.

Third, and finally, external relations were central to the overall trajectory of the European Community, even if their profile remained below the hopes of Kohnstamm, Hager, and others. External relations are key to understanding why, in the course of less than four decades, the EC turned into the central organization of international cooperation and integration in (Western) Europe—a position its supporters had always aspired to, but that it did not clearly occupy at the beginning of the process in comparison to other organizations such as the Council of Europe or the Organisation for Economic Co-operation and Development (OECD).[5] Its trade and development policies supply examples of how it projected power toward other world regions and incrementally developed what Kohnstamm and Hager called the EC's "European personality"—that it became a meaningful actor in its own right, beyond the sum of its member states.[6] It developed such qualities for internal reasons, but also as others came to accept its legitimacy over time, its power and its very existence: the Eastern bloc moved in this direction at an informal level from the late 1960s, though officially, socialist countries only recognized the EC in 1988/89. Perhaps even more important was the sustained American support of European integration, despite the EC's trade policies challenging certain US commercial interests, particularly in the field of agriculture. Washington's willingness to tolerate this was an important factor in the EC's external relations, and one that facilitated further integration within the European Community. The EC's "actorness," as some political scientists call it, depended heavily on its external relations—not only for its place in the world, but also as a determining factor for its trajectory within Western Europe and for its member states.[7]

The road to becoming an actor of this kind was full of twists and turns. Our volume identifies and examines the factors that at the various junctures either supported or impeded Europe's international projection and the EC's development into a more prominent and efficient international player while also emphasizing the limits of its role and remit.

In doing so, we explore the substance of the EC's external relations—including its policy goals, instruments, achievements and difficulties—as well as the rhetoric and discourse that surrounded its emergence during this period. Since many grand aspirations remained unrealized, it is central to distinguish actual policy from public debates and declarations; while at the same time, books such as *A Nation Writ Large* serve as a reminder that when assessing the factors that have propelled, shaped, and limited the growth and expansion of EC external relations, public debates, and far-flung aspirations sometimes created the fertile ground upon which later political initiatives were built.

Organization of the Book

The book is organized in three parts, each of which examines a different dimension of the European Community's external relations. After an opening survey that situates the EC in the history of the Cold War, the contributions in Part One investigate the Community's relations with key countries and world regions. The mix includes a chapter on the United States, as Western Europe's benevolent hegemon in the post-1945 era, but also a chapter on the socialist world that initially denied the EC's legitimacy and right of existence. Beyond these two extremes in the international spectrum, the chapter on Japan examines the relationship to a state that provoked many concerns in Western Europe in the period from the 1970s to the 1990s. At the time, Japan was a major industrial competitor to whose aggressive export and protectionist import policies the EC had to find a strong reply. China, in contrast, remained a much smaller trade partner and rival throughout the Cold War period; our inclusion of a chapter on it reflects its importance in our own times.[8] As a final world region, the volume includes a contribution on the Mediterranean, as the EC's complex landscape of southern neighboring countries where post-colonial legacies, Cold War concerns, and globalization often intersected.

Part Two focuses on EC activities within key policy areas and domains. The European Community's restricted role in security and foreign policies and the fate of attempts to expand its remit in these fields form one center of attention. Yet such mundane fields as trade, agricultural policy, and development—each of which is discussed in a separate chapter—represent another. The EC's powers concentrated on these issues with clear implications for questions of the Cold War, North–South relations in a post-colonial world, and the history of globalization. We also discuss enlargement policies, here seen in part as a powerful tool of external relations. In doing so, each of the chapters factors in the specificities of the policy domain or policy instrument at stake.

As in Part One, all chapters evaluate and interpret the scope and nature of EC external relations, including its main drivers, the various policy goals, and objectives pursued, instruments and strategies deployed, key actors involved, and record of achievement. Wherever necessary, they also consider the relationship between EC policies and those of its various member states and convey a summary of the views of the state or world region with which the European Community interacted. The chapter on enlargement, for instance, also accounts for the applicants' views of the EC. In Part One, perceptions of the EC in the United States, Japan, China and the socialist countries also form part of the analysis. Some chapters, however, deal with an external environment that is extremely diverse or consists of a whole range of governments and states; examples include the contributions on development policy and the Mediterranean. Given the vast range of views in these cases, it remains impossible to go into detail on external opinions about the EC. However, even these chapters illustrate the contradictions and tensions that gave rise to negative or doubtful opinions on EC region-wide programs.

Part Three, lastly, offers reflections and conclusions on the empirical-historical chapters from a set of different perspectives. The contributions by Konrad H. Jarausch and Charles S. Maier contextualize the development of the EC's external relations in the wider frameworks of the histories of post-war international relations and the histories of European societies, and link the empirical findings of the Cold War period to the more recent development of the EU's capacity to act as an international actor on the global scene. The third chapter in this section, by Ulrich Krotz, offers a complementary perspective. Adding an explicitly interdisciplinary angle to the book, he discusses the theoretical and methodological implications of our historical findings on debates in International Relations, and examines how against this backdrop, history sheds new light on present and future developments.

Together, the book's three parts investigate the EC's relations with key countries and world regions while also providing the necessary contexts of Cold War, international, and European history in which to assess them and bring them into a dialogue with the empirical findings and theoretical questions driving research on the post-Cold War period.

The *Doppelgänger* Problem: Concepts and Historical Findings

When examining the EC's external relations—with the double goal of conceptualizing its nature and achievements as an international actor, and situating it in the broader sweep of post-World War II international history—we are immediately faced with a set of dilemmas and paradoxes. The first one concerns the very nature of the EC (and its immediate predecessors the European Coal and Steel Community (ECSC) and the European Economic Community (EEC), or Common Market, and Euratom). Neither a full-fledged super-state nor a plain international organization, it does not lend itself easily to comparisons with the classical agents of international relations.

Should its external relations be assessed against the template of the modern nation-state, particularly the most wealthy and influential ones with their great-power prerogatives and pretensions? Or rather against imperial formations that incorporate different communities and populations in a constantly renegotiated hierarchical order, while reshaping its surroundings and purporting to spread a normative order in and around its peripheries? A further option would be to set it in a comparative gaze at the many international organizations—OECD, the European Free Trade Association (EFTA), the General Agreement on Tariffs and Trade (GATT), the North Atlantic Treaty Organization (NATO) etc.—with which the EC interacted, and to a certain extent competed, in the multifaceted effort of managing the Western economies and coordinating the ideational and strategic posture of the Atlantic West.

None of the chapters explicitly opts for a single template from among these since the exclusive use of any one of them would be narrow, constraining, and ultimately inadequate. And yet, most of the chapters that deal with the "high-politics" realm of foreign and security policy implicitly—perhaps inevitably—frame their analysis around categories and concepts typical of the great-power state, while insightfully foregrounding the many ways and dimensions in which the EC fell short of, or diverged from, that model. N. Piers Ludlow tackles the relationship with the Cold War system and its dynamics. He identifies the many ways in which the East–West antagonistic partition of the continent shaped the environment and defined the ground rules within which integration could thrive. In a similar vein, Konrad H. Jarausch aptly comments on the "formative impact of the Cold War" system upon the EC, and of the profound ways in which anti-Communist ideology shaped its outlook.

Ludlow also emphasizes the inverse relationship, i.e. the facilitating function that European integration played in the cohesiveness of the Atlantic alliance—first and foremost by cementing the key Franco-German compact. This was, after all, the primary reason for US sustained support for the integration project, as Kenneth Weisbrode makes clear in his refined analysis of the nuanced interconnection between trans-Atlantic interdependence and a gradually rising but still subsidiary EC independence. Both authors indicate that only the end of the Cold War opened up a new landscape in which the EC (now morphed into the EU) could imagine to transcend its previous role as "supporting cast member" (Ludlow) of the Western compact.

Whether the EU actually rose to such a challenge is, of course, quite a different matter that falls beyond the chronological confines of this book. In any case, Ludlow, Weisbrode, and also Wilfried Loth (the latter's contribution focuses fully on security and foreign policy), converge in stressing how the Cold War Atlantic framework operated as a precondition for European integration and, simultaneously, as a powerful, crucial obstacle against the transformation of the EC into the kind of full-fledged foreign policy actor that Kohnstamm, Hager, Monnet, and others hoped for. If Charles de Gaulle saw, and suffered, the Atlantic compact as a suffocating constraint, the governments of other member states—and the West European political elites at large—consistently maintained a priority for trans-Atlantic solidarity as the key condition for international peace, the safest guarantee of European stability and, last but not least, a welcome barrier to the hegemonic rise of any single member state.

This last point is particularly elaborated by Loth. More forcefully than other authors, he argues for a fundamental, recurrent impetus to a foreign policy identity and role as one of "the driving forces" behind the establishment and development of the EC. But he also sees—like other contributors—the key prerogatives maintained by the stronger member states. They jealously preserved the essential nexus between national sovereignty and security. They retained an exclusive role on defence issues and a primary one in managing relationships with the United States (and the USSR). They unfailingly prioritized intergovernmental structures of foreign-policy coordination (like the European Political Cooperation (EPC), introduced in 1970) upon any genuinely integrative solution. Whether this derived from a fundamental imprint of European integration as the Milwardian *rescue of the nation-state*, as Charles S. Maier suggests, remains a controversial issue.[9] However, if one wants to find a point of convergence, a minimum common denominator among these chapters (and Konrad H. Jarausch's comment about them), is Maier's image of the Community as "a certain non-presence as compared to its component nation-states … a *Doppelgänger*, accompanying the nations that created it" seems quite appropriate, almost inescapable.[10]

Elena Calandri's essay on the Mediterranean vividly confirms that the Cold War system and the ways in which the major member states decided to play their cards in it were the key explanatory factors for this circumscribed role of EC external relations. Commercial interests, energy issues, and post-colonial legacies had a dense, substantial relevance in this directly neighboring area, and in the Middle East often conflated with it. And yet, the EC's many, often clumsy attempts at building a role of its own in the area were primarily driven by Cold War oriented concerns for stabilization. Even more cogently, those efforts always found a "glass ceiling" (Calandri) in the great-power dynamics that played out in the area, and especially the strong hegemonic role played by the United States, which reduced the EC initiatives to a declaratory function with very limited clout. As both Weisbrode and Maier point out, as much as the United States valued the EC role in consolidating trans-Atlantic interdependence, it would not countenance its ascent as an autonomous actor in the great-power game and in far-flung world regions.

What Kind of Power?

Thus, the overall view of the EC as an international actor conveyed by this set of chapters appears as a rather somber one. In the power struggles that defined international relations in the post-World War II era, the EC was not a primary agent. However, such a dejected conclusion could only flow from two assumptions that—while not entirely erroneous—are nonetheless imperfect. The first one is that only the external projection of hard power defines a crucial international role. The second related assumption is that the absence of hard power depreciates every other exercise of external influence into a subordinate, lesser activity. Scholars and observers of the EC/EU have long debated this issue. Ever since François Duchêne coined the term "civilian power" in the early 1970s, EC officials and sympathetic analysts have consistently tried to defy those assumptions, by positing that the changing nature of international relations in the age of globalization makes hard power less decisive, while the normative power deployed by the EC/EU would be more relevant to the current conditions of multiple and tighter interdependencies.[11] This claim of an entirely new type of power (rule-based, value-oriented, and fully steeped in multilateral arrangements), upon which the EC/EU built no small part of its own self-representation, was not only criticized but even ridiculed as a historical, particularly by contrasting it to a more "realist" American appreciation of strategic power.[12]

This book's chapters try to go beyond this rigid, stale binary. Throughout the historical chapters and most systematically in Ulrich Krotz's conclusive discussion, the nature of EC power (or lack of) is assessed and conceptualized in its various nuances. Yes, the EC did not become a centralized state flexing its muscles across oceans and foreign lands. But the methodological nationalism underlying such an understanding of the EC/EU, which ignores its unique features, stands in the way of a more nuanced picture. As Maier himself reminds us, the European Community's role as a fundamental stabilizing factor in post-war Europe—as a key consolidator of prosperous democracies first in Germany and Italy, then across Southern Europe, and eventually in most of Central-Eastern Europe—is an international relations achievement of historical proportions. It embodied, and eventually came to symbolize, the shift from war to peace in Europe's twentieth-century history. More crucially, it buttressed the very international order that for a long time made the projection of the EC's hard power unnecessary for its own well-being.

Moreover, the deliberate projection and indirect reach of the EC's influence proved to be very significant in many fields and instances. Angela Romano's essay on EC policies towards the socialist regimes demonstrates that when member states shared a clear strategic intent, and pursued it through effective institutional mechanisms of policy coordination, the EC's considerable economic power and allure could translate into relevant political influence. In the complex negotiations around the Conference on Security and Cooperation in Europe (CSCE), they defined an innovative agenda of extended East–West cooperation and exchange, they drew the USSR and the United States to accept it, and eventually shaped a long-lasting intra-European *détente* around their vision. Maier astutely comments that such an enhanced role for the EC was possible only in moments of East–West cooperation. It is no less true, though, that EC policies expanded and deepened the very nature of *détente*, gave it a far more solid and durable European dimension that survived the resurgence of superpowers' tensions, and ultimately affected the transformations of the socialist regimes way beyond the West's initial expectations.[13]

Here, as on other fronts, it is clear that by the 1970s the EC was emerging as a relevant actor with strong leverage and influence all around its borders—and it is this context that informed the book by Kohnstamm and Hager. The European Community's own enlargement is another process that reveals its power of attraction—as a vast, dynamic market, of course, but also as a community of values, a political symbol, and an institutional framework for democratic stability.

As Eirini Karamouzi explains in her chapter on enlargement as an external policy, the EC did not conceive of its first enlargement as a foreign-policy issue. It established a principle, though, that would later come to embody the EC's power to reshape rules and institutions beyond its perimeter; the applicant countries had to fully accept the EC's existing norms and practices (the so-called *acquis communautaire*). Thus, enlargement became a process not so much of international negotiation but rather of adaptation to the EC in order to get access to it. When the authoritarian right-wing regimes of Greece, Portugal, and Spain were toppled in rapid succession, those countries saw entry in the EC as a key factor not only for their economic development, but for consolidating and, ultimately, securing the democratic nature of their transitions. Thus, they projected upon the EC the aura of democracy's continental lynchpin that had previously been only implicit and low-key. The EC, on the other hand, came to see accession as the way to stabilize Southern Europe, uphold its alignment with the West and NATO and, in the process, enhance its "own power as a stabilizing factor" (Karamouzi). It was by no means irrelevant that the US government itself shared this notion of the EC as a new factor of geopolitical stabilization in an expanded Europe.

In the space of a few years, its role in East–West *détente* and its own Southern enlargement began to transform the EC into the "Europe" we so often refer to. It became a normative power with "a potentially inclusive identity" that can attract and mould beyond its borders not only by means of market force, but by its projections of social norms and cultural values, and by policy actions with geopolitical implications.[14] This specific dimension of the EC's external relations was of course to grow exponentially after 1989, culminating in the EU's big Eastern enlargement at the turn of the century. And even though the various rounds of enlargement still saw the big member states playing crucial roles—with the noticeable rise of Germany's weight—the most apt historical analogy in this case is no longer with the great power state but with empire. Expansion by inclusion, attraction as a means to stabilization, normative redefinition of spaces and relations, and the EC/EU's inherently multi-level polity are features that recall a complex imperial entity rather than a centralized and allegedly homogeneous nation-state. Thus, they open up to diverse—though still imperfect if not elusive—conceptualizations of the EC/EU's nature and international role.[15]

Regional or Global? The Scope of the EC's International Projection

However, a further conclusion on which this book's chapters converge is that such a strong, influential EC role remained largely, if not exclusively, regional. When considered in a wider, global scale, EC foreign relations appear far less influential and transformative. Powerful and increasingly determinative in Europe, the EC recedes to a far lesser actor on the global stage.

Lucia Coppolaro focuses on the EC's main area of strength—the commercial power arising from its large and advanced economy. As soon as the Common Market was established, the EC was the second most powerful global commercial actor, and soon grew to acquire the largest share of world trade. It could operate as a unified, single actor whose international status was undisputed. Yet, as she argues, it "was neither the leader of the trade regime nor its driving force." Until the 1990s, it operated primarily in a defensive rather than proactive role, protecting its own turf against the United States and other partners rather than shaping the global trading regime. Different reasons explain this self-limited role. Immediate interests were given priority over long-term goals and visions. The member states were often in conflict with each other, forcing Brussels to negotiate on the basis of a minimum common denominator defending existing arrangements. Thus, the EC accommodated its needs within the GATT's "US-led framework" even though the strength deriving by the EC's commercial reach could have warranted—at least in theory—more ambitious goals.

Albrecht Rothacher's analysis of EC relations with Japan reinforces this dismal evaluation. Usually outdone by the United States—which, at any rate, possessed far superior means of influence upon Tokyo—the EC did not really have a timely, in-depth reading of Japan's commercial ascent, nor a consistent attention to its developments, and was often hampered by its own liberal understanding of trade relations. It dealt with Japan's commercial challenges mostly in a defensive, reactive mode. Even though it gradually improved its own performance, it nonetheless remained the less effective partner vis-à-vis Tokyo's more focused goals and successful tactics. Here, once again, internal divisions and parallel, if not conflicting, policies by the member states mattered.

When considered alongside the Chinese relationship studied by Enrico Fardella, though, we can see a broader pattern that embraces the whole of East Asia. Chinese leaders looked at the EC, at least from the early 1970s, within a "calculated global strategy" that imagined the Europe they desired—i.e. an increasingly autonomous geopolitical entity capable of fostering a more multi-polar world. The EC, though, thought and operated rather differently. Rooted in a much more Western and Atlantic mind-set, it was far less bent on the rise of a multi-polar constellation of international power. Nor did it look at East Asia with a strategic lens. Throughout the 1970s and 1980s, its attention was focused on opportunities for trade and investment (which were, at any rate, still relatively limited in comparison to Japan or other markets) and on development support. Asia was, it would seem, a distant land rather than a priority for Brussels and the major member states. Dealing with the emerging economies of the Asia-Pacific was still a secondary aspect of an international outreach that long remained pivoted on the EC's immediate surroundings, on the trans-Atlantic dimension, and on relations with Europe's former colonial possessions.[16]

The EC rose when European colonial empires were being dismantled, and inherited some of their predicaments. France, in particular, lobbied very hard for the nascent EC to become a guarantor of privileged relations with its own former colonial territories, and to no small extent it succeeded. However, a systematic re-forging of post-colonial relations around an expansionary EC entrusted with post-imperial responsibilities, and therefore with an explicit global outreach, was quite a different matter. The essays by Katja Seidel and Giuliano Garavini illustrate the internal differences that separated— and to no small extent contrasted—the EC's Common Agricultural Policy (CAP) and its development aid policies. With the CAP erecting a protected market and turning Europe into a major agricultural exporter, the leverage that a large and dynamic domestic market could offer as tool of foreign influence was by and large sacrificed. As time went by, the post-colonial nations (and the developing world in general) managed to get better deals with the EC, due to shifting cultural frameworks no less than to external pressures on the EC. Yet—as Garavini points out—this did not really amount to a deliberate strategy to enhance the relevance of the EC as foreign policy actor. Eventually, those inner tensions abated as the rise of a neoliberal understanding of the EC's place in a globalizing economy forced a reform of the CAP and a shift to the conditionality paradigm in relations with the developing economies.

Thus, even though dreams of *Eurafrique* initially inspired some of the EC architects, such ambitious views of an expanded community with a world role soon took a back seat to the key compromises that defined the EC's nature and internal structure. Whether from the trade angle explored by Calandri or the development angle analyzed by Garavini, it is clear that—as Seidel writes—"conflicts between trade liberalization versus agricultural protectionism on the one hand and preference for domestic farmers versus development aims on the other, have shaped and at times even obstructed the external relations of the EC."

It was of course a matter of contrasting interests, often reflected in the administrative division of prerogatives and responsibilities among the various Directorate Generals (DG), that were difficult to reconcile. But there was more than that. The complex, multi-level structure of the EC, with its rickety combination of supranational and intergovernmental functions, meant that those policy compromises that were successful became the very pillars of the structure itself. The Common Market and the CAP, in particular, were the very "glue" (Seidel) of the entire project, its functional and symbolic foundations. For a long time they could not be eroded, bent, or endangered for the sake of foreign-policy ambitions, as they safeguarded the EC's internal cohesion. They supported the entire edifice of intergovernmental agreements that constituted the EC. In a way, they *were* the EC.

Thus, the ultimate paradox is that the primacy of its internal arrangements, which presided over the creation of the EC and shaped its functioning, hindered the development of the world role that those policies' undoubted success (an economic, but also an institutional and symbolic success) might have sustained and justified. If the temptation to a significant foreign role was always there, and certainly grew over time, its full-fledged realization remained a prisoner of the EC's original structure, conditions, and intent. Born to coordinate and enhance economic performance within an international context defined by the East–West conflict, and particularly by the trans-Atlantic allegiance of its member states, it maintained a secondary, supplementary role on foreign and security affairs. In the realm of "high politics," after all, its member states—particularly the large ones—did not want a European superpower, but rather a cooperative tool to be activated when necessary.[17]

In the more mundane—but for the EC also more crucially constitutive—realms of commerce and economic relations, on the other hand, its considerable power had to be geared, first and foremost, to pursuing the domestic goals that its internal compromises dictated. These activities certainly enhanced the EC's international influence but by and large kept it inward-focused. The European Community prioritized institution-building and neglected developing a clear global strategy.[18] Some lamented this, while others felt that a more ambitious approach was unrealistic. Richard Mayne, editor of the book that published François Duchêne's 1972 piece on Europe as a "civilian power," for instance, conceded that Europe had "important contributions to make to world peace, to international trade, and to the economic development of less favoured countries and regions." But he also contended that it "behoves Europeans to mind their own business."[19] As a consequence, external observers and representatives of third states could often only deplore the EC's somewhat parochial and self-centered outlook and priorities. Only rarely did they find ways to change them. But this self-referential tendency also impacted the development of the EC itself. As material foundations for Europe's ambitions, it helped producing the recurrent gap between expectations and realizations in the quest for a greater role for the EC as a civilian power.[20]

As the challenges inherent in the trends towards globalization became more pressing and more acutely felt, these solidly established patterns drove the EC towards a "strategy of regionalization"—eventually pivoted on the neoliberal move towards the Single Market and monetary union—that was at the same time defensive and forward looking.[21]

It should therefore not come as a surprise that the combined result of these chapters points to enlargement, as both Jarausch and Maier indicate, as the most relevant and significant expression of the EC's external role.[22] It embodied, successfully deployed and further enhanced the EC's peculiar blend of values, economic power, and institutional recipes as a unique combination of attractive, influential, effective resources.

While the European Community displayed comparably little ability to factor in the needs and interests of third countries and other world regions and to arrive at balanced results, exchanges with the wider world still had a massive impact. Ludlow, for instance, refers to Alfred Grosser, who once called Joseph Stalin Western-Europe's greatest federator. In a similar vein, Garavini quotes the French expert and politician Louis Armand, according to whom the Egyptian president Gamal Abdel Nasser deserved the same title, for it was he who cleared the path for a renewed French commitment to European integration in 1956.

Taken together, the contributions collected in this volume trace and explain the slow process by which the EC developed its external policies and attempted to define its place in an increasingly globalized world. In doing so, it did not follow the template of the modern nation-state and did not become a nation writ large. The complexities and contradictions of this development require careful historical analysis—to better understand the past, the global role of today's European Union, and future trends and options.

Notes

1   Max Kohnstamm, "Preface," in Max Kohnstamm and Wolfgang Hager (eds.), *A Nation Writ Large? Foreign-Policy Problems before the European Community* (London: Macmillan, 1973), vii.

2   Though this analogy to nation-states, often drawn by contemporaries, has serious methodological problems; see also Daniel Möckli, *European Foreign Policy during the Cold War: Heath, Brandt, Pompidou and the Dream of Political Unity* (London: I. B. Tauris, 2009).

3   For a succinct overview, see Christopher Hill, Michael Smith and Sophie Vanhoonacker, "International Relations and the European Union: Themes and Issues," in Christopher Hill, Michael Smith and Sophie Vanhoonacker (eds.), *International Relations and the European Union*, 3rd edition (Oxford: Oxford University Press, 2017), 3–22.

4   See also Pierre Pescatore, *Les relations extérieures des Communautés européennes: contribution à la doctrine de la personnalité des organisations internationales* (Leiden: Sijthoff, 1962); Alessandra Bitumi, Gabriele D'Ottavio and Giuliana Laschi (eds.), *La Comunità europea e le relazioni esterne. 1957–1992* (Bologna: CLUEB, 2008).

5   Kiran Klaus Patel, "Provincialising European Union: Co-operation and Integration in Europe in a Historical Perspective," *Contemporary European History*, 22 (2013),

649–673; and now also the special issue: Kiran Klaus Patel and Wolfram Kaiser (eds.), "Multiple Connections in European Cooperation: International Organizations, Policy Ideas, Practices and Transfers 1967–1992," *European Review of History*, 24:3 (2017).

6   Max Kohnstamm and Wolfgang Hager, "Conclusion," in Kohnstamm and Hager, *A Nation Write Large*, 253.

7   For the debate about the EU's actorness see, e.g., Kateřina Čmakalová and Jan Martin Rolenc, "Legitimacy of the European Union," *Cooperation and Conflict*, 47 (2012), 260–270; also Kiran Klaus Patel, *Projekt Europa. Eine kritische Geschichte* (Munich: Beck, 2018), 295–341.

8   The relationship to the Asia Pacific region, India, and Latin America—regions that we do not cover—is analysed in Pascaline Winand, Andrea Benvenuti and Max Guderzo (eds.), *The External Relations of the European Union: Historical and Contemporary Perspectives* (Brussels: Peter Lang, 2015); Pascaline Winand, *The European Union and India: Rhetoric or Meaningful Partnership?* (Cheltenham: Edward Elgar, 2015).

9   Alan S. Milward, *The European Rescue of the Nation-State*, 2nd edition (London: Routledge, 2002).

10   See the chapters by Konrad H. Jarausch and Charles S. Maier in this volume.

11   François Duchêne, "Europe's Role in World Peace," in Richard Mayne (ed.), *Europe Tomorrow: Sixteen Europeans Look Ahead* (London: Fontana, 1972), 32–47. See, for instance, Mario Telò, *Europe, a Civilian Power? European Union, Global Governance, World Order* (Basingstoke: Palgrave Macmillan, 2006).

12   In particular, see Robert Kagan, *Of Paradise and Power: America and Europe in the New World Order* (New York: Alfred A. Knopf, 2003). For more balanced and perceptive analyses of the tensions inherent in the notion of "civilian power," see Headley Bull, "Civilian Power Europe: A Contradiction in Terms?" *Journal of Common Market Studies*, 21 (1982), 149–164, and Ian Manners, "Normative Power Europe: A Contradiction in Terms?" *Journal of Common Market Studies*, 40 (2002), 235–258.

13   On the complex, controversial nexus between European *détente* and the eventual demise of socialist regimes, see Stephen Kotkin, *Armageddon Averted: The Soviet Collapse, 1970–2000* (New York: Oxford University Press, 2001); Frédéric Bozo, Marie-Pierre Rey, Piers Ludlow and Leopoldi Nuti (eds.), *Europe and the End of the Cold War: A Reappraisal* (Abingdon: Routledge, 2008); Federico Romero, *Storia della guerra fredda: l'ultimo conflitto per l'Europa* (Torino: G. Einaudi, 2009); Svetlana Savranskaya, Thomas S. Blanton and Vladislav M. Zubok (eds.), *Masterpieces of History: The Peaceful End of the Cold War in Eastern Europe, 1989* (Budapest: Central European University Press, 2010); Jussi M. Hanhimäki, *The Rise and Fall of Détente: American Foreign Policy and the Transformation of the Cold War* (Washington, DC: Potomac Books, 2013); Kiran Klaus Patel and Kenneth Weisbrode (eds.), *European Integration and the Atlantic Community in the 1980s* (New York: Cambridge University Press, 2013); Silvio Pons, *The Global Revolution: A History of International Communism 1917–1991* (Oxford: Oxford University Press, 2014); Oliver Bange and Poul Villaume (eds.), *The Long Détente: Changing Concepts of Security and Cooperation in Europe, 1950s–1980s* (New York: Central European University Press, 2017); Angela Romano, *The European Community and Eastern Europe in the Cold War: the EC's Ostpolitik and the Transformation of Intra-State Relations* (London: Routledge, 2019).

14   Charlotte Bretherton and John Vogler, *The European Union as a Global Actor* (New York: Routledge, 2006), 38; Lorenzo Ferrari, *Sometimes Speaking with a Single Voice: The European Community as an International Actor, 1969–1979* (Brussels: Peter Lang, 2016).

15   See for instance Jan Zielonka, *Europe as Empire. The Nature of the Enlarged European Union* (Oxford: Oxford University Press, 2006); Kalypso Nicolaïdis, Berny Sèbe and Gabrielle Maas (eds.), *Echoes of Empire: Memory, Identity and Colonial Legacies* (London: I. B. Tauris, 2015).

16   It does not therefore come as a surprise that views and opinions on the EC/EU in the Asia Pacific remain less positive than Europe imagines and desires. A key trading and financial partner, no doubt, but far less of a powerful, influential global actor. See Winand, Benvenuti and Guderzo, *The External Relations of the European Union*.

17   Möckli, *European Foreign Policy during the Cold War*, points out that in order to assume a significant foreign policy role the EC would have had to operate with a degree of competition and/or friction with the United States, thus opening up not only a trans-Atlantic rift, but a more serious, probably paralyzing intra-European one (370).

18   Vicki L. Birchfield, John Krige and Alasdair R. Young, "European Integration as a Peace Project," *British Journal of Politics and International Relations*, 19 (2017), 3–12; Bitumi, D'Ottavio and Laschi, *La Comunità europea e le relazioni esterne*, 12.

19   Ricchard Mayne, "Introduction," in Mayne, *Europe Tomorrow*, 12.

20   See Christopher Hill, "The Capability-Expectations Gap, or Conceptualizing Europe's International Role," *Journal of Common Market Studies*, 31 (1993), 305–328.

21   Claudia Hiepel, "Introduction," in Claudia Hiepel (ed.), *Europe in a Globalising World: Global Challenges and European Responses in the "Long" 1970s* (Baden-Baden: Nomos, 2014), 12.

22   Chris Patten, *Not Quite the Diplomat* (London: Allen Lane, 2005) defined enlargement as "the most successful foreign policy pursued by Europe" (152).

1

The History of the EC and the Cold War: Influenced and Influential, but Rarely Center Stage

N. Piers Ludlow

The European Community (EC) was, from its very outset, influenced and shaped by the Cold War. The success of the integration process, meanwhile, was not unimportant for Western Europe's role and position within the Cold War, especially during the latter stages of the East–West struggle. By the mid-1980s, if not earlier, the EC began to exercise a strong power of attraction over the neighboring states of Eastern Europe. This undoubtedly would profoundly affect their trajectory once the Berlin Wall fell, but is also likely to have been of some importance to both governmental and dissident attitudes and behaviors during the final years of the Cold War. But despite this pattern of mutual influence, to study the place of the Cold War in EC/EU foreign relations is to become aware of the highly indirect nature of the relationship between the two processes. To resort to a photographic metaphor, the Cold War is present in most historical snapshots that could be taken of the EC or of collective European decision-making during the 1958–1990 period. But it is seldom in focus, rarely at the center of the picture. Instead, it is normally a somewhat blurred background presence—undoubtedly significant, and almost certainly having an effect on other elements within each photo, but hard to look at clearly or to analyze with any degree of precision.

As a result, the easiest way to discern the influence of the Cold War on the EC is to focus instead on one of the EC's key bilateral relationships—tracing the way in which this relationship was affected by the Cold War factor. This is perhaps most obvious when looking at the interaction between the European Community and the Socialist bloc, as Angela Romano does in her chapter. But the Cold War's effect would also be detectable in the Community's interactions with the United States, with the People's Republic of China, or with its partners in the developing world, especially in Africa. As such, there will be much about the Cold War in the various geographically focused chapters of this volume, as well as in Wilfried Loth's examination of the security dimension of the EC foreign policy.

Instead, this chapter's focus will be threefold. Its first task will be to briefly review the existing literature on European integration and the Cold War, noting the way that most historians, and indeed most political scientists, have tended to downplay the mutual interaction of the two—although there has lately been some evidence of change in both disciplines. The second section will then seek to justify the claim that the Cold War and European integration were of importance to each other; before the third explains why their interaction was nevertheless seldom straightforward or direct. This final section will acknowledge the important change that occurred in the 1970s, when the EC began to equip itself with the policy mechanisms and instruments to enable it to become more of an actor in the Cold War. At much the same time, its readiness to adopt such a role also increased significantly. But the chapter will go on to argue that even in this later period, the Cold War remained secondary with regard to the Community's priorities and mechanisms—an observation that only makes all the more remarkable the centrality that the Community/Union would assume in the post-Cold War reunification of the European continent. The bit-part actor in the Cold War drama would only move center stage once the East–West conflict had come to an end.

A Belated Recognition of Interconnection

Both the political science and the historical literature on the origins and early development of the European Community took their time to recognize the interconnections between the Cold War and the European integration process. In the former, the main theoretical debates about the roots of integration centered on the institutions and policies of the early integration process, much more than on their wider international context.[1] There was little about the East–West struggle in the writings of the neo-functionalists, the intergovernmental institutionalists, the historical institutionalists, or the constructivists. The rather more numerous International Relations (IR) specialists who worked on the Cold War, meanwhile, took little interest in European integration, regarding it, to the extent that they noticed it at all, as a low-policy and primarily economic issue of scant relevance to the decisive superpower standoff.

It was really only with the ending of the Cold War that the situation began to change. First, the doyen of realist political scientists, John Mearsheimer, published a prominent piece in 1990 which effectively predicted the end of European stability now that the Cold War had come to an end, dismissing any notion that the integration process itself had contributed to the "long peace" and could sustain it in the future.[2] This publication was followed by Sebastian Rosato's attempt to build on such ideas, setting out the theory that the integration process had been a product of the Cold War and was hence doomed to collapse once the Cold War had come to an end.[3] This provoked a strong retort from scholars convinced neither by Rosato's interpretation of how the integration process had evolved, nor by his analysis of its more recent difficulties.[4] The debate, however, did have the indisputable merit of forcing political scientists at least to consider the Cold War factor—even if they doubted the overall explanatory power that Rosato claimed.

Historians were equally guilty, until comparatively recently, of ignoring any potential interplay between the East–West conflict and the emergence and development of the European Community/Union. An extensive literature developed on each with, in the case of Cold War history, a sizable literature on the European dimensions of the Cold

War.[5] From the early 1990s onwards, this work succeeded in reasserting an important degree of European agency and disproving the impression—sometimes conveyed by some of the earlier superpower-focused literature—that the countries of Europe had simply been pawns of Moscow and Washington. The integration literature, meanwhile, was able to move on from its initially somewhat sterile attempt to identify a single explanatory cause, into a much richer and more varied literature about the dynamics that caused both the start and the subsequent evolution of the process.[6] But to a very large extent, the two literatures existed in parallel without any form of engagement between them. The occasional episode featured prominently in both the integration literature and the Cold War: the Marshall Plan would be one example, the doomed European Defence Community (EDC) another. Such points of intersection, however, constituted the exceptions that proved the rule.

Over the last decade or so, a substantial improvement has taken place. Chapters on European integration have crept into some of the best overall studies of the Cold War.[7] The literature on the end of the conflict, moreover, has begun to acknowledge that the attempts by Western Europe's states to integrate their economies and even to some extent their foreign policies did have important implications for the diplomacy of 1989–1990 and its aftermath.[8] Detailed studies, moreover, have begun to look at the way in which the Community institutions began to interact with those of the Eastern bloc and, more intriguingly still, the effects this may have had on the communist regimes themselves.[9] More generally, there also seems to be a willingness to perceive Cold War preoccupations and concerns as part of the panoply of factors that shaped European states and their engagement with the integration process. Eirini Karamouzi's work on Greece would be a clear case in point, identifying Cold War considerations at work both in Athens' decision to apply and in the manner in which this application was received in Brussels, but stopping well short of any claim that such geopolitical calculations were incompatible with multiple other economic, institutional or political rationales.[10] The Cold War factor may still lurk more towards the margins of the Community snapshots referred to earlier. But in a lot of the more recent literature, it has been rather less out of focus, its interconnections with other factors of importance distinctly more apparent as a result.

Mutual Influence

The European Community was born into a Cold War-dominated world. The Schuman Plan of May 9, 1950, normally regarded as the foundational moment of Community Europe, coincides with a high point of the East–West conflict, and a moment, furthermore, when Europe was the unquestionable epicenter of the struggle—the prime battleground.[11] Josef Stalin still ruled Russia, the two rival German states had just come into being, and the fear of both Soviet invasion and communist subversion were prominent features of the Western European context. The North Korean invasion of South Korea just one month later would trigger a major war-scare in Western Europe and encourage the United States to redouble its efforts to protect European security by means of the North Atlantic Treaty Organisation. In December 1950, General Dwight

Eisenhower would be announced as the first Supreme Allied Commander Europe (SACEUR), responsible for coordinating the Western military response should the Soviets attack. Between 1955 and 1957, the Treaties of Rome establishing the European Economic Community (EEC) and Euratom were negotiated against an international backdrop that included the Suez Crisis and the Soviet suppression of the Hungarian revolution of 1956.[12] The early years of the EEC after its start of operation in 1958 were played out on a continent cut in half by the Cold War and still strongly affected by the military, ideological, political, and economic contests between capitalism and communism. The first decade of the EEC was thus punctuated with major Cold War crises, from that over Berlin from 1958 to 1961, to the suppression of the Prague Spring in 1968, passing via the Cuban Missile Crisis of 1962 and the escalation of the Vietnam War from 1964 onwards. It would have been remarkable had this wider setting not had some bearing or influence on the manner in which European integration developed.

The intellectual origins of the drive for European unity predate the East–West conflict, of course.[13] Moreover, some of the issues that European integration was designed to address, such as the underlying interdependence of European economies, had little or nothing to do with the Cold War. The huge potential for intra-European trade would have existed with or without the Cold War; the distribution of the key raw materials needed for continental European heavy industry across eastern France, western Germany, the south of Belgium and the whole of Luxembourg would have been a reality in the absence of any external Soviet threat.[14] Likewise, the widespread urge to prevent a recurrence of that extreme nationalism which had led to two World Wars—and to establish a framework within which Germany could be rebuilt—was an entirely understandable consequence of Europe's recent history and in no way related to the struggle with communism.[15] It would hence be inaccurate to argue that European integration was a direct product of the Cold War. Nevertheless, the manner in which it emerged, its early timing, and some of the key features of the fledgling integrative structures were profoundly shaped by their Cold War environment.

A clear example would be the influence of the Cold War on France's struggle to devise a response to its German problem—in other words its deep sense of insecurity vis-à-vis its powerful eastern neighbor. Broadly defined, the "German problem" for France went back at least to 1870 and the establishment of a united Germany, if not substantially earlier.[16] But the precise manifestation of the German problem that triggered French action in 1950 was significantly shaped by the early Cold War. France, after all, had had a clear approach to dealing with Germany's potential power after 1945—its strategy centered on preventing the re-emergence of a strong German state. However, this ambition had been swept aside by the United States and Britain—both of which had perceived the dangers of communist takeover if the Germans were denied any prospects in the post-war world and had realized the utility of a strong and prosperous West Germany as a frontline state in the developing Cold War. They had hence dropped their own earlier flirtations with a punitive approach to Germany and started to reconstruct a viable and potentially prosperous West German state. French protestations had been to little avail; French hopes of playing upon the Soviet Union's similar suspicions of a reborn Germany were thwarted by the growing East–West divide. By 1947 and the start of separate Western discussions about how to rebuild the western zones of Germany, French policymakers were thus forced to engage in a desperate search for an alternative strategy to solve their German problem. This strategy was unveiled on May 9, 1950 with the Schuman Plan.[17]

Similarly, Konrad Adenauer's acceptance of the French offer in 1950 (and much of his subsequent European policy) would be impossible to understand without reference to the Federal Republic's vulnerable position as a state divided by the Cold War but in a still highly precarious position within the incipient Western bloc. Economically, West Germany had no incentive to accept the Schuman Plan—not even the most ardent disciple of Alan Milward has been able to suggest a strong commercial motivation for Bonn's decision. Instead, the German chancellor's choice was deeply political.[18] One motivation, of course, was to escape from the legacy of World War II, regaining a degree of international respectability and beginning the slow process of Franco–German reconciliation. But equally important was the desire to bind Germany firmly to the West, thereby ruling out either a situation in which the former occupying powers concocted some sort of deal about Germany's fate over his head, or an attempt by a subsequent West German government to gain reunification in return for neutrality. This could best be achieved by throwing off West Germany's pariah status and instead establishing strong and enduring links with his Western neighbors—an option that suddenly became possible through France's offer of participation in the Schuman Plan. Such a strategy of *Westbindung*, however, made no sense outside of the context of the Cold War.[19] West Germany's positive response to the French offer was as Cold War inflected as the offer itself.

The Cold War mattered, too, in determining the strong level of support from the United States that the early integration process received. There were, of course, non-Cold War reasons why so many post-war US policymakers were drawn to the idea of European unity. These ranged from a desire to avoid a situation in which US forces were obliged to cross the Atlantic a third time in the twentieth century to sort out internecine quarrels amongst the states of Europe, to the recurrent American tendency to believe that most areas of the world would be richer, more stable and happier were they to imitate more closely the US way of doing things. Viewed from this last perspective, the division of Europe into multiple competing political systems, and multiple competing and separate economies, made little sense. But the United States also clearly believed that a more united Europe, freed from its internal divisions, would be a stronger bulwark against communism, a better shop window for capitalism within the growing Cold War, and a more reliable partner and ally with whom the burdens of global leadership and defense against communist expansion could be shared. The American enthusiasm for European unity apparent from 1947 was thus strongly linked to the Cold War—as was the US attempt to use the Marshall Plan framework to coax and chivvy the recipient countries into doing much more together, and to regard their economic recovery as a collective endeavor rather than multiple national efforts.[20] Given that most historians would argue that this US support was a significant aid to early European integration—maybe even a necessary precondition, such a conclusion underlines the extent to which the Cold War helped to create the environment and the conditions under which European integration could successfully occur.

Also of significance was the Cold War's role in blunting potential British opposition to the integration process. The United Kingdom's refusal to lead, and then to engage with, the process of European integration during the 1940s and 1950s is well known and need not be recounted here.[21] But it is important to realize the extent to which British benevolence towards the efforts underway amongst the Six reflected a realization that, while European unity was not something in which the United Kingdom itself felt able to participate, it was something that could have positive effects on the strength of the Western bloc in the Cold War and help avoid the type of internal strife that would have played straight into Moscow's hands. This was apparent in 1950 as the British discussed whether or not to accept the French offer of participation in the Schuman Plan.[22] It shaped much of the UK's stance vis-à-vis the ill-fated European Defence Community scheme, including the last-minute intervention by Anthony Eden that would help resolve the crisis caused by France's 1954 rejection of the scheme.[23] And it was perhaps most succinctly and accurately encapsulated in Eden's rejoinder to Harold Macmillan in 1953, when the then minister for housing appealed to Winston Churchill about the damage that might be done to British interests were the Six allowed to push ahead with integration. Once the ailing prime minister referred Macmillan's warning letter on to the Foreign Secretary, Eden replied that "on balance I had rather see France and Germany in a confused but close embrace, than at arm's length."[24] Such a view was partly a product of Eden's awareness of how central Franco–German enmity had been to both World Wars. But it also surely reflected a realization of how damaging unchecked antagonism between two major European allies could be to Western unity within the Cold War.

Nor was Eden alone in perceiving the Cold War advantage of Franco–German unity in particular, and Western European cooperation more generally. All of the states of Western Europe were acutely conscious in the late 1940s through to the early 1960s— the formative period of the integration process—that disunity could only weaken the Western front in the Cold War and that greater unity, by contrast, would strengthen it. This explains the frequently repeated comment that Stalin should be classed amongst the founding fathers of the European integration process. Alfred Grosser, for instance, claims that he would have been a worthy recipient of the *prix Charlemagne*—the prize awarded annually to those deemed to have done most to advance the cause of European unity.[25] A similar awareness of the threat from the East and realization that in such circumstances division was not a luxury that Western Europe could afford also helps to explain the alarmist conclusion of a German economics ministry report from 1963, analyzing the disruptive effects of de Gaulle's decision to veto British EEC membership, hence prolonging the artificial economic separation between the EEC and EFTA as well as angering the Americans: "If the old rift between the EEC and EFTA reappears and on top of this a new fracture between the Six and America is allowed to develop, the situation can produce only one winner: Khrushchev."[26]

Finally, the early integration process was also the undoubted beneficiary of one of the great tragedies of the Cold War—namely the exclusion of the states behind the Iron Curtain from any engagement with the non-Communist world. This enforced reduction of the potential cast list of any European cooperative endeavors was almost certainly a vital necessity for integration's initial success. For it was probably essential that the integration process begin with a highly limited number of states, and yet still be able to portray its efforts rhetorically and in the minds of the protagonists as an attempt to unify "Europe," not just a small subset of Western Europe.[27] Indeed, the Cold War-induced reduction of those European countries to be considered for inclusion extended beyond the states of the Soviet bloc itself, but also included Cold War neutrals like Sweden, Austria, or Finland, none of whom could seriously contemplate full membership so long as the East–West struggle continued. All of this meant that the Six could start small, in geographical scale as well as in policy ambition, thereby greatly facilitating their early task. Europe's more recent difficulties in trying to devise policy with more than twenty members are a potent reminder of the value of this opportunity to begin the process of integration with a mere half dozen member states.

The Cold War, moreover, would continue being a factor in the Community's development during the 1960s, 1970s, and 1980s. It profoundly affected, as Romano's chapter makes clear, with whom the Community did or did not trade or negotiate. It colored how the integration process was perceived, both by significant portions of the Western European political elite and by many outside observers. (Particularly important in this last regard was the role of the Cold War in the decision by Karamanlis' government in Greece to seek EEC membership from 1975 onwards.[28]) The Cold War continued to lubricate the relationship between the Community and the United States.[29] And it was a central preoccupation of virtually all of the European political leaders who would dominate the integration process, even though it was rarely at the forefront of their minds when they dealt with or came to Brussels.[30]

The successes of European integration also began to influence the development of the Cold War. European cooperation helped smooth and decrease a series of internal European rivalries which, if left unresolved, might substantially have weakened Western solidarity in the Cold War. In addition, integration's success helped to rebuild the self-confidence of multiple individual Western-European states—West Germany first and foremost. The Federal Republic's self-image during the post-1949 period became inextricably linked with the idea of being the "good European," the willing participant in multilateral endeavors and the state that—rather than throwing its individual weight around in a fashion that might scare its neighbors—preferred always to join with others in the leadership of the EEC. It was no coincidence that Willy Brandt, the first German chancellor to play a major and semi-autonomous role in Cold War diplomacy, tried hard to demonstrate to his Western allies that this did not signal too radical and disruptive a departure from previous West German foreign policy, in part by flanking his radical *neue Ostpolitik* with an energetic and enthusiastic attempt to push forward with Western integration.[31]

The Community system also helped lock into the Western system the Cold War mavericks, like Charles de Gaulle or later Andreas Papandreou, who might otherwise have posed a greater threat to Western unity. As I have argued elsewhere, by the late 1960s many of de Gaulle's fellow European leaders had come to view the Community structures as a vital mechanism that helped prevent the unpredictable French president from straying too far or too dangerously away from his country's Western orientation.[32] Similar calculations almost certainly help to explain Western Europe's willingness to engage constructively with the outspoken Greek prime minister in the course of his

1980s campaign to renegotiate, in all but name, the terms under which his country had joined the European Community.[33]

Somewhat before Papandreou's years in power, the Cold War and the integration process had interlocked in Southern Europe during the 1970s. During that decade a pervasive sense of crisis characterized much of NATO's southern flank. In Greece, the undemocratic Colonels' regime collapsed in the wake of the Turkish invasion of Cyprus. War seemed close between two NATO members. In Portugal, the Carnation Revolution was followed by a prolonged period of uncertainty, as moderate democrats and leftwing radicals struggled for the country's leadership. Next door in Spain, tense maneuvering was underway, as Franco's health declined. Yugoslavia's position between the blocs seemed uncertain, as its ailing leader, Josip Broz Tito, neared the end of his lengthy reign. And even in Italy the electoral success of the Communist party, the economic traumas of the mid-1970s and the scourge of far-left terrorism created a pervasive sense of fragility. In such circumstances, European integration began to come into its own as a mechanism for spreading and securing democracy, and thereby avoiding political developments that might severely damage the West in the Cold War.[34] This was all the more necessary given that the extent of anti-American sentiment, in Greece and the Iberian countries in particular, largely disqualified the United States from effective intervention of its own. NATO, too, was seen, with reason, by the Greek and Portuguese populations as having helped prop up the previous autocratic regime.[35] As a result, external support and guidance could only be provided by the Community structures, a process that became still more marked once Greece, Portugal, and Spain all applied for EC membership. Integration was, in other words, a vital tool for sorting out a situation in which a serious Cold War crisis could well have arisen within the Western bloc, and where the West's leading power was more or less disqualified from acting. By default more than by design, the European Community structures filled the void.

There is also reason to suspect, although at present we lack the documentary evidence to go beyond strong supposition, that in the latter stages of the Cold War the contrast between Western advance and Eastern stagnation gradually became a key source in the rise of dissidence in Eastern Europe. We certainly know that Mikhail Gorbachev was fascinated with the booming European Community of the late 1980s, appointing the first and only Soviet Ambassador in 1989 and expressing the vain hope that the Council for Mutual Economic Assistance (CMEA) might be able to emulate some of the Community's dynamism.[36] But the Soviet leader is unlikely to have been the only figure on the communist side of the Iron Curtain struck by, and hoping to learn from, the highly visible success of the integration process in the final half decade of the Cold War. And finally, the pre-existence of a flourishing and forceful European Community gave Europe's leaders in 1989–1990 not only the institutionalized mechanism to talk through the consequences of German unification and the end of the Cold War, but also a semi-formed framework within which the systemic threats posed by the fall of the Berlin Wall could be effectively contained. Harvey Sicherman, the sometime-US-government foreign policy advisor, asserted that "when the Berlin Wall was opened the Americans looked through the breach and saw the future while the Europeans looked through the breach and saw the past." This jibe contains a modicum of truth, inasmuch as quite a number of European leaders were momentarily haunted by the fear of a return to a less-stable European past; but it is also highly inaccurate.[37] This inaccuracy reflects Sicherman's total failure to acknowledge that Helmut Kohl, François Mitterrand and most of the other Western European leaders reacted to such fears by deliberately and enthusiastically embracing a future based on ever closer political and economic union. The establishment of a new, more integrated and tightly unified Europe was the collective European reaction to the anxieties and uncertainties unleashed by the geopolitical earthquake of 1989 to 1992.[38]

Ongoing Detachment

Despite these multiple levels of interconnection, however, a series of important factors always prevented the European Community system from dealing directly with the Cold War. The second part of this chapter needs, therefore, to trace the limits of interaction between the integration process and the East–West conflict.

In the early period of the Community's history, between 1958 and 1969, this was both clear and obvious. The early European Community had no direct dealings with the Eastern bloc at all. The Soviet bloc states refused to recognize the EEC, regarding the Community institutions as instruments of German revanchism. Similarly, there was no contact whatsoever between the EEC and the CMEA. Even more fundamentally, the fledgling European institutions lacked the mechanisms with which key foreign-policy issues such as the Cold War could be collectively discussed. The idea of establishing institutions that would allow the EEC member states to talk together about foreign-policy issues had been repeatedly aired during the 1960s, most famously with de Gaulle's Fouchet Plan proposals in the first years of the decade, but such plans had never come to fruition.[39] To some extent this reflected the deep internal divisions on key aspects of Cold War strategy and tactics amongst the leaders of 1960s Western Europe. To pledge to coordinate European approaches might thus result in the dominance of de Gaulle's semi-heretical views on the East–West conflict. In addition, the 1958 to 1970 period corresponded to a phase of Cold War history in which the dominance of the two superpowers was at its zenith. Many Europeans, it was true, resented this superpower dominance and aspired to use cooperation with their EC partners to close the power gap. This explains the repeated re-emergence of discussions about so-called "political union," despite the deep internal divisions that the issue caused.[40] But until the end of the 1960s at least, such efforts got nowhere, much to the frustration of all involved.

This situation did begin to change from 1970 onwards. As Romano's chapter describes, the decade saw the gradual development of Community engagement with the Eastern bloc. The same period also saw the beginnings of the European Political Cooperation (EPC) process and hence the start of European foreign policy coordination, one of the first success stories of which was Europe's collective role in the Helsinki process.[41] Europe seemed to have discovered a collective Cold War role during the era of high *détente* that they had struggled to achieve at any earlier point of the East–West struggle. Also of some importance was the changing shape of the

Community's internal institutional structure. The 1974–1975 creation of the European Council gave Europe's most senior leaders, who had arguably always been those most sensitive to the interplay between the Cold War and the integration stories, a much greater direct stake and voice in the system. In the 1950s and 1960s, Western Europe's most senior leaders had seldom met collectively in any Community forum; from the mid-1970s, they began to do so at least three times a year, sometimes more. The European Council, furthermore, had a specific remit to bring together Community business and EPC business, subjects which at French insistence were deliberately kept apart at all other levels of the Community decision-making structures. The regular gatherings of Europe's heads of state and government were thus not just equipped to explore the interconnections between the Community's internal development and the great geopolitical issues of the day; they also had a duty to do so. At a more systemic level, moreover, both the early 1970s and the 1980s were times of growing European discontent with the manner in which the United States was leading the Western bloc. In the early 1970s, the Nixon-Kissinger tandem met with widespread European mistrust; in the latter part of the decade, European frustrations mounted with Jimmy Carter also; the early Reagan years, too, were punctuated by repeated transatlantic disagreements.[42] The incentive for European countries to use their new collective mechanisms to express this discontent and to challenge aspects of US leadership grew accordingly.

Despite all of these factors, however, the EC did not emerge as the principal tool with which Western European countries responded to the challenges of the Cold War. Why did this not happen?

Part of the answer is that the Community totally lacked a military dimension. This mattered, because while the Cold War was never just a military confrontation, it always had a strong military dimension, perhaps particularly in an area like Europe where some of the earlier ideological and cultural aspects of the East–West confrontation had faded away. As a rival ideology, culture or economic system, Communism struggled to gain much of a foothold in Western Europe at any point after the mid-1950s, except perhaps during the southern European crisis of the 1970s referred to above. But as a military threat, the Warsaw Pact remained a genuine concern until the very end of the Cold War, since at no time between 1947 and 1990 did the West approach a point where it could match the number of men under arms deployed by the Communist bloc. And given that the West did have a rival organization in NATO, which had the missing military dimension, the Community's military impotence was a significant barrier to it becoming the central forum for Western European discussion of the Cold War. European unity might be able to become part of Europe's response to the Soviet threat; but in the absence of any effective European capability to coordinate its national military resources—and in a situation in which all military experts acknowledged that Western Europe was indefensible without a substantial commitment of US men and weaponry—it made much more sense for NATO to retain its function as Western Europe's main defense structure.

Another factor was bureaucratic specialization. None of the core European institutions had personnel with Cold War expertise. This was true of the Commission (although its first president, Walter Hallstein, was a notable exception) and of the

Council of Ministers. But it was also true of most of those national civil servants and ministers who frequently gathered in Community Brussels to take decisions together. To be sure, those who met at EPC gatherings, whether in Brussels or elsewhere, at the formal or informal meetings of European foreign ministers, or at the European Council did have the requisite specialist knowledge. But even here, a number of significant factors prevented a frontal engagement with the Cold War.

Perhaps the most basic of these was that there was too much else to do. At few times in the Community's history has the EC's agenda been empty. The 1960s were characterized by a determined effort to complete the initial agenda and timetable set out in the Treaties of Rome; the 1970s saw the Community seeking, with varying levels of success, to both inaugurate a new and wider policy agenda and protect what had already been accomplished from the onset of global economic recession; and the 1980s were divided between an initial phase of frustration and impatience, as Europe struggled to escape from the inertia of the crisis years, and a latter five-year period in which integration accelerated as never before. Regardless of the phase, however, there was more than enough to do. The temptation to bring in new factors such as consideration of the Cold War was always likely, therefore, to be kept in check by the multiplicity of EC matters that already needed to be discussed. Why clutter up an already overflowing agenda with issues that would be better discussed elsewhere? This was all the more true in this case, as to open up a debate about Cold War strategy within Community Brussels would be to throw open the discussion in a way that invited intervention from the smaller European powers, from mavericks like Greece or from a neutral country like Ireland. None of the major European powers was keen to do this.

This underlines an even more important factor: most of the larger European players—especially Britain, France, and West Germany, but sometimes Italy too—were highly reluctant to democratize the discussions of the Cold War, which they tended to conduct either bilaterally with Washington or, from the early 1970s onwards, in four-power or five-power consultations that involved the United States but excluded the smaller EC members.[43] This format gave them close access to and influence over US decision-making. It also conferred significant prestige. As such, none of the former European great powers was in a hurry to surrender such privileges for the sake of European coordination. Why spoil the intimacy of bilateral consultations with the Western superpower, or the cosy surroundings of four- or five-power consultation, for the sake of including the Belgians, the Dutch, or the Danes?

Finally and probably most fundamentally of all, it made little sense to conduct in-depth discussions of most Cold War matters in a forum from which the Western superpower, the United States, was absent. There were certainly times when a level of European coordination about how to respond to unwelcome US demands or requests was helpful, as when EPC mechanism was used to coordinate the European response to US pressure for sanctions against the Soviet Union after the invasion of Afghanistan or the declaration of Martial Law in Poland. Likewise, EPC structures were used to solidify the indignant European response during the gas pipeline affair. And there were undoubtedly moments when it was appropriate for the Europeans to work out their own stance, such as when they were due to gather, in part as EC members, in a forum such as the Conference on Security and Cooperation in Europe (CSCE) follow-up conference in Madrid, or when EC policies themselves were at stake, such as East–West trade. At times it was also useful to be able to use the structures and policies of the Community to highlight the difference between US policy stances and the preferred European policy approach. In the early 1980s, for instance, there seem to have been a number of occasions when the Community sought to give substantial development aid to Sandinista-ruled Nicaragua, at least in part to demonstrate that European countries retained a degree of policy autonomy from Reagan's America.[44]

In most cases, however, US views were too central, and each European country was too keen to preserve its bilateral dialogue with Washington, for there to be a great temptation to commit to a common European stance on the Cold War worked out in a forum at which the United States was not present. The famous *Gymnich* formula—designed to ensure that the Europeans did not use EPC mechanisms to harm transatlantic relations, and sometimes presented in the literature as a limitation on European foreign policy independence imposed at the behest of the Americans— was not simply a mechanism designed to appease Washington by stemming potential Gaullist rebellions.[45] It was a much more basic reflection of the realities of a Cold War in which all of the Community member states formed part of a US-led bloc. As a result, it was in the interest of the European countries, as well as of the Americans, that transatlantic coordination was the norm, and divergence between the United States and its Western European allies the exception. *Gymnich* was about self-limitation, more than externally imposed shackles.

The European Community's centrality as an actor during the Cold War was thus always limited, despite the growing involvement that this chapter has charted. The process of integration mattered greatly to many of the countries involved, notably to the French and the Germans. As such, it was not without importance in their wider foreign-policy stance and in their approach to the East–West conflict. Likewise, the prosperity and stability that integration was perceived to deliver made the countries of Western Europe stronger and more reliable partners for the United States in the Cold War struggle, thereby vindicating some of the calculations that had underpinned the initial US enthusiasm for European unity.

But the Community's own Cold War role remained relatively circumscribed, even during the 1980s when it could and did interact with the Eastern bloc, and when some degree of European coordination over transatlantic relations was deemed useful. The East–West conflict was the prime topic of conversation in NATO Brussels, not Community Brussels, not least because there was so much else to consider and to debate amongst those involved with the European institutions. The Community as actor had certainly been upgraded from the minor walk-on part that it had played in the early years of the Cold War, but it was still no more than a supporting cast member as the East–West conflict moved into its terminal phase.

The end of the Cold War did therefore bring about a fundamental change. The United States did not disengage totally from Europe, of course, once the Cold War was over. Nor was NATO, the enduring monument to US power and influence, wound-up, as some fleetingly called for it to be in 1990–1992. But after 1989 it became clear both to Washington and to most European capitals that the greater part of the task of dealing with the transformed post-Cold War context would be the responsibility of the European states, either individually or collectively. One or more European lead actor(s) were needed to replace an American star inclined to scale back the centrality of his own role. Indeed, one senior American source claims that the US-led push to give the European Commission the responsibility of coordinating Western aid to the countries of Eastern Europe as they liberated themselves from Communist rule—a step taken at the G7 Summit in July 1989—reflected a quite conscious tactic, making clear to the Western Europeans that it would be their task and not that of the United States to take the lead in undoing the division of Europe.[46] Hence, the new leaders of Central and Eastern Europe would initially look to Western Europe, and to Western Europe's collective structures, as they sought to establish democratic and Western-leaning regimes. The quest for EU membership thus quickly became one of the defining features of the transition process experienced by most of the former members of the Warsaw Pact, a quest that for most would culminate in membership in 2004 or 2007.[47] The Cold War came most clearly into focus, as far as EC/EU politics were concerned, once the conflict was over and a post-war settlement needed to be devised, rather than at any point during the 1947–1990 confrontation itself.

Notes

1 Ben Rosamond, *Theories of European Integration* (Houndmills: Palgrave, 2002).

2 John J. Mearsheimer, "Back to the Future: Instability in Europe after the Cold War," *International Security*, 15:1 (1990), 40–48.

3 Sebastian Rosato, *Europe United: Power Politics and the Making of the European Community* (Ithaca: Cornell University Press, 2011); Sebastian Rosato, "Europe's Troubles: Power Politics and the State of the European Project," *International Security*, 35:4 (2011), 45–86.

4 Ulrich Krotz, Richard Maher, David M. McCourt and Andrew Glencross, "Debating the Sources and Prospects of European Integration," *International Security*, 37:1 (2012), 178–199.

5 John W. Young, *Cold War Europe 1945–89: A Political History* (London: Edward Arnold, 1993); David Reynolds, *The Origins of the Cold War in Europe: International Perspectives* (New Haven: Yale University Press, 1994).

6 Wolfram Kaiser and Antonio Varsori (eds.), *European Union History: Themes and Debates* (Basingstoke: Palgrave Macmillan, 2010).

7 Melvyn P. Leffler and Odd Arne Westad, *The Cambridge History of the Cold War, Vol. 2* (Cambridge: Cambridge University Press, 2010), 179–197.

8 Mary E. Sarotte, *1989: The Struggle to Create Post-Cold War Europe* (Princeton, NJ: Princeton University Press, 2009); Frédéric Bozo, Marie-Pierre Rey, N. Piers Ludlow and Leopoldo Nuti (eds.), *Europe and the End of the Cold War: A Reappraisal* (Abingdon: Routledge, 2008); Frédéric Bozo, Andreas Rödder and Mary Sarotte (eds.), *German Reunification: A Multinational History* (Abingdon: Routledge, 2017).

9 Angela Romano and Federico Romero (eds.), "European Socialist Regimes Facing Globalisation and European Co-Operation: Dilemmas and Responses—Introduction," *European Review of History: Revue Européenne d'histoire*, 21:2 (2014), 157–164; Angela Romano, "Untying Cold War Knots: The EEC and Eastern Europe in the Long 1970s," *Cold War History*, 14:2 (2014), 153–173.

10   Eirini Karamouzi, *Greece, the EEC and the Cold War, 1974–79* (Basingstoke: Palgrave Macmillan, 2014).

11   William I. Hitchcock, *France Restored: Cold War Diplomacy and the Quest for Leadership in Europe, 1944–1954* (Chapel Hill: The University of North Carolina Press, 1998).

12   Enrico Serra (ed.), *Il Rilancio dell'Europa e i trattati di Roma* (Brussels: Bruylant, 1989).

13   Anthony Pagden, *The Idea of Europe: From Antiquity to the European Union* (Cambridge: Cambridge University Press, 2002).

14   Alan S. Milward, *The Reconstruction of Western Europe 1945–51* (London: Methuen, 1984); Alan S. Milward, *The European Rescue of the Nation-State* (London: Routledge, 2000).

15   Raymond Poidevin, *Robert Schuman: Homme d'état, 1886–1963* (Paris: Imprimerie Nationale, 1986).

16   Raymond Poidevin and Jacques Bariéty, *Les relations franco-allemandes, 1815–1975* (Paris: Armand Colin, 1979).

17   Poidevin, *Robert Schuman*.

18   Hans-Peter Schwarz, *Adenauer: Der Aufstieg, 1876–1952* (Stuttgart: Deutsche Verlags-Anstalt, 1986).

19   Ronald J. Granieri, *The Ambivalent Alliance: Konrad Adenauer, the CDU/CSU, and the West, 1949–1966* (New York: Berghahn Books, 2004).

20   Geir Lundestad, *"Empire" by Integration: The United States and European Integration, 1945–1997* (Oxford: Oxford University Press, 1998).

21   Alan S. Milward, *The UK and the European Community, Vol. 1: The Rise and Fall of a National Strategy, 1945–1963* (London: Whitehall History Publishing, 2002).

22   Roger Bullen and M. E. Pelly, *The Schuman Plan, the Council of Europe and Western European Integration, May 1950–December 1952* (London: Her Majesty's Stationary Office, 1986), 30.

23   Spencer Mawby, *Containing Germany: Britain and the Arming of the Federal Republic* (Basingstoke: Macmillan, 1999).

24   Bullen and Pelly, *The Schuman Plan*, 846–847.

25   Alfred Grosser, *Wie anders sind die Deutschen?* (München: C. H. Beck, 2003), 200.

26   Archives of the Auswärtigens Amt, Bestand B-150, Bestellnummer 2, Ref. 200 (IA2), Bd.1236, Sprechzettel für Herrn Minister zur Kabinettsitzung, 25.1.1963, EA3–905 883, January 22, 1963.

27   Compare and contrast the high-flown rhetoric of the preamble to the Treaty of Paris (establishing the ECSC) and the reality of integrating two economic sectors of only six countries.

28   Karamouzi, *Greece, the EEC and the Cold War, 1974–79*, 19–21.

29   James Ellison, *The United States, Britain and the Transatlantic Crisis: Rising to the Gaullist Challenge, 1963–1968* (Basingstoke: Palgrave Macmillan, 2007).

30   See e.g. Garret Martin, *General de Gaulle's Cold War: Challenging American Hegemony, 1963–1968* (New York: Berghahn Books, 2013).

31   Andreas Wilkens, "New Ostpolitik and European Integration: Concepts and Policies in the Brandt Era," in N. Piers Ludlow (ed.), *European Integration and the Cold War: Ostpolitik-Westpolitik, 1965–1973* (Abingdon: Routledge, 2007), 67–80.

32   N. Piers Ludlow, *The European Community and the Crises of the 1960s: Negotiating the Gaullist Challenge* (London: Routledge, 2006), 117–118.

33   A major study of Papandreou's years in power and his interaction with Western Europe is under preparation by Eirini Karamouzi.

34   Mario Del Pero, Víctor Gavín, Fernando Guirao and Antonio Varsori (eds.), *Democrazie: l'Europa meridionale e la fine delle dittature* (Florence: Le Monnier, 2010).

35   Eirini Karamouzi, "Telling the Whole Story: America, the EEC and Greece, 1974–1976," in Antonio Varsori and Guia Migani (eds.), *Europe in the International Arena during the 1970s* (Brussels: Peter Lang, 2011), 355–374.

36   Marie-Pierre Rey, "Gorbachev's New Thinking and Europe, 1985–1989," in Bozo, Rey, Ludlow and Nuti (eds.), *Europe and the End of the Cold War*, 23–35.

37   Harvey Sicherman, "NATO Germany and Pragmatism's Finest Hour," *Orbis*, 41:4 (1997), 619.

38   N. Piers Ludlow, "Not a Wholly New Europe: How the Integration Framework Shaped the End of the Cold War in Europe," in Frédéric Bozo, Andreas Rödder and Mary Sarotte (eds.), *German Reunification: A Multinational History* (Abingdon: Routledge, 2017), 133–152.

39   Jeffrey Glen Giauque, *Grand Designs and Visions of Unity: The Atlantic Powers and the Reorganization of Western Europe, 1955–1963* (Chapel Hill: The University of North Carolina Press, 2002).

40   See e.g. Carine Germond, "Les Projets d'Union Politique de l'Année 1964," in Wilfried Loth (ed.), *Crises and Compromises: The European Project 1963–1969* (Baden-Baden: Nomos Verlag, 2001), 131–155.

41   Angela Romano, *From Détente in Europe to European Détente: How the West Shaped the Helsinki CSCE* (Brussels: Peter Lang, 2009).

42   Daniel Möckli, *European Foreign Policy during the Cold War: Heath, Brandt, Pompidou and the Dream of Political Unity* (London: I. B. Tauris, 2008); Kristina Spohr, *The Global Chancellor: Helmut Schmidt and the Reshaping of the International Order* (Oxford: Oxford University Press, 2016); Kiran Klaus Patel and Kenneth Weisbrode (eds.), *European Integration and the Atlantic Community in the 1980s* (Cambridge and New York: Cambridge University Press, 2013).

43   For the emergence of this group see N. Piers Ludlow, "The Real Years of Europe?: U.S.–West European Relations during the Ford Administration," *Journal of Cold War Studies*, 15:3 (2013), 136–161.

44   A PhD on interaction between Nicaragua and the countries of Western Europe during the first half of the 1980s is under preparation at the LSE by Eline van Ommen.

45   Möckli, *European Foreign Policy during the Cold War*, 316–322.

46   Robert L. Hutchings, *American Diplomacy and the End of the Cold War: An Insider's Account of U.S. Policy in Europe, 1989–1992* (Washington, DC; Baltimore: Woodrow Wilson Center Press; Johns Hopkins University Press, 1997), 69.

47   Vojtech Mastny, "Eastern Europe and the Early Prospects for EC/EU and NATO Membership," in Bozo, Rey, Ludlow and Nuti (eds.), *Europe and the End of the Cold War*, 235–245.

Part One

World Regions

2

The EC and the United States: Partners in Search of Diplomacy

Kenneth Weisbrode

The European Community began with a set of European attitudes toward the United States and with expectations of what Americans required "Europe" to be and do, and, just as often, what it ought not to be and do. The EC was a subordinate but important actor in this relationship, and a necessary but dependent Cold War participant. At times, some actors appeared to take partnership for granted, with American opposition or inattention, paradoxically, coinciding with moments of European assertiveness. On balance, influential Americans and Europeans projected upon the EC a particular image of European diplomacy—commercial, principled, and modest. This image contrasted with the one many Americans and Europeans had of the European movement at home—political, calculated, and bold. Many of them also saw little real contradiction between the two.

The history raises two questions: whether it is possible to identify a clear external role for the EC after 1957 and, if so, whether it has comparative significance regarding other actors, primarily nation-states, covered in this volume—which is to say, whether there is a meaningful correlation between EC–US relations and EC external relations in general.

The best answer to both questions is, maybe. For the sake of argument, however, we propose two affirmative answers in order to ask a third question: how much did EC–US relations matter? There is an axiom among historians of European integration that very little of it would have happened without the political, financial, and moral support of the United States. Yet, support came in many different shades. It is one thing to say that the United States was the midwife of the European Community; it is quite another to say that the United States made and sustained it in its image.[1]

This chapter advances neither point exactly. Instead, it demonstrates that, from the beginning, the leaders of the European Movement and their American collaborators maneuvered themselves into a mutual accommodation with an EC that was not sufficiently independent to pose a real challenge to American leadership but also

I am grateful to my students in the History of European Integration seminar at Bilkent University, particularly Burcu Feyzullahoğlu, for useful background research and discussion.

had to show itself, especially to critics, to be both viable and distinctive. The actors were partners in the interdependent sense of the term that the leader of the European Movement, Jean Monnet, had often used, with the relative extent of seniority and juniority determined by the particular matter at hand—that is to say, functionally. In the principal issue of shared interest—trade—they fashioned a relationship that combined the roles of partner and rival with varying degrees of ambivalence. In others—culture and defense, for example—a formal relationship or pattern barely existed at all.

It is not remarkable, then, that the EC and the United States did not fashion a clear diplomacy in combination. Their occasional efforts to shape one in response to "internal" and "external" challenges varied too much to suggest a systematic case study for social scientists in this regard. But to historians it offers a rich and worthwhile example of the interrelationship of foreign and domestic policy and actions. Some aspects of each have remained constant, as well as consistent, namely, that European integration, for all that it was an internal cause for its European proponents, has remained a foreign policy priority for successive American administrations; and that the actual reasons for this are nearly impossible to separate from the declaratory ones: Western unity, prosperity, and peace. Monnet stated it well when he wrote that "[w]hat we are building up in Europe and with other free countries, did not, in my view, arise only from our common dangers. The Common Market is not a defensive organization: it is a means of achieving a better way of life and a better chance of peace, by abolishing economic and political anachronisms."[2] The impetus, at least according to him, was more historical than geopolitical.

The EC–US partnership, however, adopted a particular character over time that had both historical and geopolitical significance. They were never allies in the traditional sense. Interdependence is not the same thing as co-dependence. Rather, they were partners with more limited and less concrete terms of engagement confined mainly to their own relations and content with autonomy in principle so long as it did not bring defiance. Here the EC played a number of roles: auxiliary, catalyst, lever, even foil, to which one should add the more positive ones of booster of morals and grantor of legitimacy insofar as the EC added value to the post-war liberal orientation of American diplomacy. The exercise of partnership, however strong it may have been in principle, was proscribed by particular roles at particular moments; the interdependence it sought bolstered rather than diminished the structural particularity of its two primary constituents, especially the European, as a "civilian actor in the international system," alongside the contrary reinforcement of others, primarily NATO, into whose military bailiwick no other organization—following a brief and failed attempt in the mid-1950s—was permitted to enter.[3] This is not to say that the EC became the civilian counterpart of NATO, for the latter was meant to be more than a military alliance; yet the coexistence of the two in rather distinct realms served to reinforce the basic difference between an alliance and a partnership and, therefore, the limited and ambiguous nature of the latter in transatlantic relations.

The two partners probably never could have constituted a genuine or lasting duopoly in any event. Nor had the EC developed a clear overall foreign policy, in spite of its emergence as the world's leading commercial bloc. The United States was too hegemonic and exposed for any real duopoly to work, while the EC was too young, its decision-making too ponderous and conflicted, its institutions too tenuous, and its members still too wedded to the prerogatives of nation-states, most of all in their foreign relations. The largest of these, with the notable exception of West Germany, had also begun to dismantle extensive overseas empires, which made it difficult for some of their governments to lower the flag and contemplate some other orientation. Their American counterparts were certainly aware of that sensitivity, although it would go too far to suggest that they exploited it to their country's advantage. In principle, both sides supported interdependence, as well as independence for the EC. When the latter appeared to become an end in itself, as during the initial phases of the Kennedy Round of trade negotiations on the General Agreement on Tariffs and Trade (GATT), beginning in 1964, or during the 1973 Arab–Israeli war, proponents of partnership on both sides made appeals to interdependence as a way of limiting or even vitiating any alternative independent course of action. But this was never done to the extent of substituting the one for the other as a matter of doctrine.[4]

The exercise of partnership in this manner raises doubts over the validity of the concept with respect to the EC and the United States. When push came to shove, the partners usually reimposed the status quo, sometimes by agreeing to disagree, other times by a partial compromise, which in nearly every instance had the effect of underscoring the asymmetrical character of their partnership. It featured hardly any diplomacy at all in the usual sense and took place reflexively without the standard elements—treaties, embassies, summits. Although in a few areas the two actors can be said to have sustained different policies during these years, there was none, so far as one can tell, where they made use of a direct and powerful opposition at the highest levels that called into question the basis of the Atlantic Alliance. At the same time, the EC came to define its external nature through its capacity to endorse or oppose the policies of its ostensible American partner. This capacity was preoccupied at the outset mainly with transatlantic trade but, as the other chapters demonstrate, could also apply elsewhere.

It is said that ambiguity can sometimes be a constructive element in international affairs. It can also be a destructive one if the assumptions underlying it are mismatched. Hence the need to revisit the EC–US partnership: first by examining the history of bilateral relations, such as they were, and the attitudes, ideas, concepts, and decisions that underpinned them; and then by describing its apparatus as an indication of its nature.

History

When, how, and why did the EC acquire a "foreign policy" toward the United States? The questions are not as straightforward as they may appear. External relations and policy are not synonymous; a foreign policy is not the sum total of actions that have effects beyond the borders of the EC.[5] For a policy to exist as such, it must be held in common, must govern a range of decisions and actions, and must be both self-conscious and public—that is, with declarations, behind which may or may not exist actions that augment or contradict it, as the case may be. Writing three decades ago, Roy Ginsberg claimed that the EC had no foreign policy with regard to the United States for the simple reason that a common policy neither existed nor could exist within the institutional and geographical boundaries of the EC.[6] Many diverse relations, yes; but no policy.

The task of identifying policies is somewhat easier to complete on the other side of the Atlantic. It responded to actions in more or less four stages.[7] The US role from the earliest days, although intimate and extensive, appeared almost deistic. "We have not been consulted or involved in the proposals, if made, in any way," wrote the American Secretary of State, Dean Acheson, perhaps with some exaggeration, upon hearing of the forthcoming presentation of the Schuman Plan.[8] Nonetheless, his deputy described it as "imaginative, useful and having considerable merit," while Acheson's successor, John Foster Dulles, then a consultant to the State Department, regarded the idea behind the plan as "brilliantly creative."[9] Still, wrote another diplomat, the United States "should continue to manifest its support … without direct involvement."[10] This would remain the basic approach, at least on the diplomatic level, toward the consolidation of European institutions and their evolving external role, until the 1970s.

Post-war American relations with a collective body of European states began not with the Schuman Plan or the North Atlantic Treaty, but with the Organization for European Economic Cooperation (OECC) which emerged from the Marshall Plan in 1948. The OEEC would later be treated in most respects as "complementary" to these other organizations, especially North Atlantic Treaty Organization (NATO), notwithstanding some effort to drive a wedge between them.[11] The OEEC was in any case "a purely technical and advisory institution … an essentially pragmatic affair."[12] It would be superseded in 1961 by the Organisation for Economic Co-operation and Development (OECD), which became no longer entirely European; indeed, this coincided with an aim in the 1960s to help underwrite a more global, or at least a more liberal, Europe. There had been attempts—notably during the balance-of-payments crisis during the early part of that decade—to see the OECD play a stronger role with greater Commission representation from within.[13] But a transatlantic consensus for that role was lacking. Neither the OECD (nor the OEEC for that matter) became a powerful vehicle for such a consensus in order "to pursue simultaneously European regionalism and worldwide multilateralism."[14] Both organizations were, strictly speaking, objects rather than subjects of foreign policy.

The EC therefore began with a paradox. The European Coal and Steel Community (ECSC) and its later counterparts, the Common Market (EEC) and the European Atomic Energy Community (EURATOM), originated with the belief that they were kernels of something greater in the pursuit of peace and prosperity. That was one reason why integration was strongly supported by the United States from the start; yet, at the same time, the modest but positive reputation of groups like the OEEC persisted, and the prospect of such institutions acquiring an external, independent political role was denied until the mid-1970s; that is, well after the EC had begun to exercise such a role, mainly in trade, and only when the EC–US relationship had at last begun to move beyond one of "patron and client."[15] Americans tended to depict any bold manifestations of independence, to the extent they were tolerated, as "short-term" means that would be justified, or excused, by greater ends. This viewpoint had been echoed in Europe for some time already.[16]

To trace and demarcate this shift toward quasi-independence alongside a (paradoxical) reaffirmation of interdependence requires us to delve into the minds and mental maps of principal actors—primarily politicians and bureaucrats—and to speculate along the lines of the chicken and the egg: which came first, the deliberate articulation of a divergence, or the implicit or explicit realization that events demanded it?[17]

To this causal question involving events, actors, and attitudes, one must insert another element: fads. European integration was at the top of the list of transatlantic policy fads virtually from the moment World War II ended, if not earlier. Fads, or fashions, as some prefer to call them, have a way of spreading as they rise and fall. They gradually, or sometimes rapidly, infect, shape, or pervert a number of policy areas by focusing attention, setting the terms of debate, consuming political oxygen, and influencing, even dictating, personnel and policy choices. In this instance, it is important not only to acknowledge how prevalent the fad of European integration was in the United States, but also, on the one hand, how prevalent the fad of transatlantic cooperation was in Western Europe, and, on the other hand, how internally divisive both fads also were in both places.

The difficulty with fads, however, is that they are intangible and metamorphic. A chronology of integration, even before the EC came into being, shows many ups and downs, including one or two near reversals with particular fads and their translation into policies. One of the best known relates to the saga of the European Defence Community (EDC) in the early 1950s. It is a complex and still rather perplexing one with the United States and France as the main actors. The EDC—more or less a European army meant to finesse German rearmament after US redeployments brought about by the Korean War—was initially a French proposal. The Americans had been cautious at first but, following the conversion of President Dwight Eisenhower and his Secretary of State, John Foster Dulles, entered into the negotiations with passion, only to have the French reject the EDC outright in mid-1954. A rearming West Germany would join NATO the following year.

The EDC failure left a scar. American diplomacy resumed a low profile toward European integration. Yet, the EDC, at least in part, proved an important stimulant to grander efforts: the Messina Conference (1955) followed by the Rome Treaties (1957). It is difficult to imagine much of this having happened when it did had there been no EDC debacle or if the United States had not been so fervent in the project's promotion. It may not have been obvious to everyone at the time, but that debacle was probably salutary, much as Wilfried Loth and Piers Ludlow have reiterated for the Suez crisis in 1956 insofar as it prompted overtures by the West German Chancellor, Konrad Adenauer, toward France, culminating, according to Loth, in the French vote in favor of the Rome Treaties.[18] That West Germany benefited much in the aftermath was not a problem: "[T]he definite conclusion was that we should not allow ourselves to be so restrained in our support of a real European federation," wrote an American diplomat back in the summer of 1952, "even though the membership be restricted and even though there was the possibility that Germany might eventually become in fact the dominating element therein."[19] That this ultimately happened was not the fault of the EC, the United States, integration, or partnership; nor was it a self-evident result of a single historical process. Rather, the quality of "actorship" revealed itself to be self-limiting and almost passive, as the above quotation suggests, in allowing a trend or fad to proceed by way of actions that themselves had been devised to restrain it, without entirely thwarting it. That process took place, arguably, in a manner once described by the economist Herbert Simon as "satisficing" by which positive results sometimes come from suboptimal choices.

One reason for the complex and counterintuitive process of integration by a self-limiting partnership was that their proponents remained divided over the means to advance it. Divisions were important because they help one to understand the rise and fall of particular bureaucracies and policies, and because they allow for the reconstruction of political and economic questions, negotiations, and "issues" in the intellectual and cultural setting in which actors understood them. The primary division among integrationists—European as well as transatlantic—at mid-century was over the shape or "architecture" of partnership. Self-described Atlanticists and Europeanists embraced sympathizers across the Atlantic; each, at the same time, drew firm distinctions on both sides. Broadly speaking, Atlanticists tended to place a priority on transatlantic over European integration, or at least tended to advance the latter—which was still important to them—in the service of the former. Europeanists did the opposite. Atlanticists put forth an image of the transatlantic partnership that resembled a solar system with planets orbiting around a sun, ideally somewhere in the mid-Atlantic though, for some, extending loosely to the south and to the east across the borders of several virtual and actual near abroads. Europeanists, by contrast, advanced a more fixed image of partnership of what they called the dumbbell, with only two planets, or poles—Europe and America—joined by a strong rod. "Far from diluting the European Community within an Atlantic Community," claimed one of their pamphlets, "this partnership should imply strengthening the unity of Europe, which should thereby be enabled to talk on equal terms with the United States ... "[20]

Intramural rivalries did not always sound healthy. Some Atlanticists said Europeanists wanted to supplant a strong and permanent alliance with a weaker partnership that could foment rivalry. This, they pointed out, was implicit in the design: how could one side of the dumbbell be independent and sovereign but the other not, to include having, if it so desired, an independent foreign policy, not merely toward the other side of the dumbbell but also toward the rest of the world? Some Europeanists in turn charged Atlanticists with masking a system of American hegemony with a vague community concept—several little balls orbiting not some mid-Atlantic sun along a functional route but instead a very large ball called the United States. That system did not look too different from an empire. Meanwhile they claimed that it was unfair to equate independence with non-alignment; in fact, they stated, an ostensibly independent foreign policy would make the transatlantic alliance even stronger.

Still others downplayed the differences. "[R]ight from the beginning Europe's efforts to integrate enjoyed the splendid support of the United States," recalled the German politician and President of the European Commission, Walter Hallstein:

> Its moral value was in no way diminished by the fact that it also served a practical
> purpose in the context of America's world-wide defence system: it helped to secure

the European front, the European frontier. Quite the reverse: European integration was not only sought, welcomed, and encouraged. It was also jointly defended.[21]

By the middle of the 1960s, however, their conciliatory voices were overpowered by diverging ones, which had become so acute they were labelled theological. It is therefore necessary to describe the American role and place in the emergence of an EC foreign policy by emphasizing that nearly every question posed to policymakers was discussed with the contending maps in mind. Integrationists had regarded US economic preponderance as the solution for many of Europe's problems, but prosperity had returned to much of Western Europe. The Common Market became a potential competitor. It had developed to the point where rivalry, or at least the specter of protectionism and trade diversion, had begun to look real. The European economy, developed and protected under American auspices during the previous decade, had now become both much bigger and more protectionist, while the United States had lost its primacy in many non-European markets as the EC itself began to diversify.[22] This coincided with the growing balance-of-payments deficit in the United States, made worse, in the latter half of the 1960s, by the Vietnam War. The crisis had spread to Europe, where the "dollar glut" led to an effort to manage and then to bridle monetary and fiscal policies, a pattern that would hold until the Nixon administration employed both, notably the former, more explicitly as political tools.[23] The Kennedy and Johnson administrations had earlier reacted to the problem with liberalization and an export boost—that is, placing the onus on lowering the deficit not by devaluing the dollar or by drastically cutting government spending, but instead by pushing hard for trade and investment in favor of growth.

Thus the Kennedy Round (1964–1967) and the Dillon Round before it (1960–1962) mattered a great deal diplomatically as well as commercially, with the former coming close to a make-it-or-break-it moment in both the GATT and elsewhere, e.g. in East–West trade.[24] Failure to come to an agreement on liberalizing trade appeared to threaten not only the growth of European and American economies but also the expensive defense protectorate the United States provided across the Atlantic. These were the presumed costs. There were also benefits. As described elsewhere in this volume in more detail, the EC also became recognized as an actor by way of its participation in these negotiations, with the Dillon Round advancing a common external tariff in harmony with national tariffs, and the Kennedy Round seeing the EC negotiate as a single bloc, albeit in the furtherance of free trade.[25] The former reset the parameters of commercial diplomacy; the latter transformed its substance. Taken together, the two sets of negotiations, especially the Kennedy Round, proved to be both impetus and catalyst for a more formidable, albeit unsettled, Commission.[26] This was not entirely an unwelcome development for the Americans, or for that matter, for several European governments, including the French.[27]

The results again were suboptimal but significant. The EC agreed to the liberalization of industrial tariffs but succeeded in protecting much of its agricultural sector and the Common Agricultural Policy (CAP). The US and EC economies did not collapse from deficits or a balance-of-payment crisis. The GATT, already prompted by Kennedy's Trade Expansion Act of 1962, ultimately did a great deal to liberalize trade and also had the effect of drawing the EC together as a single actor, with the Commission in particular as an important, flexible, even entrepreneurial "new factor in international life," according to Hallstein, as it and its negotiator, Jean Rey, made their worldwide diplomatic debut.[28] The EC's priorities may have been more immediate—that is, less "systemic"—than those of the United States, which retained the main responsibility for the successful conclusion of the negotiations, but the Europeans nevertheless assumed their own combined responsibility, and place, in the US-led trading system.

Transatlantic difficulties posed by the balance-of-payments deficit and related matters were compounded by the saga of British membership in the Common Market. The United States pushed hard for it, notwithstanding concerns over the place of the Commonwealth and the trade diversion that might ensue if its members were allowed a special status in, or if they were excluded from, the Common Market. The problem discomfited some like Hallstein, who fretted about a failure to build upon the Anglo-American "special relationship," or rather about its compounding a number of other longstanding worries.[29] The Kennedy administration responded with an innovation called the "Grand Design." The policy had two pillars—the United States and Western Europe—and three components: commerce, defense, and ideology. "In effect, the United States sought a special relationship not with the UK," the historian Thomas Zeiler has written, "but with all of Western Europe in a united Atlantic community."[30] Kennedy's "Declaration of Interdependence," delivered on July 4, 1962, was meant to align them in a "genuine partnership of equals," featuring stronger EC–US relations and a more integrated Atlantic Alliance.[31]

The response of the EC to all this is probably best described as bemused. Nor did the Grand Design win the hearts of Atlanticists. Even a few Europeanists concluded that it was premature.[32] Did the EC seek to be this kind of pillar? Not really. But what was the alternative? Could the Alliance continue to enjoy the closest relations in defense and security and still tolerate what Lyndon Johnson's White House assistant, Francis Bator, called "an economic cold war"?[33] By contrast, was the EC now explicitly or even implicitly understood to be so prominent a participant in the Atlantic Alliance?[34] Also, evidently not. Even if that were the case, would not the realization call for more, not less, restraint when important economic interests were at stake?

This was a moment, in other words, when both the EC and the United States grappled with a new role for the former in the transatlantic system but held to the familiar, asymmetrical roles they had been playing. The EC had to become part of that system even though it did not use its commercial power to reshape it. EC external actorship remained an almost inevitable product of the way it makes internal decisions. That this was less the case for the United States during this period is not in itself remarkable; rather, it was the counter-effort to demonstrate that internal priorities in decision-making worked in support of the relationship that already existed. That relationship was never jeopardized by EC assertiveness in trade negotiations, or in monetary and fiscal affairs, because it adhered to the boundaries and basic formula of a limited partnership. Trade negotiators thus could make various short-term concessions to protectionism (for example, in agriculture) while maintaining an overall commitment to free trade. So long as the EC competed with the United States within the bounds of partnership and did not attempt to mobilize partnership for any greater end in a way that countered US interests, the EC could sustain such assertiveness.

The Grand Design therefore was not to be. Its proponents blamed the demise on the French President, Charles de Gaulle, nearing the end of his political career, and on his nationalist rearticulation in the form of anti-Americanism (or, as he would have said, anti-Anglosaxonism).[35] Then Richard Nixon—perhaps in homage to de Gaulle, whom he admired, or perhaps to what he may have understood as a more realistic position— renationalized the transatlantic partnership. So, the above questions were never firmly resolved.[36] Nations, even groups of nations, dealt again more bilaterally and less in the realm of community-building.

One setback then followed another: the floating of the US dollar with the suspension of gold convertibility in 1971; the imposition of new levies; a serious clash over the 1973 Arab–Israeli war; and an oil embargo. Walter Hallstein termed the moment a potential "general crisis of confidence."[37] It may have been worse than that. The tone of EC–US relations at the time was one of bitter frustration.[38] Europeans not only resented being granted a "Year of Europe" (1973) by the American Secretary of State, Henry Kissinger, in order to underscore their "regional" status as against the global one of the United States, but Americans also resented particular Europeans for challenging US leadership publicly. Nixon at one point imagined in Europe "a Frankenstein monster."[39] Whether the moment signified a temporary breakdown or something more dire for the Cold War alliance is open to debate. The habit of deference to the United States may have waned; yet there was not a permanent substitute on offer. Instead there was another exertion from within.

So came the next "qualitative leap." As with the post-EDC recovery that brought about the creation of the EC, the late 1970s and early 1980s laid the groundwork for an institutional renaissance, culminating in the period after 1985.[40] How much did the United States have to do with it? It may have been ironic that Kissinger had predicted back in 1973 a convergence of two Euro-Atlantic "procedures … one is in NATO and one is with the Nine. With regard to the latter," he said, "by 1980, you will have one foreign policy. At some point the two procedures will merge …."[41] Americans did more than make predictions. Appearances notwithstanding, the United States was a critical actor during the Geneva and Helsinki negotiations that resulted in the Helsinki Final Act (1975) of the Conference on Security and Cooperation in Europe (CSCE), having accepted a European approach to Cold War *détente* that included an opening to the Eastern bloc, and not simply, as Nixon and Kissinger had defined it, a relaxation of tensions with the Soviet Union. American and European leaders—Kissinger and French Foreign Minister Michel Jobert, for example—made for a good deal of disharmony, but by the second half of the decade a recovery in the partnership was underway. The EC and especially the Commission under Roy Jenkins became more visible. The next few years saw the first ever visit to the European Commission by an American president (Jimmy Carter) and inclusion of an EC representative in the summits of the leading industrial nations.

Some tension persisted over the imposition of martial law in Poland in 1981, the plan to build a Soviet gas pipeline to supply Western European markets, and the Soviet invasion of Afghanistan in 1979. EC leaders looked upon these developments cautiously, recognizing on the one hand that a good deal of its trade was conducted with the East, which on principle strengthened its own international position, and, on the other hand, that an independent US–Soviet *détente*, for good or for ill, left them vulnerable to forces beyond their control.[42]

There was another, more inherent, concern. Many if not most of the EC's external relations had become technical and specialized, and were overseen by negotiators at low levels, some from departments and agencies with little experience or interest in diplomacy. This fed a perception in the United States, especially, "of a tangled and complicated economic organization, involved in inexplicable internal and endless argument."[43] Brussels bureaucrats could exasperate even the most composed and experienced diplomats. "Americans," according to the stereotype, "tend to oversimplify matters and to take extreme positions. They are enthusiastic at the beginning but expect spectacular or concrete results …."[44] Europeans fashioned themselves the opposite. Alongside high-profile American negotiations with the Soviet Union prefacing a dramatic end to the Cold War came a return to the low profile or "hands off" approach to the EC and quiet, nearly undetectable, support for the negotiations leading up to the Single European Act in 1986.[45]

The chronology of this volume ends in 1992 with the creation of the EU and the establishment of formal diplomatic relations. However, neither supplanted the transatlantic partnership and that raises one final question. Did those who contemplated a stronger partnership, or, alternatively, a looser one, predicate their preference on the Cold War, or on its demise? The former is more plausible. Yet, as David Allen has noted, a viable and more integrated EC was, at least implicitly, at the center of the latter: "It is certainly the case that both the United States and the Soviet Union have moved very rapidly from regarding their own relationship as fundamental and their relationship with the West Europeans as marginal to a position where they both see the EC as the key to the new Europe even if their conceptions of that Europe differ."[46] The crux, he added, was the prospect (and soon, the reality) of a reunited Germany. It was at this point (November 1990) that the EC and the United States issued a joint declaration, not only reaffirming common transatlantic goals but also identifying the EC "and its member states" as the repository of those goals.[47] The language signaled a return of sorts to the image of the dumbbell. Only now, according to the American Secretary of State James Baker, it looked more like a four-pointed star, with NATO and the CSCE joining the United States and the EC.

Baker's image would make for a nice synthesis as another "two-plus-four" formula, complementing the one that overlaid the negotiations for German reunification. However, it is difficult to reconstruct the history of EC–US partnership so neatly. There were elements of a linear progression of both institutions and partnership from the Marshall Plan/OEEC/High Authority period to the Grand Design, followed by a regression and a nadir, then culminating in another progression up to 1992. Unsurprisingly, that chronology more or less runs in parallel to the Cold War.[48] However, there were too many variations in the story, too many competing and contending views on what partnership really meant, too many reversals and recoveries, and too many imbalances to produce a straightforward narrative, let alone a progressive one. Historians of European integration therefore have tended to trace it thematically.[49] Some areas and subjects moved forward while others lingered or moved back. The history of this partnership, to include the role of each actor in the transatlantic and

European redefinition of the other, was neither natural nor illogical. Reconstructing it requires something like a combined gyroscope and stopwatch, each with different settings, but both pointed in the same general direction—toward greater internal and external integration.

Apparatus

A notable element of the formal EC–US relationship has been its modesty. The United States did not appoint a permanent ambassador to the EEC until 1961, and he was one of three American ambassadors in Brussels, joining the one to Belgium and the US permanent representative to NATO. The EC did not have a representative of ambassadorial rank in the United States until 1971, and he joined more than a dozen European ambassadors already there. Few of these official representatives were memorable figures, apart from a couple of Americans. Besides David Bruce, who earlier, as the Marshall Plan director in Paris, also served as the US observer to the High Authority, the one best known to historians is J. Robert Schaetzel, who represented the United States in Brussels for six years from 1966. He is remembered mainly for his outspoken bitterness at his own government's neglect.

One reason for modesty, especially in the early years, was the concern that the European project would be seen as too American. Miriam Camp expressed it well back in 1952:

> [I]t would be a mistake for the United States to formalize a relationship with these organizations too quickly. There is already an excessive tendency to regard the development of the Schuman Plan and European Political Community as things which the Europeans are doing because the U.S. wants them to be done rather than because the European countries concerned believe in them … we can not afford to take a completely "hands-off" position if things seem to be going badly. There will undoubtedly however be a continuing problem of restraining our people from premature or excessive interference.[50]

She added, more succinctly, a few months later:

> We should be constantly on guard against the natural impulse to get too deeply involved in the details and resist the urge to impose our own pattern of development on other countries … If an enduring union of the Six Countries is to be established, it must be created because they want it, it must be European in concept and reflect their traditions, not ours.[51]

It was only in 1983 that the Americans, prompted by Secretary of State George Shultz, began regular ministerial meetings with counterparts in the European Commission. These meetings were confined to economic subjects. It was not until the latter part of that decade and into the first years of the next that the EC assumed all the trappings of a diplomatic post, with some 160 ambassadors accredited to it at the beginning of 1991.[52]

The bureaucracy itself remained small. The EC's Directorate of External Relations (DG I) had an American desk similar to those in national foreign ministries. The latter often maintained direct contact with their American counterparts (cabinet departments) or through functional attachés, but DG I coordinated many of these relations with a mandate for policies coming from the respective Council working group and from the Committee of Permanent Representatives (COREPER).[53] Many issues are also still handled intergovernmentally, either through the presidency or directly with the foreign ministries of member states. Even in GATT negotiations (e.g. during the Kennedy Round) the Commission still took many of its instructions from the Council.[54]

Within the US government, political and economic relations with the EC fall within the purview of the State Department's Bureau of European Affairs (EUR). Although this bureau was probably the most consistently powerful of all the regional offices during much of the twentieth century, it has covered a very large geography and remains, like most such bureaucracies, dominated by country desks. There was an important early exception to this, however. Shortly after World War II, the State Department established the Regional Affairs (RA) office within this bureau. It was a small office with a very big remit. For a time it oversaw US policy towards nearly every major European issue and program, focused mainly on economic reconstruction, the OEEC, and related matters. RA's early intellectual force was the above-mentioned Miriam Camp, who had a British husband (W. A. Camps) and spent much of her life in the UK.[55] Her office became the primary bureaucratic interlocutor with the nascent High Authority, with its staff serving as an important force within the US bureaucracy for the promotion of Monnet's ideas, and their interpretations of them.[56]

These details about RA are significant not merely for understanding the evolving American approach to the EC as reflected in bureaucratic flowcharts, but also for contrasting it with the absence of any such office in Europe—DG I notwithstanding— for managing transatlantic relations, including political and military ones, across institutional boundaries during this formative period. The relationship was overseen, on the American side, by a powerful regional office within a powerful regional bureau, which was succeeded by a much less powerful office within the same bureau; and, on the European side, by multiple national bureaucracies whose prestige varied over time in liaison with a nascent Commission and Council.

Bureaucratic comparisons are complicated by the frequency and intensity of interaction among particular actors. From the earliest days of the partnership, individual Americans exerted considerable influence upon the internal roles and decisions of Europeans, from the setting of currency exchange rates, to the drafting of competition law, to the allocation of agricultural and other subsidies. In this respect the lopsided EC–US relationship was basically and perhaps fundamentally different from the others described in this book. Much of the real business of partnership took place less by way of official bureaucratic channels than unofficially, informally, and intermittently, at least until the holding of biannual meetings, which were followed by annual ministerials in the 1980s.[57]

A good deal has been written about this informal interaction, otherwise known in its transatlantic setting as the "Monnet method."[58] The term was popularized by Monnet's biographer and amanuensis, François Duchêne, in spite of the fact that the method and its namesake once gave their chronicler a nervous breakdown. It was not a conventional way to conduct diplomacy, at least according to most prevailing assumptions about what diplomacy is, since its practitioners were not all official representatives of states and few of its results came in the form of treaties and pacts. On the other hand, traditional diplomacy has never really been confined to such people and documents; the Monnet method—a movable feast of seminars, conferences, articles, speeches, and "advocacy groups"—was not much different from the quasi-official salons that date back to modern diplomacy's earliest days. Thus it should not be surprising that the first significant representative of the High Authority in Washington was Leonard Tennyson, a journalist and one-time assistant to Ambassador W. Averell Harriman who was recruited by George Ball, Monnet's lawyer who later became under secretary of state, to open a small information office in 1954.[59] Or that Monnet himself and a number of his colleagues—Pierre Uri, Jacques Van Helmont, Richard Mayne, Max Kohnstamm—travelled back and forth across the Atlantic on what most people would regard as diplomatic missions. Monnet had been doing that since World War I. Kohnstamm resided in Washington as the principal interlocutor on the European Atomic Energy Community (EURATOM) negotiations with a constant presence in the State Department.[60] The pattern was reproduced by many others, in many other locales on both sides of the Atlantic well before anyone could plot an official EC diplomatic apparatus on a map.

Informal activities and networks have since been supplemented by regular summits and other components of interstate diplomacy. This took a while to happen. It was only in 1977 that for the first time a representative of the EC attended an annual meeting of the G-7. The diplomatic summit would appear here to be a less meaningful, more superficial vehicle than Monnet's *Kaffeeklatsch*, but only if one does not count all the preparation and agreements that are pre-negotiated or the other important, intangible elements that go into them, beginning with the relationships, working habits, and life histories of the principal actors. The celebrated recent transatlantic friendship of the high officials Pascal Lamy and Robert Zoellick, for example, is hardly an anomalous one in this history. Partnerships sometimes feature and can rely upon such informal friendships more than formal alliances do.

Conclusion

The EC–US partnership survived the Cold War that fostered it because it matured, along with the EC itself, into a multifaceted, integral body of institutions that it had tried to become and, at the same time, to avoid becoming too quickly. Does an aspirational conclusion to partnership have historical significance even if the aspiration itself—a full and proper diplomacy—was so elusive? Most diplomatic historians, taking their cue from Richelieu, would say, yes, for there are few concrete ends, or beginnings for that matter, in what he called continuous negotiation. The best diplomacy succeeds by de-emphasizing conjuncture and points of achievement in the name of aspiration; certainly this must be the case for our subjects, one whose motto is to form a more perfect union, and the other to make an ever closer union. Both modifiers—"more" and "ever"—are significant. The political cultures of the EC and the United States were and are not only aspirational but also procedural, as diplomats and bureaucrats often say. So, too, were their mutual relations. The point here is somewhat obvious but it is often overlooked in their history.

Procedures and processes did not advance on their own. American negotiators may have dismissed the existence of a "European" policy, much as the representatives of European member states continued to insist on national prerogatives in everything from trade to culture; yet, at the same time, a preponderance of actors performed their roles as though the EC and its partnership with the United States amounted to more than a talking-shop, façade, or temporary association of convenience. In other words, the institutional character one observes emerging during these decades went from a latent force—only hinted at by the historical evidence, and therefore demonstrably inconclusive—to a more explicit axiom whereby non-European actors, notably Americans, came to conduct negotiations, define external relations, and discuss the effects and consequences of such relations more and more frequently in reference to "Europeans" than to any single member state. The irony is that this tendency came, at least initially, from Americans in anticipation of what they said Europeans ought to be, then joined by Europeans who insisted on the same, sometimes in the face of American opposition. A further irony is that diplomacy—at least state-based diplomacy—was one of the integrationists' least visible emphases. As late as 1973 the scholar and politician Ralf Dahrendorf could still insist that national prerogatives in foreign policy had not yet been supplanted by the "foreign relations" of the European Community.[61] Perhaps the capacity to know one's place was an important reason for the latter's survival in an American-dominated Western alliance.

Or it may not have been so simple, because knowing one's place was not easy for the EC to determine by itself. Therefore, action often came in response to a challenge from across the Atlantic, not least of which was uncertainty and perhaps the failure of American diplomacy to specify how far either type of integration—intra-European or transatlantic—ought to progress, and the related difficulty in adjusting expectations and attitudes to this ambiguity in order to avoid making America the "stone against which to sharpen a European identity."[62] Yet, following the EDC crisis in 1954 and culminating in the early 1970s, Europeans and Americans came around to such an adjustment: a modified dumbbell, as it were, with Atlanticism subsuming Europeanism but featuring over time an externally strengthened EC. This is demonstrated by the direction of the relationship in later decades, leading to an EU with a bona fide external policy apparatus, yet absent a major diminution of the Atlantic Alliance.

The two "isms" grew to be consistent through the combined determination of the EC to play a role, as the EC, in the world, and the counter-determination by the United States to ensure that this role, whatever else it may or may not have done, would not infringe upon or hinder the transatlantic solidarity each side valued so highly. Whether or not such solidarity, in turn, required more coherent foreign policies on the part of the EC is open to question. At least one of our authors has noted, in reference to the Kennedy Round, "that when faced with the choice between European integration and Atlantic liberalization, the Six chose Europe."[63] This choice was not clear-cut or consistent. For transatlantic solidarity was also not *sui generis*. It played at the center of the Cold War, which in turn demanded a peaceful, prosperous, and integrated Western Europe as both bulwark and beacon to the East and South.

Did the Cold War square the diplomatic circle around two uncertain, sometimes muddled, partners and patterns of integration? An answer of yes, not maybe, would make for a convenient conclusion but it is also insufficient. Few Europeans would reduce the history of European integration in the second half of the twentieth century to a Cold War appendage; fewer would cast it in the primary service of an imperial United States. There are more than a few reasons why European integration could have taken place without the imperative of the Cold War; the same could also be said for the interest and support of Americans for integration. But when one speaks not of European integration generally but of a putative role of the EC vis-à-vis the United States, it is difficult to offer an alternative historical reconstruction absent the Cold War. Even Gaullists, including the General himself, never went so far as to promote their challenge as a threat to the Atlantic Alliance. The challenge was to its implementation and to its management, notably in military matters, but not to its existence. De Gaulle offered a Western alternative, not neutrality or defection. The same could be said for most of his rivals in the European movement, particularly those who became proponents of the liberalization of East–West relations, i.e., *Ostpolitik*. More than a few probably harbored hopes for an alternative to the Cold War and a way to supersede the divisions of Europe, with the beacon overtaking the bulwark. That might have meant a reconfiguration of the inward and outward missions of interdependence, with interdependence cast in the service of independence rather than the reverse.[64] But few, if any, Americans or Europeans advanced a separate and distinct "European" foreign policy at the expense of the Atlantic Alliance as the means toward this end. Also, most of them continued to insist upon a meaningful distinction between European unification and integration.

Miriam Camps, who was among the first to insist upon that distinction and had as strong a claim as any to the promotion of an Atlantic Community, once observed that "[t]he underlying source of much of the strain in transatlantic relationships is the uncertainty and confusion on both sides of the Atlantic about the kind of international system we are trying to build."[65] It is reasonable, therefore, to conclude that an external policy apparatus and identity for the EC had to remain modest and subservient, virtually up to the point it became formally constituted within the international system. That makes the EC no less significant for what it was from at least the middle 1960s: implicitly and incipiently independent. The more prescient of its American supporters not only admitted this possibility; some even encouraged it. But its skeptics and naysayers probably had the most to do with ushering forward its existence and, at the same time, a viable transatlantic partnership.

Notes

1   The spectral doubling of the EC and its member states described by other contributors to this volume could also apply to the EC–US partnership; however, I prefer to imagine it as more akin to a geopolitical "fleet in being."

2   Fondation Jean Monnet pour l'Europe, AMK C 24/3/296, Monnet to Walter
    Lippmann, July 17, 1963 (draft).
3   Roy H. Ginsberg, *Foreign Policy Actions of the European Community: The Politics of
    Scale* (Boulder, CO: Lynne Rienner, 1989), 1.
4   I am grateful to Angela Romano for clarification of this point. I regard them as
    having been related, but not identical, aims.
5   See Roger Morgan, "Introduction: European Integration and the European
    Community's External Relations," *International Journal of Politics*, 5:1 (1975), 3–10,
    esp. 4–6; Ginsberg, *Foreign Policy Actions of the European Community*, 4. See also
    pp. 90–115 for two dozen tables and charts illustrating the type and nature of
    "foreign policy actions." My views on the relationship of both to diplomacy are
    found in Kenneth Weisbrode, "Diplomacy in Foreign Policy," in *Oxford Research
    Encyclopedia of Politics* (Oxford: Oxford University Press, 2017).
6   Ginsberg, *Foreign Policy Actions of the European Community*, 4.
7   Ibid., p. 136 identifies them: 1948–1962, 1963–1970, 1971–1980, 1981–1986.
8   Foreign Relations of the United States (hereafter FRUS), 1950, Vol. III, *Western
    Europe*, Doc. 373, The Secretary of State to the Acting Secretary of State, May 9, 1950;
    cf. François Duchêne, *Jean Monnet: The First Statesman of Interdependence* (New
    York: W. W. Norton, 1994), 201n2, suggesting some American foreknowledge.
9   FRUS, 1950, Vol. III, *Western Europe*, Doc. 376, The Acting Secretary of State to the
    Secretary of State, at London, May 10, 1950; FRUS, 1950, Vol. III, *Western Europe*,
    Doc. 377, The Acting Secretary of State to the Secretary of State, at London, May 11,
    1950.
10 FRUS, 1950, Vol. III, *Western Europe*, Doc. 380, The Ambassador in France (Bruce)
    to the Secretary of State, May 23, 1950.
11 FRUS, 1952–1954, Vol. VI, pt. 1, *Western Europe*, Doc. 32, The Director of the Office
    of European Regional Affairs (Martin) to the Deputy to the United States Special
    Representative in Europe (Merchant), April 22, 1952.
12 David Coombes, *Politics and Bureaucracy in the European Community: A Portrait of
    the Commission of the E.E.C* (London: George Allen and Unwin, 1970), 17.
13 Author's conversation with Abe Katz.
14 Wendy Asbeck Brusse, *Tariffs, Trade and European Integration, 1947–1957: From
    Study Group to Common Market* (New York: St. Martin's, 1997), 80.
15 Ginsberg, *Foreign Policy Actions of the European Community*, 129.
16 E.g. FRUS, 1961–1963, Vol. XIII, *Western Europe and Canada*, Doc. 1, Memorandum
    of Conversation, February 6, 1961; Robert Marjolin, *Le Travail d'une Vie: Mémoires
    1911–1986* (Paris: Éditions Robert Laffont, 1986), 206–220.
17 See Brusse, *Tariffs, Trade and European Integration, 1947–1957,* 142 and 212–215.
18 The pattern was repeated during the 1973 October War and the clash over Cyprus
    the following year: a crisis and reaffirmation of both the EC and the transatlantic
    partnership following a quiescent interim. See below.
19 FRUS, 1952–1954, Vol. VI, pt. 1, *Western Europe*, Doc. 56, Memorandum by the
    Acting Deputy Director of the Office of Western European Affairs (Knight) to the
    Deputy Director of the Office of European Regional Affairs (Parsons), July 9, 1952; cf.
    FRUS, 1952–1954, Vol. VI, pt. 1, *Western Europe*, Doc. 138, The Minister in France
    (Achilles) to the Deputy Under Secretary of State (Matthews), asking, "Do we really
    want Europe to unite?," November 28, 1952.
20 "Partnership for Progress: A Program for Transatlantic Action," Atlantic Institute (April
    1963), in Pierre Uri Papers, Archives of the European Union, PU–99, 1963–1978.

21 Walter Hallstein, *Europe in the Making*, trans. Charles Roetter (London: George Allen and Unwin, 1972), 21.

22 Ginsberg, *Foreign Policy Actions of the European Community*, 134.

23 Richard T. Griffiths, "'Two Souls, One Thought'? The EEC, the United States, and the Management of the International Monetary System," in Douglas Brinkley and Richard T. Griffiths (eds.), *John F. Kennedy and Europe* (Baton Rouge: Louisiana University Press, 1999), 210–211.

24 Gian Paolo Casadio, *Transatlantic Trade: USA-EEC Confrontation in the GATT Negotiations* (Westmead: Saxon House, 1973), 145 and 151.

25 Casadio, *Transatlantic Trade*, 2–5, 18–22 and 181–182.

26 N. Piers Ludlow, "A Supranational Icarus? Hallstein, the Early Commission and the Search for an Independent Role," in Antonio Varsori (ed.), *Inside the European Community: Actors and Policies in the European Integration, 1957–1972* (Baden-Baden: Nomos, 2006), 46–47.

27 Lucia Coppolaro, "The European Economic Community in the GATT Negotiations of the Kennedy Round (1964–1967): Global and Regional Trade," in Varsori (ed.), *Inside the European Community*, 356–357; cf. Casadio, *Transatlantic Trade*, 26.

28 Quoted in Ludlow, "A Supranational Icarus?," 38.

29 Hallstein, *Europe in the Making*, 268–269.

30 Thomas W. Zeiler, *American Trade and Power in the 1960s* (New York: Columbia University Press, 1992), 58.

31 Quoted in Pascaline Winand, "United States-European Relationships, 1961–1963," in Anne Deighton and Alan S. Milward (eds.), *Widening, Deepening and Acceleration: The European Economic Community 1957–1963* (Baden-Baden: Nomos, 1999), 19. The latter was to be accomplished by the Multilateral Nuclear Force, a short-lived effort whose passion and failure recalled that of the EDC a decade earlier.

32 Ginsberg, *Foreign Policy Actions of the European Community*, 138.

33 Quoted in Zeiler, *American Trade and Power*, 260.

34 Cf. Dermot Keogh, "Irish Neutrality and the First Application for Membership of the EEC, 1961–1963," in Deighton and Milward (eds.), *Widening, Deepening and Acceleration*, 290–291.

35 Lawrence L. Hamlet, "The Core of Decision-Making," in Reinhardt Rummel (ed.), *Toward Political Union: Planning a Common Foreign and Security Policy in the European Community* (Baden-Baden: Nomos, 1992), 87–88.

36 Ginsberg, *Foreign Policy Actions of the European Community*, 139.

37 Hallstein, *Europe in the Making*, iii.

38 Geoffrey Goodwin, "The External Relations of the European Community—Shadow and Substance," *British Journal of International Studies*, 3:1 (1977), and 52.

39 FRUS, 1969–1976, Vol. E–15, pt. 2, Doc. 9, Nixon to Kissinger, March 10, 1973.

40 Eberhard Rhein, "The Community's External Reach," in Rummel (ed.), *Toward Political Union*, 38.

41 FRUS, 1969–1976, Vol. E–15, pt. 2, *Documents on Western Europe*, Doc. 40, Memorandum of Conversation, December 9, 1973. "Procedures" referred to the forum for consultations over a post-Tito Yugoslavia and over the Middle East.

42 Casadio, *Transatlantic Trade*, 142–145.

43 Archives of the European Union, BAC 3/1978, No. 928/3, 1969–1970, J. Robert Schaetzel, speech, February 12, 1970.

44 BAC 3/1978, No. 927/2, 1968–1969, C. Heidenreich, memorandum, January 7, 1969.

45 Author's conversation with Rozanne Ridgway.

46   David Allen, "West European Responses to Change in the Soviet Union and Eastern Europe," in Rummel (ed.), *Toward Political Union*, 120.

47   Cited in Christopher W. Murray, "View from the United States: Common Foreign and Security Policy as Centerpiece of US Interest in European Political Union," in Rummel (ed.), *Toward Political Union*, 214. The declaration is at 358–360.

48   In contrast to the immediate period after the Cold War when the timing of respective enlargements of the EU and NATO appeared less coordinated than might have been expected.

49   E.g. Frédéric Bozo, Marie-Pierre Rey, N. Piers Ludlow and Leopoldo Nuti (eds.), *Europe and the End of the Cold War: A Reappraisal* (New York: Routledge, 2008).

50   FRUS, 1952–1954, Vol. VI, pt. 1, *Western Europe*, Doc. 66, Memorandum by the Officer in Charge of Economic Organization Affairs (Camp) to the Director of the Office of Western European Affairs (Byington), July 18, 1952.

51   ibid., Doc. 129, Draft Circular Telegram by the Officer in Charge of Economic Organization Affairs (Camp), October 24, 1952.

52   Rhein, "The Community's External Reach," 38.

53   See Ibid., 37–38. I also thank Tom Niles and Albrecht Rothacher for these details.

54   Coombes, *Politics and Bureaucracy*, 69 and 166–216.

55   She took his surname, Camps, when she married him.

56   Within the US State Department, RA held sway over many promotions given the number of matters over which it had jurisdiction, from defense to trade to economic assistance. Whatever issue, negotiation, or problem crossed a European border, RA had a role. By 1962 RA had become so big that it was split in two: RPE, or regional political and economic affairs; and RPM, or regional political and military affairs.

57   Ginsberg, *Foreign Policy Actions of the European Community*, 135.

58   See, for example, Sherrill Brown Wells, *Jean Monnet: Unconventional Statesman* (Boulder: Lynne Rienner, 2011). This method refers not to the better-known one he advocated—the functional integration of economic sectors—but instead to the one he practiced as a lobbyist and organizer.

59   The idea was reportedly Monnet's, and came during the EDC crisis that year. See Tennyson's Oral History, European Union Archives, 3–4.

60   Kohnstamm Oral History, European Union Archives, 74.

61   Ralf Dahrendorf, "It Is Not Easy For a Community to Have a Foreign Policy," *International Journal of Politics*, 5:1 (1975), 14.

62   Quoted in Goodwin, "The External Relations of the European Community," 43.

63   Coppolaro "The European Economic Community in the GATT Negotiations," 362.

64   Again, I am grateful to Angela Romano for this point.

65   Quoted in Casadio, *Transatlantic Trade*, xi.

3

The EC and the Socialist World: The Ascent of a Key Player in Cold War Europe

Angela Romano

This chapter offers a critical appraisal of the European Community's relations with the socialist world in the period 1957–1992. "Socialist world" is here restricted to its European scope: the Soviet Union and its allies (all members of the Council for Mutual Economic Assistance—CMEA or Comecon—and referred to as "the socialist bloc"), and socialist yet non-aligned Yugoslavia.

Not until 1988/89 did the socialist bloc countries establish official relations with the EC. The thirty-year non-recognition policy and the long-held idea of a Community insulated from Cold War dynamics long discouraged historical inquiry.[1] Most literature on EC–Eastern Europe relations is political-science-based and concerned with either the long road to Eastern enlargement or the elaboration of the EC/EU's foreign and security policy. The underlying argument is that the EC only engaged with Eastern European countries after 1989, when it adopted measures to favor the latter's transition from socialist to democratic regime, whereas during the Cold War it was ambivalent or even indifferent towards Eastern Europe.[2] John Pinder, for example, argued that the EC could have been more conciliatory towards the East European countries, but was uninterested in making concessions because they "had not made the breakthrough on the road to market economy and pluralist democracy."[3] Historians who recently started to explore the EC's involvement in East–West relations are revealing a different picture. Some demonstrate that the EC and its member states played a fundamental role in shaping the early 1970s Conference on Security and Cooperation in Europe (CSCE).[4] Research examining the 1970s and early 1980s confirms an active role of the EC in European Cold War relations, and shows the Community's reach into (and allure for) COMECON countries.[5]

The literature on EC–Yugoslav relations during the Cold War era is likewise limited and quite unanimous in dismissing the EC's Yugoslav policy as one of neglect and ignorance of Yugoslavia's fragile situation.[6] Benedetto Zaccaria's recent research proves that the EC in fact had a clear political goal of stabilization in the Mediterranean; identified Yugoslavia's political non-alignment as a key asset in this respect; and consistently adopted a forthcoming policy aimed at strengthening the Balkan economy.[7]

This chapter argues that, after initial neglect, the European Community steadily became an important actor in Cold War European relations, and was gradually recognized as such by the traditional subjects (states) and purposefully created organizations acting in the field (such as North Atlantic Treaty Organization (NATO) and CMEA). Not only did the EC polity break into the Cold War structure of superpower-led blocs, it did so with a view to breaking it in the long run, and consistently acted to effect change in East–West relations.

The chapter is organized in four sections that periodize the evolution of the EC's attitude to the socialist world. The sections have identical structures. First, they briefly introduce the international situation with reference to Cold War dynamics, in which the EC's relations with socialist countries were perforce embedded. Second, they describe the EC machinery and rules in place to deal with socialist countries, and appraise the role of the main EC players (Commission, member states, European Parliament) in preventing or fostering such a policy. Third, they report cases that elucidate the EC's attitude/policy toward the socialist bloc countries and the latter's attitudes towards the Community. Fourth, they compare and contrast this with the peculiar Yugoslav case. Finally, each section appraises the relationship between the EC on the one hand and United States and NATO on the other with regard to policies towards Yugoslavia and the socialist bloc countries (for example, division of labor, coordination, or divergences). In the conclusion, the chapter offers an overall assessment of the main driving forces and actors behind the development of the EC's relations with the socialist world, and summarizes the main features of these evolving relationships.

The Time of Neglect: 1957–1968

The EC was born in a Europe divided by the Cold War and organized in blocs. Created for reasons other than Cold War rivalry, the EC was nonetheless embedded in the Western camp, as its six founding states were democratic, market-oriented regimes that belonged to NATO and relied heavily on US military protection. The many discussions about the creation of a political union in the 1960s bore no results, as the six governments disagreed on the level of autonomy they desired from the hegemonic ally, as well as on its feasibility. Nor was there consensus about how to relate to the Cold War. Consequently, they maintained a division of labour between NATO and the EC, with the latter devoted to economic and institutional issues largely detached from the Cold War.[8] This attitude continued in the mid-to-late 1960s, when international flows of trade, communications, and tourism between the two halves of Europe increased markedly. At the time, all socialist regimes sought cooperation with the West; for their part, West European governments proved keen to establish and/or reinvigorate political and economic relations.[9] This new approach also reverberated in the Atlantic Alliance, where the 1967 Harmel Report added the promotion of dialogue and cooperation with the East to NATO's classic function of defense.

At EC level, no mechanism existed for discussing East–West relations, nor was the Community equipped to develop a specific trade policy towards socialist countries.

The Treaty of Rome was mute on the subject, except for a protocol on inter-German trade that described the latter as "non-foreign."

In 1958, the Commission's director-general for External Relations, Günther Seeliger, identified several pressing political reasons for a common European stance on trade with the socialist countries. Some were high politics concerns such as the need to assert the European belief that trade would help reduce the Cold War divide—vis-à-vis US hostility to any such commerce. Other reasons were related to the completion and protection of the Common Market, such as the necessity to envisage a coordinated European response in case of large-scale Soviet-orchestrated commercial dumping. However, Seeliger's paper did not enthuse his direct superior: Jean Rey, the Commissioner for External Relations, gave priority to establishing an overall common commercial policy with a view to completing the Common Market.[10]

The entry into force of the EC agricultural regulations in January 1962, which also applied to imports from the East, prompted the Commission to try to regulate member states' agricultural exports to the state-trading countries, too. Likewise, and throughout the 1960s, the Commission asked the member states to consider taking action for coordination of the member states' trade policies with the socialist bloc; for instance, shortening bilateral trade agreements, which were usually ten years, to contribute to easing the path towards a coordinated EC policy. Notwithstanding the predominant commercial character of the Commission's approach, it is hard to dismiss the supranational institution as a subject unaware of Cold War dynamics. When the Federal Republic of Germany negotiated a bilateral trade agreement with Romania in 1963, the Commission considered that "since there are no diplomatic relations per se, the Federal Government must view the conclusion of such agreements with the Eastern Bloc countries as an opportunity to discuss issues other than economic relations."[11] Evidently, the idea put forward by Seeliger in 1958—that trade could serve as a tool to overcome the Cold War divide in Europe—was alive and gaining ground among the Brussels Eurocrats.

The political value of trade with socialist countries was certainly clear to national governments, whose *détente* policies largely relied on economic tools. In fact, they competed in socialist markets and proved unwilling to agree to the harmonization of trade measures at EC level, with the exception of national import quota lists, which were introduced in 1968.

This attitude of the member states provided room for maneuver to the socialist regimes, which already refused to acknowledge the Community's existence and legitimacy. Their approach originated in their view of the EC as an instrument of Western aggression, potential German revanchism, and discrimination in international economic exchange.[12]

However, the remarkable growth of the EC economies and the successes of the Common Market induced a gradual change of attitude in the East. In September 1962, an article by Soviet leader Nikita Khrushchev considered "the possibility of economic cooperation and peaceful economic competition, not only between the states with different political systems but also between their economic alliances."[13] This more-realistic attitude was largely caused by the economic repercussions that the Common Market was having on the socialist economies' agricultural sectors. Cautiously yet gradually, some

Eastern European governments started informally approaching the Commission with the intent to negotiate sectoral agreements that could mitigate charges and quotas imposed by the EC. This was the case for Poland, Czechoslovakia, and Hungary between 1964 and 1968; Romania's ambassador in Brussels regularly frequented the Commission's offices. Yet, in observance of the official position agreed within COMECON, all the socialist bloc governments persisted in refusing to formally recognize the EC.

The political economy choices adopted by the socialist regimes in the mid-1960s also fertilized the ground for direct relations with the EC. All the socialist countries embarked on programs of rapid modernization through acquisition of Western products, know-how, and technology; the official socialist economic doctrine recognized foreign trade and participation in the world economy as key factors for economic growth. This boosted trade across the Iron Curtain, enhanced the importance of the EC market, and inevitably increased socialist economies' exposure to the impact of the EC's evolution trajectory.

By contrast, the Rey Commission's approach to non-aligned Yugoslavia was marked by attention to high politics. The Commission was manifestly supportive, and pressured the member states to conclude a trade agreement with Yugoslavia in order to give it some "political and psychological relief." As Yugoslavia was both a socialist country and a founding member of the Non-Aligned Movement, the Commission thought that a more forthcoming attitude towards Belgrade would enhance the image of the EC in socialist and developing countries alike.

However, when the EC Council agreed to open negotiations on tariffs (July 30, 1968), it limited the Commission's mandate to industrial domains: the French government excluded the agricultural sector in order to protect French producers from competition from Yugoslavia's cheaper products. Only after the Soviet intervention in Czechoslovakia in August 1968 did the member states agree on the Commission's approach to Yugoslavia, which prioritized international political considerations over national economic concerns. The Italian and German governments, in particular, became Yugoslavia's major advocates for strategic Cold War reasons, with Italy keen to improve the Balkan country's internal economic solidity to avoid instability at its borders. Concerns that the Soviets might threaten Yugoslavia after dealing with Czechoslovakia prompted the EC Council's agreement to open negotiations on a comprehensive trade treaty.[14]

The Commission's leading role in relations with the Yugoslav government was also facilitated by the latter's forthcoming attitude towards the supranational institution. From 1959, the Yugoslav embassy in Brussels had regular contacts with the Commission to promote exports to the Community, which represented the most important market for Yugoslav agricultural produce. Moreover, the 1965 Economic Reform gave impetus to economic openness to the West as a means to transform the inefficient Yugoslav economy into a more productive, market-oriented system.[15] In addition, the Commission's attention to Yugoslavia's political dimension in the Cold War did not pass unnoticed in Belgrade. In its quest for tangible arrangements with the EC, Belgrade identified the Commission as a key interlocutor; and in September 1968, after the Prague events, Yugoslavia became the first socialist country to open diplomatic relations with the EC institutions and appoint an ambassador to the Community.[16]

The Time of Assertion: 1969–1975

This period sees the full flourishing of East–West *détente*. The newly elected US President Richard Nixon opened an era of superpower negotiations that would comprise summits, expanded economic exchanges, rules of conduct, and above all the agreements limiting strategic nuclear arms. On March 17, 1969, the Warsaw Pact re-launched its proposal for a pan-European conference (what would become the CSCE), which NATO accepted in principle in December 1969. The West German government, now led by social-democrat Willy Brandt, joined in East–West cooperation. The *Neue Ostpolitik* deliberately aimed at changing the image of West Germany from enemy to partner of the socialist countries and effecting rapprochement with the East as a means to achieve reunification of the German nation in the long run. The socialist regimes and the capitalist countries of Europe grew entangled in a complex web of business interactions, financial flows, and economic interdependence; Western corporations, private banks, and businesses on the one side and socialist managerial elites on the other were also active in developing regular patterns of East–West connection.[17]

The international environment was thus conducive to an EC policy towards the socialist countries. Important changes in the EC member states' governments made it happen. Brandt's *Ostpolitik* went hand in hand with a strong forward motion on EC integration. Most importantly, the resignation of Charles de Gaulle from the French Presidency in May 1969 and the more cooperative stance of his successor, Georges Pompidou, opened the door to the first EC enlargement—bringing in Britain, Ireland, and Denmark—and to initiating political cooperation. At the keystone Hague Summit of December 1969, member states acknowledged that the soon-to-be nine-member Community would be the largest trading power in the world and hence have the weight to play a prominent international role. Within a year they instituted European Political Cooperation (EPC), an intergovernmental mechanism of foreign-policy coordination. East–West relations featured prominently in EPC's first ministerial meeting in November 1970, which decided to develop a distinct collective approach to the CSCE despite existing NATO consultations on the subject. Indeed, the EC member states perceived their common conception of *détente* as being different from the American one. Whereas the US dialogue with the Soviets seemed to aim at perpetuating the status quo, West European *détente* was conceived as a process to overcome the Cold War order in Europe and ease the liberalization of socialist regimes in the long run. Ministers also realized that the proposed CSCE agenda item on economic cooperation, which aimed at overcoming discriminatory blocs in Europe, clearly invited a specific EC response (NATO economic proposals for the CSCE totally ignored the Community!). The EC governments aimed at preserving the Community's future development and (possibly) gaining its recognition by the socialist countries.

EPC was equipped with a complex machinery to deal with the CSCE: it comprised expert working groups, and increasingly involved the EC Commission in the elaboration of this collective policy. It also developed procedures to coordinate the EC member states' stance within NATO.[18] In May 1971, an EPC ministerial meeting set the guidelines of this embryonic collective Eastern policy: cooperation with socialist countries should not prejudice the development of the Community; any agreement likely to strengthen the Soviet hold on its allies, such as the establishment of EC–COMECON relations, should be refused; and overall, establishing relations between the Community and each socialist country was a non-negotiable priority goal. As perfectly summarized by EC Commission President Franco Maria Malfatti to the EC Parliamentary Assembly on June 8, 1971, "the Seventies should see the consolidation of a new atmosphere between us and the countries of the East."[19]

The EC Nine proved a remarkable unitary force in shaping most of the CSCE Final Act according to their common vision of *détente*. They also succeeded in preventing the adoption of provisions prejudicing the Community and its future development, and in promoting the image of the EC as a constructive force in Europe. The proliferation of contacts between CSCE participants allowed the EC to acquire information about the Eastern bloc's internal dynamics, and hence grow more confident of its own bargaining position. The EC member states held firm in their refusal of an EC/CMEA accord on Soviet terms (including trade and excluding direct relations between the Community and individual countries). Then, they used the implementation of the Common Commercial Policy (CCP) as a means to pressure the socialist regimes into recognizing the Community. In November 1974 the EC Commission sent all socialist governments a letter explaining that from January onwards member states would no longer sign or renew bilateral trade agreements, as competence would pass to the Commission; contextually, it offered all-areas negotiations. In the meantime, the EC Council adopted unilateral import arrangements, which it would revise unilaterally every year pending the socialist countries' reply to the Commission's offer.

Given the economic crisis-driven protectionism in Western Europe, this arrangement promised no good for the East, particularly for export-oriented countries such as Hungary, Poland, Romania, and Czechoslovakia. Export earnings were vital for their modernization efforts; and economic growth had become a *sine qua non* for political stability and regime legitimization, especially after the repression of the Prague Spring in 1968. As their governments became more inclined to approach the Community, or even recognize it, so as to negotiate a better deal, a major discussion started within COMECON, where East Germany and the Soviet Union demanded a bloc response to the "EC question." Pending a common COMECON stance—or wishing to sidestep it—some socialist governments had started to explore national roads to the EC. On January 31, 1972, Romania formally applied for beneficiary status in the EC generalized scheme of preferences (GSP), which it received as of January 1, 1974. In 1973 the Bulgarian government (the most loyal to Moscow) also showed interest in the GSP during bilateral talks with the French, who replied that Sofia should address the EC Commission. In August 1974, some Polish representatives approached the Commission to explore the possibility of trade talks, and emphasized Warsaw's interest in opening relations with the Community; the timing was not coincidental—the transfer of trade competence to the Commission would occur at the end of the year.[20]

The governments of the export-oriented socialist bloc countries probably had in mind the example of Yugoslavia, which signed its first trade agreement with the EC on March 19, 1970. The accord met many of Belgrade's requests, particularly in the agricultural field, and set up a Mixed Commission that would allow Yugoslav needs and interests to be appraised continually. Yugoslavia also benefited from the Commission's highly political approach, which gained a new perspective in this period. External Relations Commissioner Ralf Dahrendorf highlighted Yugoslavia's international role in the Mediterranean area, which was at the time marked by instability and by a growing Soviet naval presence. Accordingly, in June 1971, the Yugoslav dossier was passed from Director General XI (DG XI), responsible for state-trading countries, to DG I, more specifically to the desk dealing with Mediterranean countries. This also met the Yugoslav preference not to be treated within the East/West context.

The Commission was acting in accord with the member states: in May 1972, EPC agreed on a strategy of support for Yugoslavia's "territorial integrity and independence" via consolidation of the EC–Yugoslav economic relations while respecting Belgrade's non-alignment.[21] While this ruled out association or preferential agreements, it facilitated the signing of a five-year commercial treaty in June 1973. Nonetheless, national interests resurfaced in response to the economic crisis following the 1973 oil shock, and protectionist measures, particularly by France and Germany, hit Yugoslav exports. Belgrade insisted that such an attitude would drive Yugoslavia towards the Soviet sphere of influence, and the Nine's diplomats on the ground confirmed that the country's severe economic crisis had potential political repercussions.[22]

The decisive drive to overcome national economic concerns came from quadripartite diplomacy outside the Community. Yugoslavia had been one of the pillars of Western containment strategy in the region for twenty-five years. With Tito an octogenarian and in precarious health, the American, British, French and West German governments worried that Moscow could attract or pressure the post-Titoist leadership back into the Soviet sphere. Neither the controversies that emerged between Washington and Belgrade during the Yom Kippur War and escalated in the Cyprus crisis, nor Yugoslavia's direct support to the national liberation movement in Angola in early 1975, altered the Western priority of keeping Yugoslavia "with the West but not in the West."[23] It was crucial to avoid Yugoslavia becoming economically dependent on the COMECON market, which would expose Belgrade to Moscow's pressures; hence EC–Yugoslav relations should be strengthened, whatever the price.

By contrast, US–West European coordination was poor on both the CSCE and relations with the socialist bloc. For the Nine, the CSCE represented a terrific opportunity to assert the EC's international role and shape a new kind of relations in Europe, where they perceived and resented a superpower condominium over their heads. For the Nixon administration, the CSCE was merely a convenient little tool for strengthening the relationship with the Soviet Union. Nixon and Kissinger had scant interest in promoting human contacts across the Iron Curtain (if not open annoyance)—an attitude that alienated the EC Nine. The next US administration proved more helpful during the final months of the CSCE, with President Gerald Ford committed to provisions encouraging progress on freedoms for all European citizens. Yet the fundamental rationales remained different on both sides of the Atlantic. Washington did not convert to European *détente*, in the sense of the process of overcoming the Cold War by expanding contacts, and still reasoned in terms of the global superpower game: "the CSCE, and its Third Basket on human issues, became the stick to punish Soviet aggressive, or at least insufficiently cooperative, policy in the rest of the world."[24]

The Years of Preservation: 1975–1984

In the second half of the 1970s, Soviet-sponsored activities in Africa and President Jimmy Carter's vigorous stance on human rights strained the superpowers' *détente*. Two major crises at the turn of the decade—the Soviet invasion of Afghanistan in December 1979, and the worsening Polish crisis culminating in the imposition of martial law in December 1981—brought the superpowers back to confrontational stances. Carter was outraged by the Soviet move in Afghanistan and adopted sanctions; his successor, Ronald Reagan, stepped up confrontation with Moscow to harsh rhetoric, economic warfare, and an arms race. Amidst these sharp tensions, all EC governments continued a policy of *détente*, and strengthened their political cooperation with a view to asserting an autonomous EC Eastern policy.

The EPC machinery was put to work to deal with CSCE follow-up meetings (or "Helsinki process") and to elaborate a collective policy towards the Socialist bloc. In 1974, the member states added a top layer to their intergovernmental cooperation: the European Council gathering the heads of state and government. As the European Council became gradually structured and integrated with both the EC and EPC, summits regularly dealt with East–West relations.[25] The European Council usually endorsed the work done in EPC; yet it added political weight to common actions, and proved a valuable tool to maximize West European cohesion ahead of discussions with the US administration.[26] In October 1981, the EC foreign ministers adopted the London Report on EPC, which, among other things, established that the Commission should participate in all EPC meetings. By so doing they recognized both the need for and the gains from such a close relationship in situations where political and economic factors were closely interrelated (for example, relations with socialist countries), and intended to allow for joint EPC/EC actions. The first such example was their common response to the imposition of martial law in Poland. In March 1982, the EC Council of Ministers adopted a number of restrictions on Soviet goods within the scope of the common commercial policy, but made no reference to the Polish situation. The link had been established within EPC, which agreed to use Community's mild restrictions to convey a warning to Moscow while avoiding open hostility.[27] During the previous months, the EC governments' most serious concern was that a worsening of the Polish crisis might lead to a Soviet intervention; this would inevitably put an end to *détente* in Europe. They did not read the imposition of martial law by Polish authorities as a fatal blow to *détente*, but considered it paramount to avoid igniting additional tensions. Accordingly, the EC members resisted US pressure for economic sanctions, and at the Brussels European Council of March 1982 openly pointed to the positive pro-*détente* political value of East–West economic relations.

Beyond crisis management, the EC's Eastern policy mostly comprised action in the CSCE process and the forging of relations with socialist countries. The CSCE branch—largely dealt with by EPC—plainly benefited from the Helsinki experience; the Nine were cohesive in both the Belgrade (1977–1978) and the Madrid (1980–1983) follow-up meetings. In particular, they proved determined to approach the CSCE in a constructive way and strove to improve relations among European countries at a time of superpower confrontation. At Madrid, EPC even added a more visible military security dimension to the CSCE agenda by endorsing a French proposal for a Conference on Disarmament in Europe.

More remarkably, the EC succeeded in consolidating unofficial relations with the socialist bloc countries. The EC Commission was projecting an image of honest broker to the East. In its 1974 offer, the Commission had addressed most socialist economies' known concerns, namely import quotas, agricultural imports, most-favoured-nation treatment, safeguard mechanisms, and problems of payment. Moreover, at the time of economic crisis the Commission, which had competence on establishing import quotas, proved more forthcoming to the socialist countries than the individual EC member states. While the latter often asked for high protectionist quotas to defend their industries from external competition, the supranational institution proved determined to build exchanges with the East on the basis of actual reciprocity of gains and concessions.

In any case, the member states provided the Commission with effective leverage in the pursuit of recognition: in December 1977 the EC Council decided to apply the common commercial policy to textile and steel imports from state-trading countries, meaning that the latter would have to negotiate bilateral agreements directly with the EC.

Facing serious harm to their exports, Poland and Hungary agreed to negotiate with the Commission and signed a five-year textile agreement with the EC. Within four months, Czechoslovakia became the first East European country to conclude a steel arrangement with the Community; it was soon followed by Hungary, Romania, and Poland. Even Bulgaria approached the EC Commission on several issues: it applied to join the GSP in 1978; signed its first agreement with the EC in January 1979, on steel; and within three months concluded a four-year agreement on textiles. More impressively, the Bulgarian government asked the Community for a wide-ranging agreement, which it wished to be more comprehensive than the EC–Romania accord. Indeed, a sort of competition broke out among socialist bloc countries to get the best deal with the Community. Apart from intra-CMEA competition, Sofia worried about the effects that Greece's imminent EC membership would have on Bulgarian exports. Overall, progress on West European integration—new policies, enlargement—proved worrisome for socialist regimes and had sobering effects on their attitude towards the Community.

This held true even for the GDR (German Democratic Republic) and the Soviet Union, whose governments had vigorously opposed direct relations with the EC. They entered into negotiations with the Community following the implementation of the common fisheries policy in January 1977 and the EC Council's request that they should either negotiate fishing quotas with the Commission or withdraw their fleets from the EC's common waters. Having economic and strategic interests at stake, both governments agreed to enter talks. Eventually they broke off the negotiations when they realized that the Community would not renounce the (Berlin) territorial clause, which the Kremlin denounced as incompatible with the existing Quadripartite Agreements on Berlin—a crucial feature of the European Cold War order.

That the socialist governments—including the Soviets—no longer ignored the Community's weight is also visible in their cultivation of regular contacts with the

Commission. Although unofficial, these interactions came very close to classic diplomacy in their substance: consultations spanned the CSCE process as well as broader international issues such as the world economic order, GATT rounds, and relations with developing countries. The socialist governments used these conversations to appraise the possible economic and political implications of EC policies for their countries; for instance, devoting strong attention to the EC monetary-union project, and to EC–China negotiations. Their persistent denial of official recognition had become a mere façade—the EC's economic force proved impossible to resist and its growing international political weight hard to ignore.[28]

Testimony to the EC's political importance, at least in the region, is supplied by the Yugoslav government's call for an EC public declaration of readiness to support Yugoslavia's economy—which was substantiated in the EC–Yugoslav Joint Declaration of December 1976—and its eventual agreement to sign a *preferential* agreement with the Community in April 1980.[29] The latter had been conceived by the EC Commission, in particular by Commissioner for External Relations Wilhelm Haferkamp, to prevent Yugoslavia becoming isolated in the Mediterranean area. Between June 1975 and June 1977, the new democratic regimes of Greece, Spain, and Portugal had officially applied for EC membership; in the same years, the EC concluded cooperation agreements with the Maghreb and Mashreq countries. Yugoslavia's consequential loss of EC market shares could only be avoided by adopting a preferential approach within the framework of the EC's Global Mediterranean Policy. Uncertainty about Soviet plans after the invasion of Afghanistan and the prospect of imminent leadership transition due to the deterioration of Tito's health induced the Yugoslav authorities to accept the preferential agreement as "a necessary evil" to anchor Yugoslavia to the EC market in this delicate political juncture.[30] However, both sides used extreme discretion during the negotiations in order to avoid provoking Soviet reactions.

The new EC strategy actually represented a *Western* guarantee for the country's entry into the much-feared post-Tito era. The Atlantic allies agreed that NATO should not be directly involved, and that Yugoslavia should be economically linked to the West through the EC.[31] In an unprecedented move, the Carter Administration even supported an expansion of the Community's preferential links to Yugoslavia within the GATT framework.[32]

Conversely, there was no transatlantic consensus on how to deal with the socialist bloc during the renewed superpower confrontation of the early 1980s. Although NATO remained the major forum for attempts at reconciling positions, bilateral channels, quadripartite meetings, and G-7 summitry were equally used. President Reagan constantly tried to broaden the unilateral US policy to a multilateral one including Western Europe, but was largely unsuccessful; the EC member states had no intention of renouncing *détente* and its benefits for the sake of the superpowers' global rivalry. When major crises erupted between 1979 and 1981, the West Europeans, though not acquiescing to the Soviets, continued their established policy of change through rapprochement, and rapprochement through trade and financial relations. When the transatlantic clash reached its peak over the Siberian pipeline affair, with unilateral US sanctions hitting also West European businesses, the European Council of March 1982 explicitly "recognised the role which economic and commercial contacts and cooperation have played in the stabilization and the development of East–West relations as a whole and which [it] wish[es] to sse continue on the basis of a genuine mutual interest."[33] The EC polity also refused sanctions because they threatened the development of the Community's bilateral relations with socialist countries, which the Commission and the member states had pursued with determination for fifteen years. Moreover, neither the Commission nor the member states intended to force change in the socialist regimes; countries were rewarded for their keenness to recognize or deal with the Community, not for their domestic reforms—Romania got better treatment than Hungary at the time!

The Time of Institutionalization: 1985–1992

After his re-election in 1984, Reagan resumed the superpowers' dialogue. The appointment of Mikhail Gorbachev to the Soviet leadership boosted this dialogue to regular bilateral summits and negotiations for the reduction of strategic arms arsenals (START). At continental level, Gorbachev fully aligned the Soviet stance to the idea of pan-European relations as enshrined in the CSCE process. The juncture at international level was thus most favorable for consolidating the EC's Eastern policy.

At EC level, the member states adopted the Single European Act (SEA)—the first treaty to amend the Treaties of Rome—in which, among other things, they committed to move towards a common foreign policy (Art. 30.1) and strengthened foreign policy coordination instruments. The SEA brought EPC into the treaty framework and provided for closer coordination between EPC actions and the use of Community's instruments of external economic policy. Accordingly, the treaty confirmed the participation of the Commission in EPC, and improved the exchange of information between EPC and COREPER (the Committee of Permanent Representatives, made up of the head or deputy head of mission from the EC member states in Brussels), which prepared EC Council meetings on the economic aspects of external policy. The SEA also brought the European Parliament into play: through the new co-decision procedure for the Community's budget, the Parliament gained a major say on EC grants to East European states, on which it would prove more forthcoming than the Council. Even before the SEA, however, the EP had shown a lively interest in policy towards the East, and produced a string of reports on various aspects of the subject.[34]

The improved machinery for political cooperation would prove key for the effectiveness of the EC Eastern policy from 1988 onwards. In the meantime, the Community harvested the fruits of its *Ostpolitik*. The EC and COMECON had been discussing the possibility to sign an agreement since 1978, but the talks had soon stalled on the scope of such an accord: the Soviets and the GDR wanted it to cover trade, so as to hamper socialist countries' bilateral relations with the EC; the latter pursued the exact opposite goal, also relying on some COMECON members' known reluctance (Poland, Hungary) or open opposition (Romania) to give up their sovereignty to COMECON. Gorbachev unequivocally changed the Soviet stance on this issue. In May 1985, he told Bettino Craxi—Italy's prime minister and president of the European Council during the first semester of that year—that it was time to seek a common language on political matters to the extent that EC member states acted as a political entity. EC–COMECON negotiations started in September 1986, aimed at establishing official relations in the context of their respective competences. The Joint Declaration signed in Luxembourg on June 25, 1988 did just that, calling for cooperation on matters of mutual interest, and inviting follow-up accords defining the fields and forms of such cooperation. Although it did not mention Berlin—it had proved impossible to convince the Soviets to accept the territorial clause—the Declaration affirmed that agreements would apply to those areas where the EC Treaty applied.

The Community's trade agreements with each COMECON country followed soon after. The Belgian government and the Delors Commission called for a consistent common Eastern policy, in which coordination between the Community's and the member states' policies towards Eastern countries should be the rule. Until spring 1989 most governments proved reluctant to limit their freedom of maneuver. Once the magnitude of the events in Eastern Europe became apparent, however, they realized that they could not tackle the challenge posed by regime transformation separately, and supported a leading role for the Community (and the Commission) in dealing with Eastern Europe. Yet Britain, France, Germany, and Italy insisted on retaining room for national cooperation agreements to continue running in parallel to the Community ones.

The Madrid European Council of June 26–27, 1989 affirmed the determination of the EC polity to play an active role in encouraging reforms in the East: conditionality came to mark the EC's Eastern policy. Indeed, during the negotiation of trade and cooperation agreements, the Community differentiated among the Eastern countries on political grounds. For instance, it suspended negotiations with the Bulgarian government from May 1989 to March 1990 because of the latter's infringement of the Turkish minority's rights; negotiations with Romania proceeded with stops and starts due to the government's slowness on reforms and frequent violence in the country.[35]

These agreements were soon overtaken by more advanced accords forged in 1990 following the collapse of socialism in Eastern Europe. The Commission reacted quite quickly to the fall of the Berlin Wall: in a special meeting convened on the very next day, it acknowledged that the GDR was a special case and would join the Community either as the thirteenth member state or as part of the Federal Republic of Germany. Member states' positions were undecided (for example France) or cautious (for example Britain), but German Chancellor Helmut Kohl's unilateral announcement of a ten-point plan for a confederation of the two Germanies forced a common decision, and the December European Council accepted the prospect of German unification. After the elections in East Germany in March 1990 led to a German–German agreement for rapid unification, the increasingly dominant view in the Community turned to favor East Germany's integration in the EC via unification with West Germany, which would require neither revision of the Community treaties nor formal negotiations. The ad hoc European Council of April 28, 1990 in Dublin accepted this course of action.[36]

The situation was different for the other East European countries. The Community was faced with new Eastern leaders declaring "re-joining Europe" a policy priority and arguing that EC membership would help them consolidate democracy just like it had for Greece, Spain, and Portugal.[37] A "widening versus deepening" debate within the EC ended with the decision to bar enlargement to East European states in the near future.[38] Their economies were too weak to compete within the EC—even East Germany's economic activity had collapsed after unification—and would benefit from a long transitional period before accession. In the meantime, the Community would address their demands for closer ties and ensure that their reforms would succeed by offering far-reaching association agreements (called "Europe agreements" to mark their enhanced political significance). In August 1990 the Commission established that the agreements would be tailored for each country (specificity principle), and that the prospective associate should give evidence of its commitment to five conditions: the rule of law, human rights, a multi-party system, free and fair elections, and a market economy. Initially, only Czechoslovakia, Hungary, and Poland met the requirements; they opened their negotiations in December 1990. The EC Council agreed to start negotiations with Bulgaria in September 1991, and only in mid-December with Romania. The preamble of all Europe agreements stated that the associate's final objective was EC membership, and these agreements provided a framework for gradually integrating the associates into the Community.

The EC's new Eastern policy comprised other instruments too, all of which adopted the conditionality principle. As early as December 1989, the EC Council approved PHARE (Poland and Hungary: Assistance for Restructuring their Economies), the Community's aid program to assist the reform process in Poland and Hungary. Operational in early 1990, it was extended to the other East European countries within a year.

In addition, the Community emerged as the leading actor in the West's relations with Eastern Europe. At the G-7 summit in Paris on July 14–16, 1989, Western leaders agreed to work together, along with other countries and international institutions, to support the reforms in Poland and Hungary. To manage this undertaking, they asked the EC Commission to take initiatives. The G-7 decision signaled a change in the US attitude towards East European countries (but not yet the USSR) to come closer to West European views: aid was now considered an appropriate policy instrument to facilitate economic reforms and help them integrate into the world economy, ultimately contributing to a new European security order. Moreover, Washington now recognized that the Community had a special responsibility for its East European neighbors.

The Community also played a major role in setting up a multilateral organization concerned with promoting private investment in Eastern Europe: the European Bank for Reconstruction and Development (EBRD). The idea came from French President François Mitterrand in October 1989, and was adopted by the Strasbourg European Council in December. Negotiations began in January among the G-24 countries, the seven East European states, the Soviet Union, Cyprus, and Malta.[39] The EBDR was founded in 1991 and was the first multilateral organization obliged to link loans to political conditionality: only countries *applying* the principles of multi-party democracy, pluralism, and market economics would be eligible for loans.[40] Hence, the EBRD's mission complied with the EC's Eastern policy principles. Moreover, the Community and its member states together were its main shareholders, with 51 percent of the capital.

Conversely, the end of the Cold War meant the loss of the EC's leading role in the Balkans. Initially, the collapse of the regimes in Eastern Europe and Gorbachev's refusal to uphold them freed EC–Yugoslav relations from Cold War cautiousness to preserve the country's non-alignment: on November 27, 1989, Belgrade asked to open negotiations for Yugoslavia's association to the Community.[41] Fully supportive of this course, and the recognized leader in the West's assistance to the Balkan country for twenty years, the EC Commission also prepared technical and financial assistance measures that would support the economic reform program in Yugoslavia in the framework of the G-24 assistance.[42]

However, when the break-up of the country started in 1990–1991, the EC's instruments lost momentum, and finding agreement among the member states on the response proved difficult and lengthy. The disintegration of the Yugoslav federation demonstrated the limits of EPC/EC's capacity to act as a security actor in the region, eventually epitomized by the (European) call for NATO intervention in the Balkans.

Conclusion

Contrary to long-held scholarly assumptions, the EC did not ignore the socialist world during the Cold War. In fact, Cold War rationales were the main driver of the Community's involvement with both the Socialist bloc and non-aligned Yugoslavia.

The EC's relations with the socialist bloc countries were prompted by EC member states' common ambition to overcome the Cold War order in Europe and their belief that by deepening interdependence across the continent through trade, economic cooperation, and cultural and human contacts they would loosen bipolar restraints and effect change in the long run. In the meantime, a second major driver came to urge common EC action towards the Eastern states by the early 1970s, namely the necessity to persuade the latter to officially recognize the Community's existence and competence, specifically on trade.

Yet the goal of consolidating EC's specific policies and further integration influenced the collective Eastern policy only to a limited extent. It is more accurate to say that common policies were used as tools to induce the socialist regimes to adopt a more cooperative attitude, that further integration (above all political) empowered the EC and made it harder to ignore, and that enlargements had the unintended consequence of limiting state-trading countries' trade options aside of the EC market. As argued in my work to date, the EC's Eastern policy originated mostly from EC governments' unease with the superpower condominium in Europe, which was consolidating over their heads, as well as their concern over the Soviet proposal for a pan-European cooperation overcoming trade blocs, which threatened the existence of the Community. They therefore worked to assert an autonomous voice *vis-à-vis* the superpowers with regard to European relations, and to shape a new continental order according to the specific EC imprint—that is interdependence and multilateralism. Not by chance was the CSCE the first field of action and a constant tool of the EC Eastern policy.

The Cold War, however, also set the limits of the EC policy towards the socialist bloc countries, as until the late 1980s Moscow's rigid bipolar logic made it impossible to consider the wide range of close agreements that the EC could offer to third countries.

As relations with the socialist bloc were part and parcel of the Cold War, national governments were the most important actors involved, both individually and collectively. Until 1969, most EC member states' governments kept the EC detached from Cold War high politics: each preferred to pursue a national Eastern policy and seek Western coordination within NATO and quadripartite meetings. The changes in French and West German governments in 1969 led to the relaunch of integration, the first EC enlargement, and the creation of an ad hoc political cooperation mechanism—EPC. Now all member states shared not only the same goals and approach to the Cold War, but also the political will to make the Community a key player in East–West relations and gain a certain degree of autonomy from the United States. National governments became key promoters of a consistent common policy towards the socialist bloc countries, which became part of every member state's own Eastern policy. Governments changed color, but their approach to East–West relations stayed the same, and so did their commitment to the collective EC policy. Actually, one observes a strengthening over time of member states' will to improve EPC and also link it better to Community actions, whether by conviction (Benelux, Italy, West Germany) or by necessity to achieve greater policy effectiveness (Britain, France). This process culminated in the post-1989 period, when the Community was entrusted with a leading role in policy towards Central and Eastern European countries.

The Commission grew more enmeshed in Cold War-related issues after 1970, because relations with the socialist world had obvious economic implications that impinged on the EC's specific competencies. Up to late 1981 some member states (particularly France) tried to limit the Commission's participation in EPC to discussion of economic aspects of foreign policy, while the supranational institution attempted to get involved in political discussions. However, as trade was a powerful tool in Cold War/*détente* policy, member states came to recognize, even formally, the complementarity of EPC and EC and the usefulness of connecting the two; consequently, the Commission gained a stronger political role in the elaboration of the common policy towards the East. Moreover, upholding the Commission vis-à-vis socialist bloc countries was a key goal of EPC policy, and member states acted accordingly to a large extent. The penchant of the four larger member states for retaining as much room as possible for national Eastern polices (cooperation agreements, national policy on exports) did not go as far as damaging the collective/EC endeavor.

The steady collective Eastern policy of the EC governments achieved its main goals: *détente* was preserved in the continent, the CSCE process continued, and the European socialist bloc governments established unofficial relations with the Community—some reluctantly and others quite convincingly. The Soviets responded with attempts at opposing, then controlling, these changes; they failed, and progressively came to accept the Community's way of reorganizing relations within the continent. Successive US governments' reactions were an ambivalent and varying combination of support and opposition. Nixon's era of negotiations with the Soviets invited and boosted West Europeans' *détente*. Yet the latter's insistence on changing the status quo and promoting personal contacts across the continent annoyed Washington because it disturbed superpower *détente*. After a small window of harmony with Ford, and some misgivings during the Carter years, the transatlantic debate on how to deal with the

Soviets turned harsh during Reagan's first term. The US president adopted a clearly confrontational policy towards Moscow, constantly pressured his EC allies to do likewise, and did not hesitate to hit their interests directly when he considered Western Europe as too interdependent with the East. Eventually it was Reagan, not the EC, who came round. Hence, the EC's collective Eastern policy impacted on both superpowers, and ultimately made them change their strict Cold War approaches.

From the early 1970s (at the first CSCE meeting) the EC was increasingly recognized as a key actor in Cold War Europe; then, in the fast-changing post-1989 scenario "the Community was expected, by its member states and by outsiders, to lead in the region."[43] Only ten years later did NATO start enlarging eastwards.

The Cold War rationale was also the most important driver of the EC's relations with Yugoslavia, though the aim here was to guarantee the status quo. As Zaccaria has demonstrated, the EC's Yugoslav policy was motivated primarily by a desire to prevent any expansion of Soviet influence to the Balkans; accordingly, supporting Yugoslavia's independence and non-alignment became a priority. Yet this imperative also limited the scope of EC–Yugoslav relations, ruling out overtly preferential or association agreements until the end of the Cold War.

In this case too, the EC member states were very important actors, with the Italian and West German governments being the strongest advocates of anchoring Yugoslavia to the Community. Yet the Commission was also a major protagonist in shaping, and actually initiating, EC's policy towards Yugoslavia, in which it emphasized the political aspects of economic concessions. The Commission's stronger role was also boosted by the Yugoslav authorities, which increasingly treated the supranational institution as a political interlocutor. The leading role of the Commission was fully supported by the member states, in recognition of the higher stakes for the Community after the accession of Greece, Spain, and Portugal; indeed, in the mid-1970s the EC's Yugoslav policy became part of its Mediterranean Global policy. Although the EC's Yugoslav policy was to a large extent a response to external challenges, the EC's intent to project its influence across the Mediterranean should not be overlooked.[44] However, the member states saw the EC's political involvement in the Yugoslav question as a means to consolidate NATO's Southern Flank without openly challenging the Soviet Union. Indeed, the strengthening of EC–Yugoslav relations was agreed within the frameworks of quadripartite meetings between the United States, France, Britain, and West Germany, and then also endorsed within NATO. There was a harmony of views across the Atlantic on the means and goals of this Yugoslav policy, especially when Tito's declining health and uncertainty about the future leadership's strategy made Western perception of the Soviet threat in the area more acute. While effective during the Cold War, the EC's Yugoslav policy had scant impact on the country's longer-term stability—and ultimately its very existence.

Notes

1   On this matter see Piers Ludlow's chapter, "The History of the EC and the Cold War: Influenced and Influential, but Rarely Center Stage" in this volume.

2   Peter van Ham, *The EEC, Eastern Europe and European Unity* (London and New York: Pinter, 1993); one slight exception is Karen Smith, *The Making of EU foreign Policy: The Case of Eastern Europe* (New York: St. Martin's Press, 1998), which looks favorably on the early 1980s EEC's intervention in the Polish crisis.

3   John Pinder, *The European Community and Eastern Europe* (London: Pinter Publishers, 1991), 18–19.

4   Angela Romano, *From Détente in Europe to European Détente: How the West Shaped the Helsinki CSCE* (Brussels: Peter Lang, 2009).

5   Angela Romano, "More Cohesive, Still Divergent: Western Europe, the US and the Madrid CSCE Follow-Up Meeting," in Kiran K. Patel and Ken Weisbrode (eds.), *European Integration and the Atlantic Community in the 1980s: Old Barriers, New Openings* (Cambridge: Cambridge University Press, 2013), 39–58; Sara Tavani, "The Détente Crisis and the Emergence of a Common European Foreign Policy: The 'Common European Polish Policy' as a Case Study," in Claudia Hiepel (ed.), *Europe in a Globalizing World 1970–1985* (Baden-Baden: Nomos, 2014); Angela Romano, *The European Community and Eastern Europe in the Cold War: the EC's Ostpolitik and the Transformation of Intra-State Relations* (London and New York: Routledge, forthcoming). On the Community's reach into COMECON see Angela Romano, "Untying Cold War Knots: The EEC and Eastern Europe in the Long 1970s," *Cold War History*, 14:2 (2014), 153–173; Suvi Kansikas, *Socialist Countries Face the European Community: Soviet-Bloc Controversies Over East-West Trade* (Brussels: Peter Lang, 2014); Angela Romano and Federico Romero, "European Socialist Regimes Facing Globalisation and European Cooperation: Dilemmas and Responses," special issue of *European Review of History*, 21:2 (2014), 157–164.

6   Branislav Radeljić, *Europe and the Collapse of Yugoslavia: The Role of Non-State Actors and European Diplomacy* (London and New York: I. B. Tauris, 2012); Rafael Biermann, "Back to the Roots: The European Community and the Dissolution of Yugoslavia: Policies under the Impact of Global Sea-Change," *Journal of European Integration History*, 1:10 (2004), 29–50.

7   Benedetto Zaccaria, *The EEC's Yugoslav Policy in Cold War Europe, 1968–1980* (Basingstoke: Palgrave Macmillan, 2016).

8   N. Piers Ludlow, "An Insulated Community? The Community Institutions and the Cold War, 1965 to 1970," in N. Piers Ludlow (ed.), *European Integration and the Cold War: Ostpolitik–Westpolitik, 1965–1973* (London: Routledge, 2007), 137–143.

9   Wilfried Loth, "The Cold War and the Social and Economic History of the Twentieth Century," in Melvyn Leffler and Odd Arne Westad (eds.), *Cambridge History of the Cold War, Vol. 2* (Cambridge: Cambridge University Press, 2010), 520.

10   Ludlow, "Insulated Community," 139.

11   Quoted in Gérard Bossuat and Anaïs Legendre, "The Commission's Role in External Relations," in Michel Dumoulin (ed.), *The European Commission 1958–72: History and Memories of an Institution* (Luxembourg: Publications Office of the European Union, 2014), 365.

12   Marie-Pierre Rey, "Le retour à l'Europe? Les décideurs soviétiques face à l'intégration ouest-européenne, 1957–1991," *Journal of European Integration History*, 11:1 (2005), 7–28, here 8–10.

13   Quoted in Andrei Grachev, "The Soviet Leadership's View of Western European Integration in the 1950s and 1960s," in Anne Deighton and Alan Milward (eds.), *Widening, Deepening and Acceleration: The European Economic Community, 1957–1963* (Baden-Baden: Nomos, 1999), 40.

14 Benedetto Zaccaria, "The European Commission as a Cold War Player: The Case of EEC-Yugoslav Relations during the 1960s and 1970s," in Vincent Genin, Thomas Raineau and Matthieu Osmont (eds.), *Reshaping Diplomacy: Networks, Practices and Dynamics of Socialization in European Diplomacy since 1919* (Brussels: Peter Lang, 2016), 156–159.

15 Ivan Obadic, "A Troubled Relationship: Yugoslavia and the European Economic Community in Détente," *European Review of History*, 21:2 (2014), 329–348, here 332–339.

16 Zaccaria, "The European Commission," 169.

17 Pavel Szobi, "Between Ideology and Pragmatism: the ČSSR, the GDR and West European Companies in the 1970s and 1980s," *European Review of History*, 21:2 (2014), 255–269.

18 See Angela Romano, "A Single European Voice Can Speak Louder to the World: Rationales, Ways and Means of EPC in the CSCE Experience," in Morten Rasmussen and Ann-Kristina Knudsen (eds.), *The Road to a United Europe: Interpretations of the Process of European Integration* (Brussels: Peter Lang, 2009), 257–270.

19 Quoted in Romano, "Untying Cold War Knots," 160.

20 Ibid., 160–164.

21 Zaccaria, "The European Commission," 161–162.

22 Benedetto Zaccaria, "Assessing Yugoslavia's Place in Western European Stabilisation Policies in Southern Europe, 1974–1976," *Journal of European Integration History*, 22:1 (2016), 67–84, here 76.

23 French Foreign Minister Jean Sauvagnargues, quoted in ibid., 78.

24 Angela Romano, "Détente, Entente or Linkage? The Helsinki CSCE in U.S.–Soviet Relations," *Diplomatic History*, 33:4 (2009), 703–722, here 722.

25 Emmanuel Mourlon-Druol, "More than a Prestigious Spokesperson: The Role of Summits/the European Council in European Political Cooperation (EPC), 1969–1981," in François Foret and Yann-Sven Rittelmeyer (eds.), *The Commanding Heights of the European Union: The European Council: Institution, Actors, Resources* (Abingdon: Routledge, 2014).

26 Angela Romano, "G-7s, European Councils and East-West Economic Relations, 1975–1982," in Emmanuel Mourlon-Druol and Federico Romero (eds.), *International Summitry and Global Governance: The Rise of the G-7 and the European Council, 1974–1991* (London: Routledge, 2014), 198–222.

27 Tavani, "Détente Crisis"; see also Smith, *The Making*, 38–40.

28 Romano, "Untying Cold War Knots," 166–171.

29 Benedetto Zaccaria, "The European Community and Yugoslavia in the late Cold War Years, 1976–1989," in Wilfried Loth and Nicolae Paun (eds.), *Disintegration and Integration in East-Central Europe, 1919–post 1989* (Cluj-Napoca: Nomos, 2014), 268–269.

30 Zaccaria, "The European Commission," 166–168.

31 Zaccaria, "Assessing Yugoslavia," 81.

32 Benedetto Zaccaria, "Under the Shadow of the Soviet Union: The EEC, Yugoslavia and the Cold War in the long 1970s," in Svetozar Rajak, Evanthis Hatzivassiliou, Eirini Karamouzi and Konstantina E. Botsiou (eds.), *The Balkans in the Cold War* (London: Palgrave Macmillan, 2017), 249.

33 Quoted in Romano, "More Cohesive, still Divergent," 56–57.

34 Aline Sierp, *Democratic Change in Central and Eastern Europe 1989–90: The European Parliament and the End of the Cold War* (Brussels: European Parliament, 2015).

35   Pinder, *The European Community*, 23–33.

36   Smith, *The Making*, 86–87.

37   Quoted in ibid., 88.

38   See Eirini Karamouzi's chapter, "Enlargement as External Policy: The Quest for Security?" in this volume.

39   In 1971, the developing countries that were members of the United Nations and organized in the Group of 77 established the "Intergovernmental Group of Twenty-Four on International Monetary Affairs and Development," or G-24. The G-24 was meant to facilitate coordination of the positions of developing countries on international monetary and development finance issues and to ensure that their interests were adequately represented in negotiations on international monetary matters.

40   Smith, *The Making*, 48–49 and 80–82.

41   Zaccaria, "European Community and Yugoslavia," 278–280.

42   European Commission, Press Release Database, "The Commission Proposes Closer Relations with Yugoslavia," 30/05/1990, http://europa.eu/rapid/press-release_IP-90-428_en.htm (last accessed October 29, 2018).

43   Smith, *The Making*, 49.

44   See Elena Calandri's chapter, "The EC and the Middle East/Mediterranean: Hitting the Glass Ceiling" in this volume.

4

The EC and the Mediterranean: Hitting the Glass Ceiling

Elena Calandri

In comparison with other foreign-policy domains, the European Community's involvement with the Mediterranean has a long history—as one might expect, given the geographical proximity and historical background. At the signing of the Rome treaties in 1957, the Six committed to offer "association" to Morocco, Tunisia, Libya, and Somalia, and allowed Moroccan and Tunisian goods free-of-duty access to the Common Market—a privilege extended to Algeria after the Evian agreements of 1962. Soon afterwards, ideas for interregional bonds were put forward. In 1959, the Community accepted applications from Greece and Turkey "to join the Community." The Mediterranean was, so to speak, "present at the creation."

Nevertheless, EC Mediterranean policy during the Cold War did not draw an incremental curve. As has been remarked, Community activity followed a peculiarly uneven path.[1] Rather static in the first decade, it bloomed at the beginning of the second, when it became a major test for European "civilian power" with two initiatives: the Global Mediterranean Policy (GMP) and the Euro–Arab Dialogue (EAD). In the 1980s, it vanished into a piecemeal and defensive approach. As a further remarkable feature, this involvement faced an extraordinarily fragmented context. Unlike the East-Central European states, bound by Council for Mutual Economic Assistance (CMEA) into one unique, stable, homogeneous and predictable partner,[2] the Mediterranean was a geopolitical concept including fifteen to twenty Southern European, North African and Near Eastern countries. Their past, current, and potential links to EEC members were different and varying, including their political allegiances, cultural, and socio-economic features and mutual attitudes. Under the "Mediterranean" heading fell bilateral relations, trade schemes, conflicts such as Cyprus and Palestine, and problems like terrorism, the environment, energy, and migration. But EEC language also encompassed the elusive definition of the Mediterranean as a broader region. Because of interdependencies and "patterned interactions" resulting in conflicts, cooperation, formal, and informal institutions, it included the Middle East following the engagement of riverine Arab countries in the Arab–Israeli conflict; but it could also reach out to the Gulf area, following energy security issues and political Islam.[3] In such a dense and interdependent environment, mono-causal decisions—and, from the vantage point of the historian, explanations—are impossible.

In sharp contrast to the wealth of often well-informed and perceptive literature of practitioners, observers, and academics of other varieties, historians have shied away from this topic, and EC–Mediterranean relations still lack an adequate base of historical research and publications.[4] Of course, the rapprochements of Greece, Portugal, and Spain have been investigated, and the stabilization of Mediterranean Europe via enlargement—discussed in this book by Eirini Karamouzi—is considered one of the indisputably Cold War-motivated achievements of the Community, as Piers Ludlow also argues in his chapter.[5] EC policy toward the Middle East conflict has also been partially investigated.[6] Usually, however, these sub-regional themes are treated in isolation from the regional environment.

Of Mediterranean policy proper—with the notable exception of Federica Bicchi's comprehensive account—the 1960s are considered by existing literature as a time of evasion, and accordingly ignored.[7] The 1980s have begun to be investigated, but still lack archival sources and framework literature.[8] The only process present in mainstream historiography of European integration is the early 1970s passage "from patchwork to framework" and the climax and rapid decline of the aforementioned GMP and EAD.[9] Considered in earlier analysis as a blooming of integrationist feelings, recent research has mostly applied a realist approach in which intergovernmental dynamics dominate and France's leading role is emphasized.[10] In fact, Mediterranean–Middle Eastern policy is part and parcel of the Six/Nine drive to transform the Community into an international actor, in the framework of an Atlantic Alliance and a bipolar system under United States hegemony. Therefore, the Mediterranean policy is a recurring theme in the literature on US–EC relations; but it often appears more as the pretext than as the true bone of contention.[11] As for "the rest," ground-breaking studies assuming the Southern viewpoints stress the resistance of Third Mediterranean Countries (TMC) to EC integrative efforts, and their inability to confront its economic preponderance.[12]

Here, we discuss the Community's emergence as an international actor by identifying phases combining institutional/formal changes with alterations in the interweaving of some dominating themes. As we mean to follow how the Mediterranean involvement of the Community was shaped and implemented, we will use the term Mediterranean in a flexible and adaptable sense, following the semantic change determined by changing historical conditions.[13] We argue that the Cold War was the primary impetus and motivation for EEC involvement in the Mediterranean, emphasizing the structural influence of American vision and interests.[14] Even when they were key determinants, however, Cold War concerns interacted with other structuring themes. Global trade rules and interests and the place of the EC in the international economy set tight limits on EC action. Against this backdrop, national foreign policies and an intergovernmental dynamic continued to dominate. Visions of post-colonial relations, of the purposes of European integration, and of development strategies, geopolitical and economic interests more often clashing than agreeing, confronted regional events perceived as more and more problematic. Attempts to solve this competition through a regional approach were launched. Compounded by the political, economic and juridical dimensions of the integration process, they produced an interplay between bilateral relations and regional schemes in which the EC remained entangled rather than being able to turn it into the basis of a mature international role.

1958–1970: The EEC as a Double-Hearted
Mediterranean Cold Warrior

EEC action in the Mediterranean began as a derivation of Western solidarity and Cold War concern. The member states and the Hallstein Commission agreed that the EEC ought to be a political anchor and an economic support for the less-developed members of the Atlantic Alliance and of the Organisation for European Economic Cooperation (OEEC). During the negotiations for the OEEC Free Trade Area (FTA), they accepted the American urge not to leave "out in the cold" the five underdeveloped OEEC members: Ireland, Iceland, Portugal, Greece, and Turkey.[15]

Even if the failure of the FTA relieved the Six from moving from words to deeds, the idea that the restored Western Europe would take back part of the charge the United States had shouldered in south-eastern Europe since the Truman Doctrine was not lost. Greece's June 1959 application, while expressing the desire to "join Europe" and thereby be acknowledged as a full member of "the West," assumed that the EEC would provide economic and political support.

Greece's association agreement, signed in July 1961, established mechanisms for a customs union as a prelude to Greece's full membership, instituted an Association Council, and committed US$125 million in assistance for five years. The Treaty of Athens embodied solidarity toward a weak and exposed ally and showed that "association" was apt to serve Western political aims. It also benefited member states' economic interests. Greece was a good market for the FRG (Federal Republic of Germany) and Italy—first and second exporters to the country, respectively—and an emerging partner for France.[16] After decades of agonizing about the rescheduling of debt repayment, the Six also intended the Community to be a technocratic instrument to stem Greece's assumed financial untrustworthiness. Association to the EEC was therefore an economic and political tool to bind a peripheral ally into the Western camp and the European integrated economy, and to promote its economic compliance with the liberal capitalist model. Greece, on its side, assumed a heavy, even if long-term, commitment to keep up with the West European standard.

This early use of Community soft power did not go unchallenged. While the Six accepted that for political reasons the Greek application could not be rejected, the negotiations revealed the difficulties of liberalizing trade between developed and underdeveloped countries. The six governments resented what they considered to be an exceedingly one-sided repartition of advantages, for which they blamed the political hubris of External Relations Commissioner Jean Rey. Other riverine countries already queuing for preferential treatment indeed showed that each Mediterranean agreement would bring more involvement in an area of undifferentiated economies, depending on their exports to Europe of a limited set of agricultural products, which the French *Midi* and Italian *Mezzogiorno* considered their quid pro quo in the Common Market. Italian fears of a *regional* domino effect and protectionist attitude set a model that other Southern European countries would later adopt.

Fear of a *global* domino effect impairing free trade motivated the United States' unease with the Athens Treaty. The State Department welcomed prospective enlargements and encouraged European financial assistance to less developed countries, but refused to consider trade preferences as a legitimate form of assistance and disliked "association," which echoed the French imperial heritage. Prioritizing its grand design of free trade and globalism, it wanted the EEC to decrease its custom duties globally via General Agreement on Tariffs and Trade (GATT) negotiations, not selectively in bilateral agreements, unless they were credibly inscribed into the building of a politically motivated free-trade area or customs union.[17] The twenty-two year transition allowed by the Athens Treaty hardly complied with this requirement.[18] For the State Department, the Athens Treaty became the "bottom line" for any other Community agreement.[19]

This double-thinking reverberated on the second Mediterranean applicant, Turkey—due to its key geopolitical position, the truest test for Cold War influence on EC policy in the area—whose application began to be seriously negotiated in late 1961, in the middle of a delicate crossroads in Western economic diplomacy.[20] After Greece, all agreed that Turkey's severe underdevelopment would make a deal exceedingly difficult. The strong yet insufficient leverage of Cold War imperatives was proved after the Cuba crisis. At the November 1962 meeting of the Council of Ministers, the Six agreed that a closer relationship with the EEC was needed to boost the Turkish allegiance to the West, but mischievously left the last word to the United States. In Washington, the clash between security concerns (the corroboration of Turkey's bonds with the West) and economic drivers (the defence of GATT's role and of domestic economic interests) rebounded for months, among fears that the whole world trade system was at stake: "the EEC could (not) become only slightly pregnant."[21] In the end, President Kennedy himself invited the State Department to be "more forthcoming" toward Turkey's pleas and US support for Turkey's association entered the US–Turkey deal for the replacement of the Jupiter missiles.[22]

This contrasted process produced oddities, to say the least. In September 1963, Turkey signed an association treaty, which established a political bond with the EEC, with the goal of full membership and US$175 million in financial aid. But later the Six showed little understanding for the country's early stages of industrialization, import substitution strategy, and state-driven economy, and so they requested reforms, rapid liberalization and reciprocity in trade—assuming they would bring convergence toward the West European economic model. As a major bargaining chip they promised a gradual implementation of free movement of workers to be completed in 1986 at the latest—an isolated example of how the migrant labor issue could be an integral part of EC–Mediterranean integration.[23] But in Turkey, the EC image was soon tarnished by balance of payment difficulties, a protectionist culture and public resentment, even more so as, in the changing conditions of the European labor market, emigration after 1973 was in fact limited.[24]

The interplay of US security and economic concerns had a different impact on the 1970 Spanish commercial agreement. Barred from membership because of Franco's dictatorship, Spain obtained an open-ended arrangement giving free access to the Common Market for its industrial goods. This time, in spite of vocal domestic opposition, the Nixon administration renounced opposing this preferential agreement following Spain's threat to refuse the US Air Force new facilities and military rights, badly needed after Wheelus Field in Libya was lost after Muammar Gaddafi took power. The exclusion of agricultural products, which suited Italy and the French southern regions, also matched American agricultural interests.[25]

In conclusion, a reluctant EC's developing and stabilizing role in Southern Europe—Malta and Cyprus obtained association agreements in 1970 and 1972 respectively—was certainly inspired and legitimized by Cold War concerns, but in the 1960s neither the Six nor the United States willingly acknowledged the Community's political, developing, and stabilizing role in the Mediterranean as a whole.[26]

1967–1974 Dealing with Regional Crisis, Rising to Political Actorness

The Six-Day War was a turning point in Mediterranean history.[27] The Arab defeat precipitated a superposition between the US–USSR rivalry and the Israeli–Arab one, allowing the Soviets to strengthen their military presence and economic and political influence, particularly in Egypt and Algeria. In Europe, the war and the beginning of Palestinian armed struggle and terrorism raised awareness about dependence on oil supplies and the influence of Middle East conflict on security and economic development. With the exacerbation of the Arab–Israeli conflict as well as the Algerian–Moroccan row and the Cyprus quagmire, the Community began to be seen as an instrument for coordinated action to protect common interests in regional peace-making. The form and effectiveness of this involvement depended on the ability to overcome fractures, particularly France's exit from NATO and its pro-Arab position.

This enhanced Mediterranean engagement was prepared by a set of bilateral agreements signed with all the riverine countries except Albania, Libya, and Syria. Although limited in scope and duration, this set of agreements was no small achievement if one considers that during the first decade relations had been stalled by a collusion between the economic strategies of the North African and Near Eastern partners, post-colonial tensions, de Gaulle's *souverainisme* and personal Arab diplomacy, Italian protectionism on agricultural products and the Northern EC members' lack of interest.[28]

Even if attempts to agree upon criteria for guiding external relations had been doomed to failure under those conditions, a set of temporary guidelines was elaborated in 1967 by the Commission, in the aftermath of the second French veto to the UK and the *coup d'état* in Greece. The freezing of Greek association, the ongoing dictatorship in Spain and Portugal and the demands of the European Free Trade Association (EFTA) countries required a rationalization of the approach toward third countries. Therefore, the Commission maintained that association could only be a stepping-stone toward membership, which in turn was barred to states with authoritarian regimes. However—building on the newly agreed Part IV of GATT, which allowed giving up reciprocity in dealing with underdeveloped countries—it asserted the Community's right to establish preferential agreements with Mediterranean countries.

The bilateral agreements negotiated between 1968 and 1972 demonstrated a *political domino effect*. As a US study recollected:

The Germans and the Dutch have linked the Israeli agreement, which they want for political reasons, to the Spanish agreement pushed by the French. The French accepted the Israeli agreement [which they had vetoed for years for political reasons (author's note)] on the understanding that parallel agreements would be negotiated with the UAR and Lebanon to maintain 'balance' in the tense Middle East situation.[29]

Other dynamics contributed to the shift toward a regional approach. Having barred Southern European countries from association and membership, these and the Southern Mediterranean countries could be dealt with as a group. The Commission now saw a regional approach fit to deal with the impending complication in energy supplies. Such an approach would keep a balance between rival parties claiming for access to the Common Market and assistance, and it was likely to make the Arabs accept a closer bond between the Community and Israel.[30] A further push arrived when the Hague conference of December 1969 made clear that Great Britain would soon enter the Community. Countries dependent on trade with Britain claimed the right to compensation for the future increase in UK customs duties. Enlargement would impose the adaptation of all existing agreements, and their harmonization.

In sum, concerns deriving from the Middle East conflict interacted with enlargement to broaden EC involvement in the Mediterranean. This was compounded by a propensity to regionalist thinking. The choice for a regional initiative expressed confidence in the role model of European integration and was seen as a way to buttress the EC as an international actor and a "civilian" power. This new set of conditions meant that EEC policy was increasingly determined by local and regional concerns, interwoven with a Cold War preoccupation that coincided only in part with the American ones. More importantly, however, the Six/Nine politicized their Mediterranean engagement.

Broader political conditions explain the changing quality of the Community's Mediterranean policy of 1970–1974. First, the global rise of the development issue offered a political argument and a language for extending relations in the area. A Mediterranean policy including not only preferential trade but also financial aid and technical and cultural cooperation—that is, a comprehensive, developmental approach to the region—responded to the expectations of the developing countries and was relied upon to counter US criticism of the Community's preferential agreements. Second, a reading of political shifts in Algeria, Malta, and especially in Libya through the Cold War lens overstated Soviet influence in the Mediterranean. Italian Foreign Minister Aldo Moro soft-pedaled opposition to agricultural exports and urged the Six to act through both the EEC and the newly-born European Political Cooperation (EPC).[31] Last, the Parliament and some Commission officials, notably Ralf Dahrendorf in his capacity as External Relations Commissioner in 1970–1972, advocated a Community right and duty to play a political role in the area, against the backdrop of the Nixon administration's alleged "passivity."[32]

The "Global Mediterranean Policy" was launched in grand style at the October 1972 Paris summit. In Point 11 of the final *communiqué*, the heads of state or government declared that they would "attach essential importance to ... the fulfilment of its commitments to the countries of the Mediterranean Basin with which agreements have been or will be concluded, agreements which should be the subject of an overall and balanced approach." Conceived by Pompidou as the launching of the enlarged political Europe, the Paris Summit included the Mediterranean policy in the definition of the Community as an international political actor at the moment in which *détente*, the changing North–South balance, and the new language of "globalism" and pacific coexistence created room for a European "civilian power."[33]

However, the Community engagement in the Mediterranean contained many elements of ambiguity and second thoughts. In its concrete form, the GMP was born from a French twofold battle *against* EPC involvement in the area and *against* a worldwide development policy prompted by Britain, the Netherlands, and Germany.[34] With regard to the first, Pompidou, who rejected the bipolar vision of the Mediterranean and was engaged in an Arab oil and armaments diplomacy, was concerned that a security-driven approach would automatically involve the United States in EPC consultations, in an area in which Franco–American rivalry over influence and roles dated back to the early years of the Atlantic Alliance.[35] The French government preferred to take the issue back into Community hands. As for the second, after a June 1972 Council meeting *à neuf* had seemingly agreed to replace the Yaoundé association with a global development aid policy, Pompidou joined forces with the Commission to defend the "*acquis communautaire*," that is, Yaoundé and the Mediterranean agreements. Hence, a "Global Mediterranean Policy" was a *pis-aller* that, being "global," would dissipate the need for EPC involvement and the risk of US involvement, and would justify Mediterranean preferential agreements under a developmental mission.

Such internal weakness gave the GMP feet of clay. The emphasis on "globalism" hardly masked the fact that the priority addressees were Spain, Israel, and the Maghreb states.[36] This approach aimed at weaning them away from the "Eastern Arabs" and anti-Israeli militancy, and away from Moscow's influence. In this sense, the GMP used EEC political and economic influence not only to "contribuer à garantir la paix dans cette région," but also to offset what some perceived as the downgrading of US engagement. Yet, little agreement existed among the Nine about the contents of future agreements. Italy and France refused concessions on agricultural products, and Germany defended trade against financial aid. France and Dahrendorf maintained the "political and moral" value of reciprocity in EC external agreements. Britain plainly refused the cooperation dimension, as well as the regional approach.[37]

Moreover, the burden of Franco–American quarrels persisted, and resistance to preferential trade agreements remained strong outside the Community. The most determined effort to prevent the European initiative from colliding with Atlantic bonds was made by the Heath government, whose interest in Mediterranean affairs was modest. They were keen to go along with France and committed to "Europe," but they were also driven by the conviction that "British political interests in the Mediterranean were coincidental with the strategic ones."[38] This approach resounded in the position of the Nixon administration, which shot chained balls against the GMP. Despite Kissinger's positive view of Pompidou and support for closer EC–Spanish relations, the

US government was keenly defending national trade interests and was suspicious of a Europe built through separation from the United States.[39] In 1973, the new External Relations Commissioner Christopher Soames agreed upon a "modus vivendi" with US Under Secretary for Economic Affairs William J. Casey, in which the Nine renounced reciprocity in agreements with South Mediterranean partners, as in relations with the African Caribbean and Pacific Group (ACP) countries.

Whatever arrangement was emerging between the Community and the United States was wiped away by the "Year of Europe," the Yom Kippur War, the oil shock, European ventures in the Euro–Arab Dialogue and the ensuing months of Euro–American dispute that climaxed in February 1974 at the Washington conference on energy.[40] According to protagonists and later observers, the Mediterranean policy and even the European opening to Arab oil producers were not the major stakes of the dispute, which was mainly about US leadership and mutual power relations.[41] Certainly, European regional actorness clashed with the US vision, both because of its interest in the area and because of alliance hierarchy, leading to the worst crisis in Atlantic relations during the Cold War. The EC Mediterranean initiative had a special place in the American urge to obtain a place at the EPC table.

As the dust settled, EC ability to lead a policy in the area legitimized by common Western goals was undermined. Far from being favorable to the Community role in the Mediterranean, *détente* reinforced the US drive for centralization of decision-making and the decrease in US–USSR tensions reduced, instead of reinforcing, the space for Community initiative. Besides supporting free trade, promoting global development aid and defending domestic interests, Washington doubted the European ability to replace the United States as economic and political guarantor in the area. Whereas it acknowledged that France was willing to engage, it had no confidence in its ultimate goals when it came to European integration, and it doubted that its lead would be followed by the other European countries.[42] Europe may well be a "regional power," as Kissinger argued in the "Year of Europe" speech, but it was not legitimate to have a role in its Mediterranean neighborhood. Washington also counted on Soviet self-restraint in the area during *détente*. French ambiguities and the hesitations of other member states worked against the EC role in the area, allowing the brutal reaffirmation of the hegemonic US role and a definition of "Western" interest dominated by US priorities.

1975–1985: "Mediterranean Enlargement" and Fragmentation

The collapse of the Community regional ambition was compounded by local events in creating a new situation. First, the 1974 Cyprus crisis and the ensuing fall of the Colonels' regime put Greece back on its membership track. Together with the Carnation Revolution in Portugal and the death of Francisco Franco in 1975, which removed the impediment to future membership for the Iberian countries, this put an end to the "regional approach." Prospective Southern European members and southern and eastern Mediterranean countries belonged hereafter to two different worlds.[43]

The return of democracy in Portugal, Greece, and Spain dismantled one of the foundations of the regional approach. The Community accepted without hesitation the relaunching of its major Cold War mission—that is, continental stabilization; still, the lengthy enlargement process showed once again that moving from words to deeds opened a gulf of difficulties, which Eirini Karamouzi investigates in her chapter. Among these, France raised the impact of enlargement on Third Mediterranean Countries (TMC) in 1978. The 1980 Commission opinion was optimistic: the increased difficulties for Southern Mediterranean products in the Common Market, saturated by whopping Spanish agricultural output, was expected to be balanced by increased exports into the new member states. For these countries, membership would result in diminished customs duties, increased consumption and higher rates of growth.[44] The British Foreign and Commonwealth Office opposed trying to solve political problems with economic instruments, advocating to allow more time for the applicants and to the Community to prepare for enlargement. They instead proposed inviting Greece, Portugal, and Spain into the EPC, thus giving them political backing also thanks to a duly reinforced cooperation with the United States. In both cases, the attempt to take care of the regional environment, however notable, did not go far. The EC prized its role as a continental promoter of democracy, and the success, and the difficulties, of the enlargement process took precedence over the perception of "disenchantment" and the anticipation of problems in the South Mediterranean partners. This was confirmed as the Spanish and Italian governments joined forces to ensure that no concessions on sensible agricultural products to the TMC would be allowed before the end of the enlargement negotiations.[45]

The legacy of 1973 on European policy toward the Middle East conflict was an opening to Palestinian rights.[46] Certainly, in 1975, Israel was first to sign, a second-generation agreement within the GMP, including a free-trade area and European Investment Bank loans; and the Nine refused to discuss the Palestinian issue or to accept a Palestine Liberation Organisation (PLO) delegation in the Euro–Arab Dialogue, even if the "Dublin formula" allowed a compromise.[47] But after the controversial "Schumann Document" of 1971, the November 6, 1973 appeal for consideration of "the legitimate rights of the Palestinians" and the June 1977 Declaration asking for "a homeland for the Palestinian people" obtained a more general support, and confirmed a cautious opening to Arab causes. In addition, in 1972, and reiterated in 1976, the Community began aid to Palestinian refugees through the United Nations Relief and Works Agency for Palestine Refugees in the Near East (UNRWA). The 1980 Venice Declaration pleaded for the Palestinians' right to self-government, as well as the PLO's right to represent them, and offered participation by the Ten in an eventual international system of guarantee. It tried thereby to revive an independent European initiative with a mildly pro-Arab stance that contrasted with the pro-Israeli position of the Reagan administration.[48] The Declaration was rejected by Israel, however, and two missions held in 1980 and 1981 by the Dutch Presidency ended in nothing. This happened in a period of intense internal conflict, as demonstrated, for example, when the 1983 Athens Council closed without an agreed final *communiqué*.[49] In general, however, no illusions existed about the ability of the Community to have a true impact on the conflict. Later attempts to adopt a more active stance were short-lived, facing a recrudescence of the conflict with *intifada* (1987–1991).

The political cooperation, as well as the negotiations of the new bilateral agreements with the non-European Mediterranean countries within the framework of the GMP, happened in a Community environment almost avowedly governed by intergovernmentalism. This had a restricting effect, as no leader, agreement or coalition emerged to promote engagement in the area. In the major crises of the period—the Turkish occupation of Northern Cyprus, the 1982 Israeli invasion of Lebanon or the 1986 US bombing of Tripoli—the EPC was weakened by the lack of wide consensus and in some cases basic cooperation (on the last occasion, US bombers were famously taking off from British bases while Lord Howe sat in an EPC meeting of uninformed Community Foreign Ministers). France and Britain, in particular, held distant assessments of the purposes and limits of common Mediterranean endeavors. Valéry Giscard d'Estaing further developed the French–Arab and energy-driven diplomacy and maintained a selective attitude regarding the involvement of the Nine in Mediterranean affairs. While via EPC he led an effective reaction to the Turkish invasion of Cyprus in 1974, he forbade the EPC forum from discussing the problems of the Maghreb countries and Libya.[50] He continued, however, to support Political Cooperation engagement in the Middle East conflict, and became the strongest supporter of the Euro–Arab Dialogue. The EAD was soon claimed as a French brainchild and engagement.

As opposed to the developmental approach of the GMP, the EAD was the regional response to the perceived shift in global economic power relations. On the European side, it was thought to be an egalitarian exercise that responded to economic security aims, that is, cooperating with capital-rich, oil-producing and Western-oriented states to reignite European growth by securing energy supplies and engaging in the industrialization, modernization, and development of the Arab world and possibly Africa.[51] While the EAD is often said to have been voided of purpose by the ban on oil discussion, on an American request willingly implemented by Saudi Arabia and by lack of Arab interest after the European refusal to discuss the Palestinian issue, closer analysis shows that the economic dimensions were not without interest for both sides. Britain, which was an open supporter of the voluntary, informal, pragmatic political cooperation, was not unfavorable to the EAD, which it considered a useful forum to lubricate relations with the Arab countries, and where discussions on financial capital movements were considered of the utmost importance.[52] After the Camp David Agreement, however, the EAD was suspended without concrete results.

A more concrete legacy of the 1970s was the new set of open-ended bilateral agreements. After the 1975 free-trade agreement with Israel, in 1976 Tunisia, Morocco and Algeria obtained developmental associations including free access to the CM for industrial goods, limited preferential treatment for agricultural products, technical aid, economic cooperation, financial assistance, a common institutional framework, and social rights for migrant workers.[53] The ratification was lengthy and unenthusiastic, and implementation neglected.[54] Negotiations with the Mashreq were completed in 1977 (Egypt, Syria, and Jordan) and 1978 (Lebanon).[55] All of these engagements bore the brunt of severe disagreements about the legitimacy and priorities in EC aid policy, and the Mashreq obtained poorer conditions than the "Western Arabs." The Labour governments of Harold Wilson and James Callaghan opposed a regional, politically motivated aid policy in the area, refused development as a rationale for action in the Mediterranean, and sought to tilt the balance of aid to Mediterranean and Asian countries. The Mediterranean associations should not give preferential development aid, and the Mediterranean countries were not entitled to priority *vis-à-vis* "non-associated" countries—that is, Asia and the Latin American countries for which Community assistance was initiated in 1976. The financial protocols resulted from hard intergovernmental bargaining, and a procedure closely controlled by the governments robbed the Commission of autonomy in spending decisions. As for trade preferences, the opening of the EC market to industrial goods was severely hampered by the imposition in 1978 of limitations on export quotas for the Mediterranean partners.

In evaluating the impact in 1988 against the backdrop of the TMC's fast deteriorating economic and social conditions, the Commission assessed that the Mediterranean was by then the third commercial partner of the Community (12.8 percent) after the European Free Trade Association (25 percent) and the United States, and the Community ran a yearly commercial surplus of 7 billion ECU.[56] Between 1979 and 1987, EC support had been 3 percent of the total amount of international aid, with member states giving another 14 percent, the United States 31 percent and the Organisation of Petroleum Exporting Countries (OPEC) 28 percent. To the Mediterranean went an 11.5 percent share of total EC public development aid, against 67 percent to ACP countries and 21.5 percent to the "non-associated." While industrial exports to the Common Market grew at more or less the same rate as those from other areas, the overall data masked important differences, with Yugoslavia, Turkey, and Israel absorbing the greatest share and many Arab countries virtually unable to sell on the EC market. The restriction on textile exports had severely hit Morocco and Tunisia, in particular. Agricultural exports were limited due to EC self-sufficiency following enlargement and persistent protectionism. Worryingly, the fall in agricultural activity was producing a set of problems—desertification, urbanization, environmental problems, but also shortages of food for domestic consumption—that was increasing due to fast demographic growth. In sum, the results of more than fifteen years of EC engagement were mitigated, but the Commission argued that domestic conditions, more than insufficient external intervention, explained the acute disarray of the regional economy.

1985–1992: In the Trenches of Fortress Europe

With the Cold War entering its final phase and losing influence following the decline of Soviet presence in the area, the Community Mediterranean outlook became increasingly dominated on the one hand by the fast deteriorating economic and social conditions of the Middle Eastern and North African countries, and on the other by local security threats, terrorism, Islamic anti-Western militancy, arms races, and nuclear proliferation. Responses to these challenges were increasingly determined by the adoption of neoliberal prescriptions for regional development and a securitization of the southern border.

The decline of oil prices that started in 1982 and accelerated in 1985–1986 had heavy implications for the Arab countries. As it has been summarized:

> The purchasing power of the Arab World was severely curbed, especially for oil-exporters, which had been the main driver of growth and internationalization over the previous decade. The redistribution of oil-rents, through aid and official investments between the Arab Gulf states and their 'poor' neighbours in the region fell sharply from 8.2 billion US dollars to 4.3 billion US dollars in 1980 and 1984 respectively … From 1982 on, the economies of the Middle East and North Africa entered a prolonged recession … From 1980 to 1987, the population of the Arab world grew by 25 per cent, from 162 to 202 million of people, and in 1981 the urban population exceeded the rural one for the first time … Between 1980 and 1989 the real GDP per capita for all MENA countries declined from 7161 to 5953 US dollar … the long term outstanding debt of all Middle East and North Africa increased from 15 billion US dollars in 1976 […] to 160 billion US dollars in 1991.[57]

The Community reaction to this deteriorating situation was inspired by neoliberal principles and prescriptions: structural adjustment, free-market capitalism, encouragement of small and medium-size industry, more infrastructures, and agro-industrial production. In a March 1985 declaration on the Mediterranean policy of the enlarged Community, the Council engaged the Community to maintain existing trade flows, and to support the Middle East and North Africa Region (MENA) countries in reducing their food deficit and working toward self-sufficiency and diversification in agricultural production. These goals would be supported by continuing financial and technical cooperation and by promoting regional and multilateral cooperation, with the fast-growing demographic problem increasingly occupying center stage. In September of the same year, the Commission adopted new guidelines for the next five years. The Community adopted a new, "tough" attitude to the Mediterranean "resting on few resources and strong conditionality." The resources for financial aid declined in real terms, and trade measures, together with budgetary discipline, were put forward as the way out of the economic and social crisis. After entering the Community, the Spanish government and Spanish members of the Commission adopted proactive initiatives, obtaining, for example, the establishment of a European Guarantee Fund to reduce the foreign debt of countries such as Algeria, Tunisia, Morocco, and Egypt, and instruments to promote small and medium enterprises. In 1989, under the initiative of commissioner Abel Matutes, the Council stated that European stability and security depended on the security and stability of the Mediterranean. General conditions, however, proved unsuited for elaborating a course of action based on positive interdependence.[58]

In the late 1980s, the Mediterranean was seen as a hub of political instability and security risks, but the United States' reasserted prominence and unilateralism made agreement on Community initiatives exceedingly difficult. An example was the lengthy dispute on a common declaration over the Lebanon crisis, which was shelved at the end of the December 1983 Athens European Council meeting after

US complaints. The already mentioned American bombing of Tripoli and Benghazi in April 1986 unveiled a basic lack of agreement—even if the Twelve later agreed upon mild sanctions against Libya, to penalize terrorism, but also to mark a difference from the American use of military force.[59] The close intertwining between the Israeli–Palestinian conflict and other regional security issues—Lebanon, Palestinian and Libyan and Syrian-sponsored terrorism, nuclear proliferation, radical Islam— expanded the political definition of the Mediterranean to permanently include the Middle East, a phenomenon that would peak with the 1990 Gulf War. In such a context, the EC's lack of military force and security resources, and the limits of a pure economic soft power, were resounding.

Indeed, the major discontinuity and the true mark of the late 1980s was the rise to political prominence of migration—a theme that, as noted, was no longer the pure concern of labor ministries, but moved up in the agenda of defence, internal security and foreign policy institutions. In fact, large-scale labor migration flows from North Africa to north-eastern Europe had existed between the 1950s and the early 1970s, sanctioned by bilateral agreements between receiving and sending countries. The European need for cheap manpower in industry, agriculture, and sometimes services had met employment and balance-of-payments problems in Mediterranean countries, and raised the expectation that "rotating" workers would come back with skills and expertise that would contribute to their mother countries' development. Migration was assigned a relevant role in development strategies in many Mediterranean countries. In spite of its economic and social relevance for both sides, the management of the migration flow and of the migrant workers that settled in Europe remained a low-key, and slightly unsuccessful, issue in relations between sending and receiving countries.[60]

The freeze on labor recruitment enacted in Northern Europe in 1973–1975, while stopping the already weak "return" flows, did not halt the flows from south to north. The economic imbalance between North and South, the abundance of labor force in the latter, the existence of a rich underground labor market in Southern Europe and family reunification in Northern Europe still drew significant currents of migrants across the Mediterranean, in particular from the Maghreb countries (see Table 4.1).

Table 4.1 *1979 data, estimated by the Commission.*

COUNTRY OF ORIGIN	Country of Employment									Total EEC
	B	DK	D	F	IRL	I	LUX	NL	UK	
ALGERIA	3 200	186	1 583	361000	5	..	..	..	600[1]	367 000
MOROCCO	37 250	1155	16 109	181400	17	..	..	33 656	2000[1]	272 000
TUNISIA	4 700	107	10000[1]	73700	3	..	..	1 085	200[1]	90 000

Source: EC Commission, Directorate general for information, Cooperation agreements between the EEC and the Maghreb countries, February 1982.

Labor migration of non-EC nationals and guest-worker policy remained a field for national policy and intergovernmental consultation during the 1970s and accordingly found little room in EC–TMC agreements.[61] In the late 1970s, cooperation agreements, the portability of pension rights, family allowances and ending discrimination in the field of social security for Maghreb nationals living in the EEC were agreed upon. But priority in recruitment, while becoming an issue between Turkey and the other Mediterranean sending countries, lost any concrete meaning following the general closure of the European labor market, and high unemployment, in the following decade.

Only in March 1985 did the Commission send the Council the first guidelines for a Community policy on migration, but it failed even to obtain Council approval to set up a prior communication and consultation procedure on migration policies in relation to non-member countries. While moving toward the implementation of the Single Market, member states refused common rules on migration and implemented national policies to reduce immigration, especially of the unskilled workers that the domestic labor markets were unable to absorb.

From a Mediterranean perspective, the Schengen Treaty on the removal of internal border controls and, even more so, the 1990 Convention implementing the treaty became first and foremost instruments for containing immigration from the South. Common rules for external borders drove the Southern European countries, particularly Italy and Spain, to adopt visas to migrants from North Africa, but also from Yugoslavia, and reduce accesses to the North European member states.[62] However, the guest workers' communities living in Europe, continuing illegal flows and returning migrants remained strong elements of interdependence between the EU and the Middle East and North Africa Region (MENA). Euro–Mediterranean diplomacy and political and economic cooperation increasingly accepted the need, particularly expressed by South European countries, to tackle the MENA countries' underdevelopment in order to curb expatriation to Europe and migration pressures: "while the migration question has not figured as an explicit issue in the negotiations leading to the new association agreements, it seems to have played a central role in driving the discussion and shaping the agenda."[63] In the 1990–1996 Renewed Mediterranean Policy, grants and loans were substantially increased, with total funds made available for the region (including Turkey, Cyprus, and Malta) peaking at five billion ECU. Funds were reserved for regional projects to promote South–South co-operation.[64] People-to-people contacts were encouraged through decentralized cooperation such as MED Campus, Med Urbs and Med Media, the first real attempt to involve civil society through cooperation networks of universities, cities, journalists, women and migrants. Resources and measures directed at small- and medium-sized enterprises, while mirroring the stress the EC put on the market economy path to development, were also geared to promote the return of small entrepreneurs to their countries of origin.

Conclusion

Even if the Mediterranean was a playground for the Cold War and played a role in the early EC Mediterranean agreements, other themes and drivers—global economic trends, integration process dynamics, enchained economic interests, special allegiances, national foreign policies—determined EC engagements. The driver for EC Mediterranean policy that rose to prominence in the 1967–1974 timeframe was responding to regional conflicts interwoven with the East–West confrontation. The EEC's rising economic power, and worries about regional security threats, apparently found in the Mediterranean the ideal region for a "civilian" international influence. For the United States, whose prominence in the Mediterranean and the Middle East was a permanent factor in EEC policy, the EEC was a useful and legitimate resource to deal with the stabilization of Southern Europe; but its projection into the Mediterranean was resented, especially as the regional geopolitical asset became deeply intertwined with the Arab–Israeli conflict. In a crucial neighboring area, the EEC hit the glass ceiling of US hegemony and of Atlantic primacy over European integration.

Moving from bilateral to multilateral approaches, the EC sought a response to a variety of problems, but the economic and political conditions did not allow implementations. In the EC, however, Mediterranean engagements, both economic and political, were never unanimously accepted as necessary, or even opportune, even when European interests were acknowledged to be at stake. Even actors with a stake in the region, such as France and Italy, exhibited double-thinking that sapped the bases of engagements. It took six years after the fall of the Berlin Wall, in December 1995, before the EU launched a resounding and multi-layered Mediterranean initiative, the Barcelona Conference, where the (by then) fifteen member countries and the MENA countries set up the Euro–Mediterranean Partnership.

Notes

1   Federica Bicchi, *European Foreign Policy Making toward the Mediterranean* (London: Palgrave Macmillan, 2007), 8.
2   See Angela Romano's chapter, "The EC and the Socialist World: The Ascent of a Key Player in Cold War Europe" in this volume.
3   Barry Buzan and Ole Weaver, *Regions and Powers: The Structure of International Security* (Cambridge: Cambridge University Press, 2003).
4   E.g. Avi Shlaim and George Nicolas Yannopoulos (eds.), *The EEC and the Mediterranean Countries* (Cambridge: Cambridge University Press, 1976); Richard Pomfret, *Mediterranean Policy of the European Community: A Study of Discrimination in Trade* (London: Palgrave Macmillan, 1986); Bichara Khader (ed.), *The EEC and the Arab World*, special issue of *the Journal of Arab Affairs*, 12:1 (1993), 113–124; Filippos Pierros and Jacob Meunier, *Bridges and Barriers: The European Union's Mediterranean Policy, 1961–1998* (Aldershot: Ashgate, 1999); Sarah Collinson, *Shore to Shore: The Politics of Migration in Euro-Maghreb Relations* (London: The Royal Institute of International Affairs, 1996).
5   See Piers Ludlow's chapter, "The History of the EC and the Cold War: Influenced and Influential, but Rarely Center Stage" in this volume; Mario Del Pero, Victor Gavin, Fernando Guirao and Antonio Varsori, *Democrazie. L'Europa meridionale e la fine delle dittature* (Milano: Mondadori Education, 2010); Eirini Karamouzi, *Greece,*

the EEC and the Cold War 1974–1979: The Second Enlargement (London: Palgrave Macmillan, 2014).

6   Daniel Möckli and Victor Mauer (eds.), *European–American Relations and the Middle East: From Suez to Iraq* (New York: Routledge, 2011); Muhamad Hasrul Zakariah, "Oil, War and European Initiatives for Peace in the Middle East 1973–1974: British Attitude and Perspective," *Middle Eastern Studies*, 48:4 (2012), 589–611.

7   See Angela Romano's chapter, "The EC and the Socialist World: The Ascent of a Key Player in Cold War Europe" in this volume.

8   See the thematic issue "Europe and the Mediterranean in the Long 1980s", *Journal of European Integration History*, 1 (2015).

9   Ricardo Gomez, "The EU's Mediterranean Policy: Common Foreign Policy by the Back Door?," in John Peterson and Helene Sjursen (eds.), *A Common Foreign Policy for Europe? Competing Visions of the CFSP* (London and New York: Routledge, 1998), 134.

10 Besides Bicchi, *European Foreign Policy*, see Aurélie Elisa Gfeller, *Building a European Identity: France, the United States, and the Oil Shock, 1973–74* (New York: Berghahn Books, 2012); Silvio Labbate, *Illusioni mediterranee. Il dialogo euro-arabo* (Firenze: Lemonnier, 2016).

11 Daniel Möckli, *European Foreign Policy during the Cold War: Heath, Brandt, Pompidou and the Dream of Political Unity* (London: I.B. Tauris, 2008); Maria Gainar, *Aux origines de la diplomatie européenne: Les Neuf et la Coopération politique européenne de 1973 à 1980* (Brussels: Peter Lang, 2012); Marc Trachtenberg, *The Cold War and After: History, Theory and the Logic of International Politics* (Princeton: Princeton University Press, 2012).

12 Giuliano Garavini, *After Empires: European Integration, Decolonization, and the Challenge from the Global South 1957–1986* (Oxford: Oxford University Press, 2012).

13 Yugoslavia remains outside the purpose of this chapter, as the Mediterranean dimension of the Conference on Security and Cooperation in Europe did not include Yugoslavia.

14 See the chapter by Kenneth Weisbrode, "The EC and the United States: Partners in search of diplomacy in this volume".

15 Elena Calandri, "Stratégie de développement, option identitaire: la Turquie et l'Europe occidentale, de l'Aide Multilatérale à l'Association à la CEE," in Marta Petricioli (ed.), *L'Europe méditerranéenne* (Brussels: Peter Lang, 2008), 267–290.

16 Lorenz Plassmann, *Comme dans une nuit de Pâques? Les relations franco-grecques 1944–1981* (Brussels: Peter Lang, 2012).

17 The latter was supposed to be a better solution, as the United States expected EEC tariffs to be lowered as a consequence of GATT negotiations.

18 Doc. L/1715, January 30, 1962 at https://docs.wto.org/gattdocs/q/GG/L1799/1715. PDF; Doc. L/1790, June 12, 1962, at https://docs.wto.org/gattdocs/q/GG/L1799/1790. PDF; the GATT Working Party Report of September 1962 at https://docs.wto.org/gattdocs/q/GG/SPEC/62-236.pdf (last accessed October 31, 2018).

19 National Archives and Records Administration (NARA), College Park, MD, Record Group 59 (RG 59), Bureau of European Affairs, Office of Atlantic Political and Economic Affairs, Alpha-Numeric Files 1948–1963, box 10, George T. Churchill (GTI) to Biller (EUR-RPE), August 1, 1963.

20 Pascaline Winand, *Eisenhower, Kennedy and the United States of Europe* (New York: Saint Martin's Press, 1993).

21 NARA, RG 59, Bureau of European Affairs, Office of Atlantic Political and Economic Affairs, Alpha-numeric Files 1948–1963, box 10, Airgram, not sent (Spring 1962).

22 NARA, RG 59, Bureau of European Affairs, Office of Atlantic Political and Economic Affairs, Alpha-Numeric Files, 1948–1963, box 10, William A. Helseth, For the record, Conversation between the President and Ambassador Hare, January 14, 1962, confidential; See Elena Calandri, "Gli *Stati Uniti e il ruolo internazionale della CEE: l'associazione della Turchia 1959–1963*," *Anno V n.s.*, 2 (2016), 253–276.

23 Emmanuel Comte, "Migration and Regional Interdependence in the Mediterranean (1980s–mid 1990s)," *Journal of European Integration History*, 1 (2015), 109–123, here 114–115.

24 EC policy became more forthcoming after the Islamic revolution in Iran, which in May 1979 prompted an overdue meeting of the Association Council, the resumption of financial aid and social rights for *Gastarbeiter*. The September 1980 military coup soon interrupted the new course. In spite of German and British campaigning for a realistic appreciation of Turkey's importance as a bastion of Western security structure, the Community froze aid. Cooperation was only resumed in 1986, and Turkey's 1987 application to join the Community obtained a lukewarm Commission opinion: HAEU, GJLA 253 SEC (89) 2290 Final/2, Commission's Opinion on Turkey's Request for Accession to the Community, December 20, 1989.

25 The largely unexpected consequence of the 1970 agreement was to boost the Spanish economy, which during the 1960s had developed competitive industrial sectors: Matthieu Trouvé, *L'Espagne et l'Europe—De la dictature de Franco à l'Union européenne* (Brussels: Peter Lang, 2009).

26 Here the term "association" did not imply a permanent bond, and mutual trade liberalization was, as in the Turkish case, delayed to future negotiations and an eventual "second period."

27 Ennio Di Nolfo, "The Cold War and the Transformation of the Mediterranean," in Melvyn Leffler, Odd Arne Westad (eds.), *The Cambridge History of the Cold War, Vol. 2* (Cambridge: Cambridge University Press, 2010), 238–257.

28 On economic strategies, see Massimiliano Trentin, "Le distanze del Mediterraneo. Europa e mondo arabo tra sviluppo e nazionalismo," in Ennio Di Nolfo and Matteo Gerlini (eds.), *Il Mediterraneo Attuale tra Storia e Politica* (Venezia: Marsilio, 2012), 283–304. On post-colonial tensions, see e.g. the 1964 nationalization of French properties in Tunisia: Houda Ben Hamouda, "France, the European Community and the Maghreb, 1963–1976: From Inertia to Key Player," in Elena Calandri, Daniele Caviglia and Antonio Varsori (eds.), *Détente in Cold War Europe: Politics and Diplomacy in the Mediterranean and the Middle East* (London: I.B. Tauris, 2013), 195–206; Chloé Berger, "L'émergence d'une politique européenne en Méditerranée dans les années 1960. Le cas des relations euro-maghrébines," in Houda Ben Hamouda and Matthieu Bouchard (eds.), *La construction d'un espace euro-méditerranéen: genèses, mythes et perspectives* (Brussels: Peter Lang, 2012), 79–90. On Italian protectionism on agricultural products, see Elena Calandri, "Europa e Mediterraneo tra giustapposizione e integrazione," in Massimo De Leonardis (ed.), *Il Mediterraneo nella politica estera italiana del secondo dopoguerra* (Bologna: Il Mulino/ISPI, 2003), 47–60.

29 NARA, NSSM 91, EC Preferential Trade Arrangements, March 27, 1970, 28.

30 Spain directed one-third and Israel one quarter of its exports to the EC.

31 Guia Migani, "Re-discovering the Mediterranean: First Tests of Coordination Among the Nine," in Calandri, Caviglia and Varsori, *Détente in Cold War Europe*, 49–60, here 51; as early as 1964 Moro had advocated an EC–Mediterranean free-trade area for industrial products; now Italy reduced opposition to concessions on agricultural exports.

32   Giuliana Laschi, *L'Europa e gli altri. Le relazioni esterne della Comunità dalle origini al dialogo nord-sud* (Bologna: il Mulino, 2015), 247.

33   Éric Bussière and Émilie Willaert, *Un projet pour l'Europe. Georges Pompidou et la construction européenne* (Brussels: Peter Lang, 2010).

34   Elena Calandri, "Understanding the EEC Mediterranean Policy: Trade, Security, Development and the Redrafting of Mediterranean Boundaries," in Claudia Hiepel (ed.), *Europe in a Globalising World* (Baden-Baden: Nomos, 2014).

35   Laurence Badel, *Diplomatie et grands contrats. L'État français et les marchés extérieurs au XXᵉ siècle* (Paris: Publications de la Sorbonne, 2010).

36   NARA, RG 59, Subject-Numeric File 1970–1973, box 1027, Tel. Paris 19096, October 6, 1972, GOF Views on proposed Mediterranean policy and revision of EC–Spanish agreement.

37   HAEU, BAC 86/2005 SEC 72/3967, Note à l'attention de MM. les Membres de la Commission, 212e réunion du Conseil du novembre 6, 1972 avec la participation des représentants des états adhérents, confidentiel, November 18, 1972.

38   Quoted in Effie G. H. Pedaliu, "'We were always realistic': The Heath Government, the European Community and the Cold War in the Mediterranean, June 1970— February 1974," in John Young, Effie G. H. Pedaliu and Michael Kandiah (eds.), *British Foreign Policy: From Churchill to Blair* (London: Palgrave Macmillan, 2013), 159–178, here 160.

39   NARA, RG 59, Subject-Numeric File 1970–1073, box 1027, William P. Rogers, Memorandum for the President, U.S. Policy toward Spain, April 25, 1972, secret; Trachtenberg, *The Cold War and After*, chap. 7, 214. On US lack of confidence on France's aims in the Mediterranean see NARA, NSSM 87, Trends new options in North Africa, February 1970, and NARA, NSSM 90, US Interest in and Policy towards the Mediterranean, March 1970.

40   See notes 11 and 12.

41   Henry Kissinger, *Years of Upheaval* (Boston: Little, Brown & Co., 1982), 899–900; Trachtenberg, *The Cold War and After*, 226–234.

42   NARA, NSSM87, Trends and new options in North Africa, February–March 1970; NARA, NSSM 90, US Interest in and Policy towards the Mediterranean, March 1970.

43   On the economic dimension of the growing North–South polarization, see Massimiliano Trentin, "Divergence in the Mediterranean: The Economic Relations between the EC and the Arab Countries in the Long 1980s," *Journal of European Integration History*, 21:1 (2015), 89–108, here 105, quoting Joan Esteban, "Economic Polarization in the Mediterranean Basin," *Els Opuscles del CREI*, 10 (2010); see also Trentin, "Divergence in the Mediterranean," 93–94.

44   Ministère des affaires étrangères, La Courneuve, Série Europe, Europe occidentale 1976–1980, Note, February 4, 1989.

45   Alfred Tovias, "Spain's Input in Shaping the EU's Mediterranean Policies 1986–1996," in Raanan Rhein (ed.), *Spain and the Mediterranean since 1898* (Abingdon: Routledge, 1999), 216–234; Pietro Calamia, "La svolta europea del 1985. Il ruolo dell'Italia," *Rivista di studi politici internazionali*, 79:1 (2012), 15–25.

46   David Allen and Alfred Pijpers, *European Foreign Policy-Making and the Arab-Israeli Conflict* (The Hague: Martinus Nijhoff Publishers, 1984); Patrick Müller, *EU Foreign Policymaking and the Middle East Conflict. The Europeanization of National Foreign Policy* (London: Routledge, 2012).

47   Labbate, *Illusioni mediterranee*, 60–67.

48 Hans W. Maull, "The Strategy of Avoidance: Europe's Middle East Policies after the October War," in John C. Hurewitz (ed.), *Oil, the Arab-Israeli Dispute and the Industrial World* (Boulder, CO: Westview Press, 1976); David Allen and Andrin Hauri, "The Euro-Arab Dialogue, the Venice Declaration, and Beyond: the Limits of a Distinct EC Policy 1974–89," in Daniel Möckli and Victor Mauer (eds.), *European-American Relations and the Middle East: From Suez to Iraq* (London: Routledge, 2011), 93–108.

49 Istituto Sturzo (Rome), Giulio Andreotti Papers, Serie Europe, box 350.

50 Archives du Ministères des Affaires étrangères, La Courneuve, Série Europe 1976–1980, Commnauté européenne, boite 4171, Direction Europe, Europe occidentale, *Note a.s. Inclusion de l'Afrique du Nord dans la Coopération politique,* November 19, 1977.

51 Haifaa A. Jawad, *Euro-Arab Relations: A Study in Collective Diplomacy* (Reading: Ithaca Press, 1992).

52 Muhamad Hasrul Zakariah, "The Euro-Arab Dialogue 1973–1978: Britain Reinsurance Policy in the Middle East Conflict," *European Review of History*, 20:4 (2013), 95–115.

53 Richard Pomfret, "Main Economic Trends in EC-Israel Economic Relations since the Creation of the Common Market," in Ilan Greilsammer and Joseph Weiler (eds.), *Europe and Israel: Troubled Neighbours* (Berlin/New York: De Gruyter, 1988).

54 In particular on the Algerian side, see Calandri, "Understanding the EEC Mediterranean Policy."

55 Massimiliano Trentin, "The Distant Neighbours and the Cooperation Agreements between the EEC and the Mashreq, 1977," in Calandri, Caviglia and Varsori, *Détente in Cold War Europe*, 221–233.

56 Including the three Maghreb, the four Mashreq, Turkey, Yugoslavia, Cyprus, Israel, and Malta.

57 Trentin, "Divergence in the Mediterranean," 95–96.

58 The "Renewed Mediterranean Policy" adopted in 1990 implied continuity, even if it acknowledged the limits of existing policies.

59 These included a reduction in the number of Libyans serving in official capacity in European countries, coupled with some measures affecting trade.

60 Sarah Collinson, *Europe and International Migrations* (London: Pinter, 1993).

61 Marcel Berlinghoff, "Labour Migration: Common Market Essential or Common Problem? The EC Committees and European Immigration Stops in the Early 1970s," *Journal of European Integration History* 23, no. 1 (2017), 155–176.

62 Simone Paoli, "France and the Origins of Schengen: An Interpretation," *Journal of European Integration History*, 22 (2016), 247–272.

63 Collinson, *Shore to Shore*, 68.

64 The Marrakech Treaty instituted the Union for the Arab Maghreb between Morocco, Tunisia, Algeria, in 1989.

5

The EC and China: Rise and Demise of a Strategic Relationship

Enrico Fardella

After the establishment of official diplomatic relations in 1975, the relationship between the People's Republic of China (PRC) and the European Economic Community (EEC) moved from a peripheral form of cooperation to one of the most important pillars of the contemporary international system.

The evolution of such a crucial relationship has not, however, been followed by an adequate expansion of academic analysis. Most of the existing literature stresses in the first place the analysis of the economic momentum, and the dynamics of its sectors, as the core element of Sino–European relations.[1] As such, it has mostly overshadowed the geopolitical impact and political designs—Chinese designs in particular—that lay behind the growth of economic interchange. The intrinsic weakness of the EC's ability to project a unified medium/long-term political strategy and the opaqueness of Chinese political discourse—and access to Chinese primary sources—have been the main factors that contributed to the transformation of the visibility of the economic dimension, and the European perspective, into the dominant protagonists of the existing academic discourse.[2]

Europe and China were the most important third actors in the Cold War system. As territorial entities and political and economic spaces located at the crossroads of the mutual spheres of action of the two superpowers, they both played important roles in the evolution and reshaping of the bipolar system. The Cold War defined the outlines of these two spaces. On the one hand, it accelerated the decline of Europe as a central player—a process already started during World War II and intensified by the dismantling of the colonial system—and, on the other, favored the shift in the center of gravity of the international system towards Asia, and hence an "Asianization" that is still in progress today.

This chapter will analyze these elements in order to locate the linear growth of economic interaction within a wider interpretative landscape. This will be done in two main steps: a historical analysis of the birth and evolution of independent European and Chinese foreign policies will be followed by a more in-depth examination of the specific threads that composed the matrix of EC–PRC "reconciliation." In the conclusion the authors reconnect this "history" with the present by sketching a broad overview of the evolution of Sino–European relations in the post-Cold War international system.

China's European Policy and the Foundations of EEC–China relations (1950s–1970s)

In 1949, when the triumph of Mao's communist revolution led to the foundation of the PRC, most of the Western countries, led by the United States, refused to recognize the new government in Beijing. In the first years of its existence the EEC, with a mostly intra-continental and economic agenda, was obviously influenced by the China policies of its constituent members, and demonstrated no ambition to bypass the prism of the Cold War and reach out to Beijing.

The years that followed changed this trend. The confrontation of the first years of the Cold War led to the consolidation of the two blocs and the creation of the bipolar monopoly of nuclear arsenals. This in turn progressively inspired the emergence of *détente* in the 1960s as a bipolar monopoly of peace. Both the relaxation of superpower confrontation and growing dissatisfaction with this new condominium eventually reinforced the search for independence among the superpowers' allies, Europe and China *in primis*, and prepared the ground for new forms of mutual engagement.

At the beginning of the 1960s, a number of basic trends in Western Europe merged to inspire a "new perspective" toward China that eventually came to inspire the EEC's China policy in the following decade. Growing concerns about the relationship emerged among Washington's European allies over a transatlantic relationship that was increasingly perceived as an unfairly imbalanced relational hierarchy. Strategic parity between the superpowers and European dependence on American's nuclear umbrella and economic designs (specifically the Marshall Plan) created an existential dilemma for European independence and sowed the intellectual seeds in Europe for alternatives to the dictates of the bipolar logic. If in the 1950s the EEC already represented a promising new autonomous and innovative continental mechanism, in the following decade it became almost natural for some Europeans to look through the Iron Curtain for what Egon Bahr called "change through rapprochement."

China stood at the very far end of these new threads of the Cold War fabric. The intensification of the Sino–Soviet dispute in the 1960s seemingly offered the West a vast geopolitical opportunity in Asia and beyond: the emerging hostility between the two biggest members of the socialist bloc impaired its Asian outreach and fractured its unity and appeal at a global level.

In the early 1960s China's heretical stance toward Moscow and its need for economic recovery, after the disastrous economic experiment of the Great Leap Forward, deeply reinforced Western interest and activated a new set of policies aimed at rapprochement with Beijing.

The United States could not easily grab this opportunity, as the Vietnam War and the defence of Taiwan bogged it down in an adversarial relationship with Beijing.

China's criticism of Moscow—which paralleled some of Europe's discords with Washington—did attract the attention of those European political figures who were looking for hedging strategies to maximize European autonomy in the international system. At the same time the traditional allure of the immense potential of the Chinese market created a strong lobby among European industrialists backing any political initiative in favor of Beijing.

This was particularly evident in the French overture of 1964. The normalization of diplomatic relations between France and China came at the crossroads of two separate historical courses: the rise of the People's Republic of China in its search for a new sphere of influence in the international system (autonomous from the Soviet Union) and the decline of a European colonial power that now found it difficult to adapt to the emerging superpower hierarchy and the demise of Euro-centrism in the post-war era.

Sino–French normalization signaled the beginning of the new rapprochement between China and Europe, and, more broadly, between China and the West.[3] In the 1970s, Western European countries helped to facilitate and consolidate this historical shift by successively recognizing the PRC—Italy (1970), Belgium (1971), and West Germany (1972)—and establishing trading strategies aimed at integrating the Chinese market and economic policies into the capitalist system.

This process set the stage for the establishment of EEC–PRC relations in 1975. Two years earlier, in his "Year of Europe" speech, US Secretary of State Henry Kissinger contrasted American "global responsibilities" with Europe's merely regional interests.[4] From 1975 onward the EEC's China policy proved the short-sightedness of Kissinger's assumptions; to this day it remains one of the main pillars of the new European global outreach.

The new Sino–European "socialization", however, was driven from the outset more by Beijing's strategic calculus and proud search for independence in international relations than by European designs. From the very beginning, Europe's outreach to China was a simple by-product of the ecumenical spirit of European foreign policy, which aimed at engaging Beijing to dilute tensions and favor peace—and trade—in Europe and beyond. On the other hand, China's European policy belonged to a much more elaborate global strategy that identified the superpowers' search for hegemony as the potential trigger of a global war that threatened China's survival and its dream of resurgence. As a consequence of this vision, China's European policies have been mostly driven by its positioning vis-à-vis the hegemonic powers.

The logic of independence has always been predominant in the Maoist struggle: the movement for class emancipation in China was instrumental to the success of Mao's movement of national liberation. The ideology that legitimized China's adherence to the Soviet bloc—the so-called "leaning to one side"—[一边倒, *yibiandao*]—was instrumental in safeguarding China's national interest in light of the emerging bipolar confrontation and healing the territorial losses imposed on China by Stalin and Roosevelt in Yalta.

Since the end of the war against Japan, Mao displayed quite a revisionist description of the bipolar Yalta system. In his meeting with the American reporter Anna Louise Strong in August 1946 he identified, in fact, a tripolar international system, pointing out the existence of a vast area in between the two superpowers—comprising capitalist, colonial and semi-colonial countries in Europe, Asia and Africa, including China—

that he labelled "the intermediate zone [中间地带, *zhongjian didai*]." According to Mao, the main contradiction in the international system was not the conflict between capitalism and socialism—namely between the US and the Soviet Union—but the American attempt to gain control over the intermediate zone in order to encircle and defeat the socialist bloc. In Mao's mind, the United States was trying to expand its influence both by suppressing revolution in the colonial and semi-colonial world and by turning its capitalist allies into vassals.[5] In Mao's vision, China could play a central role in the struggle for independence of the intermediate zone both as the vanguard of defense of the socialist camp and the leader of the anti-imperialist struggle. This would create the conditions for the rise of a "third" pole—an intermediate anti-hegemonic pole—in which China could play a leading role. Mao's definition of China's position in the world order implicitly challenged the bipolar world order and, consequently, sowed the seeds of the Sino–Soviet split from very beginning of the alliance.[6]

The concept of the "intermediate zone," however, survived only for one year. From September 1947 the Cominform started dividing the world in two camps, with Western Europe and the United States as main enemies of the socialist camp. The Central Committee of the Chinese Communist Party (CCP) followed this interpretation and the "intermediate zone" theory disappeared from Chinese public discourse.[7] As Niu Jun correctly noted, however, in the very first months after the founding of the PRC the CCP tried to reactivate the logic of the theory and divide the United Kingdom, France and other European countries from the United States. This favored the establishment of diplomatic relations with countries like Sweden and Denmark, for example, but also justified the status of "semi-diplomatic relations" with the United Kingdom and China's peaceful stance towards Hong Kong and Macao.[8]

The implementation of the "leaning-to-one-side" policy flattened these nuances, positioned the PRC on the same line as the USSR and activated the division of labor that led the CCP to become the center of revolution in Asia. Thus in the 1950s, China avoided becoming deeply or directly involved in European affairs and mainly followed the Soviet line. As a consequence, when the Treaty of Rome was signed in March 1957 to create the European Economic Community, Beijing's official reaction was very critical. The PRC's official paper *Ta Kung Pao* [大公报, Dagongbao] accused the Europeans of passively backing American Cold War policies and the domination of the US dollar. The EEC, it wrote, could not improve the position of Western Europe but merely exacerbated the divisions of Europe and Germany while its energy component— the European Energy Atomic Community (EURATOM)—intensified the threat of war by supporting West Germany in developing nuclear weapons. If the Europeans were genuinely looking for peace and wanted to boost economic cooperation within the continent, the newspaper argued that they had to follow the Soviet proposal for establishing a collective security system in Europe.[9]

At the Moscow Conference in November 1957, Mao seemed to believe that the international situation was favoring revolutionary trends—"the East wind"—against the capitalist forces—"the West wind"—and he decided to further radicalize China's foreign policy by strengthening its support for the revolutionary movements in Asia, Africa and Latin America.[10] According to a report by the Chinese Ministry of Foreign Affairs that attracted Mao's attention, more than thirty African countries were going to become independent in the following decade, and this was obviously going to create strong competition not only between China and the superpowers but also between China and the Western European countries. Africa became the central stage of Chinese revolutionary policies, placing further strain on China's relations with Western Europe (as symbolized by Beijing's strong support for Algeria in its war of independence with France).[11]

With the deepening of Sino–Soviet discord at the beginning of the 1960s and the parallel growth of the American military presence in Vietnam, the Chinese security environment deteriorated further. Mao now decided to revise his previous policies and reinforce cooperation with Europe in order to bolster China's international stance. Support for revolution still had priority, but the relationship with Europe could be developed at the same time—as long as the latter did not conflict with the former. At the CCP Central Committee working conference in September 1963 this conviction led Mao to expand the front from the "first intermediate zone" (the undeveloped countries of Asia, Africa and Latin America) to a "second intermediate zone" composed of the imperialist and developed capitalist countries of Europe, North America, Australia, and New Zealand that he believed were dissatisfied with both the United States and the USSR.[12] "They say we have a 3A [Asia, Africa, Latin America] policy, but ours is a 3A+E [Europe]+A [Australia]," as Mao said to the representative of the Indonesian Communist Party.[13]

Sino–French normalization in January 1964 was a direct result of this foreign policy shift. China's support for the Algerian struggle for independence had been the most symbolic element of its revolutionary foreign policy and had obstructed any progress in Sino–French normalization. The signing of the Evian Accords in 1962 paved the way for Mao's proposal of the "second intermediate zone," which in turned functioned as an ideological framework for normalization with Paris.[14]

The shift is particularly relevant for understanding the future evolution of Mao's approach to the West and in particular to the EEC. At the beginning of the 1960s, Mao's assessment of the international system pushed him to find a formula—namely the "two intermediate zones"—that allowed him to reconcile China's support of revolution in the developing world with its interest in cooperation with capitalist countries, first and foremost in Western Europe. At the time, the target of China's anti-hegemonic campaign was still the United States, and this influenced China's perception of the EEC as a disunited and weak community incapable of escaping Washington's control.[15]

In late 1968 this paradigm started changing. The Soviet military intervention in Czechoslovakia—legitimated by the Brezhnev Doctrine of limited sovereignty—and the subsequent Sino–Soviet border clashes in 1969 turned the Soviet Union into China's main enemy. During the same period the ideological campaigns of the Cultural Revolution threatened China's internal stability. The emerging Soviet threat—or "social-imperialist" as the Chinese called it at the time—coupled with growing internal turmoil persuaded Mao to rein in the revolutionary "tension" and shift to the "consolidation" of its results in an attempt to restore order within the country. This prepared the ground for the revision of Mao's revolutionary foreign policy and the opening to the United States. In November 1968, Beijing responded with "unprecedented speed" to the

American offer to reopen the Warsaw channel and mentioned for the first time the possibility of "coexisting" with the United States.[16]

Beijing's outlook on the EEC was obviously influenced by this epoch-making strategic shift. The Chinese leaders believed that the Soviets aimed at controlling Europe in order to concentrate their hegemonic ambitions towards China. As the Chinese Ambassador Wang Shu told German Foreign Minister Hans-Dietrich Genscher in 1975: "If the Soviet Union wants to dominate the world, it first has to take Europe as a necessary step."[17]

The international transformations were pushing China's and Europe's horizons closer to each other. Both felt at the mercy of the antagonistic forces that dominated the bipolar world, and this widened the space for cooperation between them. As Zhou Enlai said in November 1968 at the Albanian Embassy in Beijing, Western Europe should be part of the "united front" to fight superpower hegemony and "thwart the criminal plot of American imperialists and Soviet revisionists who aim to divide the world between themselves." During the same period, China expressed its support for a unified Europe for the first time: the Director of the Department for Western Europe and America of the Chinese Ministry of Foreign Affairs told Western diplomats that Western Europe had to accelerate the pace of unification and that China was interested in expanding its trade with strong European economies.[18]

The Sino–Italian negotiations for the establishment of diplomatic relations started at this crucial moment and ended in November 1970 with the establishment of official relations between Rome and Beijing. This new climate in Sino–Western relations, symbolized by China's admission to the United Nations in October 1971 and Nixon's visit to China in February 1972, boosted the development of diplomatic contacts between the EEC member states and Beijing: Belgium (1971), West Germany, the Netherlands and Luxembourg (1972) all achieved normalization with the PRC.

In 1969–1970 the Chinese media suddenly amplified their coverage of the EEC's activities, analyzing every move with greatly expanded emphasis, in order to stress the EEC's key role within the capitalist world. This emerging interest was still accompanied by overall criticisms of the internal divisions and weakness of the Community, which was seen more as a passive battlefield for superpower hegemony than an emerging unified political pole. The parallel improvement in Sino–Western European relations in those months progressively changed China's stance towards the Community and this became—internal disunity notwithstanding—a positive process with the potential to create a new pole in the international system. As Premier Zhou Enali told the French Minister of Planning, André Bettencourt, during his official visit to China in the summer of 1970, China perceived a powerful and independent Western Europe as a "precious element of global equilibrium."[19]

After the PRC joined the United Nations, its relationship with the EEC seemed bound to develop faster. The most relevant obstacle in Sino–European relations (the Taiwan issue) had now vanished and the EEC appeared stronger—thanks to the accession of the United Kingdom, Ireland, and Denmark—and more inclined to operate independently of the United States in its foreign policy and cooperate with the

Third World—as the Euro–Arab Dialogue and the signing of the Lomé Convention seemed to prove. At the time, after the turbulence of the Cultural Revolution, the EEC seemed the best option for Beijing to reinforce its domestic economy and armed forces by attracting European technologies.

Mao conceptualized this growing compatibility between China and Europe in his new "Three World Theory [三个世界的理论, *sangeshijie de lilun*]" officially launched in 1974—first at an official meeting with the Zambian president and then more broadly in a presentation by Deng Xiaoping to a special session of the UN focused on development—as a theoretical organization of China's evolving foreign policies.

Mao believed that the old Sino–American order of imperialism and hegemony was being shaken to its core and that new forces were emerging from the developing countries in Asia, Africa and Latin America. On the basis of these new fractures the world seemed to consist of three parts: the First World represented by the United States and the USSR; the Second World, represented by the developed regions, including Europe and the Third World composed by the developing countries in Asia, Africa, and Latin America. The two superpowers vied for world hegemony and sought control over the other two worlds, but according to Mao the Third World possessed enough strength to resist by uniting and allying "with other countries subjected to superpower bullying as well as with the people of the whole world, including the people of the United States and the Soviet Union."[20]

The Three World Theory inherited the global tripartite division of Mao's first intermediate zone theory but provided it with a powerful new driver: development. After the Cultural Revolution, Mao started emphasizing development—more practical and less ideological than the notion of class struggle that inspired his previous theories—as the main objective of "revolution." Soviet imperialism had annihilated the socialist bloc and had even surpassed the United States as the main hegemonic obstacle to the development and independence of the rest of the world. This allowed China, as a legitimate member of the Third World, to cooperate with all countries that wished to achieve independence and development without the control of the superpowers. Within this new framework Europe—the main battlefield of superpower competition and one of the world's most highly developed regions—became China's favored partner.

From the beginning of the 1970s an integrated and anti-Soviet Western Europe became one of the central pillars of China's foreign policy as it sought to move closer to Western European countries. In 1972 Beijing proposed to open a Chinese diplomatic representation at the EEC in Brussels and began to actively support EEC integration, not only in the economic sphere but also in the political and military, as Zhou Enlai remarked to Italian Foreign Minister Giuseppe Medici during his official visit to Beijing in 1973.[21]

The kind of European integration that the Chinese favored, however, aimed at weakening the Soviet Union by reinforcing the political and economic consolidation of Western Europe and enhancing relations with the Soviet satellites in Eastern Europe. Beijing strongly opposed any negotiations or compromise, such as the initiatives inspired by the logic of *détente*, that might facilitate intra-European dialogue with the participation of the Soviet Union. The logic of *détente* between the superpowers and within Europe conflicted with the Chinese desire to isolate the social-imperialist threat from Moscow. In a sort of inverse proportionality, when the logic of *détente* prevailed Beijing's space for action diminished, and vice-versa. China strongly criticized the Helsinki process and its final declaration of 1975, fearing that its success could allow the Soviet Union to turn its hegemonic ambitions to Asia and apply the same model there.

In the 1970s China actively worked to chill the climate of *détente* and push the EEC members into a more adversarial stance towards Moscow. Chinese diplomacy was now seen by many in Europe as potentially risky: according to Italian and Polish diplomats for example, Beijing's friendly relations with Romania, celebrated by Premier Hua Guofeng on his visit in 1978, threatened to lead Moscow to tighten its control over the rest of Eastern Europe in order to prevent emulation of Bucharest's independent policy. In those years, the EEC countries walked a very thin line trying to harmonize a partnership with China with the *détente* process with Moscow: heightened tension with the Soviet Union was perceived as potentially destructive for the process of European *détente* and integration.[22]

The launch of Deng Xiaoping's "reform and opening" at the end of the 1978 marked a turning point in this process. The reform of China's economic policy—favored by the transition from "class struggle" to "development"—was Deng's "revolution" as it structurally connected the opening to the West, as a positive source of capital and civilian/military technology, to the success of the reform itself.

Within this framework the relationship with the EEC acquired a new dimension: it helped China to resist Soviet hegemonic urges but was also an essential part of China's economic progress and the success of Deng's reform. This process of "internalization" of Sino–EEC relations produced the "golden age" of Sino–EEC relations from the late 1970s to the end of the 1980s and prepared the ground for a "strategic partnership" that was to become one of the most important pillars of the post-Cold War international system.

EEC–China Strategic "Reconciliation" (1970s–1990s)

In the early 1970s, the European Community stood at the crossroads of its political and economic development. A new conciliatory Franco–British entente permitted the accession of the United Kingdom, Ireland, and Denmark in 1973 and the creation of a stronger Europe of Nine.

The new dynamism in the "old continent" was paralleled by a troubled moment in international relations. The end of the Bretton Woods system in 1971 and the outbreak of the oil crisis in 1973 (a result of the Yom Kippur War), marked an important turning point for the EEC and pushed it into independent responses to deal with this new set of systemic challenges. EEC international activism started to be expanded and China became one of the main focuses of the European agenda. At that stage China and the EEC both had a strong interest in moving closer: both needed to reinforce their trade and their position in the international market; Sino–European relations seemed to be a good option for that.

On the European side, the constraint of American disapproval quickly disappeared with Washington's new attitude towards Beijing at the beginning of the 1970s. For all these reasons, between 1973 and 1975 both sides agreed on the necessity to establish diplomatic relations in order to boost their economic partnership.

In this very first stage of Sino–European reconciliation, political coordination in respect to China took place outside the legal framework of the Rome Treaty, namely at European Political Cooperation (EPC) level. The EPC was the process of information and consultation among member states in the field of foreign policy inaugurated by the Davignon report in October 1970, and aimed to maximize their influence in international affairs through a single coherent European approach.[23] This was the first step to strengthen cooperation and coordinate diplomatic action in all areas of international affairs affecting the interests of the EEC. Despite initial optimism over the prospect of a common foreign policy toward China, the EPC meetings agreed that member states would develop their relations with China individually, while at the same time recognizing the importance of the European Commission's role in dealing with Beijing. The Commission was institutionally responsible for external initiatives in the field of commercial and trade affairs, and it would thus have been impossible for European countries to elaborate a China policy without its support. Moreover, Community channels provided an advantageous vehicle to complement the European's national policies, which the governments had hitherto been unable to develop.

The invitation to Christopher Soames, vice president of the European Commission in charge of foreign affairs, to visit China in 1973 marked the turning point in China's rapprochement with the EEC. The Chinese did not attribute any official status to this visit as the EEC in October 1970 had signed a textile agreement with Taipei that was interpreted by Beijing as a de facto improvement of European–Taiwanese ties. The expiration of the textile agreement in October 1973 opened the door to the Sino–European diplomatic initiative and in May 1975, Vice President Soames officially visited China after a formal invitation sent by the Chinese Embassy in Brussels.

During his visit to China, Soames met Li Qiang (Minister of Trade Affairs), Qiao Guanhua (Minister of Foreign Affairs) and Zhou Enlai (Prime Minister). The Chinese leadership underlined its faith in a unified Europe and its desire to establish diplomatic relations with the EC and open negotiations for a trade agreement. Li Qiang was particularly vocal in his recognition of the EEC as a strategic partner in the anti-hegemonic struggle. He stressed EC's positive trend towards unity and its virtuous efforts to safeguard its independence and resist external pressure.[24]

At a press conference on May 7, 1975, Soames finally announced the establishment of diplomatic relations, setting aside the Taiwan issue.[25] As Peter Kirk (British member of the European Parliament) pointed out: this event marked one of the most important historical transitions in the history of European Community foreign policy.[26] Although Sino–EEC diplomatic recognition did not have an immediate direct impact on the international balance of power—still dominated by the United States and USSR—it did acknowledge the respective other's future international potential and, by so doing, helped to enhance its status at a global level.

From 1975 to the end of 1976, however, a new process of radicalization in Chinese politics, symbolized by the leadership of the so-called Gang of Four, once again strained the evolution of Sino–EEC relations.[27] The death of Mao Zedong in September 1976 and the suppression of the Gang of Four soon after reactivated the channels of communication. In February 1977, the Chinese Ambassador informed the commissioner for external relations, Wilhelm Haferkamp, that the PRC wanted to resume dialogue. The visit of the vice chairman of the Bank of China Bu Ming to Europe in May 1977, as the head of a Chinese banking delegation, was particularly emblematic in this respect. Bu Ming held a meeting with François Ortoli, Vice President of the European Commission, and stressed China's interest in concluding the trade agreement with the European Community.[28]

The European Commission welcomed this new Chinese stance, although it was concerned about the domestic situation. In April 1977, during his visit to Washington, Commission President Roy Jenkins asked the Americans for their opinion on China's internal situation. Jenkins feared that if the rumors of ongoing factional struggles within the leadership were true, this could trigger a new period of instability and weaken the space for pragmatism in Chinese domestic and foreign policies.[29] Washington's response is unknown, but it is plausible that the US assessment of China was favorable as, in July 1977, a European delegation unexpectedly visited Beijing, setting the stage for the conclusion of a trade agreement.

During the negotiations for the agreement, Zhang Bodin from the Chinese Ministry of Foreign Affairs raised the question of the "safeguard clause" and its potentially harmful impact on the Chinese market.[30] The EEC could apply the safeguard clause to any Chinese products causing material injury to domestic producers. It was a very delicate issue for the Chinese side because the balance of trade between the PRC and the EEC had always favored the latter. The Chinese delegation proposed a corrective mechanism that would have helped correct these trade imbalances. In addition, the PRC sought application of the most-favored nation clause in order to obtain the same trade advantages (low tariffs, high import quotas) granted to other countries.[31] From the EEC's perspective both Chinese requests were extremely demanding, and they eventually led to a stalemate in the negotiations.

In September 1977, the Chinese Ambassador, Huang Hsiang, met the President of the European Commission, Roy Jenkins, in Brussels and stressed China's desire to close the agreement within the year. Two months later, in November 1977, the European Council authorized the European Commission to negotiate the trade agreement with the PRC and the negotiations quickly moved to their final stage, assisted by a mutual political will to overcome the economic constraints that had prevented them reaching this important objective earlier.

In April 1978, Li Qiang finally signed the trade agreement at the Berlaymont, the headquarter of the European Commission in Brussels.[32] The agreement was very general in nature, simply expressing the determination of the parties to create favorable conditions for trade. It also created the EEC–China Joint Committee for Trade to monitor trade and examine any problem that might arise.

The signing of the 1978 trade agreement had a twofold economic and political effect. There was a profound impact on trade between China and the EEC: between 1970 and 1985 European Community exports to the PRC increased by 188.13 percent (see Figure 5.1).[33]

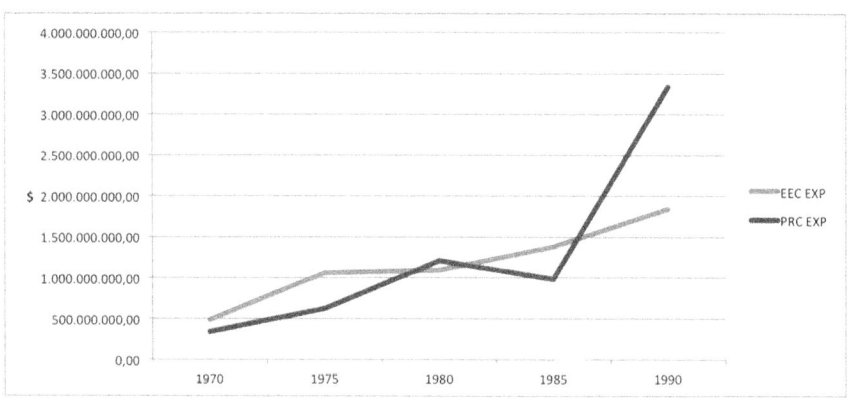

Figure 5.1 Trade Between the European Community and the PRC (constant price US$).
Source: data from UN Comtrade Database (http://comtrade.un.org). Last accessed: April 10, 2017.

In 1985, West Germany accounted for 31 percent of total EEC exports, Italy 20.79 percent, France 20.47 percent and the UK 13.41 percent (Figure 5.2).

Most importantly, at a political level the signing of the trade deal clearly demonstrated China's support for the European project; it eventually became a symbol of trust between the two, as expressed by the Chinese Minister of Trade Affairs, Li Qiang, at that time:

> The social system of our country and the countries of Western Europe are different, but all of us are faced with a common task, the task of safeguarding our independence and our sovereignty. We have much in common and we must mutually support each other. We support Western Europe in its plan to unite in order to strengthen itself and in order to fight against hegemony. We wish to see Europe united and powerful and we are certain that the countries of Europe would like to see China prosperous and powerful.[34]

The threat of Soviet military hegemonism was pushing the Chinese closer and closer to the EEC. Beijing aimed to strengthen its military potential and the EEC represented a promising source of military equipment and dual-use technology.[35] The self-reliance of the Mao era was shifted from 1978 into an open cooperation that looked at the European Community members as the key partners' in China's effort to modernize its economy and armed forces. EEC countries—first and foremost France and the UK—promptly answered Beijing's call for civil-military cooperation, creating a channel of exchange that supported the growth of bilateral trade by adding a security dimension.[36]

A combination of domestic and foreign policy factors created an ideal environment for the development of China's relations with the EEC countries at the end of the 1970s. Domestically, pervasive stagflation made the prospect of access to the Chinese market an attractive option for Britain, France and West Germany.[37] At a global level, China's compelling interest in acquiring dual-use technologies to reinforce the PLA (People's

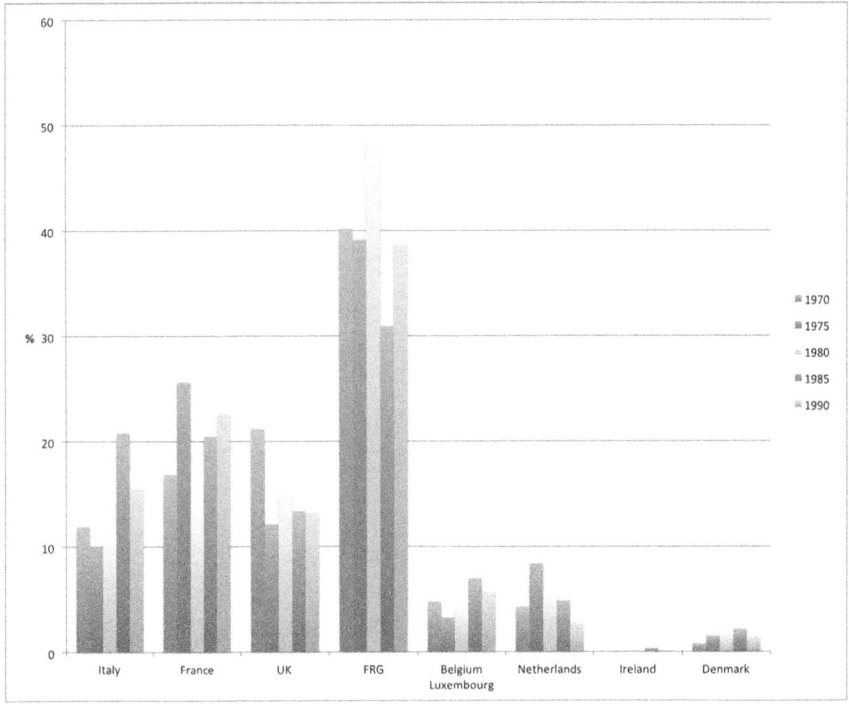

Figure 5.2 Exports from Individual Countries as a Proportion of Total EEC exports (percent).

Source: Based on data from the UN Comtrade Database (http://comtrade.un.org). Last accessed: April 10, 2017.

Liberation Army) and counter Soviet hegemony gave the EC member states a great opportunity to play an active role at the international level. The relationship with Beijing became an increasingly useful stratagem for Europe in order to pressure the Soviets in Asia and foster *détente* on the European front of the Cold War.

Chinese expectations, however, were confronted with Western trade barriers. Since the end of the Second World War the United States had created a legal framework that blocked the sale of goods, services and technologies to Communist countries in order to hinder their economic and industrial development.[38] This framework was legally absorbed by the Coordinating Committee for Multilateral Export Controls (CoCom)—established after the Second World War by the Western powers to restrict arms transfers towards the Soviet Bloc—that imposed a total prohibition against exportation of any goods, services and technology towards China.

Both the UK and France, as well as most of the other EEC members, wished to bypass US restrictions in order to expand their bilateral relations with China.[39] The British government insisted on a relaxation of the CoCom restrictions, arguing in 1973 that the supply of military items to the Chinese (such as the Spey jet engine and its technology) did not represent a security threat of such significance as to justify a permanent embargo.[40] Furthermore, the British argued, the sale of this equipment would reinforce the dynamic that animated the Sino–Soviet split and push the Soviets to divert resources from Europe to Asia.[41] As David Craine put it: "everybody in Europe liked to keep the polar bear at the east end of the zoo."[42]

France followed the British line and decided to sell dual-use technology to the PRC. In 1973, the French government submitted a request of exception to CoCom for the sale of French Super Frelon helicopters to China, but met with strong American opposition.[43] The US delegate argued that the helicopter, although a civilian model, could potentially be used for military purposes, such as troop transport. The French delegate responded that a similar objection could be made to any kind of civilian equipment. Furthermore, the cost and technical complexities of conversion minimized the risk.[44]

The UK and France became the main drivers of the new trade policy within the CoCom, in overt opposition to American objections. In the 1970s, they favored expanding trade with the PRC in the field of dual-use technologies. According to UN Comtrade data, European exports of dual-use items to China increased significantly during that decade. In 1972, for example, 47.81 percent of French and 37.89 percent of British exports to Communist China had a strategic connotation. The equivalent figures in 1975 were: UK 65.93 percent and France 54.18 percent.[45]

China made the acquisition of technology a high priority, especially in the fields of transportation, electronics and IT, telecommunications, and energy. The PRC benefited from European technology in three main ways: purchasing military technology directly, obtaining civilian technology with military applications, and developing its own modern weapons system through joint ventures with European firms (the so-called "know-how exchange").

From a European perspective, technology transfers were perceived as a natural part of trade, but possessing a strategic benefit that went beyond trade. A modernized and militarily robust China was seen as a potentially strategic asset in the struggle against the Soviet Union. It was in Europe's interest then to help China to improve its stability and strength.[46] At the beginning of the 1980s, French President François Mitterrand—during a visit to China—recognized that "the PRC was an important pillar and force of peace, especially between the US and the USSR."[47]

Strategic technology cooperation between Europe and China also embraced the European Space Agency (ESA).[48] Beijing was clearly keen to cooperate with ESA for several reasons. Firstly, the Chinese needed to acquire know-how in instrumentation, data handling, automatic computer processing, test methods and procedure, check-out and quality assurance. Second, China accorded political importance to space travel and wanted to establish good cooperation with Europe, inasmuch as Europeans established the only example of peaceful multinational cooperation in space.[49] A first Chinese delegation led by Lei Hung, member of the Council of the Chinese Electronics Society, was received at ESA's Paris headquarters in September 1977.[50] This prepared the ground for the most important ESA visit to China, led by its Director General Roy Gibson in 1979. The delegation was hosted by the State Science and Technology Commission and the Centre for Space Science and Applied Research of the Chinese

Academy of Sciences.[51] During the meeting they agreed to pursue a very structured collaboration and ESA agreed to assist China in introducing foreign technologies.[52]

The visit to China by Commission President Roy Jenkins (February 20 to March 2, 1979) significantly improved Sino–European relations following the ratification of the 1978 Agreement. During his meeting with Li Qiang, Jenkins expressed his endorsement of the new and ongoing process of reforms and declared that China's program of modernization was likely to be one of the major events of the twentieth century for the world economy. Chinese economic growth, according to the president of the EEC Commission, had in fact the potential to provide the industrialized world with stimulating opportunities at a time when all other prospects for growth seemed gloomy.[53]

In July 1979 the Sino–European Joint Committee met in Beijing for the first time, and achieved two important goals to further economic relations: first they reached a textile products trade agreement, while other Asian countries were still subject to quotas. Second, China started to benefit from the Generalized Scheme of Preferences (GSP), a system that allowed exemption from customs duties for all industrial goods and partial exemption for certain processed agricultural products exported to the EEC.

In May 1985, China and the EEC replaced the 1978 agreement with the Agreement on Trade and Economic Cooperation (TEC) that embraced industry and mining, agriculture, science and technology, energy, transport and communication, environmental protection, and development cooperation.[54] The TEC signaled a fast growing cooperation between the two sides and a growing role of the EEC in support of China's industrial and technological development: from 1981 and 1986 around 48 percent of imported technologies and 44 percent of the loans received by Beijing came from the EEC.[55]

Initially EEC–China relations remained explicitly economic. The economic agreements had been conceived as tools to intensify and diversify trade and actively develop economic and technical cooperation in line with mutual interests. As David Scott points out, however, the political-strategic dimension became particularly important, especially in the 1980s.[56]

The Chinese greatly appreciated the strengthening of the European integration process and EEC growing confidence in asserting its "European identity" in international affairs vis-a-vis the United States. The signing of the Single European Act in 1986—the historic revision of the 1957 Treaty of Rome that set the construction of a single European market by 1992—reinforced the EEC's coherence as an international actor. With the collapse of the Soviet Union these considerations became even more relevant. As Deng Xiaoping told the Central Committee: "the situation in which the United States and the Soviet Union dominated all international affairs is changing. [...] When the world becomes three-polar, four-polar or five-polar, China will be counted as a pole, as would Europe."[57]

The Tiananmen Square events of June 1989 briefly interrupted the Sino–European honeymoon. With a vocal document titled "Declaration on China" The European Council Summit of June 1989 strongly condemned the brutal repression of the student movement carried out by the Chinese army and recommended the Commission to adopt specific measures against China.[58] Financial credits were frozen, military cooperation halted, and bilateral meetings suspended. Human rights in China was flagged as an international issue and an arms embargo—still active today—was imposed on China.[59]

Alongside these seemingly rigid and punitive measures, a few weeks after the Tiananmen crackdown the EEC shifted into a conciliatory attitude towards Beijing based on the idea that isolation endangered the virtuous cycle started by Deng's reform and opening. The support to a policy of engagement became a practical choice that combined the growing economic interest of the European countries towards the Chinese market with an ethical and liberal horizon that saw China's economic reform as a premise of political democratization. The pacification of Sino–European relations after Tiananmen took place in fact in a relatively short period of time and was facilitated by the end of the Cold War in Europe that seemed officially sanctioning, according to Francis Fukuyama, the "End of History."

Sino–European relations were then relaunched in 1995 when the European Commission published its "Long-Term Policy for Relations between China and Europe" in an attempt to reconcile abstract human rights demands with real economic interests.[60] Despite differences of opinion inside the Community, the attraction of the Chinese market and the benefits brought by economic cooperation reminded the Community of the importance of the Sino–European reconciliation.

Since then in fact, the economic relations between China and Europe blossomed, turning the EU, in 2018, into China's biggest trading partner and China into the EU's second largest trading partner. A more regular and institutionalized political dialogue was being developed to sustain the growing economic interdependence: the EU–China annual summit was established in 1998, in 2003 the relationship achieved an official "comprehensive strategic" dimension, and in the "EU–China 2020 Strategic Agenda for Cooperation" the two sides started looking at a future of growing cooperation in all major areas, including security and infrastructural connectivity.[61]

Most recently, the virtue of the strong economic links between the two sides has been put into question by the European countries. The openness of the European Union to investments, in fact, has not been matched so far by China, whose domestic market remains until today mostly restricted to foreign operators. The massive rise of Chinese acquisitions on the European market started in 2014 therefore instilled a sense of growing frustration among the European Union members, who started discussing at the beginning of 2018 a new set of restrictions to foreign investments substantially aimed at China. This new European stance, in a time of fierce anti-China policies being implemented by the Trump administration in Washington, might risk expanding into a Western anti-China front that risks erasing the achievement achieved in these decades of bilateral cooperation.

Conclusion

Since the founding of the EEC in 1957, the bilateral relations with China have been influenced by the structural differences of the two actors: if China acted like an independent and unified force in the international system, the EEC was a composite aggregation of countries whose foreign policy was being influenced by their internal competitions and their alliance with the United States.

This structural difference was reinforced by the demise of European global influence—symbolized by the end of the colonial system—and by Mao's vision of China as the leader of a "third" anti-hegemonic and anti-imperialist pole in the international system.

From the beginning, these factors made the EEC much "closer" to China than the contrary: China's EEC policy was steady and efficient as it was part of China's global strategy. EEC China policy was slower and weaker as it lacked a truly shared "global" vision that could inspire it.

In its initial conception, Europe's reaching out to China was a simple by-product of the ecumenist spirit of European foreign policy aiming to engage Beijing to dispel tensions and promote peace—and trade—in Europe and beyond. In contrast, China's European policy was part of a much more calculated global strategy that identified the superpowers' search for hegemony as an imminent risk of global war that would threaten China's survival as well as its dream of political and economic resurgence. This difference allowed China since the beginning to better control the timing and the course of bilateral relations.

The Sino–European reconciliation in the 1970s thus had a double meaning. For China, it accelerated the multipolarization process of the international system whilst precipitating its resurgence on the international scene. For Europe, it helped rekindle some of the *grandeur* its member states had lost since being eclipsed by the superpower duopoly, as well as representing an important demonstration of the potential strength of the nascent European Community.

The deepening of the relationship—alongside the expansion of its width—since the end of the Cold War conserved the original anti-hegemonic inspiration of the previous decades in its attempt to rebalance the unipolar moment of the United States. The European Union searched for economic glory as a legitimacy for its own existence but also as a rebalance of its weakness in diplomacy and security vis-a-vis Washington. The Chinese played with the legendary allure evoked by their immense market to reinforce Europe's dependence on China, Europe's internal divisions and China's capacity to *divide et impera*.

These trends, however, progressively became a threat to European cohesion itself: they eventually perverted the virtuous premises of the bilateral relations providing a fertile ground for the painful revision in course today.

Notes

1   See Dick Wilson, "China and the European Community," *The China Quarterly*, 56 (1973), 647–666; Markus Taube, "Economic Relations between the PRC and the States of Europe," in the special issue "China and Europe since 1978: A European Perspective," *The China Quarterly*, 169 (2002), 78–107; Franco Algeri, "EU Economic Relations with China: An Institutional Perspective," in the special issue "China and Europe since 1978: A European Perspective," *The China Quarterly*, 169 (2002), 64–77; Roger Strange, Jim Slater and Limin Wang (eds.), *Trade and Investments in*

China: The European Experience (London and New York: Routledge, 1998); Francis Snyder (ed.), *The European Union and China, 1949–2008* (Oxford and Portland: Hart Publishing, 2009) presents a good collection of documents from Western European archives but, as much as the aforementioned sources, it ignores Chinese sources. Giovanni Bressi, "China and Western Europe," *Asian Survey*, 12:10 (1972), 819–845 can be seen as an interesting model as it provides an in-depth analysis—although only limited to the beginning of the 1970s—of Chinese political designs that inspired the evolution of China's EC policy.

2   The author will use the term "Sino-European relationships" to describe the liaison between Western European countries and the PRC. The analysis will be focused mainly on the relations between the nine EC member states (Belgium, Denmark, France, FRG, Italy, Ireland, Luxembourg, the Netherlands, and the UK) and China.

3   Jeremy Suri, *Power and Protest: Global Revolution and the Rise of Detente* (Cambridge, MA: Harvard University Press, 2003).

4   Marie Julie Chenard, "Seeking Détente and Driving Integration: The European Community's Opening Towards the People's Republic of China, 1975–1978," *Journal of European Integration History*, 18:1 (2012), 25–38.

5   Mao Zedong, "Hé měiguó jìzhě ānnà. Lùyìsī. Sī tè lǎng de tánhuà," (Conversation with American correspondent Anna Louse Strong) August 6, 1946 *máozédōng xuǎnjí* [Mao Zedong Selected Works] Vol. 4, 1193–1194.

6   Enrico Fardella, Christian Ostermann and Charles Kraus, *Sino-European Relations in the Cold War and the Rise of a Multipolar World* (Washington DC: Woodrow Wilson International Center for Scholars, 2015), 234–235.

7   Mao Zedong, "Mùqián xíngshì hé wǒmen de rènwù" [The present situation and our task], December 25, 1947, *máozédōng xuǎnjí* [Mao Zedong Selected Works] Vol. 4, Ed. 1991, 1259–1260.

8   Niu Jun, "Wèi quèdìng de kāiduān: Nèizhàn mòqí de zhōnggòng duì měi zhèngcè zài tàntǎo" [Unclear beginning: a reassessment of CCP's US policy at the end of the Cold War], *guójì lěngzhàn shǐ yánjiū* [Cold War International History Research: 2012], 2.

9   Giovanni Bressi, "China and Western Europe," 824–825.

10 Niu Ju, "The Second Intermediate Zone," paper presented at the workshop "Same Dreams, Different Beds: Sino-European Relations and the Transformation of the Cold War," organized by Enrico Fardella, Christian Osterman and Charles Kraus at the Cold War International History Project (Woodrow Wilson International Center for Scholars), June 13, 2014. On Mao's decisions after the Moscow conference see Mao Zedong, "Zài mòsīkē gòngchǎndǎng hé gōngrén dǎng dàibiǎo huìyì shàng de jiǎnghuà" [Speech at the Moscow's Communist and Workers Parties Conference] November 18, 1957, zhōnggòng zhōngyāng wénxiàn yánjiū shì biān, *Jiànguó yǐlái máozédōng wéngǎo* [Mao Zedong's presentations since 1949] Vol. 6, zhōngyāng wénxiàn chūbǎn shè, 1992, 630–644.

11 Zhōnggòng zhōngyāng wénxiàn yánjiū shì biān, *Máozédōng niánpǔ yījiǔsìjiǔ-yījiǔqīliù* [Mao Zedong's records, 1949–1976] Vol. 4, zhōngyāng wénxiàn chūbǎn shè, 2013, 314.

12 Mao Zedong, "Zhōngjiān dìdài yǒu liǎng gè" [The Two Intermediate Zones], September 1963–July 1964, Zhonghua Renmin gongheguo waijiao bu, zhonggong zhongyang wenxian yanjiu shi bian, *Máozédōng wàijiāo wénxuǎn*, 506–9.

13 Zhōnggòng zhōngyāng wénxiàn yánjiū shì biān, *Máozédōng niánpǔ* [Mao Zedong's records, 1949–1976] Vol. 5, zhōngyāng wénxiàn chūbǎn shè, 2013, 256.

14   Fardella, Ostermann and Kraus, *Sino-European Relations*, 152–153. See also Guan Chengyuan, "Zhongouguanxi liushinian suixiang" [An overview on sixty years of Sino-European relations], *Ouzhou Yanzhou* 5 (2009), 7–11.

15   After Sino–French normalization and the opening of a Chinese commercial office in Italy in 1964, the Chinese diplomats at the PRC Embassy in Switzerland wrote the Ministry of Foreign Affairs that "each step made by Western Europe towards us is a positive result in our fight against the US." People's Republic of China, Ministry of Foreign Affairs, Central Archive, Doc. 110–01765-01, "The situation of Sino-Italian relations," Swiss Embassy to MOFA, December 4, 1964.

16   Chen Jian, *Mao's China and the Cold War* (Chapel Hill: The University of North Carolina Press, 2001), 244.

17   Conversation between Foreign Minister Genscher and Chinese Ambassador Wang Shu, April 26, 1976, in Fardella, Ostermann and Kraus, *Sino-European Relations*, 520.

18   Giovanni Bressi, "China and Western Europe," 829–831.

19   Ibid., 833–834.

20   See https://www.marxists.org/reference/archive/deng-xiaoping/1974/04/10.htm (last accessed October 23, 2018).

21   Harish Kapur, *China and the European Economic Community: The New Connection* (Lancaster: Nijhoff, 1986), 27; On China's support for EC integration see also Xie Yixian (ed.), *Zhongguodangdaiwaijiaoshi (1949–2000)* [China's Modern Diplomacy, 1949–2000], (Beijing: China Youth Press, 2002), 319–320.

22   Ministero degli Affari Esteri, Segreteria Generale, Visite di Stato/Visite Ufficiali, Cina-Romania-Grecia-Spagna, 1978 Vol. 5, "Repubblica Popolare Cinese: rapporti tra la RPC e i paesi del patto di Varsavia (tranne l'Urss): Elementi di conversazione; Elementi di fatto."

23   Chenard, "Seeking Détente and Driving Integration," 25–37.

24   Harish Kapur, *The End of an Isolation: China after Mao* (Boston: Martinus Nijhoff Publishers, 1985), 84.

25   Francis Snyder (ed.), *The European Union and China, 1949–2008: Basic Documents and Commentary* (Oxford: Bloomsbury, 2009), 67–80.

26   Debates of the European Parliament, June 18, 1975. Source: *Official Journal of the European Community*, June 18, 1975.

27   Historical Archives of the European Union (HAEU), Edoardo Martino Collection, EM-124, Chine, March 8, 1974–19 October 1999.

28   Kapur, *China and the European Economic Community*, 40–41.

29   HAEU, Emil Noël Collection, EN-1153, Notes de C. Tickell, chef du Président Roy Jenkins, October 12, 1979.

30   The safeguard clause allowed the Community to unilaterally impose or tighten quotas in the event of a sudden influx of Chinese imports.

31   HAEU, Edoardo Martino Collection, EM-124, Chine, March 8, 1974–October 19, 1999.

32   HAEU, Emil Noël Collection, EN-1142, Visit of the Chinese Trade Minister Li Qiang in Europe, April 3, 1978.

33   Data have been collected from the *UN Comtrade Database* and they showed the evolution of exports (constant price) between the European Community (Italy, France, UK, Belgium, Federal Republic of Germany, Netherlands, Luxembourg, Ireland, and Denmark) and the People's Republic of China in 1970, 1975, 1980, 1985, and 1990.

34   Kapur, *China and the European Economic Community*, 50.

35   HAEU, Edoardo Martino Collection, EM-124, Chine, March 8, 1974–October 19, 1999.

36   HAEU, ESA Collection, ESA-6910, ESA Inter-Office Memorandum, *The China Briefing*, July 12–13, 1979.

37   Martin Albers, "Partners But Not Allies: West European Co-operation with China, 1978–1982," *Diplomacy & Statecraft*, 25 (2014), 688–707, here 689–690.

38   The most relevant bills in this respect were the "Export Control Act" approved in 1949, the "Mutual Defense Assistance Control Act" (or Battle Act) in 1951 and the "Export Administration Act" (1969).

39   In 1971 China ordered six Trident jet aircrafts and five large gas turbine generators from Britain; while France sold, in 1973, thirteen Super Frelon helicopters.

40   The National Archives (TNA), FCO 21/1123, Possible Export of Harrier Aircraft to China from UK, 1973.

41   TNA, FCO 21/1124, Policy on Exports of Aircraft and Spares from the UK to China, 1973.

42   David Crane, "The Harrier Jump-Jet and Sino-British Relations," *Asia Affairs*, 8:4 (1981), 246.

43   TNA, FCO 21/1249, Exports of helicopters to China from France, 1974.

44   Archives Diplomatiques de la Courneuve (ADC), 119QO/846, Asie Océanie (1973–1980), Les relations militaires franco-chinoises, Paris, December 30, 1977.

45   http://comtrade.un.org (last accessed November 1, 2018).

46   Zong Cong (ed.), "Xī'ōu jīngjì yǔ zhèngzhì gàilùn" [Introduction to the economy and the politics of Western Europe], (Beijing: China Higher Education Press, 1988), 464–468.

47   Bernadette Andreosso-O'Callaghan and Wei Qian, "Technology Transfer: A Mode of Collaboration between the European Union and China," *Europe-Asia Studies*, 51:1 (1999), 123–142.

48   The strategic cooperation was enhanced through the intergovernmental method because the EC had no legal competence in these areas, as in the case of the space policy.

49   HAEU, European Space Agency (ESA) Collection, ESA-6910, Note on ESA Visit to China and Future Cooperation, April 11, 1979.

50   HAEU, ESA Collection, ESA-6910, Chinese Mission to Europe, May 31, 1977.

51   HAEU, ESA Collection, ESA-2963, ESA Delegation's Visit to China, April 1979.

52   HAEU, ESA Collection, ESA-4808, Relations with China, August 7, 1978–February 23, 1979. The agreement between ESA and China was signed in Paris in July 1980. See HAEU, ESA Collection, ESA-4808, Agreement between the Chinese Academy and ESA on Space Technical Cooperation—Draft, February 1979; HAEU, ESA Collection, Cooperation Agreement with the National Commission for Science and Technology of the PRC, October 1980.

53   HAEU, Emile Noël Collection, EN-1607.

54   Li Qingsheng, "Ouzhougongtongti yu zhongguo de jingjimaoyiguanxi" [The trade relationship between China and the European Community], *Guójì màoyì wèntí* [International Trade Journal], 1 (1989), 54–57.

55   David Shambaugh, Eberhard Sandschneider and Zhou Hong (eds.), *China-Europe Relations: Perceptions, Policies and Prospects* (New York: Taylor and Francis, 2008), 236.

56   David Scott, "China-EU Convergence 1957–2003: Towards a Strategic Partnership," *Asia Europe Journal*, 5:2 (2007), 223.

57   Ibid., 224.

58   See Council of Ministers Declaration on China. European Council, Madrid, June 26–27, 1989, https://www.sipri.org/sites/default/files/2016-03/Council-Statement.pdf (last accessed October 23, 2018).

59   Kay Moller, "Diplomatic Relations and Mutual Strategic Perceptions: China and the European Union," in the special issue "China and Europe since 1978: A European Perspective," *The China Quarterly*, 169 (2002), 10–32.

60   The official document is available at: http://eeas.europa.eu/china/docs/com95_279_en.pdf (last accessed: October 23, 2018).

61   COM (2003) 533 is available at: http://eur-lex.europa.eu/LexUriServ/LexUriServ.do?uri=COM:2003:0533:FIN:EN:PDF (last accessed October 23, 2018). https://www.fmprc.gov.cn/mfa_eng/topics_665678/ceupp_665916/t27708.shtml (last accessed October 23, 2018); https://eeas.europa.eu/sites/eeas/files/20131123.pdf (last accessed October 23, 2018).

6

The EC and Japan: From Mutual Neglect to Trade Conflicts and Beyond

Albrecht Rothacher

It took the two quite some time and sweat to learn to tango.[1] In a nutshell, it was the low politics of trade and economic competition that dominated the relationship, at the cost of hundreds of thousands of European industrial jobs. Grand global strategic considerations may have been on the leaders' minds on occasion. In the Cold War context they surely leaned towards a vague sense of Western solidarity (aided by no uncertain US prodding), later there was a commitment to free trade among market economies. Relations were essentially managed by senior trade officials and diplomats on both sides. They did well, against all odds, in spite of actions that sometimes broke with textbook conventions. Oft-predicted trade wars were avoided, and options aiming at market opening (in Japan) and cushioned restructuring (in Europe) were found and implemented, opening the way—after 1992—for a new meeting of minds and sustained comprehensive cooperation in high and low politics. This was no small achievement for the actors on both sides.

The evolution of EEC/EC–Japan relations up to the late 1980s played a significant role for both partners' external policy development. For the European Community (EC) it created the first stress test of its new common commercial policy, and later helped to expand its scope beyond purely commercial matters, as well as to open its horizon beyond post-colonial Africa and the US hegemon towards the rest of the world. For Japan, in a mirror image, it also meant extending diplomatic skills and political perspectives beyond the traditional South East Asian backyard and the United States, and gradually modifying neo-mercantilist industrial policies under sustained external pressure. In the 1970s and 1980s, relations between these emerging global actors, which frequently perceived each other in terms of stereotypes and competed in similar mid- to high-technology industrial sectors, were seen and sometimes acted upon as zero sum games with barely constrained trade conflicts. With the wisdom of

Disclaimer: Although I served in the EC/EU Delegation in Tokyo as a Junior Attaché in 1981/82, as a First Secretary (in charge of agriculture, fisheries, transportation and regional policies) during 1987/91 and as Minister Counsellor (as head of the section on macroeconomic and social policies) during 2011/15, the views expressed here are purely personal and do in no way engage my employer.

hindsight it seems astounding that such conflicts were prevented from escalating, and in the end were always diffused through either less orthodox Japanese export restraints or more virtuous Japanese market opening under US and EC pressure. In the end monetary and macroeconomic policy measures did the trick: US pressure resulted in the 1985 Plaza Agreement, revaluing the yen and forcing the Bank of Japan to flood its economy with liquidity, resulting in a massive asset bubble. After the inevitable implosion, public rescue and stimulus packages failed to revive Japan's economy and competiveness. The "Japanese threat" quickly evaporated, as did fears of "Fortress Europe," which turned out to be more of a sand castle, welcoming Japanese investment not only in the core regions but also in recently liberated East and Central Europe.

By 1990/1991 a new and enduring chapter had opened, with relations in a state of constructive normalcy: distant but strategically like-minded partners, both with mature structurally stagnant economies, both stable and rapidly aging democracies, and both soft powers with tangibly declining real global reach and in long-term decline. But that is a different page in the story of the EC–Japan relationship.

Issues, Actors, Contexts, and Perceptions

Trade issues were clearly central to EC–Japan relations, *par faute de mieux* in the absence of operationally shared high strategic interests. Japan's interests were foremost commercial: to secure her access to the Common Market. The EC Commission had to assert its new Common Commercial Policy (CCP) competences by either negotiating Japanese export restraints, or improving access to the highly protected Japanese market by tackling tariff and non-tariff barriers, and eventually arriving at a combination of both.

Among key actors on the EC side, a division of labor gradually emerged, with senior Commission trade officials and their Commissioners (Dahrendorf and Haferkamp, later also Davignon) playing key roles alongside senior national officials and their trade and economics ministers, and occasionally also heads of government.[2] Operationally, senior officials in the Commission's Directorates General (DGs) I (External relations) and III (Industry) at head of division to director general level played the key role. They coordinated with colleagues in other DGs, with member states via Committee of Permanent Representatives (COREPER) and more junior Council working groups, and negotiated with the Japanese. In 1975 a very modest EC Delegation was also set up in Tokyo (initially as a press and information office, since member states did not want to share the intelligence gained by their embassies). It quickly acquired fully-fledged trade negotiation and commercial promotion functions, shadowed by the growing role of the Japanese Mission to the EC in Brussels.

Member states slowly scaled down the functions of their trade ministries but continued to play a dual role: a European role in Council decision-making and a national one in bilateral negotiations with the Japanese on export restraints and Foreign Direct Investment (FDI) promotion in their own national markets and for export promotion in Japan. This art was perfected by British Prime Minister Margaret Thatcher (1979–1990), who skillfully arranged the reconstruction of the UK car industry by Nissan, Honda, and Toyota (then regarded as "Trojan horses" by France and Italy) in exchange for a veto on EC-wide import restrictions on Japanese cars.

In a more strategic perspective, during the Cold War era and its aftermath Japan was seen in a global setting as a US ally and anchor, its economic rise viewed with benevolence in the context of the potentially destabilizing and dangerous Soviet–Chinese antagonism. Georges Pompidou said to Richard Nixon on February 24, 1970: "Nous souhaitons une Europe économique forte avec une France politiquement indépendante. De même en Asie, nous souhaitons le développement du Japon" [We want a strong economic Europe with a politically independent France. Similarly, in Asia we want the development of Japan].[3] To Edward Heath on March 19, 1972 more as an afterthought to relations with the United States: "Nous allons donc discuter au sommet européen les relations entre la Communauté et les Etats Unis et aussi le Japon" [Thus, at the European summit we will discuss relations between the Community and the United States, and also Japan].[4] And on global strategic developments on May 31, 1973 in Reykjavík, already terminally ill, to Nixon and Kissinger: " … l'arrivée du Japon comme puissance économique primordiale avec une situation stratégique très spéciale et difficile. Pris entre l'URSS et les Etats Unis, il a choisi provisoirement de rester lie avec vous-mêmes" […the arrival of Japan as a prime economic power with a very special and difficult strategic situation. Positioned between the USSR and the United States, for the moment it has chosen to remain tied to you].[5] Helmut Schmidt also saw Japan's role essentially in a trilateral context. He appreciated Takeo Fukuda's prime ministership (1976–1978) essentially for its supportive role in containing what he and Fukada (together with French President Valéry Giscard d'Estaing and Commission President Roy Jenkins—all four former finance ministers) regarded as misguided and risky foreign, energy, and macroeconomic policies of the Carter administration.[6] Yet he observed a "limited flexibility of Japan's global strategy, constrained with limited room for manoeuvre," "an economic giant but a political dwarf," like West Germany in the 1960s, relying for all her defense needs on the United States.[7] The previous French President, Georges Pompidou (1969–1974)—who in his talks with the American, Soviet, and Chinese leaderships thought himself the foremost strategic thinker in Europe at the time—also believed that Cold War considerations no longer applied to Japan. Brezhnev's Soviet Union and Mao's China would keep each other in hateful antagonistic check. The West was safe unless it was sold out by the Americans. Japan did not really count.

On the Japanese side, relations were essentially and in substance managed by middle- to senior-level bureaucrats (at director ["kacho"] to director-general ["kyokucho"] level) at the Ministry of International Trade and Industry (MITI) (and to a lesser extent by the ritualistic generalists at the Ministry of Foreign Affairs, playing a more formalistic role), with the usually less-than-cooperative line ministries defending their sectoral turf and client industry interests.[8] As ministers usually stayed in office for at most ten months, their impact was transitory at best. Alongside indifference to US relations, on the Japanese side EC relations were never sufficiently politicized to merit the active involvement of senior politicians from the ruling Liberal Democratic Party (LDP). Private sector involvement was essentially limited to Keidanren, the business federation, representing export interests and at the time engaging in an accommodative "private economic diplomacy" with the blessings of the ministries concerned. On the European side, business federations, sectoral industry lobbies, and individual business leaders (like Giovanni Agnelli) were involved as well. Unlike in Japan, the trade unions in threatened sectors were also engaged, albeit less effectively.

Bilateral relations, which had evolved in the context of Cold War conditions, gradually mellowed into an emerging G-7 framework. Japanese prime ministers regularly reiterated their mantra of free trade threatened by US and European protectionism, but were usually rebutted by more or less informed criticisms of their own neo-mercantilist policies. None of this was of any operational consequence.[9] Regular interaction at sherpa level started to play a role, but friendships also developed—for example between Helmut Schmidt and Takeo Fukuda, and between Margaret Thatcher and Yasuhiro Nakasone—and certainly had an impact when both held power concurrently (1976–1978 and 1982–1987 respectively). Basically, however, the role of most of Japan's short-serving prime ministers at G-7 meetings, at which they were usually linguistically disadvantaged, was to smile, nod (meaning that they had understood the simultaneous interpretations, which Westerners misread as approval), and to have their prepared statements politely ignored by fellow summiteers. Schmidt, for instance—who claimed to have initiated the global economic summits together with Giscard d'Estaing, including the Japanese in order to prevent their friendless isolation—felt he had meaningful exchanges only with his friend Fukuda and warmed less to the "nationalist" Yasuhiro Nakasone (1982–1987). According to Schmidt, the other Japanese leaders, like Eisaku Sato (1964–1972), Takeo Miki (1974–1976) (whom he misspells twice as "Miko"), Masayoshi Ohira (1978–1980), and Zenko Suzuki (1980–1982), remained very polite, but entirely enigmatic in their utterings, and were thus essentially ineffective participants.[10] In Schmidt's view Japan's lack of allies in her disputes with the United States and the EC made her resort to fake concessions (*Scheinzugeständnisse*) to stave off pressure.[11]

The big elephant in the bilateral room was certainly always the United States. EC negotiators and deciders continuously and almost obsessively compared their own modest achievements in Japan with those of the Americans, which were inevitably grander thanks to their exclusive sales of overpriced big-ticket items (airplanes, arms), followed up by bilateral trade concessions. The United States applied effectively focused political pressure, with a protectionist US Congress playing bad cop (US Congressmen smashing Toshiba transistor radios on the steps of the Capitol in 1987), while the US administration employed *gaiatsu* (foreign pressure) during dramatically enacted negotiations. In fact, the entire "diversion" of Japanese exports diversifying from the US market towards the EC was triggered by the "textile wrangle" of the Nixon administration (suffering the economic and fiscal consequences of the Vietnam War) back in 1969–1971. Subsequently the United States—in response to political expediency and the intellectual fashion of the season—successively employed various approaches: pushing for sectoral market access (from beef to oranges), or for structural reforms (the dismantling of the keiretsu conglomerates as an objective of the Structural Impediments Initiative), or ultimately for a macroeconomic game-changer. The latter resulted in the 1985 Plaza

Agreement, with a massive revaluation of the yen. In response, the Bank of Japan flooded the markets with liquidity that created a massive speculative bubble; the inevitable implosion followed five years later.

Effective trilateralism never materialized, in spite of the well-intended elite cooperation of David Rockefeller's Trilateral Commission (which saw its heyday under the 1977–1981 Carter administration and has since vanished). This turned out to be an unhappy *ménage a trois*, unsurprisingly dominated by US unilateralism, protectionist US threats (with trade diversion to European markets the feared consequence), and mutual jealousies. EC negotiators would almost obsessively compare the concessions they achieved with those of their US colleagues—who usually achieved much better deals with less but more politically focused effort—as did the European media and the member states, which were not shy to comment.

During the 1970s and 1980s Japan's export drives focused on limited high-tech segments, very visible consumer durables, and heavy industrial equipment, all of which had strong employment and capital implications, and none of which could be written off as "sunset" industries. After benign neglect in the post-war years a powerful competitor suddenly emerged, felt to be competing with substandard labor costs, public protectionism, and state capitalist collusion ("Japan Inc."), threatening European key industries and skilled employment, and during the 1980s seemingly poised to take over the world's strategic industries from ball bearings and semiconductors to cars, electronics, steel, shipbuilding, and banking. European media and interest groups were not shy to decry a "yellow peril" with alien values (workaholics), copying Western technologies and know-how, and threatening the European democracy and welfare state. Stereotypes were reciprocated on the Japanese side. Europeans lived in museums and old-age homes. They had become lazy in a protective cocoon, lacked innovation and entrepreneurial drive, and even after repeated Japanese "import missions" had no products (apart from apparel, Bordeaux wines, and ties) of evident interest to Japanese importers.

At the same time, US propaganda against the internal market project (Fortress Europe), set to launch in December 1992, fell on fertile ground in Japan. In view of their own industrial policies, they could only perceive this as a protectionist plot, and the more the Europeans denied this, the less they were believed. Hence the need for a policy response, for accommodation, for *divide et impera* strategies towards member states, and for Japanese FDI within, before it was too late. Thus, *nolens volens*, lasting constructive solutions for Europe's threatened deindustrialization were achieved.

As an international actor, the EC nonetheless remained puzzling to Japanese negotiators and policymakers. The Commission having to ask for mandates to negotiate and leeway to interpret them, the need for continuous feedback from Council working groups, and member states at the same time seeking Japanese concessions and investments in their own national interest. Japan represented a more classical if equally notoriously divided picture. The ministers, as mentioned, changed so frequently that their names could barely be remembered. Japanese bureaucrats were (and are) subject to regular rotation and rarely remain in office for more than three years. Hence they tended to represent their ministries' bureaucratic interests and consensus more than any views of their own. By the time they had mastered their brief and established relations of trust with their Commission counterparts (an essential ingredient in all successful international negotiations), they were already off to pastures new.

Prehistory: The Post-War Era

In the late 1940s Japanese cities and industry lay in ruins. As in Europe, labor unrest—initially stimulated as "democratization" by the US occupation but later strongly discouraged—was strong, and until 1949 seemed to threaten recovery. US procurement for the Korean War (1950–1953) finally got economic rehabilitation under way. Japanese export markets in South East Asia only gradually recovered, partly fueled by Japanese war reparations supplied in the guise of development aid. European colonies (French Indochina, Malaya and the Dutch East Indies) were only marginally involved, and not particularly interested, given their growing security troubles and recent bitter memories of Japanese military brutality towards their civilians and Prisoners of War.

Until the 1952 Peace Treaty of San Francisco was signed, it was officials of the US occupation who negotiated miniscule import contingents in national European markets on behalf of Japan, and when Japan (with a forcefully helping US hand in the Cold War context) joined the General Agreement on Tariffs and Trade (GATT) in 1955, most future EEC member states accepted her most favored nation (MFN) treatment only under the proviso of very limited national quotas (in Italy for instance, Japanese car imports remained limited to 2,000 per annum until the late 1980s). To the Japanese, such restrictions smacked of pre-war discrimination, and in the 1960s, when most of her exports consisted of light industrial products (like textiles, sewing machines, ceramics, canned fish, and toys) posing little commercial threat, all her diplomatic efforts were geared towards eliminating them. Most famously, when Prime Minister Hayato Ikeda visited Paris in 1964, President Charles de Gaulle wanted to discuss global strategic issues while Ikeda stuck to his trade briefs. There was no meeting of minds, and after the meeting de Gaulle is said to have called him a "marchand de transistors."[12] Yet in bilateral trade agreements with France, the Benelux countries and the UK, Japan managed to have these import quotas expanded or abolished.

The 1970s

With the entry into force of the CCP rules in 1970, the Commission was faced with the challenge of unifying its member states' divergent trade policies towards Japan: with West Germany, the Netherlands (and later Denmark) in the liberal camp, France and Italy more protectionist, and the UK (from 1973 until the advent of Prime Minister Margaret Thatcher in 1979) oscillating in between. The Commission, with Commissioner Ralf Dahrendorf in charge, soon obtained a Council mandate to negotiate a trade agreement with Japan providing for the removal of national import quotas in return for an EC-wide safeguard clause. The Japanese, who had longstanding difficulties understanding the Commission's role (and continued to prefer bilateral national negotiations, also with an eye to divide and rule), refused to accept such a clause, fearing that it would cement "discrimination" and potentially result in import constraints after only perfunctory consultations.[13] The negotiations on a trade agreement duly failed (and were only resumed forty years later after intensive Japanese lobbying and following the March 11, 2011 earthquake and tsunami). In the meantime—hurt by the 1971 Nixon shocks of sudden import surcharges and the devaluation of the dollar by a United States weakened by its losing war in Vietnam—Japan turned her attention to the only alternative market with significant purchasing power for her industrial and consumer products, which by then had been nurtured by decades-long export promotion policies into a largely cartelized, well-protected domestic market with systematically privileged keiretsu conglomerates, like Mitsubishi, Mitsui, Sumitomo, etc.[14] At that time, the export drive was mainly organized by their affiliated general trading companies, the sogo shosha.[15] Most of these have now converted into commodity and energy traders and processors, as all the major manufacturers have in the meantime learned to export directly, as well as to produce and to procure globally; for better or worse, part of "Japan Inc." had become disincorporated.

The conquest of the European car market was typical. In the 1960s the quality of Japanese cars was mocked, like the Koreans in the 1980s, and the Chinese until recently. In 1970 the soft periphery (Finland, Portugal, and Greece) was attacked first—with market shares jumping from 1 percent to 15–20 percent within a single year. Then it was the turn of Switzerland, Norway, and the Benelux countries, which also had no car industry of their own. In 1973 it was the UK, where British Leyland was quickly knocked out of existence. Germany was targeted last, while France and Italy remained protected by their residual import quotas.[16]

Similar floods of exports from this almost-unknown competitor occurred in narrow, very visible industrial sectors with high value added, threatening the employment of a very skilled workforce: consumer electronics (televisions, video recorders, radio sets), precision instruments, watches, ball bearings, motorcycles, steel, and shipbuilding. Within a few years most of Europe's motorcycle, television and watchmaking industries were wiped out. All of this happened during the first oil crisis of 1973/1974 when Japan slipped into her first post-war recession, seeking recovery first and foremost in exports to Europe (having experienced a vicious, if somewhat outdated "textile wrangle" with the United States in 1969–1971, with the Nixon administration trying to protect the declining textile industry of the US South).[17] Equally, the United States forced voluntary restraints on Japanese steel exports in 1968, which in 1976 were replaced by a "market organization system" in the United States with reference prices to be respected by both Japan and the EC. It improved the margins notably of Japanese exporters (at the expense of their customers) and further improved the competitiveness of Japanese producers.[18]

It was only in 1976 when a Keidanren mission led by its chairman Toshiwo Doko—an instrument of "private economic diplomacy" then employed by Japan—encountered unexpected criticism in Germany, that the EC's critical views of Japan's aggressive export and protectionist import policies were taken seriously in Tokyo, as the so called "Doko-Shocku."[19]

Yet to little avail. On military procurement and big-ticket items like civilian aircraft (aided by US bribes—see the Lockheed scandal of 1976 involving Prime Minister Tanaka)[20] Japan until very recently practiced a Buy-America-only policy. So during the second oil crisis of 1978/1979 the same pattern repeated, this time hitting even more political raw nerves. With a bilateral trade deficit having zoomed from US$183 million to double-digit billions and cover ratios for EC exports to Japanese imports at barely 30 percent, the Commission had little to show for the success for its CCP. Reflecting the frustration in Brussels, DG Roy Denman leaked a memo to the *Financial Times* in which (for the reading pleasure of his boss, Commissioner Wilhelm Haferkamp, a less-than-effective negotiator) he asserted that Japan was a country of "workaholics living in rabbit hutches," "sallying out of corporate fortresses to wreak havoc in a work-shy Europe, with as little propensity to import as there was carnival spirit in Glasgow."[21] Indeed Japanese "rice standards" and social dumping with exploitative long working hours were seen notably by the organized left and their media sympathizers as a threat to Europe's welfare state and hard-won working class prosperity. Haferkamp, a social democrat and career trade unionist, declared in Tokyo that the ruthless policies of the Japanese would assist Communist takeovers in Western Europe (Portugal had been at the brink at the time).[22]

Japan, however, continued with PR gimmicks, sending "import missions" to Europe, whose members publicly purchased ties and fashion apparel for themselves, but at the same time declared that the continent had become uncompetitive and unwilling to work, that it had turned into a museum and an old-people's home with nothing worthwhile to purchase for productive purposes.[23] A content analysis of the French press in 1980 revealed that 60 percent of articles covering Japan were openly hostile in tonality, using terms like menace, peril, invasion, enemy, and untrustworthy.[24] On July 30, 1980, *Der Spiegel* published a cover story depicting an aggressive sports car with slanted eyes: "Japan Autos: Europa kommt unter die Räder [Japanese cars crush Europe]." Two German trade unionists published a widely read treatise claiming that low Japanese wages and substandard working conditions forced upon a subservient, brainwashed, and repressed workforce put European jobs, wages, social standards and trade-union rights at massive risk through export dumping.[25] A Commission official posted in Tokyo at the time later published his impressions of Japan as a neo-mercantilist country with a nationalist agenda, playing systematically unfair and abusing the open trading system of the free world.[26] Other published voices of senior Commission figures, who argued instead the case for learning from cooperating with Japan, tended to be the exception.[27]

The 1980s

The Commission now increasingly resorted to anti-dumping investigations, which were not difficult to conduct. Overpricing of goods in a collusive domestic market, in which operators often competed on non-price elements from design, packaging, and after-sales services to wining, dining, and corporate gifts, was typically used to cross-subsidize cheaper exports, priced at below-production costs and hurting EC producers. Anti-dumping investigations led to fines in the form of extra tariffs and/ or price adjustments. As a tit for tat measure in 1982/1983, France replicated Japan's import barriers by forcing all Japanese videotape recorders to be cleared through the tiny customs post of Poitiers, where all sets were individually checked. Also in 1982, formal consultations aiming at "export moderation" in key affected sectors were held under GATT Article XXIII.[28] In the car market this led to "voluntary" export restraints with informal ceilings for certain national markets (allowing Japanese exporters to increase prices and profits) being replaced after year-long negotiations with a common informal import quota for all of the EC, which was only agreed in 1991 as "elements of consensus."[29] Most of the sectoral export restraints were negotiated in "confidential" deals with MITI, which then implemented them through "administrative guidance" to industry (an informal non-legal instrument allocating indicative export quotas and prices). Möhler and Van Rij argue that, given the relentless Japanese pursuit of market shares by increasing capacities, "without export moderation by Japan, European industry would not have survived."[30]

Officially, no efforts were made to calculate the job losses emanating from a decades-long double-digit-billion trade deficit in industrial products in the medium- to high-technology range, which at that time was not compensated by any surplus in services. In 1993 this author published his own appraisal that at least one million qualified productive industrial jobs in the EC had been displaced by Japanese imports, based on an estimated value added of US$30,000 per industrial worker per annum, with a bilateral trade deficit of US$31 billion (1992).[31]

More productively, and with lasting effects, the EC engaged in decades-long efforts to open the Japanese market through tedious sectoral negotiations, ranging from automotive standards and discriminatory taxes on imported liquor, leather goods, and shoes (with Japan citing the problem of the "Dowa"/"Burakumin" former outcast minority), through ski bindings ("Japanese snow is different"), cut flowers ("Japanese aphids are different"), pharmaceuticals ("Japanese bodies react differently"), and meat ("Japanese intestines are different"), to financial and insurance services, building standards, licenses for foreign lawyers, food standards, and the toleration of yakuza blackmail of foreign shipping lines; all of this on top of the world's highest tariffs on agricultural imports.[32] Ultimately the EC piously hoped for demand-driven restructuring (as outlined and promised in the Okita and Maekawa reports during the Nakasone administration): infrastructure spending and an improved social security system would finally fuel consumer spending and ultimately boost EC imports.[33] One productive survivor of the dreams of more cooperative relations at that time is the EU–Japan Industrial Cooperation Centre in Tokyo (with a branch in Brussels), set up at the initiative of Commission Vice-President Etienne Davignon (1981–1985) and Ministry of International Trade and Industry (MITI).

With the United States playing hardball in the mid-1980s, usually winning on priorities like oranges and beef, and gaining not only symbolic big-ticket sales (which the Europeans never did), one-sided Japanese concessions meant the EC's negotiators' performance always seemed disappointing.[34] Yet the United States—subject to political and/or intellectual whims and impatient with the pedestrian speed of sectoral technical talks—on occasion pushed for structural measures instead (for example, the Structural

Impediments Initiative bravely aiming at the keiretsu cartels). These, however, failed in view of the vested interests of Japan Inc.[35] Finally, in 1985, the Americans opted for the monetary nuclear option, which after the Plaza accords "succeeded" beyond expectations.

In sum, throughout the 1970s and 1980s the EC was less effective as a negotiator, because the member states could only agree on the smallest common denominator, which was the continuation of a GATT-based liberal order. Captive to their own liberal trade rhetoric, Japan's growing exports to Europe were never in any actual danger, hence allowing Japanese decision-makers to play for time, both on market access and on export "restraints." Germany and the Netherlands were consistently in the liberal camp, but France and Italy (which were most critical of Japanese policies) never seriously pushed for import protection either, and the proposition was also anathema to the European Commission.

Within the EC, Jacques Delors announced and subsequently implemented his Single Market programme. The Single European Act was agreed in 1986, to come into force by 1992. With their industrial policy tradition, the Japanese could not imagine this to be anything but a protectionist plot, and genuinely believed ill-minded US propaganda suggesting that a Fortress Europe was in the making to finally keep out unloved Japanese imports. The response was a massive shift of Japanese FDI into the EC, increasing from a mere US$29 million in 1971 to US$12 billion in 1985. The UK under Thatcher was notably successful in selling the idea of rebuilding the UK's car industry with the help of Nissan, Toyota, and Honda in return for guaranteeing free access to the entire EC market. Other member states were less welcoming to Japanese "Trojan horses." In 1991 French Prime Minister Edith Cresson, for instance, compared Japanese workers to yellow ants, forcing the French ambassador in Tokyo to explain that in French folklore ants were seen as highly intelligent, industrious, organized, and lovable creatures.[36]

Agricultural Protection: No Meeting of Minds

Both the EC and Japan maintained strong agricultural protection systems.[37] These were introduced in the post-war era to compensate the rural population for historical sacrifices during the industrialization period (supply of cheap labor, food, and soldiers), to help the countryside to catch up in terms of infrastructure, incomes, and standard of living (witness the respective provisions of the Treaty of Rome, 1957), to stabilize the rural population in view of massive urbanization, and last but not least to harness the farm vote for conservative parties. Interestingly, the Japanese Agricultural Basic Law of 1961 was modeled after the German Agricultural Law of 1955, and its implementation followed the French Law of Agricultural Orientation of 1960.[38] These policies were pursued not just in the EC and Japan, but also in other continental European countries, like Switzerland, Austria, Finland, and Norway, as well as by South Korea and Taiwan with their similar smallholding structures.[39]

Prima vista, in view of the onslaught of the liberal-minded Cairns group and notably US pressure backing its industrial farming, one could have imagined a defensive protectionist alliance of sorts between the EC and Japan in the 1980s, claiming the exceptionalism of agriculture (seasonality, artisanal nature, regional heritage, food security, and environmental needs).[40] Two so-powerful trade actors could have blocked the liberal camp in the Uruguay Round quite effectively. Yet curiously this coalition did not materialize. First, Japan claimed her uniqueness: her farm policies (implausibly since they effectively closed the domestic market to everything but feed and hence contracted global demand) did not distort international markets, as—unlike the EC and the United States—she did not subsidize her own (non-existent) exports, but instead virtuously discouraged the overproduction of rice. The EC at that time, however, viewed its export refunds as one of the sacred cows of CAP, not to be questioned or sacrificed. At the same time, Japan tried to buy off US pressure with selective concessions on beef and oranges, while continuing to stonewall on items of EC interest (pork imports; wine, cheese, and confectionery tariffs; and a range of sanitary and phytosanitary barriers).

Hence, while US *divide et impera* tactics were successful in the short term and the complexities of trade-policy decision-making on both sides did not encourage straightforward alliance-building in a controversial sector, more importantly, however, agricultural policy leaders—Commissioners Andriessen and MacSharry in the EC and the members of the "*norinzoku,*" the "tribe" of agricultural policymakers and senior experts in the ruling LDP—had decided for themselves that their protectionist policies had become too expensive, structurally dysfunctional, and untenable *vis-à-vis* both the domestic electorate and in terms of international costs.[41] The interested lobbies (in Japan, Nokyo, the powerful agricultural cooperatives; in France, the National Federation of Farmers' Union) made some noisy, yet inept countermoves, also in terms of international cooperation, but in vain. Disunited and defeated in the GATT, the reform process now made its way towards direct income support, decoupled from producer prices, and dismantled export subsidies.

The Advent of the 1990s

By the late 1980s the world had changed for the better. The Soviet empire collapsed. East Europe was in urgent need of capital and management input, hopefully also from Japan (although little in fact arrived: Suzuki in Hungary, Matsushita in the Czech Republic, and Toyota in Poland). The EC's Single Market had strengthened European industrial competitiveness, putting an end to national champions in small fragmented markets. Japan's industrial and financial might imploded into lost decades of stagnation and ruined public finances. China now emerged as a more fearsome sustained competitor playing by its own ruthless rules, initially relying on capital imports and the acquisition of foreign technology, but as an industrial mass producer still operating at much lower skill and technology levels than both the EC and Japan. After the end of the Cold War, US dominance over both partners became less salient. Trilateral cooperation was proposed by Prime Minister Takeo Fukuda in 1978, but in spite of some influence over the Carter administration (1977–1981) David Rockefeller's carefully recruited Trilateral Commission never achieved any lasting influence—conspiracy theorists notwithstanding.

With Japan's asset inflation bubble bursting around 1989 and ushering in decades of stagnation that even dozens of reflationary deficit spending programmes have failed to revive in a saturated, mature, and rapidly aging economy, the country quickly lost her threat perception (and most public and academic interest) in Europe, only to be replaced by China and the now-fading fad of the BRICS (Brazil, Russia, India, China and South Africa). In Japan itself—which during the boom years cultivated myths of national uniqueness ("*Nihonjinron*") and paternalist guardianship of conservative "Asian values" (as distinct to decadent arrogant Western values)—the growing antagonism of her Korean and Chinese neighbors due to unresolved historical issues and geopolitical rivalry has made a return to Western values and geopolitical like-mindedness palatable in public and elite opinion.

Hence by 1990 Deputy Vice Foreign Minister Hisashi Owada (also the father of Japan's unhappy Crown Princess) was able to announce his initiative for improved long-term bilateral relations. To this, the EC responded with its Hague Declaration of 1991. While market-access problems persist in Japan, mostly due to business interests but also still bolstered by habitual administrative complications, peace broke out all over. An ineffective "regulatory reform dialogue" replaced formerly straightforward market-access negotiations. In 2001 a "Ten-Year Action Plan" promised the moon in terms of over-ambitious bilateral jumelage (twinning) and unending all-encompassing dialogue (and achieved little once the initial enthusiasm evaporated after a few years). And finally, the current Free Trade Agreement/Strategic Partnership Agreement talks still suffer from the habitual foot-dragging of domestic line ministries defending the interests of even miniscule domestic lobbies, from Hokkaido's sugar-beet growers to makers of railway signaling equipment. The rest, as we know it, is contemporary history.

Notes

1   The author would like to thank Franz Waldenberger (Tokyo) and the participants of the editorial conferences in Maastricht (2015) and Florence (2016) for their most helpful comments and pertinent suggestions.

2   Roy Jenkins—although himself, like Helmut Schmidt, a friend of Prime Minister Fukuda as well—in his *European Diary 1977–1981* mentions Japan and its trade problem only in passing (London: Methuen Publishers, 1989), 96–99 and 156–157, and Jacques Delors does not mention Japan at all in his memoirs *Erinnerungen eines Europäers* (Berlin: Parthas Verlag, 2004), although photographs of his meetings with PM Nakasone (1986) and Emperor Akihito (1993) are reproduced with apparent pride.

3   Eric Roussel, *Georges Pompidou 1911–1974* (Paris: Perrin, 2004), 354.

4   Ibid., 505.

5   Ibid., 553.

6   Piers Ludlow, *Roy Jenkins and the European Commission Presidency, 1976–1980: At the Heart of Europe* (London: Palgrave Macmillan, 2016), 38; Helmut Schmidt, *Menschen und Mächte* (Berlin: Siedler Verlag, 2015), 432.

7   Schmidt, *Menschen und Mächte*, 421 and 435.

8   Rolf Möhler and Jan Van Rij, "1983–1987: Export Moderation as a Panacea or Can Japan Change?" in Jörn Keck, Dimitri Vanoverbeke and Franz Waldenberger (eds.), *European Union-Japan Relations: From Confrontation to Global Partnership, 1970–2012* (Milton Park: Routledge, 2013), 58–77.

9   Hitoshi Suzuki, "The Rise of Summitry and EEC-Japan Trade Relations," in Emmanuel Mourlon-Druol and Federico Romero (eds.), *International Summitry and Global Governance: The Rise of the G7 and the European Council, 1974–1991* (Milton Park: Routledge, 2014), 153–173.

10 Note that Sato never participated in any summit, since the first was held in Rambouillet in November 1975. So much for the accuracy of political memoirs. See also Schmidt, *Menschen und Mächte*, 431.

11 Schmidt, *Menschen und Mächte*, 436.

12 Hisanori Isomura, "Un demi-siecle de relations politico-culturelles entre le Japon et la France," *CCI France Japon,* May 22, 2012; *Der Spiegel,* May 26, 1969.

13 Masamichi Hanabusa, *Trade Problems between Japan and Western Europe* (Farnborough: Saxon House, 1979), 6; Albrecht Rothacher, *Economic Diplomacy between the European Community and Japan, 1959–1981* (Aldershot: Gower, 1983), 150.

14 For details on Japan's post-war industrial development policies in the synthetic fibre, electronics and automotive industries, ranging from credit and foreign exchange allocations, tax breaks, R&D subsidies to cheap industrial land and import protection, see Ryuichi Inoue, Hirohasa Kohama and Shujiro Urata (eds.), *Industrial Policy in East Asia* (Tokyo: JETRO, 1993), 30–64, 118–142, and 194–228, respectively.

15 Kiyoshi Kojima and Terutomo Ozawa, *Japan's General Trading Companies* (Paris: OECD, Development Centre Studies, 1984), 21.

16 Rothacher, *Economic Diplomacy*, 191.

17 Mac Destler, Haruhiro Fukui and Hideo Sato, *The Textile Wrangle: Conflict in Japanese American Relations, 1969–1971* (Ithaca: Cornell University Press, 1979).

18 Patrick A. Messerli, "La siderurgie europeenne face a la crise mondiale," in Yves Meny and Vincent Wright (eds.), *La crise de la siderurgie europeenne 1974–1984* (Paris: Presses Universitaires de France, 1985), 165.

19 Endymion Wilkinson, *Misunderstanding: Europe vs. Japan* (London: Penguin Books, 1980), 207; Hitoshi Suzuki, "Negotiating the Japan-EC Trade Conflict: The Role and the Presence of the European Commission, the Council of Ministers and the Business Groups in Europe and in Japan, 1970–1982," in Claudia Hiepel (ed.), *Europe in a Globalizing World: Global Challenges and European Responses in the "Long" 1970s* (Baden-Baden: Nomos, 2014), 216.

20 James Babb, *Tanaka: The Making of Postwar Japan* (Essex: Pearson Education, 2000), 96; Albrecht Rothacher, *The Japanese Power Elite* (New York: St. Martin's Press, 1993), 103–108.

21 Roy Denman, *The Mandarin's Tale* (London: Politico Publishing, 2002), 221.

22 Albrecht Rothacher, *Die Kommissare: Vom Aufstieg und Fall der Brüsseler Karrieren. Eine Sammelbiographie der deutschen und österreichischen Kommissare seit 1959* (Baden-Baden: Nomos, 2012), 104.

23 Hanabusa, *Trade Problems*, 98; Wilkinson, *Misunderstanding*, 228 and 259.

24 Wilkinson, *Misunderstanding*, 210.

25 Ariane Dettloff and Hans Kirchmann, *Arbeitsstaat Japan: Exportdrohung gegen Gewerkschaften* (Reinbek: Rowohlt, 1981).

26 Malcolm Trevor, *Japan—Restless Competitor: The Pursuit of Economic Nationalism* (London: Routledge, 2001). For a contemporary US view on the role of Japanese investments in the car, electronics, media, real estate and finance industry, see Robert L. Kearns, *Zaibatsu America: How Japanese Firms Are Colonizing Vital US Industries* (New York: The Free Press, 1992).

27 Reinhard Büscher and Jochen Homann, *Deutschland und Japan. Die späten Sieger?* (Zürich: Edition Interfrom, 1990).

28   An idea emanating from Laurent Fabius, Minister of industry at the time. Möhler and Van Rij, "1983–1987," 60.

29   Christopher Kendall, "The Elements of Consensus: Liberalizing EC-Japan Passenger Trade in the 1990s," in Keck, Vanoverbeke and Waldenberger (eds.), *European Union-Japan Relations*, 230.

30   Möhler and Van Rij, "1983–1987," 76.

31   Albrecht Rothacher, "Europa-Giappone: dietro il siparo di bamboo," *Relazioni Internazionali*, 6 (1993), 16–23, here 18. Originally commanded for an EC–Japan high-level academic conference at the EUI in 1992, I was disinvited from giving the paper after Japanese protests (since the EUI then—as always in vain—had tried to raise Japanese funds). To be fair, I had also argued to set up a new international trade organization replacing GATT without Japanese participation, which I had then, after four years of market access negotiations in Tokyo, felt to be incurably neo-mercantilist.

32   Interestingly Denman, who for years was the EC's top trade negotiator, in his very readable and insightful memoirs called the Dowa a "religious sect" (ibid., 18), which is clearly nonsense, since they represented a historically socially discriminated group of former outcasts dealing with leather and meat processing and limited to special settlements (*buraku*) during the Tokugawa shogunate (1603–1867). Up to the 1990s at least, their offspring defended their traditional trades—associated on occasion with the criminal underworld—against import competition in a militant and sometimes violent fashion, in a "liberation movement" associated with the Socialist and Communist parties. Tokyo bureaucrats dealing with them were usually scared stiff. The Japanese media never touched the issue. Politicians would pretend not to understand it. Japan's dockworkers unions were then controlled by organized crime. The stevedoring works at Japanese harbors were controlled by a "Japan Harbor Management Association," which stirred fear and spread corruption in what was then the supervisory Ministry of Transport, equally a public taboo in Japan.

33   Jörn Keck, "1987–1990: Keeping Relations to an Even Level," in Keck, Vanoverbeke and Waldenberger (eds.), *European Union-Japan Relations*, 80.

34   Ibid., 82.

35   Clyde V. Prestowitz, *Trading Places: How America Allowed Japan to Take the Lead* (Tokyo: Tuttle, 1988), 272.

36   *Les Echos*, July 18, 1991.

37   This section should be read in conjunction with and as complementary to Katja Seidel's chapter, "The External Dimensions of the Common Agricultural Policy: From Developed to Developing Countries" in this volume.

38   Takekazu Ogura, *Can Japanese Agriculture Survive? A Historical Approach* (Tokyo: Agricultural Policy Research Center, 1979), 442.

39   Kym Anderson and Yujiro Hayami (eds.), *The Political Economy of Agricultural Protection: East Asia in International Perspective* (North Sydney: Allen & Unwin Australia, 1986).

40   Australian Bureau of Agricultural and Resource Economies, *Japanese Agricultural Policies* (Canberra: Australian Government Publishing Service, 1988), 297.

41   Jimmye S. Hillman and Robert A. Rothenberg, *Agricultural Trade and Protection in Japan* (London: Trade Policy Research Centre, 1988), 60; Albrecht Rothacher, *Japan's Agro-Food Sector: The Politics and Economics of Excess Protection* (Houndmills: Palgrave Macmillan, 1989), 161.

Part Two

Policy Fields

7

The EC in the GATT Trade Regime: A Power Without Leadership

Lucia Coppolaro

Trade policy is one of the most established areas of integration in the European Union (EU). In 1957, it represented the initial field in which the original members chose to pool their sovereignty, delegating to the European Economic Community (EEC) the authority to wield it and carry out relations with third countries.[1] In 2014 the EU took 14.85 percent of world merchandise trade (excluding intra-EU trade), followed by China with 14.2 percent and the United States with 13.3 percent.[2] There is no doubt the EU's role in world trade is fundamental to its external activities and that trade policy has been the linchpin of the EU's engagement and relations with the rest of the world. These considerations make the study of trade policy fundamental to understanding the EC/EU's external relations.

In spite of this relevance, the literature on the EU's external trade policy is not vast, above all in comparison to the US literature on the topic. Existing historical studies focus their enquiries either on a limited time span, or on a specific trade negotiation. Asbeek Brusse analyzed the trade and tariff negotiations that took place in the 1950s in the General Agreement on Tariffs and Trade (GATT) framework and which led to the creation of the EEC.[3] Alkema investigated the role of the EC in the Dillon Round (1961–1962).[4] Attention was also paid to the role of the EEC in the Kennedy Round (1964–1967), specifically to how the EEC became a major trading power by attending this negotiation, and to the role of the European Commission in EC policy-making on trade.[5]

With their broader literature, political scientists dominate the field. Bretherton and Vogler provided an analysis on the bases of EU actorness, investigating the complex interaction between internal and external factors in the construction of this actorness.[6] Through a limited analysis of the commercial negotiations between the EC/EU and the United States in selected commercial areas, Meunier argued that the EC/EU's complex institutional procedures forced its trade partners to give in to the EC/EU's stances.[7] Woolcock investigated the role of the EC/EU in international economic negotiations and claimed that the European Community was initially a follower behind the leadership of the United States. Only in the early 1990s was the EC/EU shown to have leadership aspirations in international trade.[8] By illustrating the EC/EU trade policy, De Bièvre and Poletti reached a similar conclusion. They showed how the EC/EU moved from regime taker to regime shaper in the early 1990s, illustrating how the attractiveness of its internal market explains the EU's structural power and allowed it to export and protect its preferences.[9]

This chapter illustrates the EC's external trade policy as it developed in the multilateral trade regime of the GATT from 1958 to 1994. The General Agreement was signed in 1947 to provide a set of rules for the orderly conduct of international trade relations and the reduction of trade barriers. GATT regulated the multilateral trading system until 1994, when it was replaced by the World Trade Organization (WTO). It sponsored periodic "rounds" of conferences—during which trade barriers were progressively reduced and more areas and sectors were brought into its discipline. Thus, in almost fifty years of activities, GATT proved to be an effective instrument of liberalization. The evolution of the EC external trade policy can only be understood with reference to and focusing on the Geneva institution. First, GATT was the pillar of the multilateral trade regime and represented the arena in which the capitalist countries—the core of the world economy—negotiated the liberalization of trade and dictated the rules of the trade regime. Second, the EC deployed its trade power in this framework. It contributed to trade liberalization and to the setting of the GATT rules and, at the same time, was constantly constrained and influenced by the evolution of the GATT regime.

By analyzing the EC's external trade policy in the framework of the GATT, this chapter tries to make two points. First, by attending the GATT negotiations, the EC established itself as a single actor and acquired international status. Even now, sixty years after the establishment of the EC, the WTO is one of the few frameworks in which the EU is able to speak with a united voice. Second, the EC was a powerful actor, but—despite its economic weight, progressively increased by the enlargement to new members—it never became a leader of the trade regime. Thanks to its market size, the EC had the bargaining power to defend its interests and inscribe its preferences in the final outcome of GATT negotiations. Thus, it played a fundamental role in reducing trade barriers, in writing the rules of the regime and, more broadly, in shaping the regime. However, conflicts among member states in Brussels, a time-consuming decision-making process and the propensity to externalize its internal conflicts prevented the EC from becoming one of the regime's leaders. Beyond this, member states' inclination to privilege immediate economic gains over enduring geopolitical interests, and their incapacity—or unwillingness—to adopt a coherent approach to the interrelated aspects of a major international trade negotiation, precluded the EC's taking on the leadership role. The responsibility of leading the GATT regime remained on US shoulders, as Washington bore the major responsibility for an outcome that it conceived in broad and long-term economic, security and strategic terms. As such, the EC external trade policy developed in a US-led framework.

Laying the Groundwork (1958–1967)

The existence of the EC in the GATT trade regime flowed directly from the member states' decision to establish a customs union. By definition, a customs union requires a common commercial policy and a common external tariff (CET) towards non-member states. This factor compelled the EC to engage with the other GATT contracting parties. Under GATT Article XXIV, contracting parties entering into a regional trade area were required to present to the other contracting parties the implementing treaty, to ensure that it was consistent with the provisions of the General Agreement. Recommendations by the other contracting parties could lead to reconsiderations and revisions in the treaty. Following these provisions, in 1958 the EEC members submitted the Treaties of Rome to the General Agreement. In discussions with the other contracting parties, the representatives of the European Commission and the president of the Council of Ministers of the EEC presented and negotiated on behalf of the Community, together with the member states. The other contracting parties readily accepted engagement in negotiations with the EC representatives, and the EC was informally accepted as a player.[10] As such, this initial appearance of the EEC in Geneva marked the first sign of EEC actorness. Then, during all the GATT years, the EEC was informally accepted as a player representing the EEC contracting parties, in spite of the fact that legally the EEC never became a contracting party to GATT. Only in 1994 did the EU become a party in its own right by joining the WTO, alongside the EU member states. In this sense, the participation in GATT activities represented an external determinant of EC actorness.

This first appearance of the EEC in Geneva in 1958 could not go unnoticed. Its six founding members—the Benelux countries, the Federal Republic of Germany, France, and Italy—represented 15 percent of world trade in goods, in comparison with 17 percent for the United States and 11.3 percent for the European Free Trade Association (EFTA) countries.[11] Moreover, the six members were part of the capitalist countries that formed the core of the GATT multilateral regime. But this initial appearance was notable for an additional and critical reason: notwithstanding the assurances of the EC members, the Treaties of Rome in its most salient features did not comply with the GATT. Without delving into details, the implementation of the CET, the removal of quantitative restrictions within the EC, the vagueness of the Treaty of Rome on the Common Agricultural Policy (CAP), and the preferential trading arrangement with the former colonies contravened the GATT on points of maximum importance.[12]

Fearing the discriminatory effects of the EEC, many GATT members were quick to notice the inconsistencies of the Treaties of Rome and to ask for modifications. As provided under GATT Article XXIV, a special committee was set up with the task of assessing the conformity of the Treaty of Rome. However, two questions troubled the work of the GATT Committee: the extremely divergent positions of the actors involved in the discussion, and the political and economic weight of the EC members. With regard to the first aspect, the EC member states uncompromisingly asserted that they had incorporated GATT provisions into their treaty, which therefore complied with the General Agreement. In stark contrast, the other contracting parties, in particular the United Kingdom, Canada, Denmark, New Zealand, and Australia, firmly disagreed. Fearing a contraction of their trade with the EEC, the other contracting parties considered the legal assessment of the Treaty as a way of obliging the Six to refrain from applying certain measures or to make modifications. As for the second aspect, the core obstacle to the work of the Committee was that—even if it made sense from a legal point of view to verify the Treaty of Rome's conformity—the size and weight of the EC made it impractical to condition its existence upon the Treaty's legalistic conformity to the General Agreement.[13] Furthermore, the Treaty was the result of strenuous bargains among the Six. Hence, for the EC, making concessions to the other GATT members meant reopening the negotiations for the Treaties of Rome. And no one in the six capitals of the EEC had the intention of doing so. On the contrary, to strengthen their bargaining stance in Geneva, they even claimed that a finding that the Treaty was inconsistent with Article XXIV would result in their withdrawal from the GATT.[14] Unsurprisingly, one year of tough legalistic discussion between the GATT members on one side and the EEC members on the other produced only bitter skirmishes.

The US representatives in Geneva did not join other GATT members' complaints against the Treaty of Rome and considered the confrontation with apprehension. The conflict threatened a weakening of GATT and the multilateral trade regime and could slow a full and quick start of the EEC's working. The Eisenhower administration had both political and economic reasons to support the EEC. The Community would represent a bulwark against communism and strengthen both Western Europe and the Atlantic alliance. From an economic point of view, the EEC would represent a more efficient market than the respective individual markets of its members and, as such, could raise the growth rate of the six members and US exports and investments to the area. Certainly, the EEC customs union with its common commercial policy would discriminate against non-member states. But Washington deemed that the political advantages that European integration provided were worth some trade discrimination, while GATT rounds aimed at reducing trade barriers multilaterally would smooth EEC regional discrimination, ensuring that the EEC would evolve into an open regional area.[15]

As such, after a year of legalistic clashes, Washington intervened to settle the confrontation. US diplomats in Geneva put forward an ad hoc political solution to resolve the problem in a pragmatic way. No formal decision on the compatibility of the Treaties of Rome would be taken, but GATT would monitor the commercial policy of the EC to ensure that an outward-looking Community developed. The priority of having the EEC fully settled convinced the Eisenhower administration to put aside any doubts on the potentially discriminatory effects of the Treaties of Rome and any discussions on its most controversial aspect. As Romero put it, 'This new, crucial advancement of European integration was allowed to entrench itself behind the shelter of the US's friendly diplomacy.'[16] The result of the Geneva talks anticipated how GATT would be dominated by the US–EEC dynamic and how the EEC trade policy would develop in a US-led framework.

Soon after the end of the Geneva talks, as part of that pragmatic solution elaborated to fit the EEC into the GATT multilateral regime, the Eisenhower administration promoted a GATT round with the aim of reducing the discrimination of the EC. However, the US Congress granted the executive only modest and conditional authority to reduce tariffs. With the clumsy procedure of bilateral item-by-item negotiations typical of GATT rounds, and within the United States' limited authority, the Dillon Round (1961–1962) reduced the average protection for all goods by 7 percent.[17] This round highlighted two problems in the promotion of freer trade. The bargaining authority of the US executive was inadequate. There could not be major results as long as Congress restricted the extent of tariff reductions the executive could offer in Geneva. Moreover, with the increased number of GATT contracting parties, the item-by-item method of negotiations had become cumbersome and ineffective. A bold new initiative was needed to encourage further liberalization.

That initiative came with the Trade Expansion Act (TEA) that the US Congress approved in 1962, as requested by the Kennedy administration. The TEA abandoned item-by-item negotiations and authorized the linear reduction of tariffs in the industrial sector by as much as 50 percent and, in some cases, even the elimination of duties. The formation of the EC was the factor that encouraged the Kennedy administration to propose a far-reaching reduction of tariffs and provided the decisive push towards genuinely multilateral, across-the-board negotiations. As laid out by George Ball, Under-Secretary of State for Economic Affairs and the person mainly responsible for the elaboration of the TEA, "[the EEC had to be used as] a justification for a major new round of trade negotiations and a precedent for reducing tariffs by percentage cuts across the board rather than the tradition item-by-item haggling."[18] For the first time since 1947, Washington had a credible negotiating partner capable of making valuable counter concessions thanks to the size of its market. This aspect was crucial to winning the US Congress' support for a new negotiation organized around new principles and a sweeping liberalization of international trade.[19]

Washington's effort to reduce trade barriers was not limited to trade in manufactures but also included agriculture, for the first time since GATT's inception. GATT had not been successful in preventing a widespread reinforcement of agricultural protectionism, and despite the fact that GATT rules applied to agricultural and industrial trade alike, the first five GATT rounds (1948–1962) exclusively concentrated on cutting customs tariffs for the industrial sector. The urgency to bring agriculture under the GATT discipline rose in 1958, when the EEC started to elaborate and implement its discriminatory CAP.[20] Against the prospect of a dramatically discriminating agricultural area, Washington considered it urgent to include this sector in the GATT conference to attempt to reduce the CAP's protectionism.

The US initiative for a far-reaching liberalization obliged the EC to delineate its external trade policy and decide how liberal its policy would be for manufactured goods and agricultural products. With regard to the industrial sector, EC members agreed to attend the round in order to reduce protectionism and increase their exports. While concerned to protect certain sectors, they were ready to reduce the CET so as to obtain reciprocal reduction of duties imposed by the United States and the EFTA countries. Improvements in European competitiveness made liberalization on a multilateral scale bearable to such traditionally protectionist countries as France and Italy. Moreover, negotiating with a single voice and the market size of the EC would give member states the power to bargain as an equal partner with the United States and to question US trade policy, a capacity the Europeans had lacked in the 1950s. The EEC's behavior in the agricultural sector was totally different. By implementing the CAP, the EC members had decided to set up a strictly regulated regional agricultural market to protect their farmers from third countries' competition. The EC's major aim was not to reciprocally reduce trade barriers in order to foster its exports, but rather to maintain CAP protectionism with its variable-levy system untouched. Thus the EC refused to reduce protection in this area.

While the US initiative spurred the member states to delineate the external trade policy of the EC, at the same time this delineation would dictate the results of the trade conference and, more broadly, shape the GATT regime. In the Kennedy Round (1964–1967), the EC performed the role of reluctant partner and, above all under the pressure of France, it tried to stretch out the bargaining process until trading partners were more willing to offer concessions. With its position, the EC was able to inscribe its preferences in the outcome of the negotiations—reducing tariffs in the industrial sector while maintaining its protectionism in agriculture. In the industrial sector, the interest of all the major participants in lowering others' tariffs led to a reciprocal substantial reduction. Duties were cut by 35 percent on average, with about two-thirds of the reductions reaching 50 percent. For its part the EC, with its liberal policy, fully contributed to the liberalization of trade.

In marked contrast were the results in the agricultural sector. The EC's lack of interest in enhancing its exports and the higher priority it gave to the establishment of the CAP explain the total absence of bargaining power on the part of the United States when it came to pushing the EC to reduce trade barriers. Moreover, eager to support European integration for geopolitical reasons, the Johnson administration chose not to question the mechanism of the CAP in Geneva, further weakening its bargaining stance. In any case, Washington held that the major gain of liberalization would come from manufactures and, as such, it had no intention of wasting a profitable bargain in this sector for the sake of agriculture. Eventually, the Johnson Administration decided to drop agriculture from the talks and conclude the Kennedy Round. The EEC ended the Round with the CAP intact, which now became a major obstacle in world agricultural trade.

The US–EEC dynamic and interests dictated the outcome of the Round. Liberalization achieved during the Kennedy Round did not affect the developing countries' trade and desiderata. The EC external trade policy played a major part in explaining this result. The preferential agreements the EC had negotiated with its former colonies under the Yaoundé Convention of 1964 did not favor liberalization, above all for tropical products. Even if different positions existed among the nations in Brussels, the EC as a whole opposed any reduction in preferences, and its opposition closed the way to any meaningful result in tropical products. Developing countries were also intent on liberalizing trade in textiles, an area in which they had achieved a globally competitive position. But here they met the firm opposition of the EC, the United Kingdom and the United States. Negotiations over textiles plainly showed the unwillingness of industrialized countries to make concessions to developing countries, despite their initial statement that the Kennedy Round would be a breakthrough for trade and development.[21]

The Kennedy Round marked the emergence of the EEC as a single and powerful unit in world trade, with the capacity to inscribe its preferences in the final outcome and, consequently, to shape the trade regime. The EC showed the ability to effectively negotiate with other GATT members and, in particular, to do so on equal terms with the United States. By setting up a customs union that had to favor export-led economic growth, the national governments had blended six national commercial policies into one common commercial policy. This internal factor required the maintenance of EC regionalism within GATT. Crucially, it spurred the member states to compromise over their conflicting interests so as to converge on a trade policy that could be deployed in GATT—and to do so despite the many quarrels and tensions existing in Brussels throughout the 1960s. Moreover, the market size and, hence, the economic weight of the EC contributed to the power and effectiveness of the EC actorness. GATT worked like a bazaar, where the contracting parties offered improved access to their markets in exchange for reciprocal concessions from the trading partner. Access to the EC market was attractive enough to put the EC at the center of the GATT bazaar.

Yet, although powerful, the EC was not a leading actor. The United States had the responsibility to steer the negotiations ahead and forge compromises at critical times. Washington considered the Round in terms of US trade interests but also contemplated the impact that failure or success could have on the GATT trading regime, the transatlantic alliance in the Cold War framework, and European integration. National Security Affairs assistant Francis Bator noted that "The central point here is not primarily the level of tariff. Rather, it is holding to a reasonable set of trade rules without which international trade would become a jungle warfare."[22] In a similar way, Secretary of State Dean Rusk underlined that without the Kennedy Round, "The Atlantic partnership concept would be weakened; Gaullist nationalism strengthened; developed and developing countries further divided."[23] On the other side of the Atlantic, in the last days of the Kennedy Round, the EC members were busy calibrating the reductions of tariffs they would have to make on canned asparagus and excavating machines. The EC played a fundamental role in reducing trade barriers and was able to enhance its preferences. However, the EC did not try to play the role of leader of the trade regime. The predisposition of member states to focus on short-term economic gains more than long-term political considerations, their incapacity or unwillingness to link trade to geopolitics and their divergences in Brussels over other aspects of the EC's development impeded them from assuming the leadership role.

Beyond Tariffs in a Turbulent Economic Framework (1968–1979)

In 1973, with the enlargement to Denmark, Ireland, and the United Kingdom, the EC increased the size of the internal market and became the biggest trading bloc in terms of share of world trade, taking 19.7 percent. In the same year, the United States and the European Community together accounted for 37 percent. Both supported trade liberalization, and both accused each other of protectionism.[24] In the meantime, their dominance of the GATT trade regime endured, despite the economic challenges of the 1970s.

By 1970, a set of policy actions by the major trading actors had created a threat to the GATT trade regime. In addition to acquiring new members, the EC was also expanding its preferential treatment to African and European nations and deepening its protection of agriculture. The EC was increasing its discriminatory effects on world trade. On the other side of the Atlantic, because of the mounting deficits in the balance of payments and the protectionist mood of Congress, the United States negotiated a series of "voluntary" quantitative restrictions with its trading partners.

With this deteriorating economic situation, the Nixon administration maintained its support for European integration for the same reasons the Eisenhower and the Kennedy administrations had. However, Nixon considered it urgent to intervene to reduce discrimination coming from the EC.[25]

Against this situation, and while the deficit in the US balance of payments increased, the Nixon administration pressed the European allies and Japan to take on more responsibilities in designing new solutions to the problems of a rapidly changing international economic system. While initially unsympathetic towards US grievances and its invitation for negotiations to clear the air, the Nixon shock of 1971 convinced the EC members of the urgency of reorganizing the multilateral trading system.[26]

Once again under US initiative, the Tokyo Round was launched in September 1973 to update the GATT multilateral trading regime. While interested in reducing tariffs as in the previous GATT Rounds, the United States and the European Community were concerned with establishing the rules and machinery for dealing with non-tariff barriers (NTBs). Movement of goods was in effect progressively hampered less by tariffs than by several official and unofficial NTBs. The Tokyo Round represented the first GATT negotiations in which the United States and the EC implemented drafting rules to limit the impact of other GATT members' domestic regulatory policies.[27]

The Tokyo Round started slowly and was then negotiated in an unstable economic environment. As soon as the new round was launched, the international economic context became far from propitious for a major trade liberalization. Inflation spiralled out of control after October 1973 in the wake of the quadrupling of oil prices. The prices of raw materials and oil dramatically increased, creating difficulties in the balance of payments of the importing countries. In 1975, the deepest recessions of the post-war period hit the industrialized countries.[28] The combination of unprecedented inflation and recession brought severe pressures to bear on Western governments and created an environment of great uncertainty in which a policy of trade liberalization was difficult to achieve.[29] For the advanced economies, however, the challenge was not only the struggle with stagflation. Most importantly, a new wave of globalization was dawning. New competitive economies emerged in East Asia and started to challenge the Western economies and hurt employment there. As such, a great degree of uncertainty existed about the future of the negotiations.[30]

The state of the economy affected the elaboration of a common EC stance for the round. In Germany, the support for trade liberalization remained strong. Within conditions of slower economic growth, Bonn saw trade liberalization as necessary to counteract protectionist policies and favor trade expansion. German stances came as no surprise. Within the EC, this country had been more successful than others in remaining competitive on world markets by making investment in capital-intensive and high-technology goods. The German government considered the demise of shrinking industries in Europe—such as textiles and shipbuilding—as inevitable considering the higher level of wages in Europe in comparison to other areas of the world. As Chancellor Helmut Schmidt noted, "Given the high level of wages in Europe, I cannot help but believe that in the long run textile industries here will have to vanish. We cannot ward off cheaper competition from outside."[31] Moreover, through liberalization Germany could pursue a double aim. First, it could promote German exports of capital and technological goods to Organization of Petroleum Exporting Countries (OPEC), East Asia, and other newly industrialized countries. Second, it could allow this group of countries to export worldwide their labor-intensive goods and, consequently, earn revenues to keep importing from Germany. Crucially, as these countries were borrowing capital from Germany, exports would allow them to service their debt.[32]

For other EC members, the difficulties in carrying out structural adjustments to face the economic changes created uncertain support for trade liberalization and led to suggestions to reorganize the liberalization process. In this second category fell France, Italy, and the United Kingdom. Unlike Germany, these countries were facing difficulties in adapting to the new conditions of the world economy and were rather slow or hesitant in implementing industrial adjustment and exploring new areas of technology. France, Italy, and the United Kingdom feared competition from the low-wage countries of East Asia, which threatened traditional sectors of their economy such as textiles and apparels, shipbuilding and chemicals.[33] As British Prime Minister Callaghan explained to the Americans, "we are all aware that there are sensitive areas in our economies where strict application of an open and liberal commercial policy can produce results which were really not anticipated in a period of world recession."[34]

It was against these positions that the EC members had to elaborate a common external policy for the Tokyo Round. The nine members easily agreed that the CAP remained non-negotiable, as in the Kennedy Round. The reaching of a common stance for the other issues on the agenda was far more complicated. France, Italy, and the United Kingdom showed themselves to be more interested in changing the GATT rules in order to facilitate the restriction of imports from the newly developed countries that, from their point of view, disturbed their domestic market. Moreover, they aimed at negotiating GATT codes on rules in order to limit the discretionary way the United States applied the escape clause, anti-dumping, and countervailing regulations. According to these EC members, the US regulations were unfavorable to the foreign producers and were a manifestation of overt protectionism and unilateralism. GATT codes would allow a harmonization of domestic regulations of the developed countries and, as such, favor a more balanced liberalization. The German government agreed that rules had to be strengthened to favor trade liberalization but saw the British, the French, and Italian requests more as a bargaining position to counter US (and German) pressure to liberalize trade.[35]

Because of these protectionist trends, the Tokyo Round remained locked until 1977. The breakthrough that freed up the negotiations was above all the result of the efforts of the Carter Administration to conclude the Round. As noted by Winham, the election of Jimmy Carter in 1976 "created an important sea-change in the US trade policy."[36] The new US president aimed at successfully concluding the negotiations to respond to multiple pressures: keeping the protectionism stance under control, both at home and offshore; strengthening the GATT regime; and responding to the interests of US producers who asked for trade liberalization to enhance their exports. Against this framework, the Carter administration raised the priority of the Tokyo Round, formulating its policy approach to give the negotiations their much-needed impetus.[37]

The effect of the new line of the US administration became evident with the unfolding of 1977. In order to move the Round ahead, President Carter took the political decision to adopt a softer line on the EC and agriculture by publicly stating that his administration would not seek fundamental changes in the CAP. In so doing, the new administration downgraded the importance of this sector and signaled that it would end the Tokyo Round even without an agreement on agriculture. Once this political reality was established, one of the major stumbling blocks was removed, even if it implied a limited yield for negotiations in agriculture. What mattered for Carter was to conclude the Round to strengthen trade liberalization in other sectors and favor economic growth.[38] Moreover, one of President Carter's first foreign economic policy initiatives was to secure a commitment to complete the negotiations from the heads of governments and states assembled for the economic summit in London in May 1977. Here, Carter played a major role in urging the European and Japanese allies to conclude the negotiations by 1978. As in the past, the US leadership was necessary to unblock the trade talks.[39]

The United States' new interest in quickly ending the Round coincided with a more forthcoming attitude by France and the United Kingdom. In France, the new government of Raymond Barre showed itself to be more forthcoming towards liberalization at a multilateral level than the previous French governments, as a way of fostering French exports and competitiveness.[40] In the United Kingdom, the difficulties in the balance of payments led to IMF intervention in 1976 and, together with IMF prescriptions, further trade liberalization in GATT.[41]

The Tokyo Round ended in April 1979. While playing its standard role of reluctant partner, the EC played a fundamental role in shaping the results. The trade concessions were remarkable, especially considering that the final phase took place during a deep recession and the second oil shock. In the industrial sector, duties were reduced by 35 percent. The size of the final tariff reductions represented a compromise between the original US proposal to reduce tariffs by 50 percent and the Community's call for smaller reductions. As for agriculture, the EC stance dictated the results in the agricultural sector. The EC obtained the recognition that its CAP was untouchable in GATT; this was considered as a major victory for the EC and a major concession for the United States.[42]

The Tokyo Round started to transform the GATT from an agreement concerned mainly with reducing duties to an institution dealing with a broad variety of mostly governmental measures that distorted trade and trade remedies—such as anti-dumping policies and safeguards, the discipline of subsidies and countervailing duties. The EC played a major role in this transformation and was able to enhance its preferences. While attending the Tokyo Round, the EC members were drafting the EC regulations on trade remedies and NTBs. This experience allowed them to play an active role in writing the rules of the GATT. Having acquired experience coping with these issues at the regional level, they were able to exploit this experience to enhance their preferences at the multilateral level. The European Community aimed at bringing into GATT discipline the US domestic regulations on anti-dumping and countervailing duties, which were highly discriminatory. For example, the drafting of the EC anti-dumping regulation coincided with the negotiations in Geneva on an anti-dumping code. Eventually, the GATT anti-dumping code largely formalized the preferences of the EC. Similarly, the other GATT plurilateral codes approved and dealing with public procurement, subsidies, product standards, customs valuation, and import licensing were largely in tune with the EC preferences and required little or no domestic regulatory changes for its members. By aiming to simplify regulations, clarify procedures and introduce uniform methods of duty calculation, the codes were concerned with clarifying the operation of existing GATT procedures and helping to ensure that all industrialized countries accepted the same obligations. The codes did not erase all the problems caused by NTBs and, for the most part, they were merely a framework agreement. But they represented a major rule-making exercise and established guidelines that reached further into the nation-state, particularly in the field of industrial policy. The elimination of all tariffs on imports of commercial aircraft, engines and parts under the Agreement on Trade in Civil Aircraft was largely determined by the particular trade and production characteristics of the sector, including a high degree of international co-production, multinational investment and market interpenetration among the United States, the Community, and Japan, who clearly expected to benefit from the arrangement.[43]

The problems of the developing countries had originally assumed a prominent place in the Tokyo Round, with the US and EC pledge to keep under due consideration the trade problems and requests of this group of countries. However, when negotiations got properly under way, the United States and the EC ignored the pledge. While openly stressing the importance of including the developing countries, they conducted their bargain in the Green Room, the GATT director-general's conference room, from which the developing countries were excluded. In the latter stages of the negotiations, the developing countries increasingly felt excluded from the negotiating process. As a result, only four developing countries signed the final agreements; none of the least developed countries did so.[44] Once again, the US–EC dynamic and preferences shaped the GATT trade regime.

Broadening the Agenda: the Uruguay Round (1986–1994)

A defining characteristic of the 1980s and 1990s was the renewed globalization of the world economy. After the turmoil of the 1970s, the world speedily entered an era of globalization as trade, migration and capital flows expanded quickly and more countries became more intensively engaged in international economic relations. The election of neoliberal governments in major countries like the United States and the United Kingdom, the widespread progressive removal of capital controls, and the dramatic development in information, communication and transportation technology were among the major triggers of the rapid new integration of national markets.[45]

Against these developments, in 1981 US President Ronald Reagan took the initiative for a new and comprehensive multilateral negotiation. The US aim was to include in the GATT regime services, protection of intellectual property rights, and investments, sectors which by the early 1980s had been acquiring a major share of the world economy. Moreover, the Reagan administration fully intended to solve the long-standing problem of protectionist agriculture by pressing the EC to reduce CAP discrimination.[46]

Initially, the EC gave a negative response to the US initiative. Most of the economies of the EC member states were still in recession, and governments aimed at maintaining the freedom to intervene and protect specific sectors. However, by the mid-1980s, domestic developments brought a major change in EC external trade policy and, consequently, towards the US initiative. Frustrated by not being able to compete internationally on the basis of national markets, many European industrial sectors called for the end of the fragmentation of the EC market and the implementation of a real common market with no barriers. This market-led development resulted in the Single European Market (SEM) program and led to the liberalization of trade, capital, and investment at the EC level. The deepening of EC market integration had two major consequences for the EC's external trade relations. First, it strengthened the EC's market power and, therefore, its bargaining position in Geneva. Second, it led to a shift away from the use of member state discretionary power to intervene to support domestic sectors, which distorted competition within the EC, to a rules-based European regime for all the NTBs. These changes led EC members to accept attendance at comprehensive trade talks in Geneva and contributed to making the EC a staunch supporter of a multilateral rules-based approach.[47]

The Uruguay Round (1986–1994) is often described as the most successful of the eight GATT rounds of multilateral negotiations. Tariffs were reduced substantially, a trade liberalization framework for agriculture was agreed upon, new areas—investments, intellectual property and services—were incorporated within the trade regime, and the WTO was established. The EC attended the Uruguay Round as a Community of twelve members—as Greece, Portugal, and Spain had joined by the beginning of the Round. The new enlargement wave broadened the market size of the EC and, consequently, its bargaining power. As in the past, the initiative for a new round came from the United States and, as in the past, the outcome of the Round was largely shaped by the preferences of the EC–US duopoly. As in the past, the EC started the new trade talks by playing its role of reluctant partner. However, throughout the Round, the EC progressively played a more assertive role in using its trade policy to shape the world trade regime.

The EC started the round from a defensive position on agriculture and, eventually, had to make concessions. For the first time since 1958, Brussels accepted a framework agreement to reduce protectionism. External pressure from the United States and other states strengthened the hand of anti-CAP forces within the EC and, with the initiation of GATT negotiations, aroused the EC's business lobby with the prospect of gains obtainable only as a quid pro quo for CAP revision. International complaints about the CAP in the Uruguay Round helped to trigger the MacSharry reforms of 1992.[48] In a parallel way, the November 1992 Blair House Accord between the United States and the EU on export subsidy and domestic subsidy reduction commitments opened the way for an agreement on agriculture in GATT. Non-tariff import barriers were converted to tariffs and all tariffs reduced by 36 percent for industrialized countries and 24 percent for developing countries. Industrialized countries reduced export subsidies by 36 percent in value and 21 percent in quantity and internal support price by about 20 percent, whereas industrial country imports quotas would be phased out over ten years.[49]

The Blair House Accord allowed the resolution of an issue on which the EC had been on the defensive. With agriculture settled, the EC could play a more assertive role in other sectors of the Uruguay Round and could press to inscribe its preferences in the final outcome. This new approach was well evident in the rules and the institutional reforms agreed in the Uruguay Round. The EC actively fostered agreements on services, investment, intellectual property, and public procurement. The EC had started dealing with technical barriers to the liberalization of trade and services in the early or mid-1970s and wrestling with competition policy in the plurilateral framework of the Organisation for Economic Co-operation and Development (OECD) in the 1980s. As such, in the Uruguay Round, it had the expertise to deal with these complex regulatory issues at the multilateral level. Eventually, the General Agreement on Trade in Services (GATS), the Agreement of Trade-Related Aspects of Intellectual Property Rights (TRIPs) and the agreement on Trade-Related Investment Measures (TRIMs) were highly compatible with the US and EC domestic regulations and, as such, required minimal domestic regulatory changes.

As liberalization deepened at the world level, the EC held it necessary to strengthen the multilateral rules and institutions. The GATT regulatory system would be weakened if its rules were not binding and enforceable in a predictable and credible way. As De Bièvre and Poletti note, as rules would be generated at the multilateral level, the EC acquired an "overreaching stake in cementing these rules and procedures more firmly in institutions that would lend them increased stability and predictability."[50] This stance was well evident in the EC's request to strengthen the dispute settlement procedure and to establish a permanent international trade organization to replace GATT. During the 1980s, the United States had often carried out an aggressive and unilateral foreign-trade policy by imposing retaliatory sanctions against, above all, the EC and Japan. The EC aimed at putting the US policy under multilateral control. Moreover, the GATT regulatory system as agreed in the Uruguay round would bear heavy costs of implementation for the developing countries, which would have to harmonize their domestic regulations on services, intellectual property, and investments to GATT. As such, the EC asked for the creation of a permanent appeal body and favored the establishment of an international institution. The United States was reluctant on both proposals. Washington was concerned about Congress' opposition to loss of sovereignty and the possibility that talks in Geneva would concentrate on institutional reforms rather than trade liberalization.[51]

Thanks also to the Canadian brokering, the European Community and the United States reached a deal, leading to a major innovation: the formal installment of automatic jurisdiction, with an Appellate Body as requested by the EC, and multilateral requests for sanctions in cases of enduring non-compliance, as requested by the United States.[52] The new WTO dispute mechanism tightened procedural disciplines and dropped earlier GATT veto power over the establishment of a dispute panel, even by the accused party. As for the establishment of an international organization, the collapse of the Berlin Wall and the communist regimes throughout Eastern Europe influenced the talks in Geneva. As these regimes were replaced by governments committed to market-oriented economic reforms, the principle of liberal trade and market-oriented prices became mainstream thinking for economic reforms almost everywhere. These far-reaching developments weakened US opposition and paved the way for the establishment of the WTO.[53]

As in previous GATT negotiations, the Uruguay Round was dominated by the United States and the European Community. This dominance was demonstrated, once again, in their relations with the developing countries. At the beginning of the Round, the developing countries opposed the broadening of the GATT agenda to services, investments, and intellectual property and the liberalization that would follow. Eventually, the European Community and the United States obtained the approval of developing countries by offering a ten-year phase-out of textile quotas and liberalization of agriculture. Moreover, the two actors imposed the "single undertaking principle." All provisions of the final Uruguay Round Agreement, as well as existing GATT commitments, would be brought within a single WTO undertaking. Membership in the new organization required agreement on almost all the provisions of the single undertaking.

Thus, the European Community and the United States were able to force recalcitrant GATT members into accepting liberalization and regulatory commitments in services, investment, intellectual property rules, public procurement, technical barriers to trade, food health, and safety standards. Apparently, the final result of the Round was a compromise between developed and developing countries. Yet, developing countries gave up substantially more than they received.[54]

Conclusion

From 1958 to the early 1990s, the EC's external trade policy evolved in a US-led GATT framework and was the result of defensive responses to the US initiatives. Yet, from a defensive position, the EC was able to shape the GATT thanks to its market size and to the interests of its member states to speak with a single voice. The EC was both a liberalizing force and a stumbling block. It played a fundamental role in liberalizing trade barriers over manufactures, in establishing the rules of the trade regime, in including NTBs and the new sectors, and in enhancing the institutions. At the same time, for thirty-five years and until the Blair House Accord, it blocked even the shiest attempt to reduce protectionist in agriculture and defended its discriminatory CAP.

There was no doubt that the EC was an actor and, moreover, a powerful one. Yet, although the EC was the biggest bloc in terms of share of world trade, it was neither the leader of the trade regime nor its driving force. The EC never proposed a new Round, it never acted to unblock stalled talks, and it never set the agenda. At the beginning of each round, above all under the French input, the EC played its standard role of recalcitrant partner. Throughout the rounds, the EC negotiators strained the bargain until the very last moment, when trading partners were more willing to make concessions to wind things up. The responsibility to steer negotiations and to take the necessary moves to unblock the talks belonged to the United States. Throughout the GATT years, Washington considered the GATT negotiations also in geopolitical terms, and at the end of each round the US administration considered whether the deal reached was worthy in terms of trade gains and for the Atlantic alliance. On the contrary, the EC member states were engaged in calculating whether the trade concessions they would obtain would be bigger or smaller than those of the other EC members or the United States. The EC's potential for a leadership role was impeded by the tendency of member states to prefer short-term economic gains over long-term political considerations, as well as their ineffectiveness in explicitly linking trade to geopolitics and their divergences in Brussels over other aspects of the EC's development.

Only in the early 1990s, in the last phase of the Uruguay Round, did the role of the EC shift from a defensive to a more proactive role. In this phase, the EC tried to export its own vision of the trade regime—which did not fully coincide with that of the United States—by enhancing a rules-based multilateral trade regime. Both the WTO and its binding dispute settlement procedure owed their existence to the EC.

The Uruguay Round would turn out to be the last one dominated by the US–EC dynamics and preferences. In the aftermath of the Uruguay Round, the EU tried to maintain its proactive stance. It was the principal proponent of the new and comprehensive round that would then be launched in Doha in 2001. This more proactive stance, however, coincided with the end of the Cold War and the rise of the emerging economies of Brazil, China, and India. The shift to a multipolar world and the relative decline of the EC and US economies—as well as the attractiveness of their markets—curtailed the EC and US bargaining power and ended their dominance of the world trade regime. Since the Uruguay Round, the United States has progressively weakened its instrumental role in the trade regime, while the increased competition on the US market brought about by globalization has emboldened protectionist interests. The difficulty with which the US Congress has renewed the fast-track negotiating authority to the US executive has cast serious doubt on the US commitment and ability to be engaged in the multilateral trading system.[55] In the last twenty years, many developing countries have become more active in the WTO and, together with the other powerful players such as Brazil, India and China, are able to challenge the United States and the EU. The power shift became evident in the Doha Round, where developing countries have been able to challenge the US–EU duopoly and changed the bargaining dynamics. The difficulty in moving the Doha Round ahead pushed both the United States and the EU to pursue bilateral agreements such as the Transatlantic Trade and Investment Partnership (TTIP), where the two actors are trying to obtain more favorable concessions than what they would get in Geneva. In a way, the United States and the EU are trying to re-establish the GATT that they had dominated for almost 50 years.

Notes

1   The author expresses her gratitude to the organizers and participants of the workshop "The History of EC Foreign Relations, 1957–1992" (European University Institute, June 6–7, 2016) and to Francesco Petrini for the many useful comments they provided.

2   Author's calculation from World Trade Organization, International Trade Statistics 2015, *Special Focus: World Trade and the WTO, 1995–2014*, Geneva 2015, https://www.wto.org/english/res_e/statis_e/its2015_e/its2015_e.pdf, table I8, 45 (last accessed on November 1, 2018).

3   Wendy Asbeek Bruce, *Tariffs, Trade and European Integration, 1947/1957: From Study Group to Common Market* (New York: St Martin Press, 1997).

4   Ynze Alkema, *Regionalism in a Multilateral Framework: The EEC, the United States and the GATT Confronting Trade Policies, 1957-1962*, PhD thesis, Florence, 1996.

5   On the first aspect, see N. Piers Ludlow, "The Emergence of a Commercial Heavy-weight: The Kennedy Round and the European Community of the 1960s," *Diplomacy and Statecraft*, 18:2 (2007), 351–368; Lucia Coppolaro, *The Making of a World Trading Power: The European Economic Community (EEC) in the GATT Kennedy Round Negotiations (1963-1967)* (Farnham: Ashgate, 2013). On the second aspect see Lucia Coppolaro, "In Search of Power: The European Commission in the Kennedy Round Negotiations (1963-1967)," *Contemporary European History*, 23:1 (2014), 23–41.

6   Charlotte Bretherton and John Vogler, *The European Union as a Global Actor* (London: Routledge, 2009).

7   Sophie Meunier, *Trading voices: The European Union in International Commercial Negotiations* (Princeton and Oxford: Oxford University Press, 2006).

8   Stephen Woolcock, *European Union Economic Diplomacy: The Role of the EU in External Economic Relations* (Farnham: Ashgate, 2012).

9   Dirk De Bièvre and Arno Poletti, "The EU in Trade Policy: From Regime Shaper to Status Quo Power," in Gerda Falkner and Patrick Müller (eds.), *EU Policies in a Global Perspective: Shaping or Taking International Regimes?* (London and New York: Routledge, 2014).

10   Karin Kock, *International Trade Policy and the GATT* (Stockholm: Almqvist & Wiksell, 1968), 122–131.

11   Eurostat, *Statistics of the EEC—External Trade, 1968* (Brussels, 1969).

12   Kock, *International Trade Policy*, 122–131.

13   Robert E. Hudec, *The GATT Legal System and World Trade Diplomacy* (Salem: Butterworth Legal Publishers, 1990), 196.

14   Richard H. Snape, "History and Economics in GATT's Article XXIV," in Kym Anderson and Richard Blackhurst (eds.), *Regional Integration and the Global Trading System* (New York: Harvester Wheatsheaf, 1993), 273–291.

15   For the US stance on European integration, see Pascaline Winand, *Eisenhower, Kennedy and the United States of Europe* (London: Macmillan, 1993).

16   Federico Romero, "Interdependence and Integration in American Eyes: From the Marshall Plan to Currency Convertibility," in Alan S. Milward (ed.), *The Frontier of National Sovereignty: History and Theory 1945-1992* (London: Routledge, 1994), 155–182, quote 171.

17   In addition to Alkema, on the Dillon round see Ernest H. Preeg, *Traders and Diplomats: An Analysis of the Kennedy Round of Negotiations under the GATT* (Washington, DC: Brookings Institute, 1970), 40–41.

18   John Fitzgerald Kennedy Library, Pre-presidential papers, Transition files, Task Force reports, Box 1073, Report to the Honourable John F. Kennedy, December 31, 1960.

19   This part of the chapter, dedicated to the Kennedy Round, is based on Coppolaro, *The Making of a World Trading Power*. On the US initiative to launch the Round, see also Thomas W. Zeiler, *American Trade and Power in the 1960s* (New York: Columbia University Press, 1996).

20   On agriculture, see Katja Seidel's chapter, "The External Dimensions of the Common Agricultural Policy: From Developed to Developing Countries" in this volume. For the treatment of agriculture in the GATT regime, see Timothy Josling, Stefan

Tangermann and Thorald K.Warley, *Agriculture in the GATT* (Basingstoke: Palgrave Macmillan, 1996).

21 Lucia Coppolaro and Francine McKenzie, "Trading Blocs and Trading Blows: GATT Conflictual Path to Trade Liberalization, 1947–1967," in Lucia Coppolaro and Francine McKenzie (eds.), *A Global History of Trade and Conflict since 1500* (Basingstoke: Palgrave Macmillan, 2013), 163–187.

22 Lyndon Baines Johnson Library (LBJL), NSF National Security Council History, Book 1-TABSI-6, Box 52, Memorandum for the President from Bator, "Your meeting tomorrow on the Kennedy Round," May 10, 1967.

23 LBJL, Bator Papers, Box 12, Memorandum of the State Department written by Hinton, May 10, 1967.

24 Data from Eurostat, *Eurostat, Statistics of the EEC—External Trade, 1975* (Brussels, 1976).

25 On the reaction of the Nixon administration to the EC enlargement, see Lucia Coppolaro, "The United States and the EEC Enlargement (1969–1973): Reaffirming the Atlantic Framework," in Jan van der Harst (ed.) *Beyond the Customs Union: The European Community's Quest for Deepening, Completion and Enlargement, 1969–1975* (Brussels: Bruylant, 2007), 135–162.

26 Thomas W. Zeiler, "Nixon's War with the International Economy," in Coppolaro and McKenzie (eds.), *A Global History of Trade and Conflict*, 188–207.

27 The best account of the Tokyo Round remains Gilbert R. Winham, *International Trade and the Tokyo Round Negotiations* (Princeton: Princeton University Press, 1986).

28 Barry Eichengreen, *The European Economy since 1945: Coordinated Capitalism and Beyond* (Princeton: Princeton University Press, 2008), 225–257.

29 European Commission archives (ECAB), BAC 48/1984, 230 1974–1975, Note Eléments de l'intervention du Représentant de la Commission au Comité des Négociations commerciales, January 30, 1975; ECAB, BAC 48/1984, 230 1974–1975, Résultats des travaux effectués par le Comité 111, January 15, 1975.

30 Lucia Coppolaro, "In the Shadow of Globalization: The European Community and the United States in the GATT negotiations of the Tokyo Round (1973–1979)," *The International History Review*, 23:1 (2018), 752–773.

31 Foreign Relations of the United States (FRUS), 1973–1976, Vol. XXXI, Foreign Economic Policy, Doc. 123, Memorandum of Conversation, November 16, 1975.

32 Centre des archives économiques et financières (CAEF), PH 029/03–02, Ministère de l'Economie et des Finances, DREE, Note Compte-Rendu de l'entretien de M. de Morel avec Mme Steeg (Directeur au Ministère Fédéral de l'Economie), October 18, 1977.

33 The National Archives of the United Kingdom (TNA), PREM 16/1916, Telegram 1621 for Stowe (Prime Minister's Party) from Hunt "Bonn Summit," June 25, 1978.

34 FRUS, 1977–1980, Vol. III, Foreign Economic Policy, Doc. 42, Memorandum From Robert Hormats of the National Security Council Staff to the President's Assistant for National Security Affairs (Brzezinski), July 8, 1977.

35 FRUS, 1973–1976, Vol. XXXI, Foreign Economic Policy, Doc. 131, Memorandum From Robert Hormats of the National Security Council Staff to the President's Assistant for National Security Affairs (Scowcroft), March 19, 1976; Ministère des affaires étrangères français—La Courneuve (MAEF), DE/CE, Service de Coopération économique, 1534, Note Opportunité et contenu possible d'un engagement sur la liberté des échanges, April 18, 1977; CAEF, PH 029/03–02, Ministère de l'Economie

et des Finances, DREE, Note Compte-Rendu de l'entretien de M. de Morel avec Mme Steeg (Directeur au Ministère Fédéral de l'Economie), October 18, 1977.

36 Winham, *International Trade*, 186.
37 FRUS, 1977–1980, Vol. III, Foreign Economic Policy, Doc. 9, Memorandum From the Assistant Secretary of the Treasury for International Affairs-Designate (Bergsten) to Secretary of the Treasury Blumenthal, March 6, 1977.
38 Ibid.
39 FRUS, 1977–1980, Vol. III, Foreign Economic Policy, Doc. 27, Minutes of the London Economic Summit Meeting, May 7, 1977.
40 Michael Loriaux, *France After Hegemony: International Change and Financial Reform* (Cornell: Cornell University Press, 1991), 230–250.
41 Martin Daunton, *Just Taxes: The Politics of Taxation in Britain 1914–1979* (Cambridge: Cambridge University Press, 2002), 368.
42 On the results of the Tokyo Round, see Winham, *International Trade*, 250–277.
43 Ibid., 250–277.
44 Ibid., 278–341.
45 On the development of globalization see Alfred E. Eckes, *The Contemporary Global Economy: A History since 1980* (Chichester: Wiley-Blackwell, 2011).
46 For the US initiative, see Ernest H. Preeg, "The Uruguay Round Negotiations and the Creation of the WTO," in Amrita Narlikar, Martin Daunton and Robert M. Sterm (eds.), *The Oxford Handbook of World Trade Organization* (Oxford: Oxford University Press, 2012), 122–140.
47 For the EC reaction on the Reagan's initiative, see Preeg, "The Uruguay Round Negotiations," 122–140.
48 John Keeler, "Agricultural Power in the European Community: Explaining the Fate of CAP and GATT Negotiations," *Comparative Politics*, 28:2 (1996), 127–149.
49 On agriculture and the Uruguay Round see Josling, Tangermann and Warley, *Agriculture in the GATT*, 133–243.
50 De Bièvre and Poletti, "The EU in Trade Policy," 29.
51 Preeg, "The Uruguay Round Negotiations," 122–140.
52 De Bièvre and Poletti, "The EU in Trade Policy," 29.
53 Preeg, "The Uruguay Round Negotiations," 122–140.
54 Ibid.
55 For the stance of the United States in the WTO, see Todd Allee, "The Role of the United States: A Multilevel Explanation for Decreased Support over Time," in Daunton, Narlikar and Stern (eds.), *The Oxford Handbook*, 235–253.

8

The EC and Foreign and Security Policy: The Dream of Autonomy

Wilfried Loth

The striving for a common foreign and security policy was one of the driving forces behind the establishment of the European Community (EC). In a world dominated by the United States and the Soviet Union, many Europeans became convinced that common action by the European states was the necessary condition for maintaining influence in world politics and securing peace. As Jean Monnet, the "father" of the Schuman Plan, wrote to French Prime Minister Georges Bidault on April 28, 1950: "World peace cannot be saved without creative efforts on a level with the dangers threatening it. The contribution which an organized and living Europe can make to civilization is indispensable to maintaining peaceful relations. For that purpose, Europe must be organized on a federal basis."[1] This was the main impetus to start the process of European integration by proposing a European Coal and Steel Community (ECSC) in May 1950. In October of the same year the same thoughts led the French government to propose a European Defence Community (EDC), which would allow the deployment of West German troops within a European army.[2]

However, whereas the ECSC began its work on August 10, 1952, the EDC project resulted in major failure. On August 30, 1954, after protracted and difficult negotiations, the French National Assembly decided by a large majority to remove the EDC treaty from the agenda. Mistrust in the effectiveness of the mechanisms proposed to control German rearmament and fears of loss of national sovereignty in defense matters combined to overturn the negotiated compromises accepted by successive governments. As a result, the rearmament of the Federal Republic of Germany was organized via direct membership in North Atlantic Treaty Organization (NATO), thereby strengthening both the structures and the relevance of this comprehensive organization of Western security in the Cold War. A Western European Union (WEU) of Great Britain, France, the Benelux countries, West Germany, and Italy guaranteed a British military presence on the continent but did not include any instruments for operating independently of the American Supreme Commander of NATO in Europe.[3]

After the failure of the EDC, the European project focused on economic integration. By establishing both the European Economic Community (EEC) and the European Atomic Energy Community (EURATOM) on January 1, 1958, the

European leaders managed to overcome the crisis of the integration process. This allowed public opinion to lose sight of foreign and security policy. Political science and historiography also neglected the foreign and security policy dimension in the construction of the EEC. So far, there is no comprehensive monograph on the topic. Basic information on the attitude of French and German governments can be found in Georges-Henri Soutou's seminal work on the political-strategic relations between these two countries.[4] Daniel Möckli, Michael E. Smith, and Maria Găinar deal with the origins of the European Political Cooperation (EPC) in the 1970s.[5] In her PhD thesis, Angela Romano has covered the role of the EPC in the emergence of the Helsinki Final Act.[6] Some first pieces of evidence on EPC activities in the follow-up meetings in Belgrad and Madrid can be found in articles by Angela Romano and in Paola Varotti's unpublished PhD thesis on German CSCE policy.[7] An article by Sara Tavani examines EPC policy in relation to the 'Polish crisis" at the beginning of the 1980s.[8]

However, as the problem of self-assertion in world politics was not resolved by the combination of NATO and WEU, the striving for common policies continued, and influenced the development of the new European institutions. Therefore, the topic is discussed in depth in my recently published overview of the European integration process.[9] Still, it needs much further exploration.

The Project of a Political Union

In a certain respect, the desire for a common foreign and security policy was decisive for the establishment of the EEC. In economic terms the six-member Common Market (France, West Germany, Italy, and the Benelux countries) did not correspond fully with the needs of either the Federal Republic of Germany or France. French political and economic leaders regarded the French economy as still too weak for unrestricted integration in such a market, whereas German Economics Minister Ludwig Erhard regarded the customs union as a statist impediment to a worldwide system of free trade that better suited the export interests of the West German economy. Therefore, it was no surprise that the negotiations on the Rome treaties lurched from crisis to crisis and finally came to a dead end. At a meeting on October 20 and 21, 1956, in Paris, the six foreign ministers failed to agree on transition regulations; French Foreign Minister Christian Pineau, as chair, declared the conference a failure. Erhard immediately urged that the negotiations in Brussels be broken off, in favor of talks with the British about their proposal for a free trade zone in Europe.

West German Chancellor Konrad Adenauer was not impressed by Erhard's economic argumentation. After the Redford Plan for reducing the American troop presence in Europe in summer 1956 underlined the danger of a Soviet–US understanding at Europe's expense, Adenauer's interest in Western European security policy grew further. Initial arrangements for activating the WEU, which he had agreed with French Prime Minister Guy Mollet, were not to be called into question by the failure of the Brussels negotiations. In order to resolve the negotiation crisis he decided to seek a compromise in top-level talks with Mollet.

When Adenauer arrived in Paris on November 6, Mollet was facing great pressure from both the US and Soviet governments over the Franco–British attack on Egypt in the Suez Crisis. Adenauer's solidarity with the French government at this moment not only facilitated the finding of a compromise in the question of transition regulations; it also enabled Mollet to present the EEC and EURATOM treaties as a means by which France could avoid future humiliations. In the light of the distressing dependency on Arab oil and Adenauer's clear distancing from the United States, Europe seemed to be the stronghold of independence. This perception helped to overcome French protectionist opposition to the Common Market. In July 1957, the French National Assembly approved the Rome treaties by a surprising majority.[10]

During the first years after the conclusion of the Rome treaties it was mainly the new French President Charles de Gaulle who advocated a common foreign and security policy: the Common Market was to constitute the starting point for a more comprehensive "political, economic, and cultural reality."[11] Such a Europe seemed urgent to de Gaulle, given that he viewed the existing dependence of the European allies on American nuclear deterrence as dishonorable and to an increasing extent also insecure: dishonorable in regard to the autonomy of the European nations, which as a consequence were permanently under threat of American coercion and had no alternative in the event of military conflict; and highly uncertain given that the production of long-range Soviet bombers capable of reaching American territory with nuclear weapons had made the US guarantee extremely questionable. De Gaulle did not doubt that this guarantee would weaken further as the Soviet arsenal was perfected, and that the transition to the strategy of "flexible response" only exposed Europe to the risk of a privileged destruction.[12]

The core of political Europe was therefore autonomy in defense policy; this presupposed that the European partners had agreed on the goal of real independence from the leading Western power—that is, they would certainly remain allies of the United States but sovereign in any decision to use their own weapons. As de Gaulle wrote in July 1961, "There can be no European unity if Europe does not constitute a political entity distinct from other entities. A personality. But there can be no European personality if Europe does not have control over the defense of its personality. Defense is always the basis of politics." That "Europe must have its personality in its own defense," was for him "all the more advisable as Europe becomes a strategic whole. It constitutes a marshalling area for one single and simultaneous battle. America can lose Europe in the battle without disappearing. Europe cannot."[13]

According to de Gaulle, the path to such a "European Europe, independent, mighty, and influential within the framework of the free world," was to be found in regular consultations between the interested governments.[14] As he suggested as early as August 1958, these consultations should "in a certain sense take on an organic character to the extent that they develop."[15] In the long term, this ought to lead to the creation of a "confederation" in which majority rule should certainly apply: "We must begin with unanimity, and then we shall see."[16] In the short term, however, de Gaulle also sought to have the existing European organs subordinated to the authority of the Council of Ministers. The tendency of the Commission to develop into a European government, which had its roots in the treaty itself, was a thorn in his side: "There is nothing above the nations, if their states do not jointly decide! The aspirations of the Brussels commissioners to give orders to the governments are risible! Risible!"[17]

De Gaulle's vision never became reality—for two reasons mainly: among his partners in the "Europe of the Six," the fear of a complete withdrawal of the US military presence on the European continent prevailed in the end, and the French president combined his efforts to establish a political union with ill-conceived attacks on the ambitions of the European Commission. In a "study commission" established by the governments of the Six, the French representative Christian Fouchet presented a draft treaty (the so-called "Fouchet Plan I") on October 19, 1961 that stated the goals of "common foreign policy" and "common defense policy" for the proposed "European Union (EU)." The Union Council was to take decisions by unanimous agreement; a European Political Commission (with its seat in Paris) was to be subordinate to it; and the European Parliament was to have only an advisory function. Decisions of the Council were to be binding only for those states taking part in the voting. Three years after the treaty came into effect, it was to be revised with the goal of a step-by-step harmonization of foreign and defense policy as well as a centralization of the existing Community.[18]

The French foreign ministry felt it could accede to the demands of its partners to the extent that a revised version (approved on January 15, 1962 by Foreign Minister Maurice Couve de Murville) incorporated the Bonn formulation whereby common foreign and defense policy was to serve the strengthening of the Atlantic Alliance. On the issue of revision after three years, a commitment was made that the European Parliament would be "more strongly incorporated" into the development and implementation of common policies. Beyond that, the envisioned reform of the existing institutions was to occur "with regard for the structures" defined in the treaties of Paris and Rome.[19] De Gaulle persisted, however, in his view that avowals of strengthening the alliance and the existing treaties be left out and that the economy be explicitly included among the areas of cooperation, which had not previously been the case. Presented on January 18, 1962, the second French draft ("Fouchet Plan II") thus contained, to a greater extent than the previous version, the danger of curtailing the possibilities for supranational development of the existing Community.[20]

Faced with general opposition to unity on this basis, de Gaulle was willing to make greater concessions: At a meeting with Italian Foreign Minister Antonio Segni on April 4, 1962 in Turin, he once again accepted the declaration of support for strengthening the alliance and clarified that the realm of economics should be dealt with "by implementing the Treaties of Paris and Rome." A new Article 3 even contained an explicit guarantee of the treaties.[21] At a meeting of foreign ministers in Paris on April 17, Couve de Murville also made the revision clause more precise. A commitment was made that after three years the European Parliament would be more strongly incorporated into the development and implementation of common policies.

These concessions were insufficient, however. In negotiations on the revision on April 17, Segni, his Dutch colleague Joseph Luns, and his Belgian colleague Paul-Henri Spaak called for greater detail on the transition to direct election of the European Parliament and the strengthening of its authority, as well as on the gradual transition to majority decision-making in the Council. When Couve did not go along with this,

Spaak declared that Belgium would sign the treaty on the creation of the EU only after Britain's entry into the EC had been signed. Luns supported him. The British application for EEC membership in July 1961 had put the Belgians in a position to secure better protection from French or Franco-German hegemony, either through Britain's membership or through a supranational orientation of foreign and defense policy. Thus, the second attempt to develop an autonomous European foreign and defense policy had also failed. The foreign ministers parted without setting a date for a new meeting or giving the Commission anything further to clarify.[22]

This second defeat notwithstanding, German Chancellor Konrad Adenauer continued to support de Gaulle's project even if the other EEC partners did not initially join them. In light of Kennedy's pressure on the Federal Republic to enable a relaxation of international tensions by revoking its policy of denying recognition to the German Democratic Republic, this course seemed to Adenauer a strategic necessity that now had to be pursued regardless of the less-than-clear prospects of success. "Depending on circumstances, we must be prepared," he declared to his colleagues, "to live in tension with the Americans for a few years. We have to put more on the Franco–German and the European horse."[23] When, during Adenauer's extended state visit to France in early July of 1962, de Gaulle posed the question of whether the Federal Republic would be willing "to create a political union with France, which de facto and perforce is limited to two members," Adenauer answered "unequivocally with 'yes': We would be willing to accept this limited union, in which a place for the other members would of course have to remain available."[24]

De Gaulle's and Adenauer's agreement meant that the Franco–German Treaty or Élysée Treaty could then be signed at the official residence of the French president on January 22, 1963. It stipulated regular meetings of the French president and West German chancellor, at least twice annually, along with at least four annual meetings of the countries' foreign and defense ministers as well as monthly meetings of top officials in the foreign ministries. The general staffs and those in charge of education and youth affairs would also meet regularly; a joint fund would be established to promote youth exchanges. The governments pledged "to consult one another before every decision on all important foreign policy issues" and in the realm of defense "to bring their basic approaches closer together in order to arrive at joint doctrines."[25]

The agreement between the two symbolic figures of Franco–German reconciliation was by no means complete. De Gaulle was still promising nothing more than the use of French nuclear weapons for the security of the Federal Republic. For his part, Adenauer did not hesitate to signal to the French president that he found the American offer of a multilateral NATO nuclear force very attractive and had therefore assured Kennedy he would participate.[26] Nevertheless, alarm bells sounded in Washington when the treaty was signed. Kennedy was determined to prevent an independent European nuclear force by any means necessary. To this end, the members of the German Bundestag were asked to ratify the Élysée Treaty with the addition of a resolution strengthening the commitment to German membership in NATO and to British membership in the EEC. On May 16, the Bundestag adopted a resolution along the proposed lines almost unanimously; there were only five votes against and ten abstentions. The Franco–German Treaty was ratified with a preamble in which the document was interpreted as an instrument for promoting the "major goals" of West German foreign policy, among them a close partnership between Europe and the United States, a joint "defense within the framework of the North Atlantic alliance and the integration of the armed forces of the states brought together by that alliance," as well as continued European integration "with inclusion of Great Britain and other states willing to join and the further strengthening of these Communities."[27]

With the preamble to the Franco–German Treaty and the departure of Adenauer in October 1963, the third attempt at establishing European political self-assertion had failed, as de Gaulle saw it. Bitterness reigned on all sides. Viewpoints were farther apart than ever as to how the EC should take political action, which states should belong to it at all, and what form the alliance with the Americans should take.[28]

The European Political Cooperation

Only after de Gaulle's retreat from power in April 1969 were the first cautious steps toward a common foreign and security policy possible. This time, the main advocates were German Chancellor Willy Brandt and Italian Foreign Minister Aldo Moro. At the summit of The Hague at the beginning of December 1969 Brandt appealed to his colleagues to work toward the creation of a Europe that would play an autonomous role in international politics. Given the hesitancy of some of the other participants, this led merely to a vague assignment for the foreign ministers to examine by the end of July 1970 "how, from the perspective of expansion, progress in the area of political unity could best be achieved."[29] As a basis for discussion Moro presented a plan envisioning nothing less than the incremental construction of a political community following the model of the Economic Community. It was explicitly to include the areas of defense and justice. In a first phase, there were to be at least quarterly meetings of the relevant expert ministers and the establishment of a secretariat; during a second phase beginning in 1975, there was to be an incremental combining of responsibilities. In a third phase after 1980, the existing Communities were to fuse into a kind of federal state, with the common Commission of the Political Community and the Economic Community as a federal government and the Council of Ministers exercising the presidential function.[30]

Curiously enough, the French now took over the role of brakeman. When a committee of the political directors under the chairmanship of the Belgian Étienne Davignon came together on April 14, the French side finally presented a paper that was significantly more reserved than all the others. Instead of a political community, it only discussed cooperation on foreign policy, and there was explicit emphasis that the realm of defense should remain outside. The decision-making freedom of the participating governments was not to be diminished, and cooperation with the institutions of the Community was to be kept to a minimum. Georges Pompidou, de Gaulle's successor as president of France, was evidently not eager to take up the old debate about the Europeans' relationship to the United States. "I don't believe in political Europe," he explained to his foreign office state secretary, "at least not at the present time. Perhaps there'll come a day, 1980 or later. But I doubt that very much too."[31] In this respect,

Pompidou was significantly less a Gaullist than Brandt. Also, he tried to avoid a conflict with the orthodox Gaullists, who meanwhile believed exclusively in the virtues of strictly national autonomy.

The compromise on which first the political directors and then the foreign ministers agreed in several stages up to July 20 fell below what had been capable of gaining a consensus during the negotiations on the Fouchet plans. The pledge made by the governments was initially limited to efforts to seek harmonization in "all important issues of foreign policy." This was to be achieved through meetings of the foreign ministers every six months and of the "political committee" four times a year (more often at the request of the chair). These meetings were to be chaired by the rotating Council chair. The Commission "will be invited to make known its view," though only if the work of the ministers should "affect the activities of the European Communities." The European Parliament was to participate as well, though only in the form of a "colloquium" with the members of its Foreign Affairs Committee, which was to take place twice a year. The issue of creating a secretariat remained open because France rejected the link with the Commission that the others wanted. At the same time, however, it was decided to produce in not more than two years another report that would contain proposals for the further development of political cooperation.[32] By officially adopting this "Davignon report" on October 27, 1970 the foreign ministers established the "EPC".

Efforts to strengthen this vague form of cooperation in questions of foreign and security policy—by French Foreign Minister Michel Jobert, his Belgian colleague Pierre Harmel, British Prime Minister Edward Heath, German Chancellor Brandt, his successor Helmut Schmidt, and others—resulted in the introduction of the European Council at the Paris summit of December 1974. The heads of state and government decided to meet in future three times a year. As a concession to the smaller states, French President Valéry Giscard d'Estaing agreed that in addition to the Commission president the foreign ministers were to participate in these summits. The "European Council" was to concern itself with foreign policy and all other questions of common interest. As a consequence, EPC was now de facto integrated into the work of the Council of Ministers.[33]

However, even in this restricted form, the common foreign and security policy of the EC had an immediate impact. At their very first gathering in November 1970 the foreign ministers agreed to work out common positions on the issues of peace in the Middle East and the planned Conference on Security and Cooperation in Europe (CSCE).[34] After the orthodox Gaullists were defeated in French parliamentary elections on March 4 and 11, 1973, Pompidou was even able to yield to pressure from Heath for nuclear cooperation: at a meeting with the British prime minister on May 23, it was agreed that there should be expert consultations on the development of the next generation of medium-range missiles; as early as 1975, this initiative was possibly to lead to "something common among Europeans."[35] In a speech to the National Assembly on June 19, Jobert challenged the partners to consider an autonomous European defense. Brandt took up this call by pressing Pompidou for concrete results as soon as possible. The head of the Political Department of the West German Foreign Office, Günther van Well, published a policy article in which he embraced the goal of an "autonomous role and responsibility for the European Union" in foreign and defense policy as well. In a conversation with Jobert, German Foreign Minister Walter Scheel explained that this political union should also include defense components by 1980. In the longer term, Europe ought to "free itself from this 'indissoluble' dependence" on the United States.[36]

Brandt's initiative remained in abeyance due to a lack of understanding and decisiveness within both the French and German governments. Jobert wanted to discuss the defense question primarily within the framework of the WEU, to which obviously neither Denmark nor Ireland belonged. When German Defense Minister Georg Leber— clearly not having coordinated with Brandt or Scheel in any significant way—encouraged France to join NATO's "Eurogroup," Pompidou decided to shelve the issue for the time being. The "Document on the European Identity" adopted by the summit in Copenhagen on December 14 and 15, 1973 therefore mentioned the goal of an independent Europe only in rather vague terms. It emphasized "that Europe must unite and speak increasingly with one voice" and affirmed the goal of a European Union "before the end of the present decade." On the sensitive issue of a European defense, it stated only that Europe must possess "adequate means of defense"; at the urging of the Federal Republic, the continuation of a "constructive dialogue" with the United States was also included.[37]

The project for a political Europe received another blow when Edward Heath was defeated at the polls in February 1974. Whereas the new Prime Minister, Harold Wilson, had been engaged in trying to somehow maintain the balance between a party majority hostile to Europe and British commitments stemming from treaty obligations, new Foreign Secretary James Callaghan roundly rejected the political union as well as the economic and currency union due to vague fears of foreign control from "Brussels." He soon gave his approval to the EPC, after initial experiences with its pragmatic coordination; yet, regarding its further development into a common foreign policy, he persistently cited contrasting national interests and perceptions. A European Union was "unrealistic" and "not desired," he declared during his first appearance in the EC Council of Ministers on April 1, 1974.[38]

Callaghan's aversion to the Political Union offered US Secretary of State Henry Kissinger an unexpected opportunity to bring the conflict over a "New Atlantic Charter" to an end that coincided with his own views after all. Encouraged by Kissinger, the British prime minister had gotten initial agreement from his EC partners at Gymnich for a NATO declaration on the occasion of the twenty-fifth anniversary of the alliance, an initiative that was supposed to be independent of policy statements that had not yet been prepared. When Callaghan presented the draft of such a declaration to the NATO Council on June 15, it was so comprehensive that it could de facto have replaced the policy statements. The Eight reacted to the lack of any mention of the European Union in the document. In the end, Schmidt and Giscard d'Estaing were satisfied with a formulation stating "that the further progress towards unity, which the member states of the European Community are determined to make, should in due course have a beneficial effect on the contribution to the common defense of the Alliance." In this form, the "Atlantic Declaration" was passed by the NATO foreign ministers in Ottawa on June 19, together with a pledge "to strengthen the practice of frank and timely consultations."[39] US President Richard Nixon attended the signing of the document in Brussels on June 26.

The Ottawa Declaration did not constitute a commitment by the Europeans to stronger incorporation into the American strategy, as Kissinger had envisioned. Still less did it speak of an autonomous role for the Europeans in international politics, as not only Pompidou and Jobert but also Heath and Brandt had sought. As was the case with the new German chancellor, the new French president also viewed securing American cooperation in dealing with the acute economic crisis as more important than rapid progress on the road to European autonomy. Given that the Ottawa Declaration included a commitment by the United States to maintain troop levels high enough to maintain the credibility of allied deterrence, the project for an autonomous European defense became less urgent once again.[40]

If the difficult balance between American support and European solidarity in defense matters prevented a real breakthrough in the question of a European defense, common and reciprocal interests in the field of *détente* policy led to a major success in the CSCE negotiations. The Six (and from 1973 onwards the Nine) had a common interest in the recognition of their Community by the Soviet bloc, as well as in preventing any barrier against the further development of the Community. At the same time, they were interested in widening economic and cultural exchanges with the states of the Warsaw Pact and in promoting liberty in these countries. By developing a common Eastern policy they also averted the danger of a neutralization of the Federal Republic and a weakening of their position due to Soviet tactics of division. To ensure that the Community really spoke "with one voice" at the CSCE, the EC ministers assigned an EPC sub-committee on CSCE to prepare common viewpoints as early as February 1971, and asked an ad hoc group of Commission officials and national delegates to prepare proposals and strategies in the field of economic cooperation. During the preparatory talks and the conference itself, from November 1972 until July 1975, the two committees in Brussels worked in permanent session while the delegations of the Nine in Geneva met daily. The delegation of the member state chairing the EC Presidency included representatives of the Commission and acted as spokespersons for the EPC decisions. When the Final Act of the CSCE was signed on August 1, 1975 the then-acting-Chairman Aldo Moro said he was signing the document in his double role of national representative and EC president.[41]

Thereby, the EC assured its de facto recognition by the Soviet bloc and paved the way for commercial negotiations with the Council for Mutual Economic Assistance (COMECON) states. The Nine insisted that the possibility to change frontiers "in accordance with international law, by peaceful means, and by agreement" was included in the Final Act. This stipulation was not only essential for the Federal Republic and its obligation to maintain the possibility of German reunification. It also unlocked the way for a political union of the Europeans with any degree of coherence and supranationality. Even more important was the insistence of the Nine on unequivocal principles and concrete measures in the field of human rights, self-determination, and free movement of people, information and ideas. Against a tendency in US conference policy to end the CSCE with a superficial agreement, they refused to agree to a top-level final phase until concrete results had been reached in this field. As Soviet leader Leonid Brezhnev wished to avoid taking the blame for the collapse of the conference, he finally gave in. Thus, in the declaration of principles of the Final Act the participating states promised to respect "human rights and fundamental freedoms including freedom of thought, conscience, religion, and opinion." In the so-called "Basket Three" they agreed on "free exchange of persons, information, and views," with no reference to consistency with national laws.[42] In this way, the Nine substantiated *détente* between Western Europe and the Soviet bloc and established a strong point of reference for the liberalization of the Communist regimes.[43]

After their obvious success in the CSCE, the Nine agreed to make *détente* and cooperation with the East a permanent task of their political cooperation. A Group of Experts on Eastern Europe was installed to provide the EPC members with analyses of developments in the Soviet bloc and proposals to improve EC–East relations. In September 1975 the Venice European Council decided to maintain the principle of speaking with one voice on all issues related to the Final Act of Helsinki and CSCE follow-up meetings.[44] At the follow-up meeting in Belgrade from October 1977 to March 1978 the Nine sought to prevent the Carter administration from having this gathering devolve into nothing more than a tribunal against Eastern bloc human rights violations. Even if they were not very successful they did however manage to have the Belgrade meeting end with a declaration proclaiming the desire to continue the dialogue of *détente* and to hold at least one more follow-up conference. The European governments could—and did—build on that in their bilateral talks with the East Bloc states.[45] When Carter reacted to the entry of Soviet troops into Afghanistan at Christmas 1979 by suspending both the *détente* dialogue and ratification of the SALT II Treaty, the Nine once again encouraged moderation. They did not participate in the comprehensive trade restrictions that Washington imposed on Moscow as "punishment." Instead, Schmidt and Giscard d'Estaing developed a coordinated travel diplomacy with the Communist leaders in Moscow, Warsaw, and East Berlin.[46]

The regular meetings of the EPC and the European Council did ensure an increasing European socialization among foreign policy actors as well as the development of common standpoints—not only in regard to the CSCE process but also to southern expansion of the EC, conflicts in Africa, relations with Latin America, and the crisis in Iran after the fall of the shah in winter 1978–1979. The European Council of Venice in June of 1980 strengthened the autonomy of the European Middle East policy in that it recognized the right of the Palestinians to self-determination and characterized the Palestinian Liberation Organization (PLO) as their legitimate representative.[47] The central question of military autonomy was omitted during this period, however. This was on the one hand the result of the Labour government's rejection of a common foreign policy, a stance that remained unchanged after the victory of Margaret Thatcher in the parliamentary elections in May 1979. On the other hand, Schmidt and Giscard agreed on a Franco–German defense alliance in July of 1980 that in essence amounted to adding an autonomous European pillar to NATO. But when first Giscard (in May 1981) and second Schmidt (in October 1982) lost power the project of such a military union lost drive on both sides.[48]

Preparing Post-Cold War Europe

Meanwhile, the desire to transcend the limits of EPC acquired new impetus through an initiative of West German Foreign Minister Hans-Dietrich Genscher, the liberal coalition partner of Helmut Schmidt. Genscher was seeking to reinvigorate the integration process and to counteract the impression of a stalemate on Europe policy, which had resulted from Thatcher's generally negative attitude. Especially, he regarded it as necessary to make the European autonomy practiced by Giscard and Schmidt multilateral so as to give it a more stable basis. With Thatcher, it was impossible to develop a coherent EPC strategy for the second CSCE follow-up meeting starting in November 1980 in Madrid. Genscher had to work hard to avoid a break-up or at least a postponement of the meeting after the initial complaints about Soviet behavior in the field of the Basket Three.[49]

To promote multilateral *détente* policy again, a plan for a "Treaty on European Union" was developed in the Europe Department of the West German Foreign Office during the spring of 1980. This was to strengthen the political goal of European unity, better coordinate established activities, and highlight possibilities for further development within a readily comprehensible framework. Genscher took up this proposal in early 1981 and did so publicly, given that he was chairman of the smaller coalition partner and was eager for the opportunity to have the Free Democrats distinguish themselves in the area of European policy. In a speech at the FDP Liberal Party's traditional New Year meeting in Stuttgart on January 6, 1981, he declared that it was "high time" for such a treaty. As goals of the EU, he cited "the development of a common European foreign policy, expansion of Community policy in accordance with the Treaties of Paris and Rome, coordination in the realm of defense policy, closer cooperation in cultural matters, and the harmonization of lawmaking."[50]

Genscher's initiative was taken up at once by Italian Foreign Minister Emilio Colombo. This Christian Democrat, who had long been an important figure in Italian politics, not only saw a chance to strengthen European institutions, a goal toward which he had already worked as president of the European Parliament from 1977 to 1979. He also welcomed the prospect of breaking the Franco–German duopoly in formulating European foreign policy, so as to have greater influence in shaping it. Two weeks after Genscher's speech in Stuttgart, Colombo joined in the call for a union treaty in a speech in Florence. Thereafter, he met repeatedly with the West German foreign minister to exchange ideas about the content of such a treaty.

Of course, reactions in the other capitals were less enthusiastic. Even in the German government Defense Minister Hans Apel was not pleased with the proposed expansion of foreign policy cooperation into the realm of defense policy. It was only due to the support of the new Federal Chancellor Helmut Kohl that the European Council finally accepted at least a Solemn Declaration on European Union. At its core, this document, adopted at the Stuttgart Council in June 1983, was still only a declaration of intent regarding the deepening of existing relations and the development of new areas of cooperation. In contrast to the joint proposal by Genscher and Colombo, there was mention of agricultural policy, social policy, and promotion of regional development; cooperation in the defense realm was limited to "political and economic aspects." In institutional terms, there was only the promise of circumspection in exercising the veto right and increased consultation of the European Parliament. In regard to binding international agreements, it was merely the case that official "positions" from Parliament would be necessary.[51]

Nevertheless, the Stuttgart declaration put the question of a common foreign and security policy back on the agenda. Through close cooperation, Kohl and the new French President François Mitterrand managed to transition existing practice into treaty form. This was the case when the Council of Ministers agreed on the Single European Act in December 1986. Due to resistance from the British and the smaller states, the institutional augmentation of the European Council was limited to a small administrative secretariat in Brussels, to which some officials of the prior, the current, and the next Council president would belong. Furthermore, the Communities and Political Cooperation were now incorporated into a common treaty text, while the European Council was anchored in the treaty as the overarching institution; however, their integration still did not go beyond the presence of the Commission at all gatherings of the Council, of the foreign ministers, and of their directors.[52]

Far from being content with this meager result of intense negotiations, Mitterrand sought to promote common foreign policy and a common defense organization through a reanimation of the cooperation between France and the Federal Republic. Behind this lay not only continuing anxiety that neutralization tendencies might achieve a breakthrough in German politics; Mitterrand also appeared increasingly worried about unpredictability and inconsistencies in the policy of Ronald Reagan, especially regarding the SDI programme for a space-based missile defense system that wantonly disregarded the security interests of the Europeans. Moreover, the French president was receptive to the vision of his friend Régis Debray, who saw in an autonomous Western Europe the possibility of promoting the democratization of Eastern Europe. In any event, Debray's "Thoughts on the Foreign Policy of France," published in early 1986, conjured up the reconciliation of both halves of Europe on the basis of shared values and democratic socialism, which was to become possible after overcoming the excesses of American liberalism as well as those of Communism.[53]

Chancellor Kohl reacted positively to the French proposals because, like Mitterrand, he too feared American withdrawal tendencies as well as the German penchant for neutrality. In his view, this latter factor was strengthened by the disarmament initiatives of the new Soviet General Secretary Mikhail Gorbachev; and so he now pressed for "very close cooperation," as he said to Mitterrand at a meeting at Chateau Chambord on March 28, 1987.[54] In July 1987, Mitterrand and Kohl agreed to frequent joint maneuvers of the French Army and the German *Bundeswehr*. Four months later, the creation of a Franco–German brigade was announced, open to being joined by Luxembourg, the Netherlands, and Italy within a prospective fusion of the EC and the WEU. On January 22, 1988, on the twenty-fifth anniversary of the signing of the Franco–German Treaty, a joint Defense and Security Council came into being.[55]

The formation of this council did not yet mean that France and the Federal Republic actually agreed on a joint defense concept; the defense council acquired no operational functions. Nevertheless, the negotiations on Franco–German institutions prepared the ground for an understanding over the appropriate reaction to Gorbachev's disarmament initiatives. Mitterrand and Kohl quickly agreed that an elimination of all nuclear weapons would be highly dangerous and that it was therefore in the vital interest of the Federal Republic that the French nuclear deterrent be preserved and further modernized. Under this condition they also agreed on the elimination of all medium-range missiles held by the superpowers in Europe and Asia. Thereby, they cleared the way for the signing of the Washington Agreement of December 1987, as a major step towards substantial nuclear disarmament. Mitterrand supported Kohl in his demand for talks on reducing the asymmetry in conventional weapons. Having been successful in this respect, both could declare that the modernization of short-range missiles demanded by NATO strategists was no longer necessary. Finally, both contributed to convincing US President George Bush of the necessity to support Gorbachev in his reforms and to proclaim the end of the Cold War.[56]

With the new Franco–German institutions Mitterrand and Kohl were also well prepared for new initiatives when the end of the Cold War strengthened the objective necessity of European defense arrangements. In a joint letter of December 6, 1990 to the President of the European Council, Mitterrand and Kohl argued strongly for "more Europe" in the fields of common foreign policy and security. Kohl committed himself more explicitly to the goal of a "common defense" than he had in his efforts for the development of a joint Franco–German defense concept in the summer of 1987. For this purpose, a "clear organic tie" between the political union and the WEU was to be created; in the long term, the WEU was to become a component of the political union and consequently was also to include those EU members that had not hitherto belonged to it. As areas in which a "genuine common foreign policy" could develop, the document cited relations with the former Eastern Bloc states and the states bordering the Mediterranean, disarmament talks, as well as development policy. Decisions would be made "fundamentally unanimously," but it would also be possible to allow for majority decision-making, especially on matters involving modalities of policy implementation.[57]

This explicit choice for an autonomous European defense was opposed not only by the British, but also by the Dutch, Danish, and Portuguese governments, which argued that one ought not to further endanger the already-threatened cohesion of NATO by emphasizing a European defense identity. In order banish the danger that the Franco–German initiative would fail, Kohl suggested to Mitterrand at a meeting in Lille on June 25, 1991 that there be another joint foray. By the beginning of October, this had resulted in a new joint letter to the Council. The document made the goal of foreign and defense policy more specific in three points. First, a draft text of treaty terms on these matters was offered, naming the WEU as the organ charged with carrying out common foreign policy but at the same time declaring that the "specifics of the defense policy of individual member states" were "unaffected." A review of these terms was announced for no later than 1996. Second, Bonn and Paris presented a draft declaration of WEU member states, which was to be appended to the Union treaty; this emphasized the "incremental expansion of the WEU into the defense component of the Union" as well as the goal of "creating a European pillar" of the Atlantic alliance. Third, the chancellor and president announced not only an expansion of Franco–German military units, but also declared that these could "constitute the nucleus of a European corps," in which "forces of other members of the WEU" would participate.[58]

Thatcher's successor John Major told Mitterrand that subordination of the WEU to the rules of the EU would be absolutely out of the question. However, after Washington had accepted the "development of a defense identity for Europe" in a declaration of the NATO Council on November 8, the British prime minister had to content himself with a weakening of the formulations of the Franco–German draft at the conclusion of treaty negotiations at the Council meeting of December 9 and 10, in Maastricht. The treaty text now contained only the statement that the common defense policy "might in time lead to a common defense"; for practical measures following from Council decisions on defense policy, there was an assumption of "accord" between the Council and the organs of the WEU. Additionally, majority decision-making on "issues having defense implications" was explicitly forbidden.[59] Through close cooperation, Mitterrand and Kohl were able to prevent any further watering down of the defense perspectives during the Council meeting in Maastricht.[60]

Conclusion

Thus, progress in the institutionalization of a Common Foreign and Security Policy remained extremely slow and cautious until the very end of the period under consideration here. This was due to the very specific nature of this field of common policy: On the one side, striving for autonomy in world politics was one of most powerful driving forces behind the European integration process. On the other side, in a world dominated by superpower confrontation and nuclear arms race, the security of the EC states was inevitably dependent on American support and guarantees. The necessary balance between NATO integration and European autonomy in defense matters was more difficult to reach as US administrations—in the era of Kennedy as in the era of Kissinger—showed little understanding for European concerns and ambitions in this field. At the same time, defense was strongly connected with national identity and nation-state structures. Its organization on a supranational level was difficult to conceptualize and even more difficult to organize.

Therefore, the question of a Common Foreign and Security Policy of the EC was a matter of a permanent controversial debate—both between the member states and within them. Progress in this field was dependent on the existence of strong leaders and agreement among them. Astonishingly enough, this was often the case, thus demonstrating the long-term force of the autonomy impetus. Yet, as in other fields of "high politics," this also meant that success was dependent on the persistence of the actors. The changes from Adenauer to Chancellor Ludwig Erhard and his Foreign Minister Gerhard Schröder in October 1963 and from Heath to Callaghan in February 1974 are the most striking examples of this specific weakness.

To a certain extent, this weakness could be compensated by a process of "low politics" which started with the formation of the EPC. The permanent exchange of experts and ministers promoted a common ground of understanding which—interruptions through changes on the ministerial level notwithstanding—was growing in the long term. Progress on the implementation of the Common Foreign and Security Policy remained dependent on joint Franco–German leadership. But it was more and more facilitated by the existence of such a common ground.

Contrary to the hopes of actors such as Mitterrand, the end of the Cold War did not effect a fundamental change in this constellation. Of course, European dependency on

US guarantees declined dramatically, and European responsibility in foreign and security affairs rose to nearly the same degree. However, the opportunities for disagreements about priorities and means grew, too. Also, the security structures of NATO and national defense complexes showed remarkable persistence. As a consequence, the Europeans committed themselves to a growing number of multinational military units and missions. Sometimes however, they showed glaring weaknesses, as in the conflict in Bosnia-Herzegovina (1995) or striking disagreement as in the Iraq War (2003) or with regard to intervention in the Libyan rebellion (2011).[61] Improving the Common Foreign and Security Policy remained a permanent challenge.

Notes

1   Jean Monnet on Georges Bidault, April 28, 1950, quoted after Éric Roussel, *Jean Monnet 1888-1979* (Paris: Fayard, 1996), 520–522.
2   See William I. Hitchcock, *France Restored: Cold War Diplomacy and the Quest for Leadership in Europe, 1944–1954* (Chapel Hill: University of North Carolina Press, 1998), 116–129 and 139–144; Wilfried Loth, *Building Europe: A History of European Unification* (Berlin and Boston: De Gruyter, 2015), 28–40.
3   Dieter Krüger, *Sicherheit durch Integration? Die wirtschaftliche und politische Zusammenarbeit Westeuropas 1947 bis 1957/58* (Munich: Oldenbourg, 2003), 347–365.
4   Georges-Henri Soutou, *L'alliance incertaine. Les rapports politico-stratégiques franco-allemands, 1954–1996* (Paris: Fayard, 1996).
5   Michael E. Smith, *Europe's Foreign and Security Policy: The Institutionalization of Cooperation* (New York: Cambridge University Press, 2004); Daniel Möckli, *European Foreign Policy during the Cold War: Heath, Brandt, Pompidou and the Dream of Political Unity* (New York: Routledge, 2009); Maria Gäinar, *Aux origines de la diplomatie européenne. Les Neuf et la Coopération politique européenne de 1973 à 1980* (Brussels: Peter Lang, 2012).
6   Angela Romano, *From Détente in Europe to European Détente: How the West Shaped the Helsinki CSCE* (Brussels: Peter Lang, 2009).
7   Angela Romano, "The European Community and the Belgrade CSCE," in Vladimir Bilandzic, Dittmar Dahlmann and Milan Kosanovic (eds.), *From Helsinki to Belgrade: The First CSCE Follow-up Meeting and the Crisis of Détente* (Göttingen: Vandenhoeck & Ruprecht, 2012), 205–224; Angela Romano, "More Cohesive, Still Divergent: Western Europe, the US and the Madrid CSCE Follow-Up Meeting," in Kiran Klaus Patel and Kenneth Weisbrode (eds.), *European Integration and the Atlantic Community in the 1980s: Old Barriers, New Openings* (Cambridge: Cambridge University Press, 2013), 39–58; Angela Romano, "Untying Cold War Knots: The EEC and Eastern Europe in the long 1970s," *Cold War History*, 14:2 (2014), 153–173; Paola Varotto, "A Main German Question: The Evolution of the West German Mulitlateral Policy of Détente in a Decade of Major Crises and Changes, 1975–1985," unpublished PhD thesis, IMT Institute for Advanced Studies, Lucca, 2015.
8   Sara Tavani, "The Détente Crisis and the Emergence of a Common European Foreign Policy: The 'Common European Polish Policy' as a Case Study," in Claudia Hiepel (ed.), *Europe in a Globalizing World, 1970–1985* (Baden-Baden: Nomos, 2014), 49–68.

9   Loth, *Building Europe*.

10 Wilfried Loth, "Deutsche und französische Interessen auf dem Weg zu EWG und Euratom," in Andreas Wilkens (ed.), *Deutsch-französische Wirtschaftsbeziehungen 1945–1960* (Sigmaringen: Jan Thorbecke, 1997), 171–187; Loth, *Building Europe*, 62–74; Mathieu L. L. Segers, *Deutschlands Ringen mit der Relance. Die Europapolitik der BRD während der Beratungen und Verhandlungen über die Römischen Verträge* (Frankfurt am Main: Peter Lang, 2008), 244–249, 257–262 and 280–309.

11 Notes of his diplomatic adviser Jean-Marc Boegner, July 13, 1958, Charles de Gaulle, *Lettres, Notes et Carnets, Vol. 8: Juin 1958—Décembre 1960* (Paris: Plon, 1985), 73.

12 See Wilfried Loth, "De Gaulle und Europa: Eine Revision," *Historische Zeitschrift*, 253 (1991), 649–651.

13 Note of July 17, 1961, Charles de Gaulle, *Lettres, Notes et Carnets, Vol. 9: Janvier 1961–Décembre 1963* (Paris: Plon, 1986), 107–108.

14 Quoted in Jean Lacouture, *De Gaulle, vol. 3: Le souverain 1959–1970* (Paris: Éditions du Seuil, 1986), 313.

15 Note by Bœgner, August 13, 1958.

16 Comment in a conversation with Alain Peyrefitte on April 24, 1963, Alain Peyrefitte, *C'était de Gaulle, vol. 1*, (Paris: Gallimard, 1994), 430. See also Benedikt Schoenborn, "De Gaulle—adversaire ou partisan de la construction européenne ?," in André Liebich and Basil Germond (eds.), *Construire l'Europe. Mélanges en honneur du Pierre du Bois* (Geneva: Graduate Institute Publications, 2015), 97–112.

17 Comment to Alain Peyrefitte on July 13, 1960, Peyrefitte, *C'était de Gaulle*, 66–69. The widespread characterization of de Gaulle as a stubborn opponent of European integration stems from equating his short-term view with his long-term perspective. See also Wilfried Loth, *Charles de Gaulle* (Stuttgart: Kohlhammer, 2015), 223–248.

18 Heinrich Siegler (ed.), Europäische *politische Einigung. Dokumentation von Vorschlägen und Stellungnahmen 1949–1968* (Bonn: Siegler, 1968), 114–117.

19 Text of the draft in Esther Kramer, *Europäisches oder atlantisches Europa? Kontinuität und Wandel in den Verhandlungen über eine politische Union 1958–1970* (Baden-Baden: Nomos, 2003), 293–297.

20 Text of the draft in *Europa-Archiv* 19 (1964), 467–485.

21 Protocol of the conversation in *Documents Diplomatiques Français 1962–1*, Paris, 1998, 381–389.

22 On the course of the conference, see the report of Couve de Murville, ibid., 433–436. On this overall, Soutou, *L'alliance incertaine*, 188–201; Georges-Henri Soutou, "Le général de Gaulle et le plan Fouchet," in Histoire Premium/Fondation Charles-de-Gaulle (eds.), *De Gaulle en son siècle, vol. 5: L'Europe* (Paris: Institut Charles de Gaulle/ Pion/La Documentation Française, 1992), 126–143; Maurice Vaïsse, "De Gaulle, l'Italie et le projet d'union politique européenne, 1958–1963," *Revue d'histoire moderne et contemporaine*, 42:4 (1995), 658–669; Yves Stelandre, "Les Pays du Benelux, l'Europe politique et les négociations Fouchet," in Anne Deighton and Alan S. Milward (eds.), *Widening, Deepening and Acceleration: The European Economic Community, 1957–1963* (Baden-Baden: Nomos, 1999), 73–88.

23 During a vacation stay in Cadenabbia, April 30, 1962, reported by Horst Osterheld, *"Ich gehe nicht leichten Herzens ..."* in *Adenauers letzte Kanzlerjahre—ein dokumentarischer Bericht* (Mainz: Matthias Grünewald, 1986), 111.

24 Conversation of July 5, 1962, French protocol, quoted in Maurice Vaïsse, *La Grandeur. Politique étrangère du général de Gaulle, 1958–1969* (Paris: Fayard, 1998), 251.

25   Treaty text in *Europa-Archiv* 27 (1963), 84–86.

26   Conversations of January 21 and 22, 1963, provided by Vaïsse, La *Grandeur*, 255–257.

27   *Europa-Archiv* 27 (1963), 84.

28   On the discussion about Political Union during the remaining time of de Gaulle's presidency see Henning Türk, *Die Europapolitik der Großen Koalition, 1966–1969* (Munich: Oldenbourg, 2006); on the development of the Franco–German treaty see Corine Defrance and Ulrich Pfeil (eds.), *La France, l'Allemagne et le traité de l'Élysée, 1963–2013* (Paris: CNRS, 2012).

29   *Europa-Archiv* 25 (1970), D42–D44; on the course of the summit in The Hague, especially Marie-Thérèse Bitsch, "Le sommet de la Haye. La mise en route de la relance de 1969," in Wilfried Loth (ed.), *Crises and Compromises: The European Project, 1963–1969* (Baden-Baden: Nomos, 2001), 558–62; Claudia Hiepel, *Willy Brandt und Georges Pompidou. Deutsch französische Europapolitik zwischen Aufbruch und Krise* (Munich: Oldenbourg, 2012) 63–72.

30   Provided by Kramer, *Europäisches oder atlantisches Europa*, 260; on Moro's advocacy of increased political cooperation, also Antonio Varsori, *La Cenerentola d'Europa? L'Italia e l'integrazione europea dal 1947 al oggi* (Soveria Mannelli: Rubbettino, 2010), 235–241.

31   Jean de Lipkowksi's notes, January 6, 1970, AN 5AG2, 1035.

32   *Europa-Archiv* 25 (1970), D520-D524; see Smith, *Europe's Foreign and Security Policy*.

33   *Europa-Archiv* 30 (1975), D41–43; see Emmanuel Mourlon-Druol, "Filling the EEC Leadership Vacuum? The Creation of the European Council in 1974," *Cold War History*, 10:3 (2010), 315–339; Gäinar, *Aux origines de la diplomatie européenne*, 315–324; Loth, *Building Europe*, 217–221.

34   Hiepel, Willy *Brandt und Georges Pompidou*, 172–174.

35   AN, 5AG2, 1015. On this and the following, Wilfried Loth, "European Political Co-operation and European Security in the Policies of Willy Brandt and Georges Pompidou," in Jan van der Harst (ed.), *Beyond the Customs Union: The European Community's Quest for Deepening, Widening and Completion, 1969–1975* (Brussels: Bruylant, 2007), 21–34.

36   AN, 5AG 2, 1012.

37   English version in Christopher Hill and Karen E. Smith (eds.), *European Foreign Policy: Key Documents* (London: Routledge, 2000), 93–97; Ine Megens, "The December 1973 Declaration on European Identity as the Result of Team Spirit among European Diplomats," in Jan van der Harst (ed.), *Beyond the Customs Union: The European Community's Quest for Deepening, Widening and Completion, 1969–1975* (Brussels: Bruylant, 2007), 317–338; Gäinar, *Aux origines de la diplomatie européenne*, 134–147.

38   *Bulletin of the European Communities* 3 (1974), 14–19.

39   https://www.nato.int/docu/comm/49-95/c740618b.htm (last accessed on October 24, 2018).

40   Möckli, *European Foreign Policy during the Cold War*, 301–338.

41   See Romano, *From Détente in Europe to European Détente*; Angela Romano, "The Main Task of the European Political Cooperation: Fostering Détente in Europe," in Poul Villaume and Odd Arne Westad (eds.), *Perforating the Iron Curtain: European Détente, Transatlantic Relations, and the Cold War, 1965–1985* (Copenhagen: Museum Tusculanum Press, 2010), 123–141.

42   Text of the Helsinki Final Act a.o. in *Selected Documents Relating to the Problems of Security and Cooperation in Europe, 1954–77* (London: HMSO, 1977), 225–283.

43   On the consequences of the Final Act see Daniel C. Thomas, *The Helsinki Effect: International Norms, Human Rights, and the Demise of Communism* (Princeton: Princeton University Press, 2001); Matthias Peter and Hermann Wentker (eds.), *Die KSZE im Ost-West-Konflikt. Internationale Politik und gesellschaftliche Transformation, 1965–1990* (Munich: Oldenbourg, 2012).

44   Romano, "The Main Task of the European Political Cooperation," 136.

45   Vladimir Bilandžić, Dittmar Dahlmann and Milan Kosanović (eds.), *From Helsinki to Belgrade: The First CSCE Follow-up Meeting and the Crisis of Détente* (Göttingen: Vandenhoek & Ruprecht, 2012); Varotto, "A Main German Question," 78–106; Wilfried Loth, *Overcoming the Cold War: A History of Détente, 1950–1991* (Houndmills and New York: Palgrave, 2002), 149–150, 155; on the following, ibid., 160–164 and 172–174.

46   Wilfried Loth, "Helmut Schmidt, Europe and the Defense of Détente," in Hiepel (ed.), *Europe in a Globalizing World*, 89–109; Stephan Kieninger, *The Diplomacy of Détente: Cooperative Security Policies from Helmut Schmidt to George Shultz* (London and New York: Routledge, 2018).

47   Daniel Möckli, "Speaking with One Voice? The Evolution of a European Foreign Policy," in Anne Deighton and Gérard Bossuat (eds.), *The EC/EU: A World Security Actor?* (Paris: Soleb, 2007), 132–151; Gäinar, *Aux origines de la diplomatie européenne*, 377–476.

48   See Loth, *Building Europe,* 252–259.

49   Varotto, "A Main German Question," 167 and 171–172.

50   *Europa-Archiv* 36 (1981), D164; Wilfried Loth, "Deutsche Europapolitik von Helmut Schmidt bis Helmut Kohl," in Franz Knipping and Matthias Schönwald (eds.), *Aufbruch zum Europa der zweiten Generation. Die europäische Einigung 1969–1984* (Trier: Wissenschaftlicher Verlag Trier, 2004), 474–488; Hans-Dieter Lucas, "Politik der kleinen Schritte—Genscher und die deutsche Europapolitik 1974–1983," in Hans-Dieter Lucas (ed.), *Genscher, Deutschland und Europa* (Baden-Baden: Nomos, 2002), 85–113; Ulrich Rosengarten, *Die Genscher-Colombo-Initiative. Baustein für die Europäische Union* (Baden-Baden: Nomos, 2008).

51   *Bulletin of the European Communities* 6 (1983), 24–29.

52   Text in *Europa-Archiv* 41 (1986), D163-D182; on the course of the negotiations, Jean de Ruyt, *L'Acte unique européen. Commentaire* (Brussels: Édition de l' Université de Bruxelles, 1987); Ken Endo, *The Presidency of the European Commission under Jacques Delors: The Politics of Shared Leadership* (London and New York: Palgrave Macmillan, 1999), 140–151; Loth, *Building Europe,* 277–281.

53   Mitterrand's reasoning in Jacques Attali, *Verbatim III* (Paris: Fayard, 1995), 12, 68–71 and 101; Soutou, *L'alliance incertaine,* 387–389; Frédéric Bozo, "France, the Euromissiles, and the End of the Cold War," in Leopoldo Nuti, Frédéric Bozo, Marie-Pierre Rey and Bernd Rother (eds.), *The Euromissile Crisis and the End of the Cold War* (Stanford: Stanford University Press, 2015), 196–212.

54   Attali, *Verbatim III*, 287.

55   Soutou, *L'Alliance incertaine,* 391–394; Loth, *Building Europe,* 300–302.

56   Ibid., 303–304; Frederike Schotters, *Frankreich und das Ende des Kalten Krieges. Gefühlsstrategien der équipe Mitterrand 1981–1990* (Berlin and Boston: De Gruyter, 2019).

57   *Europa-Archiv* 46 (1991), D25–27.

58   *Europa-Archiv* 46 (1991), D571–574, Letter of October 14, 1991.

59   EU Treaty, Art. J.4. On the course of the government conference on the Political
     Union, Jim Cloos, Gaston Reinsch, Daniel Vignes, and Joseph Weyland, *Le traité de
     Maastricht. Genèse, analyse, commentaires* (Brussels: Bruylant, 1994), 73–93; Endo,
     The Presidency of the European Commission under Jacques Delors, 170–190; Frédéric
     Bozo, *Mitterrand, la fin de la guerre froide et l'unification allemande. De Yalta à
     Maastricht* (Paris: Editions Odile Jacob, 2005), 303–325; Wilfried Loth, "Negotiating
     the Maastricht Treaty," *Journal of European Integration History*, 19 (2013), 67–83.
60   On the course of the meeting, Françoise Carle, *Les Archives du Président. Mitterrand
     intime* (Paris: Editions du Rocher, 1998), 233–236; Pierre Favier and Michel Martin-
     Rolland, *La Décennie Mitterrand, Vol. 4: Les Déchirements, 1991–1995* (Paris:
     Éditions du Seuil, 1999), 227–233; Georges Saunier, "La négociation de Maastricht
     vue de Paris," *Journal of European Integration History*, 19 (2013), 45–65.
61   Loth, *Building Europe*, 356–362, 393–397 and 415–417.

9

The External Dimensions of the Common Agricultural Policy: From Developed to Developing Countries

Katja Seidel

The Common Agricultural Policy (CAP) is as contested beyond the borders of the European Union (EU) as it is within it, if not more. While critics of the CAP within the EU mainly focus on the costs of the policy to taxpayers and consumers, for developing countries the CAP epitomizes the selfishness of industrialized states protecting their farmers against outside competition and distorting the world market in the process. Industrialized countries that are also exporters of agricultural products, such as the United States and Australia, accuse the EU of having unfairly gained its status as exporter through subsidizing its agricultural sector and protecting it from external competition. This dual attack on the CAP suggests that the policy had and, one may add, still has a strong impact beyond the borders of the EU. Moreover, one strand in the literature draws a close connection between General Agreement on Tariffs and Trade (GATT) negotiations and the first major CAP reform, the MacSharry Reform of 1992.[1] This link between international pressure and policy reform demonstrates forcefully that a domestic policy such as the CAP not only had far-reaching external policy implications but was itself also shaped by the international context. It is the multifaceted external policy dimensions of the CAP that this chapter seeks to explore.

In spite of the salience of the external policy dimensions of the CAP, most historical studies have focused on the CAP's emergence and development as a domestic policy, highlighting the role of individual member states, the Commission, and farmers' lobbies in shaping it.[2] Some of this literature theorizes why the member states set up a protectionist common policy for agricultural products in the 1960s and why, in spite of its deficiencies in terms of budgetary costs and surplus production, the policy remained largely unchanged until the 1990s. Part of the literature explains this in terms of the emergence of the welfare state, arguing that the CAP served as a welfare policy for farmers through price and purchase guarantees.[3] Another explanation, also favored by historians, explains the policy's persistence in terms of path dependence both in terms of a tradition of agricultural protectionism and subsidies reaching back to at least the 1930s as well as the durability of the CAP's core principles (market unity, Community preference, and financial solidarity) and instruments (common prices and market organizations).[4] A third group, mainly consisting of agricultural economists but also political scientists, emphasizes that the rational choice of policymakers pursuing national interests explains the CAP more convincingly than the unintended consequences of early decisions emphasized by the path dependence approach.[5] More recently, the disproportionate power and influence of agricultural lobby groups has been added to the mix.[6] This chapter will take these explanatory tools into account when seeking to explain the underlying reasons for the CAP's protectionism and its effects on the Community's external relations.

The external policy dimension of the CAP has been explored mainly as part of the history of the GATT and the relationship between the EU and developing countries.[7] More recently, agricultural economists Josling and Tangermann have analyzed the conflictual agricultural trade relationship between the United States and the EU from its origins in the 1950s to the Transatlantic Trade and Investment Partnership (TTIP) negotiations.[8]

The European market for agricultural products has been highly coveted. After the Second World War, temporary food shortages in Europe meant that the United States became a major exporter of foodstuffs to Western Europe. Colonies and former colonies also often had preferential trade terms for agricultural products with their European colonial powers. Any common agricultural policy set up by the European Community (EC) would thus affect member states' trading partners to a greater or lesser extent, depending on the principles and nature of the policy. During the period under consideration, the EC became one of the world's largest importers and, crucially, exporters of foodstuffs with exports growing from almost 3 billion ECU in value in 1968 to more than 31 billion in 1985 and the level of self-sufficiency rising from 33 percent in 1968 to 63 percent in 1985 (Table 9.1).

Both the EC's status as an importer and its newly gained status as a major exporter of agricultural products entailed major consequences for world agricultural markets and particularly for developing countries. Economists have attempted to quantify the effects of agricultural protectionism on third countries and world trade more generally. Disagreeing over the policy's exact impact, mainly due to using different parameters in their studies, there is nevertheless agreement that the CAP's production incentives such as purchase guarantees, export subsidies and high prices distorted the world market.[9] EC exporters benefited from export subsidies, paying them the difference between the EC target price and the (usually lower) world-market price. At the same time, imports were disadvantaged as a variable import levy was imposed on products upon entry into the common market, bringing the price up to the EC internal target price. These issues set the scene for a lasting conflict between the EC and other agricultural exporters in developed and developing countries as well as between the CAP's external effects and the EC's development aims and free trade agenda. There can be little doubt that these underlying conflicts between trade liberalization versus agricultural protectionism on the one hand and preference for domestic farmers versus development aims on the other, have shaped and at times even obstructed the external relations of the EC, raising the question to what extent the CAP undermined the EC's quest to become a global civilian power.[10]

Table 9.1 External trade in agricultural products (excluding fishery and forestry products)

		Imports	Exports	Cover rate (%)
Community of Six	1968	8,822	2,950	33
	1969	9,702	3,079	31
	1970	10,583	3,557	33
	1971	10,634	3,851	36
	1972	11,560	4,446	38
Community of Nine	1973	19,755	6,895	35
	1974	22,593	8,655	38
	1975	21,807	8,851	41
	1976	27,428	9,997	36
	1977	32,610	12,041	37
	1978	31,025	12,760	40
	1979	33,354	14,524	44
	1980	33,945	18,424	54
Community of Ten	1981	37,366	25,146	67
	1982	40,175	24,557	61
	1983	41,620	25,275	60
	1984	48,623	29,957	61
	1985	48,812	31,138	63

Note: in m ECU.

Source: Eurostat—Comtrade. Reproduced from: European Commission, *Twenty Years of European Agriculture*, Brussels 1987, 44. Available at: http://ec.europa.eu/agriculture/cap-history/crisis-years-1980s/20-years_en.pdf (last accessed November 1, 2018).

In order to explore these conflicts, the chapter will focus on four areas, each opening up a different external policy dimension of the CAP. First, the chapter will look at the emergence of the CAP in the late 1950s and 1960s and consider to what extent external policy considerations played a role in shaping it. Second, it will look at how the CAP influenced trade negotiations and the EC's relationship with developed countries more generally, notably in GATT. Third, the CAP's impact on developing countries will be considered. Lastly, the chapter discusses external pressures on the CAP, which played a role in shaping and eventually reforming the policy.

The Founding Principles of the CAP: Agricultural Exceptionalism Enshrined

One answer to the puzzle of the EC's dual agenda of trade liberalization and agricultural protectionism lies in the fact that the CAP was designed as a domestic policy, with strong support for the idea of agricultural exceptionalism.

The CAP's inherent protectionism should not have come as a surprise to the European Economic Community's (EEC's) trading partners, if the CAP is considered as the continuation and indeed culmination of over one hundred years of protectionist agrarian policies in many of the major Western countries.[11] During the twentieth century, national agricultural policies became highly regulative, controlling markets and prices and shielding farmers from external competition. Food shortages following the Second World War led governments to encourage an expansion of domestic food production. Even though agricultural production reached and then exceeded pre-war levels, the income gap between farming and other economic sectors grew. To counter this development, many European countries enacted agricultural legislation aimed at achieving parity of agricultural incomes with those in other sectors of the economy.[12] While this made agricultural products more expensive, there was broad societal acceptance for such policies, particularly in countries such as France and Germany. When the EEC was set up in the late 1950s, the farming sector was still an important, albeit declining, sector of the economy.

There is little evidence that the external repercussions of a common agricultural policy played much of a role during the negotiations leading to the Treaties of Rome. The treaty articles on agriculture (Articles 38–47) did not explicitly refer to the external dimension of agriculture or trade in agricultural products. They were primarily geared towards outlining the objectives of the CAP: to increase productivity and thereby increase agricultural incomes, ensuring a good standard of living for the agricultural community; to stabilize markets; and to ensure an adequate supply for consumers at reasonable prices. Third-country access to the EEC market and external trade in agricultural products were not mentioned in the treaty, while Article 40.3 specifies measures that can be adopted for the common policy, among them the "common machinery for stabilising imports or exports."

The treaty articles dealing with external trade generally present quite a contrast to the domestic orientation of the farming clauses. The EEC's international role was laid down, among others, in Article 110 of the EEC Treaty: "By establishing a customs union between themselves, Member States aim to contribute, in the common interest, to the harmonious development of world trade, the progressive abolition of restrictions on international trade and the lowering of customs barriers." Article 111 specified that it was the Commission's role to negotiate agreements with third countries, on behalf of the Council and in consultation with the Foreign Trade Committee (the "111 Committee," later the "113 Committee"). The Commission was thus the sole negotiator in matters of commercial policy (e.g. in GATT), also concerning agriculture.

In 1960 the Commission presented its proposals for the CAP. These did not necessarily make the CAP protectionist per se, as much would depend on the level of prices the Council adopted and the level of protection from external competition it agreed. The Council, that is, the national agricultural ministers, were, however, unwilling to put their agricultural policies on a new, more liberal and outward-looking footing. High farm prices and protection from world markets were seen as necessary and justified in terms of welfare and farmers' incomes.[13] They corresponded to the wishes of farmers in the member states and, in particular French and German, policymakers.[14] At the insistence of the German government, heavily influenced by the Deutsche

Bauernverband, the basic framework of the CAP, the market organizations became characterized by high internal prices relative to world-market prices, maintained through a system of intervention buying, variable import levies and export subsidies. The crucial cereals price, agreed in December 1964, was fixed well above the world-market price level at an amount that was close to the German domestic price level. The incentive for farmers to increase production to cash in on these high prices was thus considerable. These principles and instruments of the CAP were bound to have a profound impact on the EEC's relationship with third countries. "The agricultural welfare state and world trade liberalization were not easily made complementary," commented Knudsen.[15]

Arguably, the EEC's status as a major importer of agricultural products in the 1950s and early 1960s made it more justifiable to design a CAP favorable to EEC farmers. This agricultural protectionism enshrined in the CAP became further entrenched as the CAP became one of the Community's first major working policies; a consensus emerged between member states and the Commission that its substance was to be defended at (almost) all costs.

The carefully balanced CAP framework as it had emerged during the 1960s was, however, challenged by external events—one of them being the enlargement to new member states, discussed in Eirini Karamouzi's chapter. As each candidate country brought with it its own set of agricultural interests and trading networks, the agricultural chapter in these negotiations was notoriously difficult. The United Kingdom's traditional ties with the Commonwealth, for example, meant that it imported many of its foodstuffs from these countries. In the accession negotiations special arrangements had to be made, for example, for New Zealand dairy and sheep meat exports to Britain.[16] However, the substance of the CAP was never challenged.

The CAP in International Trade Negotiations: The GATT

It was in the context of GATT that the CAP first became the subject of major international negotiations. In the period under consideration the Community participated in four GATT rounds: with each one, outside pressure on the CAP increased. Remarkably, the CAP survived the first three rounds with its core principles intact. The EEC/EC refused point blank to trade the CAP for an agreement on tariff reductions on industrial goods and largely got away with it. This section considers why the Community defended the CAP at the risk of alienating its trading partners and how it managed to do so.

The relationship between the United States and the EEC/EC was at the heart of the first three negotiation rounds, the Dillon (1960–1961), Kennedy (1964–1967) and Tokyo (1973–1979) Rounds, and tested their "special" relationship. While the transatlantic relationship remained fundamental in the Uruguay Round (1986–1994), other players became increasingly important.

In theory, agriculture was subject to GATT rules like any other economic sector. In practice, at the insistence of the United States, several articles in the GATT agreement of 1947 provided exemptions for the farming sector. Article XI, for example, "permitted import quotas on agricultural products if domestic production restrictions were in force" to limit domestic output.[17] In 1955 the United States obtained a waiver effectively allowing the government to protect the domestic market even in cases where it did not limit supply; this waiver remained in place for almost forty years and was used to restrict imports of sugar, peanuts and dairy products.[18] Finally, Article XVI permitted export subsidies for primary goods, including agricultural products, as long as subsidizing countries did not have more than an (undefined) equitable share of the market for these products. Owing to US initiative, agriculture thus effectively obtained a special status in GATT. US criticism of the CAP therefore at times lacked credibility and limited the effectiveness of its calls for liberalization of trade in agriculture.

Concerned about the potential effects of the common market and the potential protectionism of the emerging CAP, the US administration initiated the Dillon Round to bring the Community to the negotiating table. US negotiators demanded guarantees such as binding ceilings not to be exceeded by the variable import levies to be put into place by the EEC, as well as guaranteed access to the EEC market based on historical market shares.[19] The EEC refused to accept restrictions on a policy that was still in the making. However, to show goodwill, it agreed to zero- or low-duty access for US soya beans, soya bean meal, other oilseeds and manioc—a decision that the Europeans would come to regret later as imports of these products increased greatly during the 1970s in the form of cheap animal feed. The main reason cited for American acquiescence to the EEC's refusal to limit the CAP was Washington's general support for European integration, which overrode their trade interests.[20] The fact that the CAP was not yet operational and its effects were difficult to foresee certainly played a role, too.

The first trade conflict emerged in 1963–1964. The infamous "Chicken War" broke out when, in line with its obligations under the CAP, the German government raised duties on poultry imports and thus effectively withdrew a tariff concession from which the United States benefited most.[21] The US government retaliated and revoked tariff concessions on a number of products it imported from the EEC. While the issue seemed trivial, the Chicken War set the tone for the increasingly fraught relationship between the United States and the EEC concerning agricultural trade.

In the GATT Kennedy Round the United States thus expected progress on the issue of agriculture, insisting that "for the first time since its inception, agriculture must be brought fully within the rules and disciplines of the GATT."[22] Notwithstanding this threatening rhetoric, it is doubtful whether the United States, which also subsidized its farm sector, would have itself agreed to what it demanded of the EEC/EC. Still, both partners differed fundamentally in their views on how to approach agriculture; for instance the EEC/EC proposed basing the negotiations on their proposal of *montant de soutien*, in other words quantifying farm support and fixing it at current levels. This would allow the contracting parties to choose their methods of support up to a certain threshold.[23] In addition, the Community proposed commodity agreements for cereals, beef and veal, some dairy products, sugar and possibly oilseeds to stabilize world market prices. The US government rejected both proposals and aimed for a lowering of the EEC/EC's agricultural support mechanisms instead. In retrospect the EEC/EC proposal does not seem so outlandish, given that in the 1980s with the producer support estimate (PSE) the Organisation for Economic Co-operation and

Development (OECD) developed a method to calculate the levels of agricultural support. Tracy speculates that had the United States agreed to negotiate with the EEC/EC on the basis of the *montant de soutien*, it would have been able to exert some influence over the level of CAP protection.[24]

When the Kennedy Round started in earnest in May 1964, the CAP was still lacking its cornerstone: the common cereals price. This affected the GATT round, causing a delay to the start of negotiations and hampering its progress. Some EEC member states joined the United States in trying to use the GATT as a lever to put pressure on the German government to commit to a common price level for cereals, taking advantage of its interest in a GATT agreement on tariff cuts for industrial products.[25]

The link between the issue of the common cereals price and progress in the GATT negotiations—ironically one the German government had itself lobbied for—increased the pressure on Germany to finally agree to the Community cereals price. It did so in December 1964.[26] The fact that the German government successfully pushed for a high cereals price, 60 percent above the world market price, shows, however, that its arguably strong interests in trade liberalization for industrial products did not interfere with the wish to protect its domestic agricultural sector. The effect of the Kennedy Round on the substance of the CAP was thus minimal. So while the Six were under pressure to finalize the CAP, the policy they agreed on turned out to be highly protectionist and non-negotiable: the opposite of what the United States had hoped to achieve.

The GATT Tokyo Round (1973–1979) unfolded against the backdrop of a major economic and monetary crisis hitting Western economies in the aftermath of the 1973 oil shock. Facing economic and financial difficulties, the United States arguably had an even greater interest in opening up markets to its exports. From the 1950s US agricultural exports increased steadily; in the first half of the 1970s alone the United States' share of world agricultural exports rose from 12 to 16 percent.[27] The CAP had become a major obstacle to US expansion in agricultural trade. Moreover, the EC had now become a net exporter of many products and was becoming a global competitor to traditional exporters such as the United States, Australia, Canada, and Argentina (Table 9.1). Not surprisingly, the CAP became a bone of contention during the Tokyo Round and was attacked by politicians and negotiators from the United States but also from other countries such as Australia.[28] At the same time the world food crisis of the mid-1970s (temporarily) reversed the trend of falling commodity prices. Thanks to the CAP, food supply to consumers in the EC remained stable during this period and food prices were maintained even below world market prices. From the perspective of EC policymakers there was thus little incentive to give in to the pressure of the US administration and put the CAP on the negotiation table.

Before the start of the negotiations, the Community had decided that the "specific nature" of agriculture meant that the agricultural chapter had to be kept separate from negotiations on industrial goods.[29] The Community successfully asserted its view and agriculture became one of the six negotiating groups. In the light of the world food crisis the EC was interested in a more stable world market, in particular for cereals, and thought that this could be achieved through international commodity agreements. This was opposed by the United States, which was keen to achieve a ban on export subsidies. This basic conflict affected the progress of the entire negotiations and led to an impasse of nearly two years, which was only resolved in the summer of 1977 when the new administration of US President Jimmy Carter prioritized a successful outcome of the Tokyo Round. For this to come about, the Americans had to compromise on agriculture as the EC refused to alter the substance of the CAP.

The Tokyo Round brought rifts in the Commission to the fore, exposing an underlying conflict between those keen to protect the domestic agricultural markets and those advocating liberalization of external trade. For the first time, officials from the Directorate-General for Agriculture (DG VI) negotiating in the agriculture group were joined by officials from the Directorate-General for External Relations (DG I). Inevitably this resulted in arguments about competences and the freedom of action of DG VI in the negotiations, which the negotiators from DG I believed were too large and ultimately harmful to the Community's trade interests.[30] While the Community was torn between advancing free trade and protecting the status quo in agriculture, the latter had become a priority in the crisis-ridden 1970s—for a deeply political reason: in a decade that gave rise to the term "Eurosclerosis," the CAP was very much seen as "one of the few really 'common' policies" and one that held the Community together.[31]

Not surprisingly, the results of the Tokyo Round were limited and included product agreements for dairy and beef as well as several bilateral agreements with individual countries on specific concessions on the import and export of particular agricultural products and the reduction of some tariffs.[32] However, it also resulted in a "Code on Subsidies and Countervailing Duties" giving a more precise definition to GATT Article XVI by requiring, for agricultural products "[…] not to grant directly or indirectly any export subsidy on certain primary products which results in the signatory granting such subsidy having more than an equitable share of world export trade in such product […]."[33] This potentially put a brake on unlimited subsidies for agricultural exports and would potentially pose a problem for the EC in future negotiations.

Indeed, liberalizing agricultural trade became one of the major issues of the Uruguay Round (1986–1994) for the United States and fourteen so-called "fair trading" nations—the Cairns Group.[34] While the United States adopted a maximalist "zero option," demanding the phasing out of all agricultural import restrictions over ten years and of all subsidies that directly or indirectly affected trade, the Community was obviously opposed to the total elimination of import restrictions, but was prepared to discuss a "progressive, concerted, substantial" reduction in subsidies. There was thus some common ground with the US position, which in fact diverged widely from actual domestic US farm policy. The proposal may thus have been launched to position the United States in the driving seat of the negotiations as a progressive and reform-orientated actor.[35] It must be seen in the context of the Reagan administration's wish to reform US farm policy and the long-established aim to further increase exports (though with the EC, the United States had always maintained a positive trade balance in agricultural products).[36] Unsurprisingly, negotiations soon reached an impasse, affecting progress in other areas of the GATT talks. Disagreement over agriculture, by then only a small part of the EC member states' gross domestic product, thus put the negotiations in jeopardy. This time the issue could only be resolved with a major reform of the CAP, discussed below.

The GATT negotiations up until the Uruguay Round saw domestic farm interests compete with trade interests at the expense of a deteriorating relationship with major trading partners, particularly the United States. Josling and Tangermann argue that the Cold War context meant that the shared external policy objectives of the United States and the EC prevented a further escalation of these trade conflicts.[37] The end of the Cold War may thus also have encouraged the United States to launch a more determined attack on the CAP. The EC's liberal policy on trade in industrial products was no longer compatible with agricultural protectionism.

The CAP and Developing Countries

The CAP and International Commodity Agreements

International commodity agreements were first concluded in the inter-war period as an attempt to regulate and stabilize prices and production in international product markets.[38] In the post-war period, negotiations on these agreements were conducted in the framework of the United Nations Conference on Trade and Development (UNCTAD). Unlike GATT, which concerned more the developed countries, the negotiations in UNCTAD involved developed and developing countries.

An analysis of international commodity agreements such as the International Sugar Agreement (ISA) can thus serve to illustrate two of the CAP's external relations dimensions: first, it can highlight the extent to which the Community's negotiating strategy on the international stage reflected the domestic focus of the CAP and, second, and related to this, it allows the potential conflict of interests between domestic interests and development aims to be drawn out.

Negotiations for the ISA had a wide geographical scope and encompassed communist countries such as the Soviet Union and Cuba. Those countries had not recognized the EC and were now encountering the Community, represented by the Commission, at the negotiating table. These talks were thus an opportunity for the EC to raise its profile and become an internationally recognized global actor. Moreover, it presented an opportunity for the Commission, leading the negotiations on behalf of the Community, to prove its worth.

The ISA is chosen as an example here as it was one of the oldest commodity agreements and one of the negotiations in which the Community participated early on. It had existed since the late 1930s and was an attempt, albeit not a very successful one, to regulate and stabilize the world sugar market by agreeing export quotas for producers and minimum prices. After the war it was revived and became linked to high-flying ideas of a more equitable distribution of food and income for producers in poorer countries, but these were soon countered by domestic farmers' interests, for example in the United States, and later the EEC/EC.[39] Indeed, in the sugar market, the CAP saw the amount of EC sugar rise above the level of consumption; between the mid-1960s and mid-1980s sugar production of the EC-12 increased by 70 percent, and the EC-12 went from importing 2.1 million tonnes annually in 1965–1967 to exporting 3.2 million tonnes in 1986–1988 (Table 9.2 shows the increase in self-sufficiency in the main agricultural crops, including sugar, between 1973–1974 and 1982–1983).[40] From the 1980s to the early 1990s the EC was the world's largest sugar producer (see Figure 9.1). Support policies for sugar production in the EC, but also the United States, thus affected the world sugar market and the ISA became a forum where the interests of developed and developing countries clashed, as well as those of exporters and importers.

Until the mid-1960s, EEC/EC member states held individual membership of the ISA; this changed when the sugar market came under the CAP and the Community took over representation of member states at the UN sugar conferences.[41] In 1968 for the first time, the Community participated in the negotiations to a new sugar agreement. The new kid on the block saw its negotiation position heavily criticized for what was perceived as selfishness. According to former Food and Agriculture Organisation (FAO) Director Albert Viton:

> Each of the delegates of the Ten [Exporters' committee of non-EEC states formed during the negotiations] spoke in blunt terms on the destructive effects of the Community's subsidies on the rural economies of the traditional cane sugar exporters and appealed for more responsible policies internationally.[42]

Viton alleged the EC position had been heavily influenced by the sugar beet lobby. Sugar beet producers, usually rather wealthy and well-organized farmers, had clout among the farming community as a whole as well as among the political establishment, particularly in France.[43] It is thus quite likely that the Community took their interests into account. In the end, the EC did not join the ISA in 1968; the EC delegation had

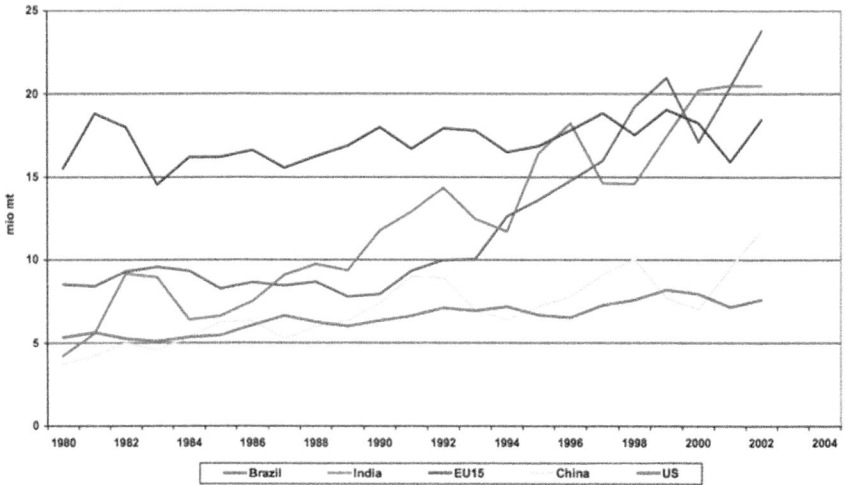

Figure 9.1 Sugar (raw equiv.) production 1980–2004, main sugar producers.

Source: European Commission, *Agricultural Commodity Markets Past Developments and Outlook*, February 2006, 63.

Table 9.2 Self-sufficiency levels in the EC

Product	1973–1974	1982–1983
Cereals	91	109
Sugar	90	141
Milk powder (whole milk)	231	317
Milk (concentrated)	130	177
Butter	98	147
Beef	96	105
Poultry meat	102	111

Source: Commission des Communautés européennes, *La situation de l'agriculture dans la Communauté—Rapport 1985.*

difficulties agreeing on a common negotiation position and the other participants at the conference, resenting the expansion of sugar production within the EC, incentivized by the CAP, were not prepared to offer an export quota high enough to be deemed acceptable to the EC.

While in 1968 the EC only aspired to becoming a sugar exporter, by the late 1970s this had become a reality. Oversupply with the commodity meant that world market prices were very low, hitting sugar-producing developing countries that did not benefit from the preferential treatment granted to developing Commonwealth and African, Caribbean and Pacific (ACP) countries (ex-colonies of EC member states) under the Lomé Conventions, ensuring that their sugar exports to the EC received the same prices paid to Community producers. At the same time, the EC refused to limit exports, for example by lowering prices to disincentivize domestic production of sugar beet. Again, Viton put this down to the influence of the sugar beet producers and processors.[44] The Community thus prioritized short-term gains for its farmers, missing out on the opportunity to contribute to a more equitable world commodity trading regime and to put into practice the pro-development rhetoric prevailing in Brussels.

While the Community was not able to join the ISA in 1968, the negotiations were a success with regard to acceptance of the Community as an international actor. The Commission's chief negotiator recalled how the 1968 conference was considered a breakthrough in the Community's external relations as other states, in particular the Soviet Union and Eastern European countries, had to accept the Community as a member of the organization, speaking on behalf of EC member states.[45] Moreover, the 1968 ISA contained a clause providing the legal basis for future EC membership of the ISA, which until then had only accepted individual states as members. The EC joined the ISA in 1984.

Development Policy Versus Agricultural Policy

The economic impact of the CAP on poorer countries has been a hotly debated subject to which there is no simple answer. A considerable number of developing countries, the ACP countries, have benefited to varying degrees from preferential access to the EC market for some of their agricultural products, while others have been excluded from such arrangements. The CAP's protectionism thus affected developing countries in different ways and to different degrees. One major channel was the depressing effect exports of EC agricultural surpluses had on world market prices. Not having preferential access to the EC market meant that many developing countries depended on selling their produce on the world market, where they often achieved only very low prices (which on the other hand tended to benefit consumers in these countries).

There appears to be no easy answer to the issue of subsidized agriculture in the developed world. Raikes concludes that a complete removal of EC farm protection (and indeed the removal of such protection from all developed nations) would, first, be unrealistic and, second, of limited value to developing countries.[46] In any case, this chapter cannot deliver an econometric analysis of the economic damage or benefits of the CAP to developing countries. Instead, this section will study to what extent the interests of developing countries, mainly the ACP states, were considered when setting up the CAP and how the relationship between the EEC/EC and ACP states in agricultural trade was shaped by the association agreements from the 1960s to the early 1990s. Did development aims prevail over interests represented by the domestic farm sector as well as those of different member states?

In 1957, on the initiative of France, the founding members of the EEC decided to maintain close economic ties with their colonies, or soon to be ex-colonies, and agreed to inscribe an association of African states into the Treaty of Rome. Often, these countries were dependent on trade links with their respective colonial power, mostly exporting agricultural products as opposed to finished industrial goods. With many of these countries achieving independence in the early 1960s, the relationship between the EEC/EC and the former colonies had to be reformed, resulting in the association agreements Yaoundé I and II (1963 and 1969), and later the Lomé Conventions (1975 and after). The Yaoundé Agreements were preferential trade arrangements with funding from the European Development Fund (EDF). Yaoundé I came into being while the CAP was being drawn up. It is thus interesting to examine whether the two policies overlapped in any way and whether the CAP accommodated agricultural interests of former colonies.

Early negotiations with African countries reveal a paradox, in that the EEC expected African countries to liberalize their agricultural sectors while at the same time the Community was setting up a highly protectionist agricultural policy. The aid given to African countries by the EEC was to facilitate rapid modernization of their production methods and increase their production.[47] This attitude of the Community towards former colonies can partly be explained by the reticence of member states such as Germany and the Netherlands to continue supporting (former) French colonies. While France would have preferred to uphold its current trading system, giving preferential access to products from former colonies, Germany and the Netherlands "branded the existing overprice system as colonial and backward" and maintained that political independence also entailed economic independence.[48] Thus, diversification efforts and speedy integration of African countries into the world market were the Community's answer.

However, the wording of the Yaoundé Agreement raised hopes that "the adequate consideration of the associated states' interests in the preparation and determination of the Common Agricultural Policy" (Article 11) would result in more considerate treatment. Senegal and other states thus expected that CAP regulations would be more favorable to them and, importantly, that they could exert some influence over them. In this they underestimated the divisions among EEC member states, with Germany and the Netherlands in favor of a clear distinction between agricultural policy and development aid. Another issue was that, as in external trade policy, the two domains were looked after institutionally by two different directorates-general: DG VI in charge of the CAP, and DG VIII dealing with development aid.

Rempe's study of Senegal can serve as an example how a coalition of member states, and to an extent DG VI, pushed for a complete separation of the CAP from development aid. The French colonial legacy meant that peanut production and export had become the main source of income for Senegal, constituting 75 percent of income in the agricultural sector and half of the active agricultural land. Up to 90 percent of the economically active population worked in this sector in the early 1960s.[49] Under French rule a trade system was established whereby France exchanged peanut products for other products; this was replaced, following independence, by a system of minimum prices and sales volume.[50]

The colonial legacy for the Senegalese economy was heavy and was threatened by the EEC's plan to establish a market organization for oils and fats. The stakes were high: if Senegal's interests were not considered in the market organization, it could have lost the EEC market. Hence, the Senegalese government tried to influence the debates on the market organization and obtain price guarantees and a market share for its peanut products, relying on Article 11 of the Yaoundé Agreement. However, member states were not keen to discuss CAP measures with associated countries during the development stage. The "consideration" of the interests of developing countries remained a dead letter and member states and the Commission proceeded to negotiate behind closed doors, merely informing associated countries about developments rather than consulting with them.

The Commission was aware of Senegal's problems and DG VIII tried to lobby DG VI to propose a favorable deal for ACP countries in the CAP regulations.[51] DG VI followed suit and proposed preferential treatment for oilseed producers from associated countries. However, the only delegation prepared to back this in the Council and the Committee of Permanent Representatives (COREPER) was France, the other member states arguing that development aid was already sufficient and refusing to accommodate third party interests within CAP regulations.

Once the new regulation on a market organization for oilseeds entered into force on July 1, 1967, Senegal would not benefit from French subsidies anymore. The member states had decided that associated states' concerns were to be dealt with in a separate regulation. Germany's hard-line position meant that the Council agreement reached at the end of June 1967 set the reference price at 186 Units of Account (UoA) (Senegal had pushed for a minimum of 190 UoA) and limited the benefits to 80 percent of oilseeds exported to Europe up to a total sum of 13 million UoA.[52] In January 1968 Senegal was forced to start selling the bulk of its peanut production on the world market and immediately felt the effect of its volatility with peanut prices hitting an all-time low.

For the newly independent African states the Yaoundé Agreements thus turned out to be a raw deal compared to their previous trade relationship with France. Hopes that the CAP would compensate for this were briefly raised but then shattered. Member states were reluctant to set a precedent with the treatment of Senegalese peanut production, expecting that other countries would also ask for a better deal for their main products in the CAP framework. The attempt of developing countries to be included into the CAP and to shape the system from within failed miserably as these states lacked unity, knowledge of the EEC system and, crucially, effective backing by EEC actors. The CAP was not bent to accommodate development aims. Instead, special arrangements such as association agreements including import quotas and market share for African, and later ACP countries came to represent the development side of agricultural trade relations.

While the position of African countries was not very strong in the Yaoundé Agreements, this changed in the first Lomé Convention. Negotiations for the Lomé Convention between the EC and 46 ACP states began in 1973 and ended in February 1975. The Lomé negotiations became necessary as with the accession of the United Kingdom poorer Commonwealth members needed to be incorporated into the EC's association framework. Additionally, the negotiations were intended to profoundly change the Community's development cooperation policy, particularly regarding the stabilization of commodity markets.[53] More generally, the balance between North and South had changed (ever so slightly) in the latter's favor: the growing assertiveness of developing countries became tangible in the founding of the UN's G77 in 1964 and the UN General Assembly adopting the Charter of Economic Rights and Duties of States in 1974.[54] A reform of development cooperation was agreed at the Paris summit in 1972, aiming at "a comprehensive development cooperation policy on a global scale."[55]

The Lomé Convention was quite favorable to ACP states in that there were no reciprocal trade requirements: ACP exports would enjoy free access to the Common Market but the reverse did not apply. The sugar protocol annexed to the Convention stipulated that sugar from ACP countries benefited from the price and market guarantees usually reserved for EC producers. The Lomé Convention for the first time put the interests of developing countries on a par with that of European farmers—but the EC only had to accept a small amount of imports and many of the products, such as tropical fruits, lacked competition from European producers.

As in external trade, the development aims and rhetoric contradicted the practice of the EC's agricultural policy. They were considered as two distinct areas, serving different clienteles, and the EC had difficulties—even if it was often willing—in reaching a compromise between the two.

External Pressures on the CAP: Adaptation and Reform

The documents of the European Commission from the mid-1970s to the 1980s leave little doubt that the CAP was perceived to have entered a period of crisis. The costs of the policy had spiraled out of control and threatened on several occasions to bankrupt the Community. The declining economic importance of the agricultural sector and the falling numbers of farm workers made it more and more difficult to justify the high levels of spending, which at its peak reached 90 percent of the EC budget in 1970.[56] In a more general and global context, it is certainly appropriate to regard the economic crisis of the 1970s and early 1980s and the perceived lack of competitiveness of the European economies compared to their American and Japanese counterparts as the backdrop against which state-subsidized and highly dirigiste policies such as the CAP were fast losing their legitimacy.

Agricultural exceptionalism had been justifiable (and affordable) in the 1960s, in the context of the rise of the welfare state and the exceptional post-war economic boom in Western Europe. The CAP of the 1980s was in this respect an outdated rusty vessel having to navigate increasingly turbulent waters. The disruption was intensified not least by the triumph of the neoliberalism of the so-called Chicago school. The political implications of the widespread pursuit of neoliberal economic and fiscal policies were important and generally called into doubt state subsidies, which were seen as causing waste and resource misallocation. In international relations neoliberals promoted free trade, including in agricultural products. The effects on the CAP were not immediate but they arguably triggered a reconsideration of the policy and its instruments.

The relationship between external and internal factors facilitating policy reform is a complex one that cannot be discussed in any depth in this chapter. However, there are strong indicators that the external dimension impacted on the CAP and provided additional pressure (or opportunity, depending on the viewpoint) to adapt and even fundamentally change the policy.

In 1982, at the first GATT ministerial meeting since the end of the Tokyo Round, the United States and other major agricultural exporters took a tough stance on agricultural subsidies. The OECD also emerged as a major player in agricultural policy debates during this period. At the 1982 Ministerial Council, the OECD Committees for Agriculture and Trade were charged to examine problems of agricultural trade and identify farm policy measures that contributed to those problems.[57] This was done through extensive statistical work and development of a tool to measure agricultural subsidies—the PSE. It made agricultural subsidies more transparent and comparable across countries. With one of the highest PSE indexes, there could no longer be any doubt that the CAP was one of the most protectionist agricultural policies in the OECD.[58]

Indeed, the Commission referred to the link between the CAP and trade more frequently from the mid-1980s onwards. In 1986 it wrote: "The world's agricultural powers have ... a clear responsibility to reorient their policies in such a way as to permit domestic adjustment of the agricultural sector ... and to reduce the risks of trade conflict."[59] The Commission did not single out the Community, but was nevertheless including it in a discourse of reform and change. While one reason was certainly the upcoming new GATT round opening in 1986, the negative image of the CAP among the EC's trading partners was another.

It was thus predictable that the Uruguay Round would pose a serious threat to the CAP. The pressure came, as outlined above, from the US Reagan Administration and the Cairns group of "fair-trading" nations. The literature debates to what extent the GATT negotiations and trade concerns (as opposed to, for example, budgetary pressures) contributed to the reform of the CAP.[60] Naturally, when preparing the CAP reform in early 1991, the Commission tried to downplay the influence of external factors on the reforms proposed by Agricultural Commissioner Ray MacSharry. However, the reform proposal of February 1991 came suspiciously timely after the collapse of the GATT Ministerial Meeting in Brussels in December 1990, which, instead of concluding them, led to a suspension of the trade talks mostly due to the unresolved issues in agriculture.

Moreover, a key concern of the Uruguay Round was the "decoupling" of prices from farm incomes, a practice on which the CAP was built and which had such distorting effects on the world market. And indeed, the MacSharry Reform opened a new chapter in the CAP by slashing prices for, in a first instance, grains and beef, but cushioning farmers' income losses with direct payments. While the reform did not make the CAP any cheaper, it removed the incentive to increase production. The EU has since extended this principle in subsequent reforms in the early 2000s under Commissioner Franz Fischler. Thanks to the MacSharry Reform, the EU was able to agree to the "Agreement on Agriculture" in late 1993, entering into force in 1995. It provided, among other things, for a 20 percent reduction in market support, the tariffication of non-tariff border measures and reduction of these tariffs by an average of 36 percent. Since the MacSharry and subsequent Fischler reforms, the CAP, while no facilitator, has at least been much less of an external trade obstacle.

Conclusion

It is paradoxical that an agricultural sector of steadily shrinking economic importance was subject to enormous efforts by the Community to protect it in international trade relations. The roots of this paradox lie in the ideological and ideational importance of agriculture in Europe, the agricultural protectionism enshrined in the CAP mechanisms, and the bargaining power of farmers' lobbies and farm ministers who were very successful in defending the status quo. The CAP as one of the Community's first fully functioning common policies embodying European integration achievements added a further stimulus to ring-fence the policy.

The defence of the CAP came at a cost: the agricultural protectionism displayed in international relations and negotiations undermined the EC's image as a champion of trade liberalization even though with industrial products the EC pushed for low tariffs and the removal of non-tariff barriers. The relationship with the United States clearly suffered; one important source for the souring of transatlantic relations in the 1970s has to be the conflict over agricultural trade. Likewise, the subsidies to farmers in wealthy industrialized nations were a bitter pill to swallow for developing countries, first and foremost the former colonies of member states whose agricultural systems had been shaped by the colonial trade system benefiting the colonial power. If their agricultural interests were accommodated, this was done in special arrangements. The CAP framework itself was not up for negotiation. Only since the Uruguay Round and with the continuous reform of the CAP has agriculture become less of an obstacle in international trade relations. This has allowed the EU to gain initiative and broaden its room for maneuver.

If the EC, and later the EU, is to be defined as a civilian power, then the complexities of the CAP in terms of the decision-making process within the Community, the policy's diverse aims and its function as the "glue" of European integration long prevented it playing a more proactive role in the international arena. In terms of relations with third countries, mainly developing ones, the CAP certainly contributed to the EU's international role, but at the same time reined in its freedom of action and limited its bargaining power.

Notes

1   Carsten Daugbjerg and Alan Swinbank, "The Politics of CAP Reform: Trade Negotiations, Institutional Settings and Blame Avoidance," *Journal of Common Market Studies*, 45:1 (2007), 1–22; Adrian Kay, *The Reform of the Common Agricultural Policy: The Case of the MacSharry Reforms* (Wallingford: CAB International, 1998).

2   Ann-Christina L. Knudsen, *Farmers on Welfare: The Making of Europe's Common Agricultural Policy* (Ithaca: Cornell University Press, 2009); Kiran Klaus Patel, *Europäisierung wider Willen? Die Bundesrepublik Deutschland in der Agrarintegration der EWG 1955–1973* (Munich: Oldenbourg, 2009); Carine Germond, "The Franco-German Tandem and the Making of the CAP, 1963–1966," *Journal of European Integration History*, 16:2 (2002), 25–44.

3   Adam Sheingate, *The Rise of the Agricultural Welfare State: Institutions and Interest Group Power in the United States, France, and Japan* (Princeton: Princeton University Press, 2001); Knudsen, *Farmers on Welfare*. For a critique of this approach see Mark Spoerer, "Agricultural Protection and Support in the European Economic Community, 1962–92: Rent seeking or Welfare Policy?" *European Review of Economic History*, 19 (2015), 195–214.

4   Adrian Kay, "Path Dependency and the CAP," *Journal of European Public Policy*, 10 (2003), 405–420; Guido Thiemeyer, "The Failure of the Green Pool and the Success of the CAP: Long Term Structures in European Agricultural Integration in the 1950s and 1960s," in Kiran Klaus Patel (ed.), *Fertile Ground for Europe? The History of European Integration and the Common Agricultural Policy since 1945* (Baden-Baden: Nomos, 2009), 47–59; Katja Seidel, *The Process of Politics in Europe: The Rise of European Elites and Supranational Institutions* (London: I.B. Tauris, 2010). For the theoretical approach, see Paul Pierson, *Politics in Time: History, Institutions, and Social Analysis* (Oxford: Oxford University Press, 2004).

5   Ulrich Koester and Stefan Tangermann, "The European Community," in Fred Sanderson (ed.), *Agricultural Protectionism in the Industrialized World* (Washington DC: Resources for the Future, 1990), 64–110; Andrew Moravcsik, *The Choice for Europe: Social Purpose and State Power from Messina to Maastricht* (Ithaca: Cornell University Press, 1998).

6   Carine Germond, "Preventing Reform? Farm Interest Groups and the Common Agricultural Policy, 1958–1984," in Wolfram Kaiser and Jan-Henrik Meyer (eds.), *Non-State Actors in European Integration, 1958–1992: From Polity Building to*

Transnational Politics and Policy-Making (London: Palgrave Macmillan, 2013), 106–128; Dieter Konold, *Agrarinteressen als Verhandlungsmasse: Die Handelspolitik der Europäischen Union zwischen nationalen Präferenzen und internationalen Zwängen* (Baden-Baden: Nomos, 2015).

7   On the EC/EU, agriculture, and the GATT see Lucia Coppolaro, *The Making of a World Trading Power: The European Economic Community (EEC) in the GATT Kennedy Round Negotiations (1963–67)* (Farnham: Ashgate, 2013); Gilbert R. Winham, *International Trade and the Tokyo Round Negotiation* (Princeton: Princeton University Press, 1986); Katja Seidel, "The Challenges of Enlargement and GATT Trade Negotiations: Explaining the Resilience of the European Community's Common Agricultural Policy in the 1970s," The International History Review (February 2019). Timothy Josling, Stefan Tangermann and Thorald Warley, *Agriculture in the GATT* (Basingstoke: Palgrave Macmillan, 1996). On the EC/EU, the CAP and developing countries, see Philip Raikes, *Modernising Hunger: Famine, Food Surplus & Farm Policy in the EEC & Africa* (Portsmouth: Catholic Institute for International Relations, 1988); Guia Migani, "Development Aid: Historic Priorities and New Dynamics," in Eric Bussière, Vincent Dujardin, Michel Dumoulin, Piers Ludlow, Jan Willem Brouwer and Pierre Tilly (eds.), *The European Commission 1973–1986: History and Memory of an Institution* (Luxembourg: Publications Office of the European Union, 2014), 393–411; Giuliano Garavini, *After Empires: European Integration, Decolonization, and the Challenge from the Global South, 1957–1986* (Oxford: Oxford University Press, 2012).

8   Timothy E. Josling and Stefan Tangermann, *Transatlantic Food and Agricultural Trade Policy: 50 Years of Conflict and Convergence* (Cheltenham: Edward Elgar Publishing, 2015).

9   Raikes, *Modernising Hunger*; David Blandford, "The Costs of Agricultural Protection and the Difference Free Trade Would Make," in Sanderson (ed.), *Agricultural Protectionism*, 398–432.

10 E.g. Sophie Meunier and Kalypso Nicolaides, "The European Union as a Conflicted Trade Power," *Journal of European Public Policy*, 13:6 (2006), 906–925.

11 Michael Tracy, *Government and Agriculture in Western Europe* (New York: New York University Press, 1989).

12 For the German case see Patel, *Europäisierung wider Willen*; also Tracy, *Government and Agriculture*, 228–231.

13 Knudsen, *Farmers on Welfare*, 144.

14 Jan Van der Harst, "The Common Agricultural Policy: A Leading Field of Action," in Michel Dumoulin (ed.), *The European Commission 1958–72: History and Memories* (Luxembourg: Publications Office of the European Union, 2007), 327–328.

15 Knudsen, *Farmers on Welfare*, 146.

16 Cf. Sir Michael Franklin (ed.), *Joining the CAP: The Agricultural Negotiations for British Accession to the European Economic Community, 1961–1973* (Oxford: Peter Lang, 2010).

17 Tracy, *Government and Agriculture*, 347.

18 Ramesh Sharma, "Agriculture in the GATT: A Historical Account," in FAO, *Multilateral Trade Negotiations on Agriculture: A Resource Manual*, no date, at: http://www.fao.org/docrep/003/x7352e/x7352e04.htm (last accessed October 25, 2018).

19 Josling and Tangermann, *Transatlantic Food and Agricultural Trade Policy*, 26.

20 Ibid.

21 Winham, *Tokyo Round*, 153.

22 Josling, Tangermann and Warley, *Agriculture in the GATT*, 54.

23 Tracy, *Government and Agriculture*, 348.

24 Ibid.

25 Coppolaro, *The Making of a World Trading Power*, 4.

26 Ibid.; see Patel, *Europäisierung wider Willen*, 256; Cf. Patel, *Europäisierung wider Willen*, 251–281 for the complexities of the German government's tenacious resistance and finally acceptance of the common cereals price.

27 Winham, *Tokyo Round*, 150.

28 Historical Archives of the European Commission (HAEC), BAC 48 1984 234, Leslie Fielding, Note to Mr D Hannay, Australia's Relations with the Community: Policy Statement by the Australian Foreign Minister, July 28, 1976, quoting Australia's Foreign Minister Peacock: "it is time to stop viewing the EEC as simply a closed agricultural shop."

29 HAEC, BAC 28 1980 633, COM(73)556, Elaboration d'une conception globale en vue des prochaines négociations multilatérales (Communication de la Commission au Conseil), April 4, 1973, 79–110, 89; Seidel, "Challenges".

30 HAEC, BAC 48 1984 230, R.E. Abbott, Note for the attention of Mr Hijzen, How to handle agriculture in the M.T.N., January 28, 1975, 235–239, 238.

31 HAEC, BAC 48 1984 235, R. Phan van Phi, President Jenkins' visit to Washington, April 18–19. General background brief on MTN, 1 April 1977, 42–45, 44.

32 Winham, *Tokyo Round*, 249.

33 Cited in Tracy, *Government and Agriculture*, 350.

34 The Cairns group consisted of Australia, Argentine, Brazil, Canada, Chile, Colombia, Hungary, Indonesia, Malaysia, New Zealand, Philippines, Singapore, Thailand, and Uruguay.

35 For a discussion of US motives, cf. Josling and Tangermann, *Transatlantic Food and Agricultural Trade Policy*, 75.

36 In 1984 the United States had a 4.5 billion ECU trade surplus with the EEC. See European Economic Community, *The agricultural situation in the Community*, 1985, 264.

37 Josling and Tangermann, *Transatlantic Food and Agricultural Trade Policy*, 44–45.

38 See e.g. Fritz Georg Gravenitz, "From Kaleidoscope to Architecture: Interdependence and Integration in Wheat Policies, 1927–1957," in Patel (ed.), *Fertile Ground for Europe?*, 27–45 for a study on the international wheat agreement.

39 See Albert Viton, *The International Sugar Agreements: Promise and Reality* (West Lafayette: Purdue University Press, 2004).

40 Marcelo Raffaelli, *Rise and Demise of Commodity Agreements: An Investigation into the Breakdown of International Commodity Agreements* (Abington: Woodhead Publishing Limited, 1995), 81.

41 Council Regulation No 1009/67/EEC 1 on the common organization of the market in sugar, December 18, 1967; Council Regulation (EEC) No 766/68 of the Council laying down general rules for granting export refunds on sugar, June 18, 1968.

42 Viton, *The International Sugar Agreements*, 155.

43 Until a sugar market reform in 2006 the lucrative nature of sugar production in the EU hardly changed nor did the detrimental effects of low world market prices on sugar producers from third countries. See e.g. John M. Kline, *Ethics for International Business: Decision-Making in a Global Political Economy* (London: Routledge, 2005), 33.

44 Viton, *International Sugar Agreements*, 219.

45 Interview, Helmut Freiherr von Verschuer with the author, Nentershausen, February 16, 2004.

46   Raikes, *Modernising Hunger*, 158–160.

47   For a study on the case of the Senegalese groundnut production, see Martin Rempe, *Entwicklung im Konflikt: Die EWG und der Senegal 1957–1975* (Cologne: Boehlau, 2012); Martin Rempe, "Airy Promises: The Senegal and the EEC's Common Agricultural Policy in the 1960s," in Patel (ed.), *Fertile Ground for Europe?*, 221–240.

48   Rempe, "Airy Promises," 226.

49   The following passages rely on Rempe's study of the case of Senegal.

50   Rempe, *Entwicklung im Konflikt*, 91–92.

51   Rempe, "Airy Promises."

52   Ibid., 239.

53   Migani, "Development Aid," 396.

54   Ibid., 394. Resolution adopted by the General Assembly 3281 (XXIX), Charter of Economic Rights and Duties of States, December 12, 1974, http://www.un-documents.net/a29r3281.htm (last accessed October 25, 2018). On the general issue of developing countries' relations with the Community, see Garavini, *After Empires*.

55   Migani, "Development Aid," 395.

56   Mark Spoerer, "'Fortress Europe' in Long-term Perspective: Agricultural Protection in the European Community, 1957–2003," *Journal of European Integration History*, 16:2 (2010), 143.

57   Josling and Tangermann, *Transatlantic Food and Agricultural Trade Policy*, 65.

58   Giovanni Federico, "Was the CAP the Worst Agricultural Policy of the 20th Century?" in Patel (ed.), *Fertile Ground for Europe?*, 261.

59   Commission of the European Communities, COM (86) 373 final, European Council of June 26–27, 1986, Agriculture in the World Context, June 20, 1986, 1.

60   Kay, *The Reform of the Common Agricultural Policy*.

10

Enlargement as External Policy:
The Quest for Security?

Eirini Karamouzi

The decision of the British electorate to leave the European Union (EU) has ultimately shaken to the core the beliefs of EU supporters in the self-evident benefits of membership. Juggling concurrent crises, and eking out barely any concrete results has called into question the orthodox view of European integration as a necessary historical process.[1] The Western Balkan applicants waiting in the wings to join the EU feel neglected and deeply concerned that the enlargement process could be put off track by a distracted "Europe," while their own people grow even more disillusioned with the EU dream. Progressively, accession talks resemble a religion: "Be good, and you'll see the benefits once you die."[2]

Before "Europe" found itself in the throes of its worst "existential crisis," the dominant view concurred that the EU had contributed significantly to the reshaping of the European order, especially since the end of the Cold War, by extending EU membership to an ever-increasing number of countries.[3] Admittedly, for the nations of former Yugoslavia, the promise of EU membership became a cause for both elites and public opinion, and aided in curbing ethnic tensions in the region. EU accession talks may have pirouetted off to the margins, but as Karen Smith wrote in 2014, "the enlargement train moves haltingly, but it is still moving."[4] At the heart of such assertions lies the fact that the promise of enlargement remains one of the most effective means by which the EU is able to play a regional role in transforming the economic and political systems of aspirant countries. Either as "an impressive exercise in empire building" or exploiting its *civilian* clout (namely its "power of attraction"), even with inconsistent and at times counterproductive use of conditionality, the experience of enlargement has been diverse, unpredictable and multi-dimensional.[5]

The current crises may cast doubt on the EU's capacity to sustain the enlargement momentum but reinforce the need for a *longue durée* historical analysis in order to better comprehend how these heightened expectations of the utility of enlargement in foreign affairs came about. Enlargement as a tool of foreign policy was fully institutionalized only with the end of the Cold War, which partly explains why the theory-oriented research on enlargement has focused on the two major rounds of 1995—which included three former European Free Trade Area (EFTA) members—

and the Big Bang enlargement of 2004. Indeed, the volume and nature of applications for membership forced European officials to devise a sophisticated and ever-growing list of demands to make the candidates compatible with existing member states whilst allowing for their adaptation to the EU system. However, political and economic conditionality and accession practices did not take place in a vacuum; rather, they grew and were gradually articulated partly through the earlier enlargement experience.[6]

Admittedly, the new international order that broke through the barriers of the Cold War was more propitious for a genuine transformation of the EU; but this chapter will show the period prior to the formal introduction of the Copenhagen criteria of 1993 to be a fertile ground for the study of enlargement politics. During the Cold War, enlargement was a quite sporadic event with no formalized framework, despite carrying both a political and a legal dimension. In fact, Article 237 of the Treaties of Rome provided scant details on the kinds of criteria and practices involved for aspiring members, thus rendering the procedure of entry much more politicized and less institutionalized.[7] Individual member states could much more easily impede the process based on threats to their diverse national interests, or even reject application as in the case of the long-drawn British EEC story in the 1960s. Moreover, early enlargement procedures were much less interventionist in their exchanges with the candidates, who were left to their own devices in tackling obligations arising from accession and with few pre-accession carrots and sticks. The lack of an institutionalized framework, with the exception of the respect for the *acquis* that had arisen from the first round of enlargement, ultimately restricted the effectiveness of the Community's enlargement policy; but it did allow for experimentation. In the long decade of the 1970s, ideas flourished, and accession talks constituted a worthwhile political exercise in which the Community started toying with the idea of enlargement as a foreign policy tool. In these discussions over possible ways of implementation, Community institutions such as the Commission and the European Parliament were pivotal and have thus far been overlooked.[8]

This chapter seeks to investigate the historical evolution of enlargement as a foreign policy tool, the gradual eminence the policy gathered as a weapon in the Community's civilian arsenal, and the progressive and unplanned discovery of soft aid instruments in ensuring different forms of security in Europe. The quest for security, "an essentially contested term," is featured in both rounds of enlargement covered in this chapter— albeit debated in different ways, ranging from the geopolitical to the cultural and above all the economic dimension.[9] The first wave of expansion to the north covers eleven years, from Britain's first failed attempt of 1961 to its accession along with Ireland and Denmark in 1973. Then, the focus shifts to the then recently democratized countries of Southern Europe with the applications, debate and final accession of Greece, Spain, and Portugal from 1975 to 1986. Interestingly enough, both rounds of enlargement engulfed the common discursive terrain of security from which both the EC and the applicants debated, and framed the prospect of membership as a way to legitimately further their own interests and foreign policy aims.[10]

The chapter will attempt to stay away from a descriptive, exhaustive analysis of the two major EEC/EC enlargement rounds that took place in the years from 1957 to 1986, mostly gauging the evolution of the practices of enlargement policy and the discovery on the part of the Community of its usefulness as a foreign policy tool, utilizing the growing body of literature recently published on the topic. In contrast to political science research that tends to prioritze the EU enlargement politics dimension, the bulk of the historical research on enlargement has been conducted from the point of view of the single nation-states.[11] These national studies highlight first and foremost the economic rationale and the (geo)political motives behind enlargement.[12] The introspective character of such research has a plethora of merits but fails to capture the transformative impact that each round of enlargement has had on the mind-set and practices of the Community's enlargement policy; it also gives scarce attention to the foreign policy discourse surrounding enlargement.

The chapter will demonstrate how both the Community's formal institutional framework as a whole and the applicants themselves experienced enlargement and started to see it as a foreign policy in itself, rather than considering enlargement's impact on the EC's foreign policy or on the process of European integration and the institutional build-up of the Union.[13] There was no strategic plan within European circles, and the historical analysis of enlargement's earlier rounds unearths an almost accidental use and appreciation of its value for the Community's foreign policy machinery. Moreover, it will shed light on member states' internal debates, as national politics are still the crucial arena for the "politicization of European integration."[14] Adding to the importance of exploring these earlier rounds of enlargement is the fact that the question of the EC's political identity also gained relevance during the 1970s and 1980s and stood at the heart of enlargement, with both existing member states and the aspiring applicants feeling increasingly compelled to define their own interests and goals. The chapter identifies how the different institutions of the Community developed a discourse of political identity in the 1960s and 1970s, introducing the idea of the Community as a political entity based on shared values. The institutions increasingly articulated these values around the concept of democracy, not merely in terms of rhetorical self-identification, but as a framework within which policies had to be formulated.[15] Teasing out the interplay of political action and situational context lies at the heart of the enlargement story.

Enlargement as a One-Off Event: 1961–1973

In 1961, the Commission considered then British Prime Minister Harold Macmillan's application for EC membership to be "a turning point in post-war European politics … regard[ing] it as fresh recognition of the economic and political values of the work of European integration undertaken since 1950."[16,17] Historians and political scientists have offered contrasting explanations for Britain's turn towards the EEC and away from the Churchillian doctrine of "with but not of Europe" that dominated Britain's attitude towards the formative years of the European Economic Community (EEC). Andrew Moravcsik rightly noted that the British application targeted "the advancement of British commercial interests," whilst others such as Bange have stressed the primacy of political considerations in bringing about the membership bid.[18] Notwithstanding such diverse interpretations, British application in the summer of 1961 presented the Community with its first taste of its potential civilian appeal via the simple force of economic attraction. To be more precise, the success of the EEC as a commercial powerhouse had brought home the realization that the country was running out of options, rendering the EC the only game in town, despite the problematic—for the Brits—supranational character of the Community. The Six's decision to hasten moves towards a common external tariff and accelerate reduction of trade barriers amongst themselves in May 1960 raised concerns within Whitehall of a possibility of discrimination, with the Chancellor of the Exchequer, Reginald Maudling, warning against the possible damage to trade.[19] Fears were made more acute as, in Macmillan's own words, "we are a country to whom nothing at this moment matters except our exports trade."[20] So from early on, trade and the size of the customs union stood at the core of the Community's civilian power with the Commission increasingly, as the years went by, elaborating and negotiating on behalf of its members bilateral trade agreements and major rounds under the GATT.[21]

Moreover, in the 1960s, there was a hope that EEC/EC membership would bolster prevalent perceptions of a "sense of relative decline" in UK's international reach and power.[22] Britain's sluggish growth—not by historical records but in relation to the comparatively higher growth rate of EEC economies—meant that "by 1950 the difference in per capita GDP between the UK and Six was 28 percent. Seven years later, when the Treaty of Rome was signed, it stood at 15 percent, and in 1961 when Britain applied, the difference had reached 10 percent."[23] With EFTA being less competitive, less sophisticated, and thus inferior in trade performance to the emerging EEC, the British membership bid constituted "the response of a political system trying to catch up with economic realities," thus further exemplifying the lure of the Community as economic powerhouse affecting a country's foreign policy choices.[24] The emerging salience of European integration as a political concern was also reflected in the Foreign Office's capture of the agenda away from the Treasury, which had tended to dominate the dossier of European affairs during the previous decade.[25] The same applied to Denmark, which ditched its neutrality policy in favor of EEC membership in a bid to solve the agricultural outlet problem as well as to further boost exports with its main trading powers of Britain and West Germany.[26] Equally, Ireland was following Britain's suit on the grounds of economic prudence.[27]

Commercial imperatives were consistently linked to geopolitical concerns underpinning Britain's European policy. For instance, Macmillan discussed how staying out would "have the effect of excluding us both from European markets *and* from consultation in European policy."[28] The single most important document on Britain's first attempt to enter the EEC, namely the April 1961 Frank Lee Report, drew attention to the fact that "the Commonwealth is not likely to flourish under the leadership of a United Kingdom shut out of growing European markets."[29] The report went on to state that the economic consequences of exclusion from the EEC would be significant in the long term because the Community's size made it a formidable competition, and Britain's alternative, EFTA, was not a coherent unit. More broadly, the economy was strained as the gap between Britain's available resources and the cost of its overseas commitments widened. Economic turmoil and the threat of political marginalization formed the basis for Macmillan's turn to Europe. Joining the EEC was, as Milward notes, "a last concession to preserve the national strategy pursued since 1950" either in terms of Commonwealth, special relationship and changing Cold War fluctuations.[30] It is interesting, therefore, how enlargement to the EEC echoed political and economic realities, entangled in a reassessment of the foundation of British foreign policy.[31] Similarly for Ireland, the smallest and most economically underdeveloped country to apply, the economic benefits of possible membership to the EEC—cemented of course by the British decision to apply—aided the country's move towards membership and marked, as Geary has claimed, "a decisive economic foreign policy change for Ireland."[32]

In January 1963, several days after General de Gaulle's veto, Harold Macmillan wrote in his diary: "the great question remains: What is the alternative to the European Community? If we are honest we must say there is none."[33] Echoing similar disillusionment, but several years later, the Labour Prime Minister Harold Wilson would also come to acknowledge how far economic realities dictated Britain's move towards the Community. Historians differ in their explanations of the rationale behind Wilson's turn towards Europe. Parr concludes that the application was a pragmatic result of the July 1966 sterling crisis, while Kaiser argues that it was a tactical effort to deny the Tories a policy upon which they could attack. Despite their differences, they both concede that, as with the first attempt, economics interacted with political considerations in the British mindset. Indeed, the British and the "friendly Five" couched the prospective enlargement in terms of prolonging Western Europe's ties to the Atlantic and ensuring that the Americans remained committed to the defence of Western Europe, especially following the French double challenge to the European Community (EC) and North Atlantic Treaty Organization (NATO) in 1966.[34] The French, however, still with de Gaulle at the helm, would not even permit the enlargement talks to commence— pointing to Britain's financial problems and capitalizing on Wilson's decision to devalue the pound in October 1966 and its balance of payment deficit.[35]

By the time Edward Heath became prime minister in 1970 and revived the failed second application, Britain's political elite hoped that joining the Community would achieve multiple goals. Rather than being relegated to the sidelines, Britain would be in a position to reap the economic and political benefits of Community membership. Importantly, accession to the Community would allow Britain to catch up to the superior economic performance the Six had experienced over the 1960s. Furthermore, membership signaled a chance for Britain to recover international influence through full membership in the dynamic Community, which was becoming an increasingly important international player. In the early 1970s, British, Irish, and Danish EC enlargement complemented the Community's 1969 strategy of completion and deepening as well as Duchêne's calls for a united Europe capable of assuming its responsibilities in the world. Enlargement, still not seen as a foreign-policy tool in and of itself, was in its earliest guise designed to fortify and complement the rising commitments of the EC in external commercial relations, aid to developing countries, social policy, environmental and industrial policies and the emerging political cooperation and monetary affairs. Heath, upon his departure from the October Paris Summit of 1972—to which he had been cordially invited by the President of France, Georges Pompidou—was filled with joy for the "the advantages the enlargement of the Community will bring to us in Britain, to Europe and to the rest of the world."[36]

The story of Britain's quick disillusionment and concomitant frustration upon accession to the EEC has been the subject of numerous recent studies, ranging from rising food prices to political outcry over the budgetary terms of membership to issues of sovereignty and European identity.[37] Moreover, the experience of the first years of membership show how the success of enlargement was dependent on the environmental context and how the policy could evolve from a successful tool of foreign affairs to a divisive domestic issue with unwelcome repercussions.[38] From 1973, the sentiment within the enlarged Community went from hope to uncertainty to despair—damaging the perception of the beneficial aspects of enlargement within the British public debate. On the Community side, the Six, in dealing with Britain, Ireland, and Denmark and in the absence of criteria, were called upon to draft a procedure for moving the enlargement dossier forward. In his authoritative study on Britain's conditional application in 1961, Piers Ludlow has convincingly argued how the Community, in an attempt to safeguard its nascent achievements and avoid any interruption to its inner workings in dealing with such a demanding applicant as the United Kingdom, adopted an accession doctrine, defensive at heart, that protected the acquis at all costs. Through this process of discovery of the available tools and the eligibility of its relevant institutions, the EC prioritized an enlargement doctrine of "take it or leave it" that would become a staple of the next rounds of enlargement and responded more to the logic of protecting the current member states' interests than to the applicant's capacity or willingness to adapt to the acquis.[39]

The Unexpected Turning Point: Southern European Enlargement, 1974–1986

When negotiations with Denmark, Ireland, Norway, and the United Kingdom were concluded in January 1972, the EC dismantled its enlargement unit, as it did not expect to deal with the issue of enlargement in the near future.[40] However, the question re-emerged in 1975, after the collapse of right-wing authoritarianism in Greece, Spain, and Portugal. With all three countries, the Community had to take into account for the very first time the changing nature of prospective members—from long-established democracies and market economies to recently democratized and economically disadvantaged states.[41] Moreover, the transformative politics and the international geopolitical reconfigurations of the 1970s, which had been less pronounced in the previous round of accession, were brought to the forefront and became intertwined explicitly with the enlargement process for the first time.

In 1975, contemporary pundits, journalists, and politicians were convinced that events on the ground in Southern Europe had reached their tipping point, leaving the EC as a whole and also its member states at a loss on how to handle the crisis.[42] The perfect storm was brewing in Western Europe's own backyard, with different elements interacting simultaneously—and what is more intriguing, against the transformative environment of superpower *détente*.[43] Despite its conservative character of stabilizing the status quo, *détente* between the two superpowers had unintended consequences in the volatile environment of Southern Europe, where the relaxation of the once constraining framework of the Cold War had further fostered domestic instability.[44] Southern European societies, still sober from the experiences of the brutal dictatorships, became less convinced by an endless crisis that the Cold War fostered, and thus during the apogee of superpower *détente* felt more confident to pursue their perceived national interests at the expense of wider Alliance interests. The biggest fear for the Western elites therefore became the lack of political legitimacy and respectability that the Cold War narrative seemed to foster in these recently democratized countries, as well as the potential ramifications of diminishing domestic popular support for the American-led Western order. The threat for Southern Europe did not emanate primarily from the East but was mostly framed and understood as the devastating effect of a possible loss of faith and ultimately disillusionment of the Southern European public opinion with the merits and benefits of a Western connection. Such fears were confounded by a series of disasters, ranging from the global monetary and energy crises to the rifts in the transatlantic relationship, that threatened to upend the basic premises of what had contributed to the "making of the West"—wrong-footing assessments of a monolithic bloc, bent on progressing in uniformity and adhering to its hegemon.

The first shock came with the unanticipated toppling of the Portuguese dictatorship on April 25, 1974, which sank the country into political turmoil and caught the West off guard. The new military-dominated regime in Portugal was undecided as to the direction in which to take the country and whether or not to hand over power to a democratically elected government. There were concerns that the country might slide towards a kind of Euro-Communism and undermine Portugal's membership in NATO. Such concerns were strongly voiced in Washington. For Kissinger, it was essential to isolate Portugal, as the country had allegedly been "lost" to Communism.[45] The Nine were equally troubled about Portugal's uncertain future, with then British Prime Minister Harold Wilson declaring Portugal a "test of *détente*."[46]

Only four months after the Carnation revolution, the Greek dictatorship instigated a coup against Archbishop Makarios that ultimately led to the Turkish invasion of Cyprus. The Cyprus issue per se was not as destabilizing to the strategy of the West. The American interest in Cyprus was essentially a preventive one: to keep its political problems from boiling over and throwing wrenches into the Greco–Turkish relationship.[47] As declared in a State Department briefing paper of early August 1974, "our strategy is directed toward removing Cyprus as a bone of contention between Greece and Turkey."[48] Indeed, it seemed that rather than from the other side of the Iron Curtain, the biggest challenge and threat for the two countries was emanating from each other. Breaking free from the restrictive Cold War ideological straitjacket, fears arose that "defense expenditure by Greece and Turkey has been motivated more by the threat each perceived from the other than by a common Soviet threat," as posited a report by the Joint Intelligence committee.[49] Kissinger was eager to cooperate with the British on the Cyprus front, especially since America's latitude had been restricted by the strong and influential presence of the Greek lobby in Congress. Moreover, Britain, as signatory to the 1960 Treaty of Guarantee of the Cypriot state, was thrust into a position of responsibility. However, the British lacked the power to take effective action, suffering from what then Foreign Secretary James Callaghan described as "responsibility without power."[50]

Following the failed coup that led to the fall of the dictatorship, and confronted with a rapidly growing anti-Americanism and the humiliating consequences of the recent double Turkish invasion in Cyprus, the newly installed government in Athens was pressured to act.[51] Prime Minister Konstantinos Karamanlis concluded that war against Turkey would be a highly dangerous option, as the seven years of the junta had left the Greek armed forces in a fragile state.[52] Instead of war, Karamanlis announced the country's withdrawal from NATO's integrated military structure and requested renegotiations on the future of US bases on Greek soil.[53]

The threat to NATO's southern flank in the aftermath of Greece's withdrawal and the country's unstable domestic political situation during transition to democracy loomed large. Although Karamanlis was firmly attached to the West and his government had made it clear that the withdrawal from NATO was the least damaging and only acceptable policy to the public at the time, fears over Greece's future policy orientation were abetted by the rise of the Left in domestic politics. The newly formed Panhellenic Socialist Movement (PASOK) under Andreas Papandreou, despite coming third in the 1974 legislative elections, was becoming a progressively more popular party, campaigning on an anti-American and anti-EC platform. An illustration of this line of thinking was evident during Chancellor Schmidt's visit to Athens in May 1975. Karamanlis went on to explain to the chancellor that, although his parliamentary control was complete and the country's NATO withdrawal had reached its limits in terms of political gain, it would be a mistake to assume that he could or would pursue policies that were unacceptable either to his opponents or to Greek public opinion.[54]

Europe's fears over Greece were exacerbated by its potential spill-over effect on the neighboring countries in the Southern European region. Franco's dictatorship in Spain seemed to be nearing the end in 1975, with the 1953 base agreement with the United States in the air. Western leaders were equally concerned about Italy's domestic instability and economic crisis. Italy in the 1970s was caricatured as an unreliable partner and "the soft underbelly" of the Atlantic alliance.[55] Anxiety heightened even more with *compromesso storico* and the probability of the Italian Communist Party coming to power. All of these factors helped to exacerbate the already dismal strategic outlook in the Mediterranean region. In contrast to the first post-war decades, when the American fleet dominated the Mediterranean, the 1970s witnessed a growing Soviet infiltration.[56] In the face of deep economic malaise, Britain had already undertaken the defense review that had led to a phasing out of its Mediterranean defence.[57] In the minds of the political elites on both sides of the Atlantic, therefore, the unstable internal order in Greece, Spain, Italy and Portugal, with its possible ramifications for the robustness of NATO's southern flank, became part and parcel of this changing setting of crisis in Southern Europe.[58]

How could the EC step in and guarantee internal stabilization in these counties? The answer on how to diffuse the crisis surprisingly came from the applicants themselves, who flocked to the EC, viewing it as the only appropriate forum to support their countries' democratization processes. Since the 1960s, the EEC/EC had engaged with the region in different shapes and forms. Athens and Ankara had signed privileged Association agreements in 1961 and 1963, respectively, which were designed specifically to lead to full membership and as such, maintain close ties with the West.[59] In February 1962, Spain, sketching out the road map along the

Greek and Turkish path, requested association membership as a first step towards accession. Whilst the French and West Germans were willing to examine the request from Madrid, the idea of association was eventually dropped for political reasons and instead a simple preferential agreement was reached in October 1970.[60] Echoing similar political concerns for the lack of democratic rule, Lisbon's link with the process of European integration was limited to a free trade agreement signed in July 1972, as a consequence of the Community's first enlargement to Britain.[61] Discussions around the idea of the EC as a community of values with the right and duty to uphold democracy were enhanced with the imposition of the Greek junta and the resulting EC decision to freeze the Athens agreement. For the EC, democratic rule was becoming an informal requirement for accession; for the Greeks, the freezing of the agreement, coupled with the forced withdrawal from the Council of Europe, lodged in the Greek consciousness the EC and the Council of Europe as the only two organizations that had, at least symbolically, denounced the dictatorship—unlike the transatlantic allies.[62]

In the 1970s, therefore, all three southern European countries approached the European question, trading on the simplified but convincing political argument of democratic promotion that transcended the merely economic focus of the previous decades. Karamanlis, upon applying for Community membership, made a case to his fellow Europeans that failure to grant him a success on the EC application front would undermine his position, jeopardizing the country's smooth democratization process and, in turn, its foreign policy direction.[63] In a semblance of the Greek strategy, Portuguese domestic elites linked the democratization process with the European option and applied to join on March 28, 1977. Soon after, the Spaniards followed. On July 28, 1977, barely one month after the first democratic parliamentary elections, the Spanish EC application was lodged. The decision was prompted by the unparalleled political consensus—across the Spanish party system and public opinion—on the question of EC membership.[64] Simultaneously, however, the Spanish government was acting with its back against the wall, since failure to act swiftly could mean losing out on the momentum building up for a second enlargement. Fears of lagging behind its other two Southern European neighbors militated against any delays.

However, it was not just the applicants themselves that were setting the agenda for the Community. The Americans—reluctantly at first but forcefully after 1975—started framing prospective membership into a guarantee of domestic stability and security for the region. The US administration was painfully aware of the tide of anti-Americanism, with its ebbs and flows, that had swept Southern Europe, limiting America's room for maneuver. To make matters worse, the trauma of Vietnam and Watergate had paralyzed the presidency, with Congress becoming more assertive. The Ford administration no longer enjoyed the same flexibility in foreign affairs, a development that would add an unexpected layer of complexity in the conduct of US foreign policy.[65] Especially, the US embargo on arms for Turkey was an illustration of how the United States "could be paralyzed to the disadvantage of NATO."[66]

In an effort to overcome such constraints, the Americans looked—not immediately in the case of Portugal but quite forcefully over Greece—to their European allies for help. A paper on transatlantic cooperation highlighted the importance they placed for the EC's regional stability role:

During the past year the EC-nine have gradually refined a common approach to problems in the Mediterranean's northern ties, based on a desire to promote stability and political moderation and using the joint instruments of trade concessions, financial assistance, and ultimate closer association with or without membership in Europe. The Nine's approach reflects a growing sense of responsibility, based on self-interests. There is a major US interest involved in accepting and encouraging the sharing of the Mediterranean burden with the Nine.[67]

Without fear of antagonizing their transatlantic partner, the Nine progressively adopted a more confident view, putting emphasis on strengthening the hand of the democratic forces in Southern Europe, and utilizing the diverse set of economic and political tools at their disposal, with EC membership as the grand prize. In practice, the Germans shared American anxieties over the predicament of Southern Europe and Greece in particular, noting that "although his [Karamanlis'] own position on NATO and on the US presence in Greece was well known, we should not expect him to alienate public support at this stage by pro-American gestures or by a conspicuous return to NATO."[68] The Germans, like the rest of the Nine, came to support Greece's wish to join the Community—knowing very well that the Community's unequivocal support would find approval with Greek public opinion and buttress the new social order, if only because the Greek government had oversold membership as being key to protecting democracy. The British shared the need for the EC to offer the solution, as by their own admission: "We are too poor to do much ourselves. Logically, we should leave it to others to make the running. ... We should therefore be ready to encourage our allies to help. The Germans and the French are the key."[69] It was therefore within the EC context that Britain also chose to act, and through this medium to consult with the Americans.[70] The policy of enlargement therefore did not seek to reduce the role of the United States in Greece.[71] Europeans had the diplomatic and political means of influence that *complemented* those of the United States.

The merits of approaching enlargement in purely political and security terms was little disputed within European circles; it was thus hardly surprising how quickly the discussion ceased to revolve around the question of whether enlargement should take place, moving on to the "how" and "when." In other words, how would you ensure that enlargement, with all its complications and technocratic character, would serve the security concerns of the applicants? It was an arduous task to flesh out a road map to membership that would accommodate the applicants' heightened hopes and dreams for security without jeopardizing the cohesion and identity of the club. The terms under which Greece would be admitted, for instance, "would set a pattern for other nations that would demonstrate to what extent the 'Six' form a closed shop."[72] The Commission's Opinion, published on January 28, 1976, understood fully the political importance of supporting the Greek application, but at the same time considered that enlargement called for speeding up the process of integration, given the serious political and economic implications of a possible accession.[73] The suggestion for a pre-accession period stemmed from several considerations.[74] It presented an opportunity for the Community to reform its institutions and at the same time to develop a substantial program for economic aid that would enable Greece to overcome its structural weaknesses and adapt more easily to the Community's obligations and mechanisms. Moreover, a preparatory period seemed to reflect the desire of some member states to delay Greece's accession without causing a political rebuff.

> Despite the problems it had raised, the Commission's Opinion concluded that it is clear that the consolidation of Greece's democracy, which is a fundamental concern not only of the Greek people but also of the Community and its member states, is intimately related to the evolution of Greece's relationship with the Community. It is in the light of these considerations that the Commission recommends that a clear affirmative reply be given to the Greek request.[75]

Therefore, notwithstanding serious misgivings about the challenges of a Greek accession, the Commission concluded that democratic concerns overshadowed all others when it came to providing a rationale in favor of accepting the Greek application. Attempting to walk the same thin line between the need to welcome a recently democratized Portugal and the impact that its accession would have on the EC's institutional and economic structures, the Nine suggested to then Prime Minister Mario Soares in his early 1977 tour of Western European capitals that he opt for the alternative formula of "pre-accession status" or "privileged association," given that further domestic political upheavals were bound to complicate and prolong the negotiations on all the issues pertaining to Portugal joining the EC.[76]

Although the Spanish application followed the Greek and the Portuguese in March 1977, it far outweighed them in terms of complexity and consequence.[77] Indeed, in an informal discussion at the European Council on June 29, 1977, French President Valéry Giscard d'Estaing revealed that Madrid's entry without CAP reform would be impossible in French domestic political terms, given the threat posed by cheap Spanish competition to the interests of southwestern France farmers.[78] The negotiations on terms of entry were bogged down as soon as some chapters opened up. In fact, Giscard chose the Assembly of French Agricultural Chambers for his speech on June 5, 1980 in which he requested "a pause in the EEC's second enlargement."[79] The Spanish government reacted fiercely, accusing Paris of adopting an obstructionist policy, while the press portrayed the French as "the villains of the enlargement negotiations."[80]

The proposed pause in the talks with the EEC was a major setback that forced the Spanish government to reshape its entire international agenda. Prime Minister Adolfo Suarez was too busy fighting for his political life to react, leaving Foreign Minister Marcelino Oreja, and the minister responsible for negotiations with the EC, Calvo Sotelo, with the task of finding an adequate response. This answer was formulated in mid-June 1980, when the Spaniards linked entry into the EEC to membership in NATO.[81] Sotelo, who replaced Suarez in February 1981, thought of the link as not only perfectly compatible, but mutually reinforcing.[82] If the linkage was not enough to convince the EC, the member states were reminded of the political imperative of bringing Spain into the EC when a group of military officers led by Colonel Antonio Tejero attempted a coup in the Spanish Parliament on February 23, 1981.[83] The plotters attempted to take full advantage of the unraveling of order following Suarez' resignation. By revealing the fragility of Spanish democracy, the attempted coup altered the perception of the interests at stake in the Community's enlargement. It gave real meaning to the Spanish thesis that its new democracy required a more propitious international environment in which to be nurtured.[84]

The Ten condemned the coup, reaffirming their desire to see a democratic Spain accede to the EC. Renewed promises by the member states, however, failed to translate into practical steps, as progress in the pace and rhythm of negotiation remained limited. The harsh realities and internal dissent that had plagued the Community since 1979 enfeebled the lure of membership and its promise as a tool of stabilization. The second oil shock of 1979 choked off the tentative economic recovery of the preceding two years, and the political situation was equally unpropitious. New leaders such as Kohl and Papandreou came to the fore, while the Community was paralyzed over budgetary issues, the British fiscal rebate and the future of the CAP.

Hopes for resolution of the enlargement question heightened when François Mitterrand came to power in 1981, followed by Spain's PSOE victory in 1982. The new Spanish Socialist Prime Minister, Felipe Gonzalez, was eager to reverse the unfortunate situation he had inherited from the previous administration, which saw his country inside NATO and outside the EEC. The promise of socialist solidarity that could deliver "Europe" for him lay at the heart of his electoral promises.[85] He would be swiftly disillusioned when Mitterrand visited Madrid in June 1982; in the president's own words:

> What I can tell you is that there is political will to bring Spain into Europe. But I will not take the risk of adding to the present miseries of Europe, an additional misery. It would be useless to build new ties, when old ties could not only bend but actually break.

He moved on to note: "The general discourse that access to the EEC is open to countries that have chosen democracy, actually conceals a willingness to obstruct. Our partners are at the very least alarmed. The hypocrisy reigns supreme. The double language is devastating."[86]

Ultimately, it was not until Mitterrand's pro-European turn, reform of the CAP, and solving of the budgetary conundrum that the possibility of the Spanish entry became a distinct possibility. Lisbon's predicament was even worse, since newly appointed Mario Soares in 1983 realized early on that the fate of his country's application hinged on the outcome of the Spanish negotiations. West Germany, as in the case of Greece, was willing to shoulder the financial burden to assuage the French fears over the impact of Spanish entry.[87] Similarly, the Commission adopted amendments to rules related to fruits, vegetables and olive oil, as well as the guidelines of the integrated Mediterranean programs; The Integrated Mediterranean Programme, a lavish project costing US$4.8 billion over six years, was cooked up by the Commission to compensate Greek, Italian and French farmers for losses they might suffer from Spanish entry into the community.[88]

However, Germany's generosity was, albeit not explicitly, linked to the condition of continued support for Spain's remaining in NATO. Unanimous cross-party support for the EC may have weakened Spain's hand, but lack of popular support for Spain's continued membership in NATO became possible leverage over the EC partners. The Socialists had stocked up votes on the Left by promising a referendum on NATO membership in the 1982 elections. After 1983, therefore, the negotiations with the EEC acquired an added political dimension, as the question of Spain remaining in the NATO alliance galvanized political debate within the country.[89] Early on, the Germans, along with the British, utilized the carrot of EC membership to convince Gonzalez to contribute to the "conversion of the PSOE from its neutralist position to being in favor of remaining in NATO."[90] The United States administration and the EC governments knew that an acceptable package for Spain on Community membership could ensure that González put his prestige behind staying in NATO.

Conclusion

Enlargement, like other EU policies, runs on deference to steadily accumulated precedent. It started off as a random event, but through successive rounds the Community actors discovered a series of instruments that transformed enlargement from an ad hoc process into a formalized policy, starting with the notion of the *acquis* and the power of economic attraction during the first round to the role of democratic stabilizer through the second enlargement and the emergence of informal criteria for admission, laying the ground for the 1993 Copenhagen criteria. Even before the end of the Cold War, the member states of the Community took the first taste of what would take place in the post-1989 rounds of enlargement and its multidimensional nature of power: the interplay between geopolitical considerations, market policy and normative power as formed against a cumulative precedential need to conform to norms and identities.[91]

However, the EC was defensive and assertive at the same time in facing up to the challenges of enlargement. In every round, the aspirant applicants encountered ample amount of incredulity among the existing member states of the Community, who were wary of the possible diluting effects of enlargement on the institutions, and of the financial costs involved. At the same time, however, they were eager to respond to the applicants' calls for security in the form of democratization, social cohesion and economic modernization. In accepting the southern Europeans' bid for membership, the Nine set out on a path that would eventually lead to far-reaching changes in the whole nature of the Community and its role as an international actor.[92] At the same time, however, and unlike the first enlargement, the Southern European countries became "European" not because of what they could offer, but because of what they lacked: fragility and weaknesses constituted the countries' assets, creating a precedent of expectations and influencing their behavior and discourse once they became members of the EU. Moreover, during the years under examination, there was a "politicization" of enlargement where the technicalities were overlooked to serve geopolitical and normative considerations, whilst at the same time member states utilized the prospect of enlargement to strike better deals within the EC, thus increasing uncertainty and limiting the impact of the promise of accession.[93] Since it was mainly the applicants that brought home the effectiveness of the tool of conditionality, it is hardly surprising that when faced with the prospect of a big-bang round, the enlargement process and criteria required underwent a major shift.

The Copenhagen "conditions of eligibility" institutionalized in 1993 were products of specific political circumstances and attuned to meet the needs of the Central and Eastern European enlargement, but they echoed the processes that had taken place in the preceding years. The historical record of the period of 1957–1992 offers the broad brushstrokes of a more complicated enlargement picture, which confirms the lack of a monolithic progress but more highlights the contingent character, reflecting the changing self-perceptions of the applicants and the evolution of the nature of the European integration process. Ultimately, accession to the EU but mostly withdrawal, as with the case of Brexit, acts as a powerful reminder of the voluntary character of enlargement; it is this freedom of choice that strengthens the policy's appeal and explains its success as a foreign policy tool.

Notes

1 On the teleological trap, please see Mark Gilbert, "Narrating the Process: Questioning the Progressive Story of European Integration," *Journal of Common Market Studies*, 46:3 (2008), 641–662.

2 Quoted in Alberto Nardelli, "This Is Why Balkan States Fear Brexit Could Kill off their EU Dream," BuzzFeed, https://www.buzzfeed.com/albertonardelli/this-is-why-balkan-states-fear-brexit-could-kill-off-their-e?utm_term=.kfRoG5mQP3#.on4brkMXOL (last accessed November 1, 2018).

3 Jean-Claude Juncker, "State of the Union Address: Towards a better Europe—A Europe that protects, empowers and defends," Strasbourg, September 14, 2016; Lisbeth Aggestam, "New Actors, New Foreign Policy: EU and Enlargement," in Steve Smith, Amelia Hadfield and Tim Dunne (eds.), *Foreign Policy, Theories, Actors, Cases* (Oxford: Oxford University Press, 2012), 431–451.

4 Karen E. Smith, "Is the European Union's Soft Power in Decline?" *Current History*, 113 (2014), 104–109.

5 Jan Zielonka, *Europe as Empire: The Nature of the Enlarged European Union* (Oxford: Oxford University Press, 2006), 44; Karen Smith, "Enlargement, the Neighborhood, and European Order," in Christopher Hill and Michael Smith (eds.), *International Relations and the European Union* (Oxford: Oxford University Press, 2011).

6 For instance, Daniel C. Thomas, "Constitutionalisation through Enlargement: The Contested Origins of the EU'S Democratic Identity," *Journal of European Public Policy*, 13:8 (2006), 1190–1210; Emma de Angelis and Eirini Karamouzi, "Enlargement and the Historical Origins of the European Community's Democratic Identity," *Contemporary European History*, 25:3 (2016), 439–458.

7 Mark Dawson, "The European Union as a Community of Law: Achieving Diplomatic Goals through Legal Means?" in Robert Hutchings and Jeremi Suri (eds.), *Foreign Policy Breakthroughs: Cases in Successful Diplomacy* (Oxford: Oxford University Press, 2015).

8 Jan van der Harst, "Enlargement: The Commission Seeks a Role for Itself," in Michel Dumoulin (ed.), *The European Commission, 1958–1972: Histories and Memories of an Institution* (Luxembourg: Publications Office of the European Union, 2007), 533–556.

9   Barry Buzan, *People, States and Fear: An Agenda for International Security Studies in the Post-Cold War Era* (Boulder: ECPR Press, 2007), 26–32.

10 Hazel Smith, *European Union Foreign Policy* (London: Pluto Press, 2002), 27.

11 There are exceptions with research on enlargement by Piers Ludlow, Eirini Karamouzi, and Lorena Ruano; Piers Ludlow, "History Aplenty: But Still Too Isolated," in Michelle P. Egan, Neil Nugent and William E. Patterson (eds.), *Research Agenda in EU Studies: Stalking the Elephant* (Basingstoke: Palgrave Macmillan, 2009).

12 A few among many: *Journal of European Integration History*, Special issue on enlargement, 11:2 (2005); Wolfram Kaiser and Jürgen Elvert (eds.), *European Union Enlargement: A Comparative History*, (London: Routledge, 2007); Christopher Preston, *Enlargement and Integration in the European Union* (London/New York: Routledge, 1997); Loukas Tsoukalis, *The European Community and its Mediterranean Enlargement* (London: Allen & Unwin, 1981).

13 Frank Schimmelfennig and Ulrich Sedelmeier (eds.), *The Politics of European Union Enlargement: Theoretical Approaches* (London: Routledge, 2015); Marise Cremona (ed.), *The Enlargement of the European Union* (Oxford: Oxford University Press, 2013).

14 Hanspeter Kriesi, "The Politicization of European Integration," *Journal of Common Market Studies*, 54 (2016), 32–47.

15 De Angelis and Karamouzi, "Enlargement and the Historical Origins."

16 Britain, Ireland, Denmark and Norway pursued membership during the 1960s and 1970s. In the case of Norway, a referendum on EEC accession produced a negative result in 1972; see also Haakon Ikonomou, "Europeans, Norwegian Diplomats and the Enlargement of the European Community, 1960–1972," PhD Thesis (European University Institute, 2016).

17 Quoted in Dumoulin, *The European Commission, 1958–1972.*

18 Andrew Moravcsik, *The Choice for Europe: Social Purpose and State Power: From Messina to Maastricht* (Ithaca: Cornell University Press, 1998), 164. Bange cited in John Young, *Britain and European Unity, 1945–1999* (Basingstoke: Palgrave Macmillan, 2000), 79.

19 Richard Lamb, *The Macmillan Years, 1957–1963: The Emerging Truth* (London: John Murray, 1995), 155.

20 James Ellison, "Accepting the Inevitable: Britain and European Integration," in Wolfram Kaiser and Gillian Staerck (eds.), *British Foreign Policy, 1955–1964: Contrasting Opinions* (Basingstoke: Palgrave Macmillan, 2000), 171.

21 Sophie Meunier and Kalypso Nicolaidis, "The European Union as Trade Power," in Christopher Hill and Michael Smith (eds.), *International Relations and the EU* (Oxford: Oxford University Press, 2011), 276; Lucia Coppolaro, *The Making of a World Trading Power: The European Economic Community (EEC) in the GATT Kennedy Round Negotiations, 1963–1967* (Surrey: Ashgate, 2013).

22 Jim Tomlinson, *The Politics of Decline: Understanding Post-War Britain* (Harlow: Longman, 2001).

23 http://voxeu.org/article/britain-s-eu-membership-new-insight-economic-history (last accessed October 29, 2018).

24 Norman Aitken, "The Effect of the EEC and EFTA on European Trade: A Temporal Cross-Section Analysis," *The American Economic Review*, 63:5 (1973), 881–892; also Alan Milward, *The UK and the European Community, Vol. 1: The Rise and Fall of a National Strategy, 1945–1963* (London: Cass, 2002), 313; cited in Sean Greenwood, *Britain and European Cooperation since 1945* (Oxford: Blackwell, 1992), 82.

25   Piers Ludlow, "A Waning Force: The Treasury and British European Policy, 1955–1963," *Contemporary British History*, 17:4 (2003), 87–104.

26   Thorsten B. Olesen, "The Dilemmas of Interdependence: Danish Foreign Policy," *Journal of European Integration History*, 7:2 (2001), 37–63; Johnny Laursen and Thorsten Olesen, "A Nordic Alternative to Europe? The Interdependence of Denmark's Nordic and European policies, 1945–1998," *Contemporary European History*, 9 (2000), 59–92.

27   Mervyn O'Driscoll, Dermot Keogh and Jérôme de Wiel (eds.), *Ireland through European Eyes: Western Europe, the EEC and Ireland, 1945–1973* (Cork: Cork University Press, 2013).

28   Ellison, "Accepting the Inevitable," 179.

29   The National Archives of the United Kingdom, Kew (TNA), CAB134/1820/EQ(60)27.

30   For a diverse set of the political considerations: N. Piers Ludlow, *Dealing with Britain: The Six and the First UK Application to the EEC* (Cambridge: Cambridge University Press, 1997); Wolfram Kaiser, *Using Europe, Abusing the Europeans: Britain and European Integration, 1945–1963* (Basingstoke: Palgrave Macmillan, 1996).

31   Ellison, "Accepting the Inevitable," 171.

32   Michael J. Geary, *An Inconvenient Wait: Ireland's Quest for Membership of the EEC, 1957–73* (Dublin: Institute of Public Administration, 2009).

33   Cited in Vernon Bognador, "Footfalls echoing in the memory: Britain and Europe: The Historical Perspective," *International Affairs*, 81:4 (2005), 693.

34   Helen Parr, "Anglo-French Relations, Détente and Britain's Second Application for Membership of the EEC, 1964 to 1967," in N. Piers Ludlow (ed.), *European Integration and the Cold War: Ostpolitik-Westpolitik, 1956–73* (Abingdon: Routledge, 2007); Stephen Wall, *Official History of the United Kingdom and the European Community Vol. 2: From Rejection to Referendum, 1963–1975* (London: Routledge, 2012).

35   Gérard Bossuat, "De Gaulle et la seconde candidature britannique aux Communautés européennes," in Wilfried Loth (ed.), *Crises and Compromises: The European Project, 1963–1969* (Baden-Baden: Nomos-Verlag, 2001), 511–538.

36   TNA, PREM15/895, Statement by Heath, October 21, 1972.

37   David Gowland, Arthur Turner and Alex Wright, *Britain and European Integration since 1945: On the Sidelines* (London: Routledge, 2010); N. Piers Ludlow, "Safeguarding British Identity or Betraying It? The Role of British 'Tradition' in the Parliamentary Great Debate on EC Membership, October 1971," *Journal of Common Market Studies*, 53 (2015), 18–34.

38   Lindsay Aqui, *Britain and the European Community, January 1973–June 1975*, Unpublished PhD Thesis, London: Queen Mary University, 2017.

39   Ludlow, *Dealing with Britain*.

40   Dumoulin, *The European Commission, 1958–1972*, 429.

41   Eirini Karamouzi, *Greece, the EEC and the Cold War, 1974–1979: The Second Enlargement* (Basingstoke: Palgrave Macmillan, 2014), 194.

42   Ennio di Nolfo, "The Cold War and the Transformation of the Mediterranean, 1960–1975," in Melven Leffler and Odd Arne Westad (eds.), *The Cambridge History of the Cold War, Vol. 2* (Cambridge: Cambridge University Press, 2011), 238–257.

43   Jussi Hanhimaki, "Conservative Goals, Revolutionary Outcomes: The Paradox of Détente," *Cold War History*, 8:4 (2008), 503–512; On the transformative character of the 1970s: Daniel Sargent, *A Superpower Transformed: The Remaking of American Foreign Relations in the 1970s* (New York: Oxford University Press, 2015).

44   Effie Pedaliu, "A Sea of Confusion: The Mediterranean and Détente, 1969–1974," *Diplomatic History*, 33:4 (2009), 735–750.

45   Mario Del Pero, "A European Solution for a European Crisis," *Journal of European Integration History*, 15:1 (2009), 15–34, here 21; Kenneth Maxwell, *The Making of Portuguese Democracy* (Cambridge: Cambridge University Press, 1997).

46   For a more detailed analysis on support for the Portuguese socialist party: David Castano, "A Practical Test in the Détente: International Support for the Socialist Party in the Portuguese Revolution (1974–1975)," *Cold War History*, 15:1 (2015), 1–26.

47   James Edward Miller, *The United States and the Making of Modern Greece: History and Power, 1950–1974* (Chapel Hill: The University of North Carolina Press, 2009).

48   Quoted in Claude Nicolet, *United States Policy towards Cyprus, 1954–1974: Removing the Greek-Turkish Bone of Contention* (Mannheim: Bibliopolis, 2001), 418.

49   Report by the Joint Intelligence Committee, Cabinet Office, April 29, 1976, in Keith Hamilton and Patrick Salmon (eds.), *The Southern Flank in Crisis, 1973–1976: Series III, Vol. 5: Documents on British Foreign Policy Overseas* (London: Routledge, 2012), 526.

50   Quoted in Andreas Constandinos, *America, Britain and the Cyprus Crisis of 1974: Calculated Conspiracy or Foreign Policy Failure* (Milton Keynes: Author House, 2009), 382.

51   Ivan-Andre Slengesol, "A Bad Show? The United States and the 1974 Cyprus Crisis," *Mediterranean Quarterly*, 22:2 (2000), 96–129; Nicolet, *United States Policy towards Cyprus*; Konstantina Botsiou, "Anti-Americanism in Greece," in Martin Griffith and Brendon O'Connor (eds.), *Anti-Americanism: History, Causes and Themes, Vol. 3* (Oxford: Greenwood World Publishing, 2007), 213–345.

52   National Archives and Record Administration (NARA), College Park, MD, RG 59, box 205, 1969–1974; Constantinos Svolopoulos (ed.), *Constantinos Karamanlis: Archives, Event and Texts, Vol. 9* (Athens: Karamanlis Foundation, 1997), 14.

53   Constantinos Svolopoulos, *Greek Foreign Policy, 1945–1981, vol. 2* (Athens: Estias Books, 2002).

54   Berlin, Akten zur Auswärtigen Politik des Bundesperublik Deutschland (AAPD), Doc. 120, Meeting between Karamanlis and Schmidt, May 16, 1975, 534–541.

55   Mario del Pero, "Italy and the Atlantic Alliance," in Erik Jones and Gianfranco Pasquino (eds.), *The Oxford Handbook of Italian Politics* (Oxford: Oxford University Press, 2015), 691.

56   Evanthis Hatzivassiliou, "The Cold War as a Frontier: The Mediterranean Cleavages and the View from NATO, 1967–1982," *Journal of European Integration History*, 1:15 (2015), 13–32, here 21; Milan Vego, "Soviet and Russian Penetration strategy in the Mediterranean since 1945," in John B. Hatterdorf (ed.), *Naval Policy and Strategy in the Mediterranean: Past, Present and Future* (London: Frank Cass, 2000), 164.

57   NARA, CFSF, 1973–1976, Telegram by D. Bruce, March 6, 1975.

58   Sotiris Rizas, *The Rise of the Left in Southern Europe: Anglo-American Responses* (London: Pickering & Chatto, 2012).

59   Jean Rey, "L'association de la Grèce et da la Turquie à la C.E.E.," *European Yearbook*, 11 (1963), 50–59; Ziya Önis, "An Awkward Partnership: Turkey's Relations with the European Union in Comparative Historical Perspective," *Journal of European Integration History*, 7:1 (2001), 105–120.

60   Juan Crespo MacLennan, *Spain and the Process of European Integration, 1957–1985* (Basingstoke: Palgrave Macmillan, 2000), 75–81; On the issue of informal EC democratic conditionality, see Daniel C. Thomas, "Consitutionalization through

Enlargement: The Contested Origins of the EU's Democratic Identity," *Journal of European Public Policy*, 13:8 (2006), 1190–1210.

61 Nicolau Andresen Leitão, "A Flight of Fantasy? Portugal and the First Attempt to Enlarge the European Economic Community, 1961–1963," *Contemporary European History*, 16:1 (2007), 71–87.

62 De Angelis and Karamouzi, "Enlargement and the Historical Origins," 439–458.

63 Karamouzi, *Greece, the EEC and the Cold War*, 35–63.

64 Carlos Closa and Paul M. Heywood, *Spain and the European Union* (Basingstoke: Palgrave Macmillan, 2004), 6–30.

65 Henry Kissinger, *Years of Renewal* (New York: Simon & Schuster, 1999), 192; Yanek Mieczkowski, *Gerald Ford and the Challenges of the 1970s* (Lexington: Kentucky University Press, 2005), 3835; John Robert Greene, *The Nixon—Ford Years* (New York: Facts on File, 2006), xxv.

66 NARA, CFSF, 1973–1976, Telegram by D. Bruce, May 29, 1975.

67 NARA, CFSF, 1973–1976, Telegram by J. Greenwald, January 27, 1976.

68 AAPD, Doc. 120, Meeting between Karamanlis and Schmidt, May 16, 1975, 534–541.

69 Hamilton and Salmon (eds.), *Southern Flank in Crisis, 1973–1976:* Telegram from Baker to Goodison, London, August 22, 1975, no 138, 480.

70 NARA, CFSF, 1973–1976, Telegram by E. Richardson, January 8, 1976.

71 Geir Lundestad, *The United States and Western Europe since 1945: From "Empire" by Invitation to Transatlantic Drift* (Oxford: Oxford University Press, 2003).

72 Quoted in Mervyn O'Driscoll, "The 'Unwanted Suitor': West Germany's Reception, Response and Role in Ireland's EEC Entry Request, 1961–1963," *Irish Studies in International Affairs*, 22:2 (2011), 163–186, here 169.

73 Historical Archives of the European Union (HAEU), Florence, Commission Working Document, no. 373, January 28, 1976.

74 See Karamouzi, *Greece, the EEC and the Cold War*, 35–62.

75 *Bulletin of the European Communities*, 1 (1978).

76 David Hannay, *Britain's Quest for a Role: A Diplomatic Memoir from Europe to the UN* (London and New York: I.B. Tauris, 2012), 76.

77 Paul Preston and Denis Smyth, *Spain, the EEC and NATO, Chatham House Papers 22* (Routledge: London, 1984), 66.

78 Archives du Ministère des Affaires étrangères, La Courneuve (AMAE), Direction des affaires économiques et financiers (1976–1980), Note on Enlargement, Paris, October 7, 1977, 1389.

79 *Le Monde*, June 7, 1980.

80 Fernando Rodrigo, "Western Alignment: Spain's Security Policy," in Richard Gillespie, Fernando Rodrigo and Jonathan Story (eds.), *Democratic Spain: Reshaping External Relations in a Changing World* (London: Routledge, 1995), 54–56.

81 Emilio A. Rodriquez, "Atlanticism and Europeanism: NATO and Trends in Spanish Foreign Policy," in Federico Gil and Joseph Tulchin (eds.), *Spain's Entry into NATO: Conflicting Political and Strategic Perspectives* (Boulder: Lynne Rienner Publishers, 1988), 65.

82 Charles Powell, *The Long Road to Europe: Spain and the European Community, 1957–1986* (Madrid: Elcano Royal Institute, 2015), 9.

83 *The Economist*, November 10, 1984.

84 Glen D. Macdonald, "European Community Enlargement and the Evolution of French-Spanish Cooperation 1977–1987," in Gil and Tulchin, *Spain's Entry into NATO*, 76.

85   Mark Gilbert, *European Integration: A Concise History* (Plymouth: Rowman & Littlefield Publishers, 2012).

86   Roland Dumas, *Affaires Etrangeres I, 1981–1988* (Paris: Fayard, 2007), 238.

87   Macdonald, "European Community Enlargement," 82.

88   *Bulletin of the European Communities* 2 (1983), 46–47; *The Economist*, December 8, 1984.

89   Benny Pollack and Graham Hunter, *The Paradox of Spanish Foreign Policy: Spain's International Relations from Franco to Democracy* (London: Pinter Publications, 1987), 138–139.

90   MacLennan, *Spain and the Process of European Integration, 1957–1985*, 168.

91   Anna Michalski, "The Enlarging European Union," in Desmond Dinan (ed.), *Origins and Evolution of the European Union* (Oxford: Oxford University Press, 2006).

92   For more recent work on the appeal of the EC to Eastern Europe and Yugoslavia, please see Federico Romero and Angela Romano (eds.) "European Socialist Regimes Facing Globalisation and European Co-operation: Dilemmas and Responses," special issue of the *European Review of History*, 21:2 (2014).

93   Karen E. Smith, "EU Membership Conditionality," in Marise Cremona (ed.), *The Enlargement of the European Union* (Oxford: Oxford University Press, 2003).

11

The EC's Development Policy: The Eurafrica Factor

Giuliano Garavini

Debates on the colonial legacy of European powers rage on. The most recent wave of immigration from Africa and the Middle East is generating widespread resentment for the alleged loss of jobs it generates, for endangering the European identity and for security concerns. On the other hand, as European societies become increasingly diverse, periodic arguments resurface over the necessity for the colonial powers to compensate for the pillaging of their former colonies, as well as for the enslavement of Africans and of other populations.[1]

The European Community's (EC's) development policy has been one of the instruments to enhance Western Europe's role and influence in the postcolonial world, as well as to deal with the legacy of colonialism. Overall, the trajectory that will be described here is one in which the nature of EC development policies, as well as its main instruments, changed significantly from 1957 to 1992. While colonial or openly "neocolonial" efforts prevailed up to the end of the 1960s; from the beginning of the 1970s to the middle of the 1980s, the EC, under strong pressure from Third World countries as well as from new European social and political movements, made an effort to reform its development policies and practices. By the middle of the 1980s up to the Maastricht Treaty, EC development aid came to resemble much more closely that of the multilateral financial institutions such as the World Bank, and the centrality of African countries as aid recipients started to be questioned as globalization and the collapse of Communism in Eastern Europe opened up new challenges and opportunities.

A few ideas underlying these pages are worth spelling out before attempting a summary of the EC's development policy. The first idea is that European integration was deeply linked to the colonial past of its member states. The global political, economic, and cultural networks set up by European powers in the nineteenth century did not cease abruptly after World War II.[2] We now know that, to the contrary, Western European powers clung to their colonies with all their strength, tried to revitalize them with new development efforts, and exerted extreme violence in the process. Eventually links were restructured but never totally severed.[3]

The second idea is that, while there is certainly a technical aspect to the development policy, development aid was a political, social, and cultural tool employed by all the powers after WWII.[4] Various kinds of development policies were often in contradiction with one another: the "liberal" development policies, also defined as "modernization," which were driven mainly by the United States and tested through the Marshall Plan; the Communist development policies; and the "trade not aid" policies of the so-called Third World countries, that had as their main discussion arena the 1964 United Nations Conference on Trade and Development (UNCTAD). As he tries to periodize and summarize the huge literature on development, Joseph Morgan Hodge noted that: "The word 'development' was the perfect hegemonic catch-all for capturing the goals and aspirations of all parties to the situation. Its basic elements were constructed in the years between 1945 and 1955."[5] It is worth noting that France created its *Fonds d'investissement pour le développement économique et social* (FIDES) in 1946, before Point IV in the United States; the same is true of the British Colonial Development and Welfare Act of 1940, which provided money coming from colonial taxation for the purpose of improving the welfare of colonial subjects.[6] Also, pan-European projects for the "development" of Africa, although they remained on paper, had already appeared in the 1920s as a reaction to compete with the United States that was basically self-sufficient in raw materials.[7]

The third idea is that, since development policies remain an instrument to exert regional or global influence, the views of the recipients should also be taken into account to fully understand the nature of these policies. Development policies have never been a one-way process from the donor to the recipient, but provided for wide possibilities of reciprocal interaction and influence.[8]

The fourth idea is that it is hard to limit the analysis of the impact of development policies to what normally qualifies as Official Development Assistance (ODA)—and not only because there are other policies such as trade preferences, industrial cooperation, and migration policies that have been directly linked by policymakers to aid. This often sheds an entirely different light on the generosity of the "development" efforts. For example, if the EC increases its development aid but at the same times introduces barriers to immigration or to trade, the nature of development policies acquire an entirely different meaning.

Eurafrica: The European Economic Community as a Colonial Actor (1957–1963)

When the European Economic Community (EEC) was created with the signing of the Treaties of Rome in 1957, continuities with the colonial era largely prevailed over discontinuities. France, Belgium, the Netherlands, and even Italy (not to mention the United Kingdom and Portugal, that would later become members) were still colonial powers that directly managed overseas territories and fought to preserve their influence for the years to come. Belgium still retained control over the Congo, Rwanda, and Burundi. Italy had a UN trusteeship over the Trust Territory of Somaliland.[9] The French Union was still present in West and Equatorial Africa and the Pacific. The Netherlands was unwilling to give up West New Guinea to the Republic of Indonesia. Only Germany and Luxembourg, albeit for very different reasons, did not have direct colonial involvement. So, while the EEC was obviously an effort at European integration, the territories it integrated were in fact both European and "non-European." The troubles of France in Algeria, or Belgium in Congo, were internal European problems. The EEC had Eurafrican origins: There were links between the creation of the EEC and ideas of a possible European colonial cooperation in Africa as embodied in the projects of Coudenhove-Kalergi (among others) in the 1920s.[10]

The most recent literature has taken very seriously the effort to revive European colonial empires, the so-called "late imperialism" of the 1950s. Tony Chafer argues: "Indeed, even as late as 1957–1958, the prime focus of policymakers in Paris was how to restructure the colonial link with Black Africa so as better to maintain it, rather than on preparing the colonies for self-government."[11] As late as 1958 French President Charles de Gaulle advanced a plan—the Constantine Plan—to raise Algerian national revenue by more than 7 percent, while at the same time promoting education and land redistribution.[12] An important objective of this "developmental colonialism" was to solve the problem of the "dollar shortage" after World War II and to allow some breathing space for the governments to invest in post-war economic recovery and sustaining the newly born welfare states.[13] This effort was radically challenged after the Franco–British failure to recover the Suez Canal in 1956. Jean Monnet recalled how Louis Armand—one of the "three wise men" charged, after the failure of the European Defence Community (EDC) in 1954, with re-launching a common European initiative through a joint atomic energy project—provocatively proposed the creation of a statue honoring Nasser as "the federator of Europe."[14] Having dealt a first very serious blow to the imperial dreams of France and the United Kingdom in 1956, the Egyptian leader had also cleared the way for a new French commitment in Europe. But while the "Suez crisis" of 1956 might have paved the way to the signing of the Rome treaties, it did not end the colonial effort altogether.

The EEC was born Eurafrican mainly due to the French willingness to retain its colonies, while at the same time sharing the political and economic burden with its more skeptical European partners—mainly the Federal Republic of Germany and the Netherlands.[15]

In 1954, 70 percent of France's food imports came from the Pays d'Outre-Mer (POM). The POM's imports from France were 34 percent of French total exports. Around 500,000 French employees were directly involved in France's overseas territories. A little less than a quarter of French public sector employees dealt directly or indirectly with the colonies. Still in 1957, the commercial network and cultural links between the metropolis and its African territories motivated French officials like Pierre Moussa to dream of a bright future for Françafrique.[16]

France made the preservation of its colonial links, mainly with Africa, a precondition for signing the Rome treaties. The result was that the EEC was "associated" with Overseas Countries and Territories (OCT), most of them part of the French and the Belgian colonial empires (Fig. 11.0). German and Dutch opposition to this association was never to the colonial idea of Eurafrica per se (to which they had no ideological objection), rather to the amount of money they would have to contribute to the OCT's development fund: The European Development Fund (EDF).

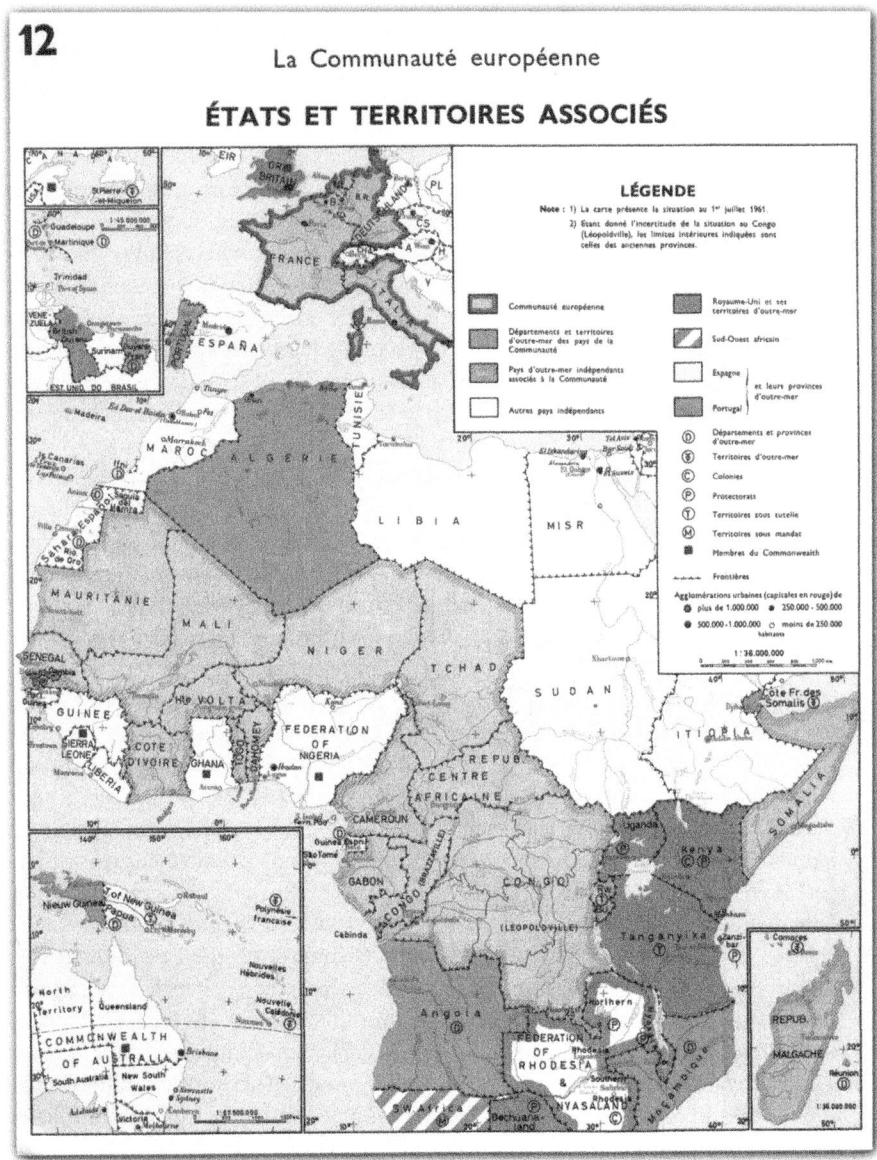

Figure 11.0 The European Community and the associated overseas territories, 1961.
Copyright © European Union

Association with the EEC implied the disbursement of development funds in favor of the associated countries, but at the same time their acceptance of free trade within the Common Market. The "associated" countries had no role and no voice in the shape or the management of the association. The governance of the Development Fund of the EEC was modeled on that of the French colonial bureaucracy and managed by French former colonial bureaucrats. The EDF would have a budget of 585.5 million units of account (UoA), with France and the FRG (Federal Republic of Germany) contributing 200 million each.

To be sure, some in the French empire in West Africa, especially Léopold Senghor, looked favorably at being represented in the EEC Parliamentary Assembly and dreamed of a Eurafrica where Europeans and Africans would forge a common culture and identity,and enjoy equal political, social and economic rights.[17] But for the vast majority of African nationalist leaders of the time, especially outside Francophone Africa, Eurafrica came to be viewed as the latest embodiment of political and economic exploitation.[18] The reality was that the countries associated with the EEC had, up to 1960, no independent foreign policy, no real possibility to decide on their own investments and development model, and no autonomous monetary policy (something that is still true for a number of countries in former French West Africa).

It is hard to assess whether the Eurafrica project collapsed due to nationalist pressures in African countries, or because of the increasing internal political conflicts over empire in Western European countries themselves. The collapse of Eurafrica was probably due to a combination of both. Nowhere was this truer than in France where, on one hand the Algerian National Liberation Front (FLN in French) became a global symbol for the struggle against imperialism, and at the same time it managed to shift the *locus* of conflict from the African continent to European territory. On October 17, 1961, 30,000 Algerians enacted peaceful demonstrations in Paris; but their repression resulted in deaths, arrests, detainment and over 14,000 interrogations. The Algerian conflict was tearing the fabric of French society and politics apart even before Algeria obtained independence in 1962. Algerian independence definitively sealed the fate of the most visible embodiment of Eurafrica. In 1962, Europe and Africa started to be perceived as two distinct geographical, political, and economic concepts that should find a new way to deal with one another; a process that was enshrined by the French in the identification of France with the European *Hexagon*, an identification would have been impossible before Algerian independence.[19]

The Yaoundé Association: "European-Style" Development and Modernization (1963–1972)

Even though the most visible aspects of the colonial legacy embodied by the Eurafrica project had been buried with the independence of the vast majority of African countries, the Yaoundé Association signed on July 20, 1963 was fundamentally in continuity with the past. It established a free trade area (structurally imbalanced in favor of industrialized countries), created new common institutions to manage it that acted according to the principle of "unanimity," and basically marked the prosecution of the French colonial experience, now without direct territorial domination. Véronique Dimier calls the Yaoundé model: "recycling empire."[20]

The Yaoundé association was born just after the creation of the Organisation of African Unity (OAU) in Addis Ababa, with its calls for an anti-colonialist struggle in Africa; thus, it can also be considered as a way to weaken those who called for the creation of an African federation.[21] The association excluded the Maghreb countries that were ruled by nationalist governments. Anyway in Algeria, in particular, the discovery of vast oil reserves was considered an opportunity to be exploited exclusively by the French industry: There was no willingness whatsoever to share Saharan hydrocarbons with the European partners.[22]

Yaoundé helped to contrast the different hypothesis of African unification that could have allowed the African countries to be more economically independent from Europe. At the same time, it was another way to contrast growing Communist influence in sub-Saharan Africa. This risk was particularly strong in Congo or Ghana, but was by no means insignificant elsewhere.[23]

During the 1960s, the EC became the most important donor for many of the African Francophone states, right behind France. The Yaoundé group included eighteen African countries—fourteen of which had been part of the French colonial empire, three of the Belgian, and one (Somalia) of the Italian. This was largely a Francophone club.

The first EC Commissioner for Development was French, while the all-powerful Director General for Development (DG VIII), the former French colonial officer Jacques Ferrandi, spent much of his time over the telephone with African ministers who were both his friends and his clients. The EDF was a paternalistic affair and provided both for patronage and for significant profits for French companies. At the beginning, DG VIII had only fifty employees to manage aid in eighteen countries. Its bureaucracy increased progressively. The first EDF spent less than 1 percent on industrial cooperation, the second less than 6 percent, and the third only a little more than 7 percent. Of the US$580 million of the first EDF, US$511 millions were distributed to states with "special relations" with France, as compared to US$30 million for the former Belgium colonies and US$35 million for New Guinea.[24] The logic behind European aid was to discourage the development of a local industry that could compete with European exports, while at the same time contributing to infrastructure development, to basic health and education and possibly to developing the raw materials export industry, considered complementary to the European industry. Africans did have a say over the disbursement of EDF funds. But EEC projects were pursued on an unpredictable case-to-case basis, this being considered the more pragmatic "Latin" approach to African development, as opposed to the "technocratic" approach favored by Anglo-Americans and northern Europeans.[25] Martin Rempe paints a nuanced picture of African agency in the EDF development projects, arguing that in some cases African input was important. But he is also prepared to admit that the intervention by European "civil society" actors was marked by a relevant degree of racism: "What is more, all societal actors shared the belief that they served the morally irreproachable cause of helping people in underdeveloped parts of the world, and this conviction was often combined with a feeling of superiority and condescension towards them."[26]

Table 11.1 Sectoral disbursement of the European Development Fund, 1958–1975

	EDF I		EDF II		EDF III	
	Unit of account (thousands)	in %	Unit of account (thousands)	in %	Unit of account (thousands)	in %
Industrialization	4175	0.73	40,225	5.61	45,598	7.15
Rural Production	94,108	16.49	26,6919	37.19	188,966	29.63
Infrastructure[1]	346,847	60.75	310,947	43.32	274,853	43.11
Educational	111,043	19.45	70,092	9.77	66,328	10.4
Others	14,729	2.58	29,489	4.11	61,918	9.71
Total	570,902	100	717,672	100	637,663	100

[1]Infrastructure encompasses transport communication, health, water engineering and urban infrastructure.

Source: Reproduced from Carol Cosgrove-Twitchett, *Europe and Africa: From Association to Partnership* (London: Saxon House, 1978), 136.

The EEC practices were strongly criticized within the Development Assistance Committee (DAC) of the OECD because its development policies smelled too much of colonial paternalism.[27] The United States wanted EEC/EC aid to be more multilateral and less regionally focused on Africa. In any case, the vast majority of Western European aid remained bilateral and was geared towards the achievement of specific national goals.[28] For example, one of the FRG's key aid objectives was to fight against the recognition of the German Democratic Republic and mainly consisted in financing German exports; while for France, development aid to Algeria was a crucial way to support its monopoly control over oil production in the Sahara.

In the 1960s, the EEC/EC became one of the main targets of criticism stemming from the developing countries within the UN system. In the negotiations that led to the creation of the UNCTAD, the EC received a harsher treatment than either the United States or the Soviet Union.[29] It was only the increasing US involvement in Vietnam that eventually shifted the accusation of "imperialism" away from Western Europe and directed it towards the United States. An internal EEC memorandum listed the following charges waged in UN debates against the EEC:

- That Yaoundé was an association that perpetuated the economic dominance of former colonial powers (for example through the system of "reverse preferences");
- That Yaoundé aimed at splitting the world economy into three big macroeconomic areas with the Americas dominated by the United States, Eurafrica dominated by the EEC, and Asia dominated by Japan;
- That the main objective of Yaoundé was to fight against any possible autonomous African federation;
- That the European Common Agricultural Policy discriminated against the agricultural products of the Third World;

- That Western Europe had benefited from Marshall aid to rebuild its shattered economy after World War II, but that it did not recognize the need for a massive flow of aid to the really poor areas of the world;
- That the very same term Yaoundé "association" was paternalistic and unfair in that, contrary to other "associations" with European countries such as Turkey or Greece, the Yaoundé associates were precluded from becoming EEC members.[30]

While it is certainly true that the EEC/EC was criticized in many Third World countries, the British Commonwealth also came under intense scrutiny—both by Commonwealth members and within the United Kingdom itself, where a widening constituency was questioning the centrality of the Commonwealth at a time when European links were becoming increasingly important. These feelings were expressed by the British Conservative Member of Parliament Peter Griffiths, writing in 1966:

We owe no debt to our ex-colonies. The great cities, the schools, hospitals, roads, bridges and airports are the legacy of colonialism. The industries, the bustling commerce and prosperous agriculture, there pay off any debt we might be said to owe [...] The debt owed is one of gratitude to the men and women from this country who brought prosperity to replace poverty, education in place of ignorance, health instead of disease, the Word of God to sweep away superstition and fear. How dare they discount the selfless efforts of missionaries and teachers, engineers and doctors, soldiers and administrators who gave them heritage and an opportunity. Independence was demanded. Now they have it. We owe them no debt. We too demand independence.[31]

The renewal of Yaoundé (Yaoundé II) and the signing of the Arusha Association (with East African Countries such as Kenya, Tanzania and Uganda: it included no development aid) in 1969 did not significantly modify the relationship between the EC and the African countries.

But the political and cultural setting in which Yaoundé had been signed, with politically moderate, anti-Communist, still rather nationalistic Western European governments—the kind of world in which the words of the likes of Peter Griffiths could carry some weight—was rapidly changing.[32] The second Development Decade that the UN opened in 1970 would start from very different premises that would affect also the nature and the logic of the European development policy.

The EC as a "Civilian Power": Facing the New International Economic Order (1972–1984)

By the end of the 1960s, the pressures for a different approach to European development policy came both from within Western European countries and from outside its borders. Western European leaders, more or less willingly, were forced to adapt to the new scenario.

From within, there was the increasingly visible presence of non-European immigrant communities, most of them migrating from former colonies, which reinforced a significant cultural shift affecting both social movements (youth movements, trade unions and NGOs) as well as established European political parties. This shift could be defined as the rise of "Third-Worldism." Coalescing around the opposition to the US intervention in Vietnam, a wide community of politicians, intellectuals, and activists from Western Europe but also from Communist Europe began supporting developing countries as their governments struggled to overcome neocolonialism.[33] If, as Albert Memmi argued in *The Colonizer and the Colonized* published in 1957, the colonizer "having become aware of the unjust relationship which ties him to the colonized, he must continually absolve himself," Western Europeans started—but by no means ended—a process of "mental decolonization" at the end of the 1960s.[34] This abrupt change of mentality and politics, often underestimated by diplomatic historians, was very clear to the observers of the time. US President Richard Nixon identified this trend for his advisor Henry Kissinger, and reflected on the widening political distances in the Atlantic:

> The way the Europeans are talking today, European unity will not be in our interest, certainly not from a political viewpoint or from an economic viewpoint. When we used to talk about European unity, we were thinking in terms of the men who would be at the top of Europe who would be in control. Those men were people that we could get along with. Today, however, when we talk of European unity, and when we look ahead, we have to recognize the stark fact that a united Europe will be led primarily by left-leaning or socialist heads of government. I say this despite the fact that Heath is still in power. Even in Britain and France we have situations where the media and the establishment strongly pull to the left at this point, and also where the media and the establishment take an increasingly anti-US attitude.[35]

External pressures greatly influenced and in a way forced this new openness by European leaders to the requests stemming from the Global South. *Détente* and the perceived imperialism of the superpowers—the Vietnam War and the Soviet intervention to suppress the Prague Spring being a symbol of this—contributed to the weakening of both the US and the Soviet models. The decreasing international appeal of the Superpowers, including the reduction of their development aid, went hand in hand with the emerging economic weight of the Third World countries, first among them the oil-producing countries of Organization of Petroleum Exporting Countries (OPEC).[36] Through nationalizations and diplomatic pressures, especially within the UN system and the Non Aligned Movement, these emerging nations managed to make their voices heard, often for the first time, in the international arena.[37]

The EC leaders, it should be remembered, had approved at The Hague summit of 1969 the first procedures to coordinate their foreign policies (European Political Cooperation, EPC) and had opened the negotiations for the first enlargement of the European Community to the United Kingdom: This would make the EC the largest trading bloc in the world, the most interconnected with the countries of the Global South and, potentially, one of the strongest actors in international economic institutions such as the IMF (The International Monetary Fund), the World Bank, and the UN. If the 1970s were the decade of "interdependence," as widely argued at the time by US political scientists, the EC itself became a community of interdependent nations and could present itself as a symbol of such a decade. For the first time it had begun to acquire its own international personality.[38] French political scientist François Duchêne formulated in 1972 the notion of the EC as a "civilian power": An entity that—in a world where the threat of force was ever less credible due to the nuclear annihilation it would inevitably produce—would influence the rest of the world with its "normative" ability (its support of international law and institutions, and the soft power of its economic weight). The goal of Europe as a civilian power would be to export through diplomacy the regulatory capacity that the European institutions in Brussels had demonstrated in resolving the historic conflicts between nations on the continent.

Expectations ran high before the convening of the Paris summit of EC leaders in 1972. This event should have paved the way for the new EC of the Nine (one that included the United Kingdom, Ireland, and Denmark). The adhesion of the United Kingdom in particular meant that the EC would now include a country that had ruled over what had possibly been the vastest empire in world history. The Nine would be forced to be less inward looking and less focused on Francophone Africa than the Six had previously been. The European Commission bureaucracy viewed the Paris summit as potentially foundational of a new approach, both internally and externally:

> It is indispensable to present to the peoples of the Community, and particularly to its youngest generations, as well as to the entire world, the image of a Community that, after the complicated process of enlargement, will pull its weight once more and be conscious of its own responsibilities [...] what is needed is a new cycle on the model of 'broadening, widening, and deepening', perhaps the following will suffice: 'Solidarity, prosperity, and global responsibility'.[39]

In Paris, the European leaders proclaimed the EC a "privileged partner" of the developing countries and, also due to the initiative of the Dutch President of the European Commission Sicco Mansholt, promised to "activate an overall policy of cooperation and development on a world scale," surpassing the exclusive regional concentration on Africa.[40]

While the Paris summit marked the willingness to strengthen both internally and externally the role of the EC, the energy crisis of 1973, coupled with the demands for a New International Economic Order evoked by the Third World countries at the 6th UN Special Session of 1974, reinforced the willingness to define a distinct European identity.[41] This EC identity, as defined by the Declaration on the European Identity presented by the EC leaders in Copenhagen in December 1973, was based on a stark denial of the colonial past and of Cold War power politics:

> European unification is not directed against anyone, nor is it inspired by a desire for power. On the contrary, the Nine are convinced that their union will benefit the whole international community since it will constitute an element of equilibrium and a basis for co-operation with all countries, whatever their size, culture or social system.[42]

This asserted cooperative nature of Western European diplomacy in the middle of the 1970s was well reflected in the debates of the Trilateral Commission created in 1973 to bring together US, Western European and Japanese elites, in order to foster dialogue among the industrialized countries and avoid unilateral protectionist measures after the crisis of Bretton Woods. Western European countries were far more dependent than the United States on raw materials imports, and their leaderships were facing stronger societal pressures by protest movements and trade unions at home. As European Socialist parties started to define a global agenda in the 1970s through the Socialist International, its leaders tried to present a strategy that would be different from the US one of splitting the Third World between oil-importing developing countries and the oil-exporting developing countries (OPEC).[43] But a Conservative politician, such as the former Dutch Development Minister Berend Jan Udink, argued to his colleagues in the Trilateral in 1974 that:

> The trilateral world will possibly try to split the emerging 'trade-unionism' of the developing countries, but this would be bad policy; we have no moral right to pressure the poorest LDC's to join with us in demanding an oil price rollback, especially in view of the fact that we have not helped the LDC's very much in the past; rather, we should tell the LDC's that we are willing to help them solve their immediate balance-of-payments problems without forcing them to put pressure on OPEC; there is no real common interest between the rich and the poor, excepting the need for a massive shift in funds from the former to the latter; besides, a mere price rollback would leave the LDC's exactly where they were before price increases.[44]

Western European countries, and in particular the Nordic countries, were leading the way in promoting international dialogue, economic cooperation and an increase in development aid.[45] Institutions such as the Vienna Institute for Development or the Institute for the Relations between Italy and Countries from Africa, Latin America, Middle and Far East (IPALMO), among many others, brought together politicians and academics from different political affiliations to promote the study of the Third World and of development policies. Development economists such as Jan Tinbergen in the Netherlands and Gunnar Myrdal in Sweden, both affiliated to the Socialist International, had been put in charge of ambitious global plans for development that would eventually culminate in the report of the Brandt Commission published in 1980 and entitled *North-South: a Programme for Survival*.[46] Overall there were strong societal pressures, but also a clear foreign policy and economic rationale, that pushed for more European engagement with the Third World and for attributing a key role to the EC in this engagement. After all, while it would be have been very hard for France to hide its colonial past, the EC, as a relatively young political entity with no military power, had a much shorter and less controversial history.

All of the pressures coming from within the EC, coupled with the pressures exerted on the EC from the developing countries, converged in the signature of the Lomé Convention in February 1975. This inaugurated a potentially new model of development policy, with new mechanisms and new institutions that partially responded to the requests coming from the Third World countries, within the UNCTAD and elsewhere, for a stabilization of the income from raw materials exports.[47]

While at the beginning the French government pressed for a simple renewal of the Yaoundé association, the outcome of the Lomé negotiations was significantly shaped by the British adhesion (with the need to include Anglophone countries) and by the action of the negotiators that would form the African, Caribbean and Pacific (ACP) group. The choice of Claude Cheysson, who had already acquired a good reputation among African elites (also because he had already favored Algerian independence in the 1950s) as new EC Commissioner for Development signaled that France would now be prepared to accept a new form of "association," more open to the demands of developing countries.[48]

Thanks to the pressures from the Foreign Minister of Guyana, Shridath Ramphal, who represented the Caribbean group as well as the G77, and through the diplomatic strength of Nigeria, representing the African group and eventually the entire ACP group, the EC was forced to renounce the "reverse preferences" and to establish a system for stabilizing the export revenues for agricultural products. This system, called STABEX, was a first step along the lines of what the G77 countries had requested globally in their call for a New International Economic Order in 1974—although the STABEX fell short of stabilizing raw materials prices in general, was unilaterally managed by the EC, and its overall budget was relatively limited.

Nigeria can be commended for having agreed to common negotiations between "associates" and "associables", "French-speaking" and "English-speaking", "AASM" and "Commonwealth members". Until 1973 the majority of the Nigerian establishment opposed special agreements with the EC arguing that: crude oil formed 80 percent of Nigerian export earnings and this product did not come under any EC tariff barriers; Nigerian agricultural exports represented less than 10 percent of its export revenues and so the country would not benefit from the STABEX; Nigeria had been able to survive during the civil war without having any agreement with the EEC; joining the other francophone countries was seen as entering the "neocolonialist" orbit of the EC; and Nigeria did not require any capital aid from the EDF.[49] A decisive breakthrough was achieved in the meeting in Abidjan, in Ivory Coast, convened under the auspices of the Organisation of African Unity (OAU) in May 1973. It was then that African countries refused to sign separate treaties and decided for a common approach:

> Thereafter, throughout the discussions, extending over a year, the ACP never negotiated otherwise than as a Group and spoke always with one voice. It was often an African voice, sometimes a Caribbean or a Pacific voice; but always a voice that spoke for the ACP [...] the Convention was a point of departure in the relations between the developing and the developed States. The negotiations were then the most effective negotiations on a package of comprehensive economic arrangements ever conducted by developing countries with any major sector of the developed world.[50]

The Lomé Convention was the product of the necessity of former Western European colonial powers to now come to terms with their colonial past through relaunching the image of the EC, and at the same of their need to preserve preferential links with providers of key raw materials that were at the same time increasingly important market outlets. At the same time, Lomé was the embodiment of the new negotiating power acquired by African countries that wanted a new system less dependent on political and economic conditionality, one that also included some elements of industrial cooperation that was basically non-existent under the Yaoundé system.[51]

After the signing of Lomé, the Nine also decided on a common participation in the December 1975 launch in Paris of the North–South Dialogue (the Conference for International Economic Cooperation, 1975–1977), where the EC participated as a single actor and where the questions of oil, development, debt and reform of international economic institutions were all discussed together and linked to each other.[52] This, as well as the signing of the Conference on Security and Cooperation in Europe (CSCE) Final Act and the common participation to the G7 starting from the London summit in 1977, confirmed the new standing of the EC, and particularly for the EC Commission, in international arenas.

In the second part of the 1970s, cooperation agreements were concluded between the EC and Mediterranean and Arab countries. The EC contributed

Table 11.2 Regional Allocation of EDF Aid Commitments (ECU/ per capita)

	Lomé I	Lomé II	Lomé III[a]
Sahel	12.7	14.0	16.2
West Africa			
Francophone	11.8	12.7	16.2
Anglophone[b]	1.5	2.1	3.8
Eastern Africa	6.8	6.5	8.2
Madagascar	58.1	58.2	81.7
Central Africa	6.7	7.0	9.0
Southern Africa	8.8	12.0	13.1
Caribbean	14.7	18.3	25.5
Pacific	11.0	16.0	21.5
Total aid commitments			
(million ECU)	1,934.0	2,516.0	3,827.0

Note: Programmed aid only.

[a] As of 31 December 1989.

[b] The unweighted averages for Anglophone West Africa are: 10.6 (Lome I), 12.2 (Lome II),15.5 (Lome III)

Source: Court of Auditors of the European Communities, Annual Reports—Part II, *The European Development Funds*, Brussels (various years).

significant funding for food aid, and, starting from 1976, it inaugurated a modest financing for "non-associables" countries—the global development policy that had been conceived at the Paris summit in 1972. In 1975, the NGO-EC Liaison Committee was established to allow for more direct involvement of a European civil society that was increasingly vocal throughout the 1970s and wanted to have a say in development policies and in the international polices of Western European countries in general.[53]

During the negotiations for Lomé II in 1979, which happened at the time of the second "oil shock"—in many ways an even more painful experience for the consumers than the first one—European negotiators were less forthcoming than five years before, and the new agreements far less innovative. The structure of Lomé basically remained the same. A new system was introduced for minerals: the SYSMIN. This was different from STABEX in that the funding was directly earmarked to increase productivity in the mineral sector, not credited to the general budget of the recipient as in the case of STABEX. The rationality for this new scheme, particularly favored by the FRG, was to secure strategic minerals for the EC in an international economic environment characterized by extreme instability. The requests for a New International Economic Order, while weakened by the lack of practical achievements in the Paris Conference for International Economic Cooperation and by increasing tensions among Third World countries, remained at the center of international debate together with the fear, highlighted by the second "oil shock," of the potential loss of supply of crucial raw materials.

"Washington Consensus," Human Rights and the Fading Eurafrica (1982–1992)

Changes in the international political and economic environment, coupled with economic stagnation and increasing unemployment in the industrialized countries of the West, contributed to a significant shift in the European development discourse during the 1980s. The EC started looking more towards its own South (Greece, Spain, Portugal) and eventually to the East, rather than towards the Global South.

Margaret Thatcher, in her diaries, claims that "1981 was the last year of the West's retreat before the axis of convenience between the Soviet Union and the Third World."[54] At the heart of the change in the international economic environment was the rise of a neoliberal discourse based on the universal validity of "structural adjustments" (devaluation, reducing state expenditure and privatizations, opening up to foreign direct investments) as the best way to be competitive.[55] These policies were in direct opposition to the prevailing developmental discourse in the 1970s, which blamed economic backwardness on the damage provoked by neocolonialism and imperialism, thus implying that colonial and neocolonial powers had to pay for their exploitation by redistributing wealth towards the South.

At the beginning of the 1980s, the bestselling French author Pascal Bruckner could write in *The Tears of the White Men* (first published in 1983) that white men needed to open their eyes to what was going wrong in a Third World where corrupt and undemocratic governments were starving their own populations.[56] African countries, in particular, were considered as economically "underperforming" and politically "failed states." Between the 1980s and 1993, the GDP in Sub-Saharan Africa declined at the rate of 0.8 percent a year, while debt in the region exploded from US$5 billion in 1970, to nearly US$50 billion in 1980, to more than US$150 billion in 1991. Basically every economic and social indicator for Sub-Saharan Africa worsened in the 1980s.[57]

Liberalizations, state-budget cuts, opening up to foreign direct investments, increased taxation, and reduction of the role of the state as promoter of industrialization and provider of services were considered the best solutions against raising external debt and economic stagnation. The North–South dialogue of which the EC had been one of the main sponsors had, by the end of the 1970s, achieved marginal results.[58] The Washington institutions such as the World Bank and the IMF, dominated by OECD countries, shifted their policy towards rigid conditionality and marginalized UN economic institutions such as UNCTAD that asked for state-to-state negotiations. Raw materials producers had to deal with a new scenario of decreasing prices for their exports and faltering state budgets. At the same time, export-oriented economies, especially in Asia, were on the rise. While the 1970s were the decade of OPEC, of raw materials producers and of the North-South dialogue, the 1980s were the decade of the four "Asian tigers"—Hong Kong, South Korea, Taiwan, and Singapore—and of the "Washington consensus." The EC, whose members held crucial positions and significant voting power in the Bretton Woods economic institutions, was at the very heart of this shift toward the Washington consensus.[59]

The French Socialist President François Mitterrand won the general elections in 1981 on a 1970s agenda. He campaigned for "French-style" socialism, nationalizations, and manifested a strongly anti-American discourse in foreign policy. His first government included Claude Cheysson, the former EC Commissioner for Development in charge of the Lomé negotiations, as Minister for Foreign Affairs. The Third-Worldist stance of the French Socialist government, also embodied by the presence of the friend of the Cuban revolution Régis Debray as special foreign policy advisor to Mitterrand, basically lasted less than a year, until the failure of the North–South summit in Cancun in 1981.[60]

The new French EC Commissioner for Development Egdar Pisani presented in 1982 a memorandum that started from the premise of the failure of the North–South dialogue and of the New International Economic Order. According to Pisani, the EC should find an original way between the "rigid conditionality" of international financial institutions and the extreme "non conditionality" of the Lomé scheme. The memorandum argued in favor of a "policy dialogue" with ACP governments, and for more protection of foreign direct investments. While Cheysson used to say to the ACP governments "EDF money is your money," Pisani argued that the EC should finance programs and not single projects, thus gaining some degree of control over the recipients' general development planning.[61] At the same time, EC development policy was more streamlined with that of other multilateral institutions.[62] The background for this shift in attitude toward developing countries was both a shift to more neoliberal politics in Western Europe, with the success of Thatcher in the United Kingdom and Helmut Schmidt in the FRG, but also a difficult economic situation under the pressure of a strong dollar, increasing interest rates, unemployment, slow growth and the crisis of mature industrial sectors such as steel, refineries and ship-building. There would be less aid money available, and this had to be used in a more effective way.

The Lomé mechanism was by now generally considered as underperforming and incapable of fostering economic growth in Africa. Trade preferences offered to developing countries were eroding due to the general decrease in tariffs and barriers. The whole idea of aid as a way of fostering state-driven industrialization in developing countries and of changing the global distribution of labor was fading into the background as a relic of the past. Between 1980 and 1989, some thirty-six African countries had taken a total of 241 loans from international financial institutions, and many were to follow in 1990. As noted by Paul Nugent:

> Whereas the European colonists had delivered Africans from pre-colonial despotism and 'intertribal warfare', their later twentieth-century counterparts saw themselves as delivering the benighted continent from autocratic and incompetent regimes who could not grasp elementary economics.[63]

During the negotiations for Lomé III in 1984, the respect for "human rights"—even though there was still significant opposition on the ACP side to political conditionality—became one of the conditions for the disbursement of EC aid. The idea was that both official development aid and the project approach had not worked well and had to be substituted by a more intrusive "policy dialogue." As Dieter Frisch, Director General for Development between 1982 and 1993, explains: "This dialogue triggered a shift away from the financing of one-off projects—the construction of a road for instance—towards institutional and financial support for sector-based policies—for instance a transport policy integrating all modes of transport, responsibility for maintaining the investment made, passenger charts, etc."[64] In the new Lomé, the concept of "mutual interest" was added alongside solidarity as a motivation for EC aid, raising the issue of ACP obligations as well as benefits.[65]

The pressures stemming from a European public opinion, highly critical of the relations between their governments and corrupt and violent postcolonial African leaders, was certainly among the driving factors in the presence of a new human rights dimension in the dialogue with ACP countries. The idea that governments that were ideologically at odds with the Western European model—such as Ethiopia, Angola, and Mozambique—could be accepted as EC partners was being questioned. NGOs acquired an increasingly significant role as agents of development policy, and their approach was highly suspicious of government and state action in both donor and in recipient countries.

The paradox of this was that the pressure on governments to reduce public expenditure and to privatize, especially in Africa, actually worsened instead of improving the performance of these countries in terms of respect for economic and social rights.[66] The other paradox was that the approach of safeguarding earnings from raw materials exports, enshrined in the 1975 STABEX, was criticized and sidelined at exactly the time when it would have been most needed: in the 1980s, the prices of raw materials dropped continuously and STABEX was conceived precisely to deal with such hard times and guarantee some income stability to raw materials exporters. The price of copper, for example, crucial to Zambia and Zaire, collapsed in 1975 and in 1986 was 56 percent of what it had been at the beginning of the 1970s. Instead of expanding STABEX to include other raw materials, its funding was reduced. It is hard here to assess if the STABEX's "philosophy" was side-lined because it was wrong, or just because there was no money or political support left.

By the middle of the 1980s, EC aid represented 15 percent of the overall aid that the EC countries distributed in bilateral or multilateral form.[67] On the other hand, EC aid had also been growing continuously at a time when bilateral aid was stagnating, or even contracting. It remained heavily concentrated on Africa until the very end of the 1980s, but strong pressures were building up both to change the EC prominent regional focus on Africa and to radically modify its objectives.

Even more important, from a symbolic point of view, was the fact that while EC aid was stagnating and changing both in terms of its nature and geographic focus, the EC governments began intra-European discussions on mobility and visas that would increasingly separate the intra-EC movement of people from non-EC mobility. As the Schengen Agreement of 1985 developed into the Schengen Convention in 1990, a new term, *extracomunitari* (non-Community nationals), was coined in Italy to describe, rather disparagingly, non-European migrants.[68]

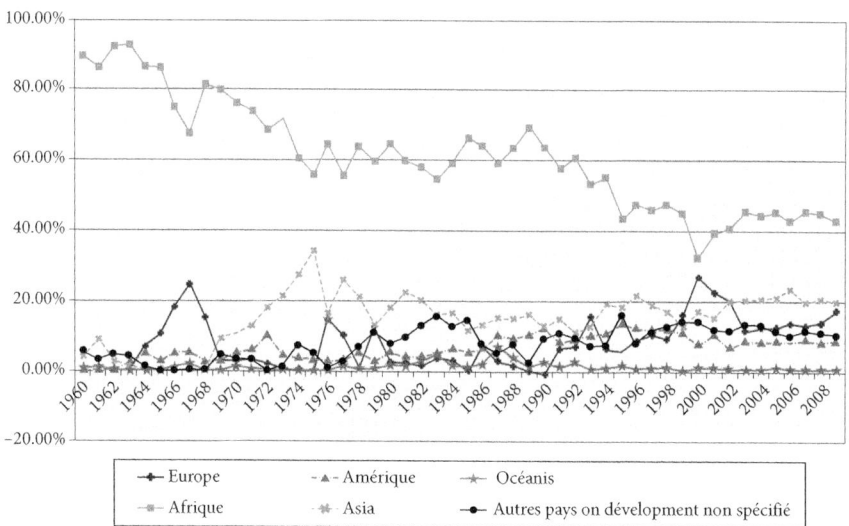

Figure 11.1 Répartition géographique de l'aide par continent.

Source: Reproduced from François Pacquement, "Eléments statistiques sur cinquante and d'aide européenne au développement," in Gérard Bossuat (ed.), *La France, L'Europe et L'aide au Dévelopment* (Paris: IGPDE, 2013).

Table 11.3 Network of EC Trade, 1958, 1971 and 1985 (percentage share)

	EC*	Non-EC Western Europe	Other Industrial Countries	USSR and Eastern Europe	China[6]	Latin America	Africa	South and South East Asia	West Asia	Residual Trade
Imports from:										
1958 EC(6)	32.1	25.8	10.8	2.6	1.3	7.4	11.5	4.6	3.0	0.9
1971 EC(6)	49.3	21.9	11.2	3.4	0.4	3.6	4.7	2.1	2.1	1.3
EC(9)	50.6	16.1	13.9	3.3	0.3	3.9	4.9	2.8	2.4	1.3
1985 EC(9)	54.2	13.3	12.8	2.6	0.4	3.0	5.4	3.4	3.2	1.7
Exports to:										
1958 EC(6]	33.9	19.5	17.9	3.1	0.4	6.7	9.6	2.9	5.6	0.4
1971 EC(6)	52.3	15.0	12.6	3.3	0.3	3.3	6.0	1.6	5.1	0.5
EC(9)	53.2	11.0	15.0	3.4	0.3	3.3	6.0	2.0	5.4	0.4
1985 EC(9)	52.3	13.9	14.2	2.8	0.8	2.1	4.7	3.4	4.8	1.0

• Intra-trade *0* Includes other socialist economies in Asia.

Source: *UNCTAD, Handbook of International Trade and Development Statistics* (New York, 1976 and 1988).

Conclusion

Only with the Treaty of the European Union (Maastricht Treaty) was a Development Cooperation policy given a clear legal base in the EU treaty. Among its objectives would be to "foster sustainable economic and social development" along with "consolidating democracy and the rule of law, and that of respecting of human rights and fundamental freedoms." Development cooperation had to be coherent with the other external policies of the EU, and its establishment officially marked the end of the concept of "political neutrality" of aid. Significantly, the ACP–EC Convention was not included in the normal framework of EU development cooperation and was left with a relevant degree of autonomy.[69]

Arguably, the Africa-focused development policy became less important as an external policy of the EC as early as the 1980s—certainly less important than it was in 1957—as Western European countries had to cope with competition by the emerging economies in Asia and elsewhere, the need to integrate the countries of Southern Europe and, eventually, to deal with the fading and then the collapse of the Soviet Empire in Eastern Europe. The EEC was born Eurafrican in 1957. By the end of the 1980s, the EC had become a key promoter of globalization and of decreasing barriers to trade and to foreign direct investments. In other words: while Africa had been the main object of EEC policy after the Rome Treaties, by the end of the 1980s it was only one of its possible partners and markets in an increasingly multipolar world. The focus on Eurafrica that implied a specific responsibility towards Africa (even if colonial in nature) shifted to a discourse on "human rights" that had a global rather than regional significance.[70]

While up to the end of the 1980s the focus of EC development aid was still Africa, the form and the objectives of this aid had changed very significantly from 1957 to the end of the 1980s. The end of the Cold War and the shift of geopolitical focus towards Eastern Europe, coupled with the end of "commodity power" in the 1970s, contributed to the decreasing relevance of Africa.[71]

A comparison between EC development aid and other forms of multilateral and bilateral development aid programs (including by EC countries themselves) would probably shed an even clearer light on the importance of Africa and on the peculiar patterns and objectives of 40 years of EC development aid. Furthermore, there is a great need for more research, following the lead of Martin Rempe, on specific development projects to assess how EC development aid fared on the ground and how it changed over time.

To this day, the ACP Convention and EDF represent a significant portion of EU development aid (in 2014–2020 it had been allocated 30 percent of the total EU spending on external assistance) and remains outside the normal framework of the EU budget: its management is intergovernmental, and the European Parliament has almost no control over it.[72] This probably remains the single greatest demonstration of the legacies of colonialism for some European countries. To conclude, one could argue that development policy has certainly contributed to the establishment of an external personality of the EC/EU but that, to this day, this policy has a very hybrid nature. On the one hand, it has become similar to the development cooperation axis of other OECD countries and of other multilateral institutions; on the other hand, mainly through the African Caribbean and Pacific Group (ACP), the EC/EU tries to retain a "special relationship" with countries that were part of European colonial empires, a relationship that is becoming once again increasingly important with the recent immigration trends from African countries.

Notes

1   On the importance of the legacies of colonial empires in Western Europe: Elisabeth Buettner, *Europe after Empire: Decolonization, Society and Culture* (Cambridge: Cambridge University Press, 2016).

2   Mark Mazower, "The End of Eurocentrism," *Critical Enquiry*, 40:4 (2014), 298–313.

3   Frederick Cooper, *Colonialism in Question: Theory, Knowledge, History* (LA: University of California Press, 2005); Martin Thomas, *Fight or Flight: Britain, France and the Roads from Empire* (Oxford: Oxford University Press, 2014).

4   Sara Lorenzini, "Sviluppo e strategie di guerra fredda: il contagio difficile," *Storica*, 53 (2012), 7–37.

5   Joseph Morgan Hodge, "Writing the History of Development (Part 1: The First Wave)," *Humanity: An International Journal of Human Rights, Humanitarianism and Development*, 6:3 (2015), 429–463; Mark Frey and Sönke Kunkel, "Writing the History of Development: A Review of the Recent Literature," *Contemporary European History*, 20:2 (2011), 215–232.

6   Corinna R. Unger, "Postwar European Aid: Defined by Decolonization, the Cold War, and European Integration?" in Stephen Macekura and Erez Manela (eds.), *The Development Century: A Global History* (New York: Cambridge University Press, 2018); Frederick Cooper, *Citizenship Between Empire and Nation: Remaking France and French Africa, 1945–1960* (Princeton: Princeton University Press, 2014).

7   Sven Beckert, "American Danger: United States Empire, Euafrica, and the Territorialization of Industrial Capitalism, 1870–1950," *The American Historical Review*, 122:4 (2017), 1137–1170.

8   Martin Rempe has gone far in assessing these reciprocal influences: Martin Rempe, "Entangled Industrialization: The EEC and Industrial Development in Francophone West Africa," in Christian Grabas and Alexander Nützenadel (eds.), *Industrial Policy in Europe after 1945: Wealth, Power and Economic Development in the Cold War* (London: Palgrave Macmillan, 2014), 236–255.

9   For this forgotten episode of late colonialism: Antonio Maria Morone, *Come l'Italia è tornata in Africa 1950–1960* (Bari: Laterza, 2011).

10 For the Eurafrican origins of the EEC, see Peo Hansen and Stefan Jonsson, *Eurafrica: The Untold History of European Integration and Colonialism* (London: Bloomsbury, 2014).

11 Tony Chafer, *The End of Empire in French West Africa: France's Successful Decolonization* (London: Bloomsbury, 2002), 11.

12 Muriam Haleh Davis, "Restaging *Mise en Valeur*: 'Postwar Imperialism' and the Plan de Constantine," *Review of Middle East Studies*, 44:2 (2010), 176–186.

13 Frederick Cooper, "Reconstructing Empire in British and French Africa," in Mark Mazower, Jessica Reinisch and David Feldman (eds.), *Post-War Reconstruction in*

Western Europe: International Perspectives, 1945–1949 (Oxford: Oxford University Press, 2011), 196–210. An extreme case of late "developmental colonialism" in: Miguel Bandeira Jerónimo and António Costa Pinto, "A Modernizing Empire? Politics, Culture, and Economy in Portuguese Late Colonialism," in Miguel Bandeira Jerónimo and António Costa Pinto (eds.), *The Ends of European Colonial Empires* (London: Palgrave Macmillan, 2015), 51–80.

14　Jean Monnet, *Mémoires*, trans. Richard Mayne (London: Collins, 1978), 422.

15　Anjo G. Harryvan and Jan van der Harst, "A Bumpy Road to Lomé: The Netherlands, Association and the Yaoundé Treaties, 1956–1969," in Marie-Thérèse Bitsch and Gérard Bossuat (eds.), *L'Europe unie et l'Afrique. De l'idée d'Eurafrique à la convention de Lomè I*, (Brussels: Bruylant, 2005), 319–343; Guia Migani, *La France et l'Afrique sub-saharienne, 1957–1963* (Brussels: Peter Lang, 2008).

16　Jean Charles Asselain, *Histoire économique de la France du XVIIIe siècle à nos jours, Vol. 2: De 1919 à la fin des années 1970* (Paris: Seuil, 1984), 84. Quoted in Martin Rempe, "Decolonization by Europeanization? The Early EEC and the Transformation of French-African Relations," *KFG Working Paper*, n. 27, May 2011.

17　Gary Wilder, "Eurafrique as the Future Past of 'Black France': Sarkozy's Temporal Confusion and Senghor's Postwar Vision," in Trice Danielle Keaton, Tracey Deenan Sharpley-Whiting and Tyler Stovall (eds.), *Black France/France Noire: The History and Politics of Blackness* (Durham: Duke University Press, 2012), 57–87.

18　Frank Gerits, "When the Bull Elephants Fight: Kwame Nkrumah, Non-Alignment, and Pan-Africanism as an Interventionist Ideology in the Global Cold War (1957–66)," *The International History Review*, 37:5 (2015), 951–969.

19　Todd Shepard, "Making French and European Coincide: Decolonization and the Politics of Comparative and Transnational Histories," *Ab Imperio*, 2 (2007), 1–21.

20　Veronique Dimier, *The Invention of a European Development Aid Bureaucracy: Recycling Empire* (London: Palgrave Macmillan, 2014); Urban Vahsen, *Eurafrikanische Entwicklungskooperation: Die Assoziierungspolitik der EWG gegenüber dem subsaharischen Afrika in den 1960er Jahren* (Stuttgart: Franz Steiner Verlag, 2010).

21　Yacouba Zerbo, "La problématique de l'unité africaine (1958–1963)," *Guerres mondiales et conflits contemporains*, 212:4 (2003), 113–127.

22　Hocine Malti, *Histoire Secrète du Pétrole Algérien* (Paris: La Découverte, 2012), 40–50.

23　On fear of the spread of communism in Africa, see for example: Zbigniew Brzezinski, "Conclusion: The African Challenge," in Zbigniew Brzezinski (ed.), *Africa and the Communist World* (Stanford: Stanford University Press, 1963), 200–230.

24　Frédéric Turpin, "Alle origini della politica europea di cooperazione allo sviluppo: la Francia e la politica di associazione Europa-Africa (1957–1975)," *Ventunesimo Secolo* (2007), 137.

25　Sara Lonzini, *Una Strana Guerra Fredda: Lo sviluppo e le relazioni Nord-Sud* (Bologna: Il Mulino, 2017), 233–248.

26　Martin Rempe, "From Development Business to Civil Society? Societal Actors in Development Cooperation," in Jan-Henrik Meyer and Wolfram Kaiser (eds.), *Societal Actors in European Integration: Polity-Building and Policy-making, 1958–1992* (Basingstoke: Palgrave Macmillan, 2013), 134.

27　Guia Migani, "La politique de coopération européenne: une politique étrangère *ante litteram*? Le rôle de la CEE au DAC pendant les années soixante," in Morten Rasmussen and Ann-Christina Knudsen (eds.), *The Road to a United Europe:*

Interpretations of the Process of European Integration (Brussels: Peter Lang, 2009), 189–204.

28   Carol Lancaster, *Foreign Aid: Diplomacy, Development, Domestic Policies* (Chicago: University of Chicago Press, 2006).

29   Giuliano Garavini, *After Empires: European Integration, Decolonization and the Challenge from the Global South, 1957–1986* (Oxford: Oxford University Press, 2012).

30   Historical Archives of the European Union (HAEU), CM 2-1962, 122, Note, Criticisms of the Community by members of the United Nations, November 8, 1961.

31   Quoted in Buettner, *Europe after Empire*, 317–318.

32   Antonio Varsori, *Alle origini del presente: L'Europa occidentale nella crisi degli anni Settanta* (Milano: FrancoAngeli, 2008).

33   Richard T. Griffiths, "Development Aid: Some Reference Points for Historical Research," in Helge Pharo and Pohle Fraser (eds.), *The Aid Rush: Aid Regimes in Northern Europe During the Cold War*, Vol. 1 (Bergen: Fagbokforlaget, 2008), 17–52; Robert Gildea, James Mark and Niek Pas, "European Radicals and the Third World," *The Journal of the Social History Society*, 8:4 (2011), 449–471.

34   Albert Memmi, *The Colonizer and the Colonized* (London: Souvenir Press, 1974), 98.

35   FRUS, 1973–1976, Vol. XXXI, Foreign Economic Policy, Doc. 31, draft memo from President Nixon to the President's Assistant for National Security Affairs (Kissinger), 10 March 1973.

36   Stephen J. Macekura, *Of Limits and Growth: The Rise of Global Sustainable Development in the Twentieth Century* (Cambridge: Cambridge University Press, 2015).

37   Jürgen Dinkel, "The 'Third World' Begins to Flex its Muscles: The Non-Aligned Movement and the North-South Conflict during the 1970s," in Sandra Bott, Jussi M. Hanhimäki, Janick Marina Schaufelbuehl and Marco Wyss (eds.), *Neutrality and Neutralism in the Global Cold War: The Non-Aligned Movement in the East-West Conflict* (London: Routledge, 2015), 108–123.

38   Lorenzo Ferrari, *Sometimes Speaking with a Single Voice: The European Community as an International Actor, 1969–1979* (Brussels: Peter Lang, 2016).

39   HAEU, FMM 58, E.P. Wellerstein, *Idées sur le Sommet*, October 4, 1972.

40   *Bulletin of the European Communities*, 10 (1972), "Paris Summit Declaration, October 1972."

41   Aurélie Elisa Gfeller, *Building a European Identity: France, the United States and the Oil Shock, 1973–74* (New York: Berghahn, 2012).

42   Declaration on the European Identity (Copenhagen, December 14, 1973) http://www. cvce.eu/content/publication/1999/1/1/02798dc9-9c69-4b7d-b2c9-f03a8db7da32/ publishable_en.pdf (last accessed October 29, 2018).

43   Christian Salm, *Transnational Socialist Networks in the 1970s: European Community Development Aid and Southern Enlargement* (London: Palgrave Macmillan, 2016).

44   Rockefeller Archives, The Trilateral Commission: Meetings of the Trilateral Study Group on LDC Priorities, March 18–19, 1974.

45   Pharo and Fraser, *The Aid Rush*.

46   Independent Commission on International Development Issues, *North-South: A Programme for Survival* (London: Macmillan, 1980).

47   Jean Marie Palayret, "Da Lomé I a Cotonou: morte e trasfigurazione della convenzione CEE/ACP," in: Elena Calandri (ed.), *Il primato sfuggente: l'Europa e l'intervento per lo sviluppo, 1957–2007* (Milan: FrancoAngeli, 2009), 35–52.

48   Lorenzini, "Sviluppo e strategie di guerra fredda," 248–255.

49   Timothy M. Shaw and Olajide Aluko, *Nigerian Foreign Policy: Alternative Perceptions and Projections* (London: Palgrave Macmillan, 1983), 84–86.

50   Shridath Ramphal, "ACP Beginnings," Interview (1.11.13): http://www. inoutconstruct.com/fileadmin/user_upload/EPG_Caribbean_SpeechRamphal.pdf (last accessed November 20, 2017).

51   Guia Migani, "The EEC and the Challenge of ACP States' Industrialization, 1972–1975," in Grabas and Nützenadel (eds.), *Industrial Policy in Europe after 1945*, 256–276.

52   Giuliano Garavini, "The Conference for International Economic Cooperation: A Diplomatic Reaction to the Oil Shock (1975–1977)," in Rasmussen and Knudsen (eds.), *The Road to a United Europe*, 153–168.

53   Kevin O'Sullivan, "A Global Nervous System: The Rise of European Humanitarian NGs, 1945–1985," in Mark Frey, Sönke Kunkel and Corinna R. Unger (eds.), *International Organization and Development, 1945–1990* (London: Macmillan, 2014), 196–219.

54   Margaret Thatcher, *Downing Street Years* (New York: Harper Press, 2012), 157.

55   On the role of the Thatcher and Reagan administrations in promoting neoliberalism, see James E. Cronin, *Global Rules: America, Britain and a Disordered* World (New Haven: Yale University Press, 2014). On the emergence of global finance see Eric Helleiner, *States and the Reemergence of Global Finance: From Bretton Woods to the 1990s* (Ithaca: Cornell University Press, 1996).

56   Pascal Bruckner, *The Tears of the White Men: Compassion as Contempt* (London: The Free Press, 1986).

57   Delfin Go, Denis Nikitin and Xiongjian Wang, "Poverty and Inequality in Sub-Saharan Africa: Literature Survey and Empirical Assessment," *Annals of Economics and Finance*, 8:2 (2007), 251–304.

58   Thomas Walde, *A Requiem for the New International Economic Order: The Rise and Fall of Paradigms in International Economic Law*, CPMLP, University of Dundee, Professional Paper n. 9, 1994.

59   Rawi Abdelal, *Capital Rules: The Construction of Global Finance* (Cambridge, MA: Harvard University Press, 2009).

60   Guia Migani, "The Road to Cancun: the Birth and Death of the North-South Summit, 1978–1982," in Emmanuel Mourlon-Druol and Federico Romero (eds.), *Summitry at the Dawn of the Global Era: Historical Enquiries into the Rise of the G-7 and the European Council* (London: Routledge, 2014), 174–197.

61   Edgar Pisani, "L'aide au développement: entre anciennes priorités et nouveaux défis," in Michel Dumoulin (ed.), *The European Commission, 1973–1986* (Luxembourg: Publications Office of the European Union, 2014), 401–420.

62   Ole Elgrstrom, "Lomé and Post-Lomé: Asymmetric Negotiations and the Impact of Norms," *European Foreign Affairs Review*, 5 (2000), 175–195.

63   Paul Nugent, *Africa since Independence* (London: Palgrave Macmillan, 2012), 327.

64   http://ecdpm.org/wp-content/uploads/2013/10/PMR-15-European-Union-Development-Policy-International-cooperation-2008.pdf (last accessed October 29, 2018).

65   Carol Cosgrove Sacks (ed.), *Europe, Development and Diplomacy: New Issues in EU Relations with Developing Countries* (London: Palgrave Macmillan, 2001), 268.

66   The classic study in this issue is: James Raymond Vreeland, *The IMF and Economic Development* (Cambridge: Cambridge University Press, 2003).

67   François Pacquement, "Eléments statistiques sur cinquante ans d'aide européenne au développement," in Gérard Bossuat (ed.), *La France, l'Europe et l'aide au*

développement. Des traités de Rome à nos jours (Paris: Comité pour l'histoire économique et financière de la France, 2013).

68   Simone Paoli, "The Schengen Agreements and their Impact on Euro-Mediterranean Relations: The Case of Italy and the Maghreb," *Journal of European Integration History*, 21:1 (2015), 125–146.

69   Paul Hoebink (ed.), "The Treaty of Maastricht and the Europe's Development Co-operation," in *Studies in European Development Co-operation Evaluation, No. 1*, Brussels, December 2004.

70   Patrick Pasture, "The EC/EU Between the Art of Forgetting and the Palimpsest of Empire," European Review, 26 (3), 545–581.

71   Enzo R. Grilli, *The European Community and the Developing Countries* (Cambridge: Cambridge University Press, 1993), 331.

72   European Parliament, *European Development Fund: Joint Development Cooperation and the EU Budget: In or Out?*, European Parliament Research Service, November 2014.

Part Three

Reflections and Conclusions

12

The European Project: A Critical Reconsideration

Konrad H. Jarausch

In the historical literature on the second half of the twentieth century, the integration of Europe plays only a marginal role. Much of the scholarly output is still dominated by syntheses of national history because many big publishing houses are convinced that the public prefers to read about its own country. Among the more general overviews such as Mark Mazower's *Dark Continent*, the "European project" appears only in passing and with a skeptical undertone at that. Tony Judt's magisterial reflection in *Postwar* devotes more space to the cooperation effort, but accuses the European Union (EU) of generating a "parochial view." Global histories like Edgar Wolfrum's *Welt im Zwiespalt* offer no sustained treatment of the issue either, since they are interested in broader transnational questions.[1] Philipp Ther's reflection on the post-communist transformation in Eastern Europe just presents a critique of the EU's neoliberal assumptions. While Andreas Rödder's history of the present devotes an entire chapter to "News from Old Europe," only Andreas Wirsching's survey of post-1989 events reserves an entire section to the EU and my own synthesis of the twentieth century *Out of Ashes* explores European developments from a modernization perspective.[2]

The present volume is therefore a welcome effort to break out of the ghetto of Europeanist scholarship by investigating the EU as an external policy actor. Its chapters approach the subject by contextualizing the European Community (EC) in relation to the Cold War and other major powers like the United States or the Soviet Union. Moreover, the chapters probe half a dozen important topics such as EU enlargement or its trade policies in order to ascertain how successful Brussels was in achieving its stated aims. The contributions are written by well-known specialists like Piers Ludlow or Wilfried Loth, drawn from different European countries. Their analyses are supplemented by texts from younger scholars like Angela Romano who have produced detailed empirical studies of specific topics. Moreover, the contributions represent a fortuitous mix of historians and political scientists. Through its rigorous design and balanced interpretations this collection of chapters intends to appeal both to EU specialists and generalist scholars interested in the European past.

The sober tone of the contributions also helps resolve the question of what kind of narrative is to be used for representing the development of the EU—a story of success or failure. On the one hand, much integration literature is written by convinced partisans of Europe who fall into the Treitschke trap of commenting on the process while advocating its goals. This celebratory approach also informs the House of European History which opened its doors in 2017, because it is "dedicated to the understanding of the shared past and diverse experiences of European people," and presents integration as a triumph of cooperation over nationalist obstacles.[3] On the other hand, the Eurosceptics dominate the conservative American and British media like the *Wall Street Journal* or the Murdoch press by predicting the imminent demise of the EU because they cannot understand what a "civilian power" is all about. Republican presidential candidates like Mitt Romney and Donald Trump have disparaged the EU as being socialist, pointing to its weak response to the Greek Euro-crisis or to rising anti-immigration sentiment that has produced backlash such as Brexit.[4] Fortunately, the chapters of this volume present a more nuanced assessment of European achievements and disappointments.

By treating the EU as a polity in becoming, this volume dispels the notion of inevitability and moral superiority, making its development amenable to critical historical analysis. Such a perspective does not overstate integration achievements but rather conceives of the evolution of the EU as a process of advances and set-backs that are contingent upon major actors and situational constellations. Far from suppressing difficulties, such an approach scrutinizes the many contradictions, crises and conflicts that have marked the European project in the past and are likely to bedevil it in the future. It also makes it possible to criticize mistaken policies like the agricultural protectionism of the CAP or the neocolonial aspects of the development policy towards Africa. The result of such scrutiny is a more complex understanding of the complicated nature of the fits and starts of integration, addressing the process of widening and deepening by looking at the actual record rather than just repeating ideological judgments.[5] What new understanding do these chapters provide when taken as a whole?

Emergence as an Actor

It is often forgotten that the process of European integration emerged out of a post-war constellation in which competing institutions sought to prevent the outbreak of a Third World War through intensified cooperation. Winston Churchill's Zurich encouragement of continental collaboration, the founding of the Council of Europe and the creation of the Organization for European Economic Cooperation (OEEC) were important first steps, but they were only one alternative solution to European problems. The founding of the Western European Union and subsequent creation of the North Atlantic Treaty Organization (NATO) in 1949 claimed priority in the realm of defense during the Cold War. The provision of the American nuclear umbrella maintained the United States as a European power through the stationing of troops, making Washington a super-protector who could determine the shape of the rebuilding on the continent. And even more broadly yet, the creation of a United Nations as successor to the defunct League of Nations, now located in New York, provided a global effort to safeguard peace in the future. Its subsidiary organizations like the United Nations Education, Scientific and Cultural Organization (UNESCO) offered another platform for East–West and North–South cooperation. Due to the failure of more far-reaching political plans, the creation of the European Coal and Steel Community (ECSC) in 1951 and the European Economic Community (EEC) in 1958 were therefore merely regional efforts at integration, limited in scope.[6]

Piers Ludlow's chapter is a reminder that the asymmetry between far-reaching federalist aspirations and limited economic powers was a birth defect that hamstrung the EC from the beginning. The Common Market was not a new state but a form of inter-governmental cooperation that assumed some transnational features in the area of trade and tariffs—a more modest institution than some of its founders like Jean Monnet had envisaged. The original focus on coal and steel had a certain logic, since the former was the dominant energy source and the latter an essential material for the rebuilding of ravaged cities. But it was only the failure to integrate defense and politics that propelled the relaunching of the European project through the Treaties of Rome and the creation of the Common Market in the functionalist hope that additional steps would naturally follow in the future. The Community institutions such as president, court and parliament already indicated a more far-reaching ambition, but the very economic success of abolishing internal customs through the creation of a shared market ultimately stabilized the European nation-states after the war—making further steps in integration all that much more difficult. The Gaullist *Europe des patries* was therefore not just a product of French delusions of grandeur, but an expression of how far the member states were prepared to go with pooling parts of their sovereignty.[7]

The volume also correctly emphasizes the importance of the Cold War context within which the Common Market was able to develop. The East–West conflict meant that integration could only include Western Europe, thereby splitting the continent and leaving the Eastern part to the less successful effort at cooperation with the Soviet Union in the Council for Mutual Economic Assistance (COMECON). Kenneth Weisbrode points to the crucial importance of the United States as original sponsor of integration which, however, retained a certain ambivalence. With growing economic recovery, the original six were bound to chafe at its proconsul paternalism and try to assert their own interests, becoming competitors in trade, and precipitating conflicts like the "Chicken War." Angela Romano demonstrates the oblique relations of the EC to the Socialist Bloc, surprised by the sustained growth of the West when Marxist analysis had predicted the demise of "late capitalism." Not sure what it should do about the Common Market, the Soviet leadership was instead annoyed by Western support of a heterodox Yugoslavia. Beyond neoliberalism, anti-Communism was therefore also part of the founding ideology of the EC. In contrast to some of the Western-centered literature, it is important to remember the formative impact of the Cold War.[8]

The emergence of the EU as an actor in its own right was therefore a contested and prolonged process that took place in several stages. Originally the Common Market influenced international relations only by its very existence and successful economic growth, making the rival European Free Trade Association (EFTA) take notice and the Mediterranean countries think about joining as well. Only during the 1970s with the establishment of the Brussels bureaucracy did the EC gradually become accepted in trade negotiations about tariff reduction (General Agreement on Tariffs and Trade, GATT) or in talks with Asian rivals. And it took until the early 1990s before the relevant institutional infrastructure was created with the transition to the EU by the Single European Act in order to have the appropriate negotiators and supporting expertise for playing an independent role. But from the beginning the European Union was hampered by the cumbersome nature of its consensual decision-making in which conflicting national interests needed to be harmonized so as to present a common front to the outside. Time and again such disagreements, for instance on agricultural protectionism versus industrial free trade, stalled negotiations and muffled the European voice. But in spite of such difficulties, the integration process was seen as successful from the outside, even becoming a model for other regions that attempted to emulate its cooperation.[9]

The consolidation of the European Community gradually attracted the attention of historians, although telling the story of a polity in becoming turned out to be more difficult than dealing with established states. Already in the 1960s political scientists like Ernst B. Haas began to chronicle the development of the Common Market in the hope that it would lead to a unification of the old continent. Social scientists therefore came to dominate the new subfield of European integration studies, both analyzing the process and advising actors on how to move it forward. Eventually historians also entered the discussion by addressing the deep pre-history of ideas of Europe and analyzing earlier, failed efforts at cooperation like the Briand-Stresemann plans in the late 1920s. The actual emergence of the ECSC, the failure of the European Defense Community (EDC) and the development of the Common Market were frustrating topics because of the discrepancy between the proclamation of grandiose plans and their more modest practical implementation. It took, therefore, a couple of decades for a sustained historical scholarship to engage the integration process.[10]

Successful Initiatives

The most important external policy of the European Community was, as Eirini Karamouzi emphasizes, the enlargement with several sets of new members. This was largely an ad hoc process in which potential newcomers petitioned the Common Market for admission. Existing members might welcome new admissions in order to increase the size of the market, strengthen its economic weight in international negotiations, and have their approach validated. But concretely enlargement tended to create new difficulties, because latecomers would render decision-making more difficult, since their interests and preferences might clash with those of existing members. While during the first round of enlargement in the early 1970s two of the new members who had belonged to the EFTA were on a similar level in wealth and self-government (while Ireland lagged behind), they nonetheless represented more of a free-trade approach that conflicted with the integration aspirations of the original founding six. This difference helps to explain Charles de Gaulle's double veto of the British effort to join the Common Market, which was only overcome once he retired from power. In order to preserve the institutional gains of prior integration, Brussels insisted on later joiners accepting the so-called *acquis communautaire* which consisted of numerous regulations and decisions that future members had to accept as a precondition of entry. Instead of renegotiating the whole set of arrangements, the European Community acted as a unit that required the potential members to treat it as a whole.[11]

Although the EU worked out an enlargement procedure relatively late, this policy had a considerable transformative impact upon potential members. The principle of conditionality suggested that petitioners had to become compatible with the Community during a prolonged transition period in which they would meet its standards. The two basic requirements included a liberal "market economy" rather than a neo-mercantilist form of government control and the existence of democratic governance rather than a rightist or leftist dictatorship. In order to reach these goals, Brussels was willing to offer material aid—a promise that made membership attractive to those states who were intent upon raising their standard of living and liberalizing their political structures. The chapter by Elena Calandri on the Mediterranean also suggests that some countries like Greece, Spain, and Portugal were recognized as "European" and therefore accepted as future members while other Maghreb nations were considered too underdeveloped economically and too different culturally in order to be included. In contrast to new membership among equals, the Mediterranean enlargement added a dimension of economic development and stabilization of democracy that dominated further EU expansion into post-Communist Eastern Europe. In the Balkans the corruption in Romania and Bulgaria slowed the admission of Slovenia and Croatia, while a reformed Serbia hovered on the door-step. But it was not clear what to do with marginal states like Albania, Macedonia, or wards of the international community like Kosovo or Bosnia. In each case this was a contested process that required domestic reform but also eventually transformed the structure of the existing community.[12]

In trade policy the EC also developed considerable influence as Lucia Coppolaro shows. In many ways, this was the original purpose of the Common Market, which promised free trade internally and a degree of protection externally. However, from the beginning this dual purpose created tensions between those members who, like Germany, wanted access to foreign markets for their industrial products and those other countries, like France and Italy, who insisted on protecting their agricultural producers. As a result, the EC played a somewhat contradictory role in the GATT rounds, initiated by the United States, which sought a general lowering of global tariffs in order to strengthen international trade. Due to its large imports and exports, the EC became gradually accepted as an actor, gaining a seat at the table. But Brussels took a paradoxical stance, vigorously defending the Common Agricultural Policy (CAP) of high subsidies for farm production, which was only gradually transformed into income supplements for European farmers. At the same time, the EU pushed for trade liberalization for industrial products. Moreover, in the negotiations for preferential status of former African colonies, it insisted on maintaining an unequal trading regime that gave the emerging countries little space for economic development. The chapters of Katja Seidel on the CAP and Giuliano Garavini show that the EU vigorously pursued the interests of its major members, following the US lead towards liberalization only reluctantly.[13]

In responding to the new challenges of globalization, the EU was even less successful: Brussels could not find a common strategy to stop deindustrialization. Surprised by the rapid rise of the Asian tigers of Japan, Korea, Taiwan, and Singapore, the European Community reacted with bluster and harassment against the unforeseen competition that undercut its prices at the same or better quality. The caustic chapter by Albrecht

Rothacher demonstrates in shocking detail the incompetence of European negotiators in fending off East Asian competition, which soon led to the collapse of European production of textiles, shipbuilding, or electronics and the take-over of the British car industry. Only the massive intervention of the United States in revaluing the yen eventually stopped the Japanese advance. The more optimistic chapter by Enrico Fardella demonstrates that the same pattern was repeated with China two decades later, since neoliberalism proved to be no match for a neo-mercantilist policy that targeted European and American markets by systematic dumping below world market prices. Western insistence on Beijing's market opening was never as effectual as the state-aided focus on capturing single industries like the production of solar panels, which was thereby ruined in the EU. Only the shift to off-shore production into other low-wage states and direct investment in the Chinese market proved to be somewhat successful counter-strategies. The best that can be said for this policy area is that the EU somewhat buffered the trade war, whereas its member states were forced to cope with the social consequences of massive deindustrialization.[14]

Among Europeanist historians these noticeable advances led to the formation of a success narrative that celebrated European integration as an alternative to traditional power politics. Taking the rhetoric of the founding fathers Robert Schuman, Konrad Adenauer, and Alcide de Gasperi literally, many scholars interpreted the closer cooperation of West European states as a positive response to the lessons of the Great Depression and the World Wars. While every setback reinforced the neo-realist Eurosceptics, the Europhiles were undaunted in their support for integration as pathway to peace and prosperity. In their vision, the progress of the EC showed that soft power and multilateralism could also be successful in pursuing interests in the international arena. Overlooking the many conflicts and crises of the actual functioning of the EU, such optimistic accounts treated integration almost as a self-fulfilling prophecy.[15]

Unresolved Problems

The chapters of this volume also point to several unresolved problems that have complicated the drive to "an ever closer union" in the past. Chief among them is, in Wilfried Loth's opinion, the area of security policy, since defense was considered as involving the core of national sovereignty. Already the initial failure of the EDC in 1954 showed that lingering mistrust of Germany prohibited agreement on a common military force, because it presupposed a political community that proved elusive less than a decade after the end of World War II. As a result, West European defense remained anchored in NATO while the East organized itself in the Warsaw Pact, therefore dividing the continent into hostile military alliances. Intermittent efforts at creating a European pillar within NATO also made little progress, because the French deterrent was not strong enough to replace the Anglo-American nuclear umbrella. At best, during times of transatlantic tension, leaders like François Mitterrand and Helmut Kohl were able to establish some integrated forces, called "Eurocorps," as the core of a future army that never materialized. Similarly, basic decisions on foreign policy that touched on national interests remained the province of nation-states, limiting the heralded European Political Community to periodic consultations among the leaders of the member countries. These discussions helped coordinate policies in some non-vital areas, but failed to turn into a supranational government. As a result, progress in defense and foreign policy has been rather slow.[16]

Some of the chapters also raise the question of association of countries not expected to become full members of the EU. Even after the rejection of membership in referenda, the relationship to Norway and Switzerland has remained rather constructive, since both countries have so closely associated themselves with the EU as to become virtual members, accepting most community regulations and even paying into Brussels' coffers while retaining titular autonomy. But in the case of Ukraine such positive association failed in spite of the high hopes and misguided promises after the Orange Revolution that Kiev would soon join the community. Leaving the country in limbo, internal divisions, prevalent corruption and Russian conquest of the Crimea as well as ethnic separatism have dimmed its prospects, forcing it to ask for Western aid without practical prospect of membership. Similarly, the question of Turkey has remained unresolved, since preparatory negotiations have proceeded in fits and starts, making progress during periods of internal reform and stalling when Istanbul oriented itself to the Muslim world. The recent re-Islamicization under President Recep Erdogan, the continuing Kurdish conflict and the frequent violations of human rights have made future accession unlikely. And finally there is the Greenland precedent of leaving the community altogether, soon to be repeated by the more significant Brexit of the United Kingdom.[17] While these issues go beyond the end of the volume in 1992, they call the automatism of enlargement into question.

Another problem, only touched upon in the foreign policy chapters, is the widespread complaint about a "democracy deficit," that has troubled integration from the beginning. Since ordinary Europeans were struggling to regain control over their lives, the establishment of the ECSC and the Common Market was an elite affair, promoted by prominent members of the political class in the original six countries who sought to rebuild the continent after its self-inflicted catastrophe. While some educated youths also were enthusiastic supporters, the general public was only willing to tolerate closer cooperation as long as it brought tangible benefits such as economic growth, military security, free travel, a wider array of consumer goods, and so on. As soon as the infamous "Brussels bureaucracy" started to go beyond setting health standards and began to regulate goods like French cheeses and German beers, the citizenry began to resent this interference in their lives. Moreover, the neoliberal orientation of champions of a free market hampered the community response to globalization and prevented the emergence of a coordinated social policy to alleviate the impact of deindustrialization. Nationalist politicians found it easy to exploit such popular resentment by blaming Brussels for everything that irritated EU citizens, leading eventually to the failure of the constitutional project in referenda in France and the Netherlands in 2005. Even successive efforts at broadening the powers of the European Parliament, creating more exciting campaigns, electing a quasi-government, and so on, did little to rekindle enthusiasm for Europe.[18] As a result, the neo-nationalism of the East Europeans and the rising xenophobia of Westerners have increasingly threatened to undo the entire European project.

A final cluster of problems that complicates the conduct of a common policy to the outside is the internal confusion about what constitutes European identity, challenged from below and above. The debates about the preamble of the constitution draft showed that there was little common memory that Europeans could agree upon, since the Western sense of the past revolved around the suffering of the Holocaust whereas the Eastern recollections focused on the crimes of Soviet Communism. Under the European umbrella regional identities have also re-emerged, calling for statehood for instance in Catalonia, and reasserting the nation as refuge against globalization pressure. At the same time the United States with its domination in popular culture and consumption styles threatened to overwhelm the smaller European countries with a youthful lifestyle that was promoted by social media created in Silicon Valley. Underestimating the impact of emotional belonging as opposed to material interests, the EU has done too little to define and defend a European model of modernity in politics, society and culture against such global assaults. While the West shares a set of basic values, the implementation of liberal democracy has increasingly diverged between the United States and Europe, with the latter standing for a peaceful, multilateral foreign policy and a social system based on solidarity as opposed to military unilateralism and individual profit-seeking. The European project will only survive if it manages to articulate its cultural foundations more clearly.[19]

This combination of longstanding unresolved problems and more recent dramatic challenges has darkened the tone of key historical assessments. In contrast to the hopeful optimism of previous decades that produced an "advancement through crisis" narrative, many current evaluations of the European prospects have become rather pessimistic, since the capacity of the EU to surmount its difficulties has been called into serious question. After the hopeful progress of the Single European Act and the Eastern expansion, already the failure of the constitutional project was an early warning sign. Soon thereafter the so-called Euro-crisis made media headlines, with the Greek default on its loans and the excessive debt of other countries suggesting that the currency union was premature without a common fiscal policy. When the appalling images of drowned bodies of African refugees washing up on Mediterranean beaches created a humanitarian outcry, the EU could only agree to strengthen its border defenses, but failed to distribute the refugees equitably among the members. And finally Brexit, the biggest shock of all, that was propelled by nationalist agitation of the Murdoch media and the resentment of the older generation in the UK, threatened to break up the European Union altogether. While most fears have fortunately proven exaggerated and the smaller EU might even be better capable of common action, these challenges have inspired gloomy predictions about the future.[20]

Interpretative Implications

The impressive chapters of this volume nevertheless show that the history of integration has much to contribute to the broader understanding of European history after World War II. Though still incomplete, the common effort at cooperation has largely overcome the hereditary enmity between the French and the Germans while also improving relations between them and the Poles. Even if a common defense has not emerged, war has become unthinkable between the members of the EU, making the Russian depredations towards the Ukraine all the more intolerable. In spite of complicated adjustment problems to globalization pressures, the Common Market has supported the rise of an unprecedented prosperity for European citizens. While migration pressures are hardening external borders, the freedom of movement within the Schengen area and the common currency have created a shared sense of space on the old continent that its inhabitants do not want to do without. Though education systems remain national, the Erasmus exchange programs are fostering a common European identity in the student generation. No doubt, the EU has also seen major failures in developing a common government, security policy, social safety net and cultural understanding. But the significance of integration achievements suggests that it is time to have their impact included into the general histories of post-war Europe.[21]

Yet the present collection also reveals several key deficits of integration history that need to be overcome in order to make it more convincing. To begin with, the frustrations and failures of the process need to be taken more seriously. Their recurrence suggests the inadequacy of a federalist success story of EU development, since the actual evolution has been marked by high hopes that were followed by frequent disappointments. The fact that after half a century of integration efforts a United States of Europe has failed to emerge is more than an occasional pothole on the way to inevitable progress, but rather a sign that expectations need to be fundamentally reframed. The curious mixture of supranationalism and intergovernmentalism that characterizes the present structure of the EU only makes sense if it is treated as a new kind of political entity that needs to be understood in its own terms.[22] Methodologically speaking, writing about integration is a form of "history of the present" that lacks a definite endpoint such as the overthrow of European communism in 1989, and therefore needs to remain open-ended in regard to its outcome. A presumed closure of an "ever closer union" can be a political goal, but it is not an adequate point of reference for historical understanding. Since historians do not know what will become of the EU, they need to eschew any simplistic teleology.[23]

Another important consideration is the need to broaden integration history into a wider account of Europeanization that focuses on processes strengthening the intra-European connections. No doubt analyses of politics, law and diplomacy will remain central in this endeavor, but they need to be expanded into additional directions, since these are themselves the product of other forces. It goes without saying that one relatively neglected but absolutely crucial area is the development of the economies, especially in the context of globalization, since the integration project has taken the form of a free market and customs union. Another question concerns the degree of convergence into a shared society with increasing transnational migration or ties between civil society groups. Then there is the problem of cultural identity in a climate of resurgent nationalism: Do EU citizens feel increasingly "European" and what might this sense of "Europeanness" entail beyond pop song competitions or soccer rivalries? Often forgotten is the dark underside of integration in xenophobic exclusion of migrants, post-colonial economic exploitation, and lingering racist prejudice against Muslims. Since the willingness to integrate is itself a product of a reorientation towards Europe, its development should be analyzed in such a broader framework of Europeanization.[24]

Finally, the history of European integration needs to be grounded in an explicit understanding of common values that represent learning processes of the twentieth century. In geographic terms the movement from local to national and beyond it to European horizons is merely an expansion of scope that is not inherently positive if one recalls the totalitarian dictatorships. For that reason the results of closer cooperation ought to be measured by their contributions to the core values that inspired the founders of integration: the immense carnage of the World Wars made the maintenance of peace a central priority; the mass murder of ethnic cleansing and genocide underlined the importance of human rights; the widespread suffering during hyperinflation and depression demonstrated the necessity of social solidarity; and the continuation of negative othering and racial prejudice emphasized the need for tolerance of various forms of diversity. In daily EU practice of wrestling about subsidies or bureaucratic regulations, these imperatives are often forgotten, leading to dry technical histories of laborious compromises on specific issues. In order to keep integration from turning into the nightmare that its opponents claim, it is essential to recall these founding values and to use them as a yardstick for writing integration history.[25]

Notes

1   Mark Mazower, *Dark Continent: Europe's Twentieth Century* (London: Penguin, 1998), 364–365; Tony Judt, *Postwar: A History of Europe Since 1945* (London: William Heinemann, 2005), 302–309; Edgar Wolfrum, *Welt im Zwiespalt: Eine andere Geschichte des 20. Jahrhunderts* (Stuttgart: Klett-Cotta, 2017).

2   Philipp Ther, *Die neue Ordnung auf dem alten Kontinent* (Berlin: Suhrkamp Verlag, 2014); Andreas Rödder, *21.0: Eine kurze Geschichte der Gegenwart* (Munich: C. H. Beck, 2015), 266–337; Andreas Wirsching, *Preis der Freiheit: Geschichte Europas in unserer Zeit* (Munich: C. H. Beck, 2012); Konrad H. Jarausch, *Out of Ashes: A New History of Europe in the Twentieth Century* (Princeton: Princeton University Press, 2015), 506–532.

3   https://historia-europa.ep.eu/en/mission-vision (last accessed October 30, 2018). Cf. Hartmut Kaelble, *A Social History of Europe, 1945–2000: Recovery and Transformation after Two World Wars* (Oxford: Berghahn Books, 2013).

4   Florian Hartleb, *A Thorn in the Side of European Elites: The New Euroscepticism* (Brussels: Centre for European Studies, 2011).

5   For an earlier overview see Desmond Dinan, *Ever Closer Union? An Introduction to the European Community* (Boulder: Lynne Rienner Publishers, 1994).

6   Walter Lipgens, *A History of European Integration, 1945–1947: The Formation of the European Unity Movement* (Oxford: Clarendon, 1982).

7   John Gillingham, *Coal, Steel and the Rebirth of Europe, 1945–1955* (Cambridge: Cambridge University Press, 1991); Alan Milward, *The European Rescue of the Nation-State* (London: Routledge, 2000).

8   Katarina Hochmuth (ed.), *Krieg der Welten: Zur Geschichte des Kalten Krieges* (Berlin: Metropol-Verlag, 2017).

9   As example of Europhile literature, Jeremy Rifkin, *The European Dream: How Europe's Vision of the Future is Quietly Eclipsing the American Dream* (Cambridge: Polity, 2004).

10   Ernst B. Haas, *The Uniting of Europe: Political, Social and Economic Forces, 1950–1957* (London: Stevens, 1958).

11   N. Piers Ludlow, *The European Community and the Crises of the 1960s: Negotiating the Gaullist Challenge* (London: Routledge, 2006); Michael Geary, *Enlarging the European Union: The Commission Seeking Influence, 1961–1973* (Basingstoke: Palgrave Macmillan, 2013).

12   Finn Laursen (ed.), *EU Enlargement: Current Challenges and Strategic Choices* (Brussels: P.I.E. Peter Lang, 2013).

13   Kiran Klaus Patel (ed.), *Fertile Ground for Europe? The History of European Integration and the Common Agricultural Policy since 1945* (Baden Baden: Nomos, 2009).

14   Henryk Kierzkowski (ed.), *Europe and Globalization* (Basingstoke: Palgrave Macmillan, 2002); Konrad H. Jarausch (ed.), *Das Ende der Zuversicht: Die Siebziger Jahre als Geschichte* (Göttingen: Vandenhoeck und Ruprecht, 2008).

15   Hartmut Kaelble and Rüdiger Hohls (eds.), *Geschichte der europäischen Integration bis 1989* (Stuttgart: Franz Steiner Verlag, 2016).

16   Wilfried Loth, *Building Europe: A History of European Unification* (Berlin: De Gruyter Oldenbourg, 2015).

17   Kiran Klaus Patel, "(BR)EXIT: Algerien, Grönland und die vergessene Vorgeschichte der gegenwärtigen Debatte," *Zeithistorische Forschungen*, 14 (2017), 112–127, here 112; David Phinnemore, *Association: Stepping-Stone or Alternative to EU Membership?* (Sheffield: Sheffield Academic Press, 1999).

18   Christopher Lord (ed.), *A Different Kind of Democracy? Debates about Democracy and the European Union* (New York: Open Society Foundations, 2015).

19   Konrad H. Jarausch and Thomas Lindenberger (eds.), *Conflicted Memories: Europeanizing Contemporary Histories* (New York: Berghahn Books, 2007); Malgorzata Pakier and Joanna Wawrzyniak (eds.), *Memory and Change in Europe: Eastern Perspectives* (New York: Berghahn Books, 2016).

20   Heinrich August Winkler, *Geschichte des Westens: Die Zeit der Gegenwart* (Munich: C. H. Beck, 2015), 400–441.

21   James J. Sheehan, *Where Have All the Soldiers Gone? The Transformation of Modern Europe* (Boston: Mariner Books, 2008); Kiran Klaus Patel, "Europäische Integration," in Jost Dülffer and Wilfried Loth (eds.), *Dimensionen Internationaler Geschichte* (Munich: Oldenbourg Verlag, 2012), 353–372.

22   Jan Zielonka, *Europe as Empire: The Nature of the Enlarged European Union* (Oxford: Oxford University Press, 2006).

23   Martin Sabrow, "Writing Contemporary German History in the Present," in Martin Sabrow and Thomas Lindenberger (eds.), *German Zeitgeschichte: Konturen eines Forschungsfeldes* (Göttingen: Wallstein Verlag, 2016), 13–27.

24   Martin Conway and Kiran Klaus Patel (eds.), *Europeanization in the Twentieth Century: Historical Approaches* (Basingstoke: Palgrave Macmillan, 2010), 1–18.

25   Jarausch, *Out of Ashes*, 784–788.

13

Reflections, Reactions, Conclusions:
The Doppelgänger

Charles S. Maier

"Yesterday, upon the stair, I met a man who wasn't there. ..." William Hughes Mearns's once-famous light verse sprang to mind as I read these chapters. As a foreign-policy actor, the European Community (EC) that emerges from this collection exudes a certain non-presence as compared to its component nation-states. This is not the authors' fault: by dint of thorough scholarship they have made its spectral appearance as robust and solid as possible. Drawing on the massive body of monographic scholarship that has now accumulated (and to which many have notably contributed), they are careful to highlight the role of Brussels in its own right, apart, say, from Paris or Bonn or Rome. Still the Community remains a *Doppelgänger*, accompanying the nations that created it. "He wasn't there again today," the poem continues, "I wish, I wish he'd go away."

Not this author, however: I hope, I hope he is here to stay. Most readers as well presumably do not want the European Union (EU) (into which the Community morphed in 1992) to go away. They are unlikely to be Brexit supporters. But these chapters help us understand why the Union, like the Community from which it sprang, has found it difficult to materialize more strongly as a protagonist in world politics. Still, despite my reading of this volume as a record of incomplete or ambiguous achievement, let me preface what follows by a confession of faith in the EU. It has embodied some of the great public aspirations of the era since the Second World War. Institutions should be measured by the solidarities they aim to create as well as the results they finally accomplish. All of them, after all, fall short of the hopes that created them.

The EC and Geopolitics

The contributions to this volume cover the thirty-five years from the 1957 Treaties of Rome until the Treaty of Maastricht in 1992, now already a quarter-century behind us. Throughout this period the Community was caught in the vortex of geopolitical transformations that transcended it. History went on around it, in particular the history of the great ideological conflict of the era. "To study the place of the Cold

War in EC/EU foreign relations is to become aware of the highly indirect nature of the relationship between the processes," Piers Ludlow writes at the beginning of his chapter. Ludlow recognizes that

> The early years of the EEC [European Economic Community—one of the two communities established by the treaties of Rome, the other being Euratom] [...] were played out on a continent cut in half by the Cold War and still strongly affected by the military, ideological, political and economic contests between capitalism and communism [...] It would have been remarkable had this wider setting not had some bearing or influence on the manner in which European integration developed. [...] The Cold War remained secondary with regard to the Community's priorities and mechanisms [...]. The bit-part actor in the Cold War drama would only move center stage once the East–West Conflict had come to an end.

As Ludlow recognizes, the longer-term history of Franco–German conflict and the geo-economics of the coal and iron in their continually contested border region provided the powerful direct impetus to the coal-steel community from which the EEC would emerge. Nonetheless, as he also concedes, had the powerful German state of 1871–1945 not been effectively divided by the encompassing Cold War, and had German defeat not provisionally placed West German resources under a residual allied control that Konrad Adenauer wanted to overcome, the creative French *démarche* of May 1950, would not have been feasible. Dividing Europe between 1945 and 1948/1949 was the prerequisite for partially integrating the Western half. By 1992 that integration was sturdy enough so that the East European nations, including the former German Democratic Republic (GDR), could be safely invited into a proven structure. The thirty-five years in which the EC took shape, survived, and "deepened" as well as "widened," were also years in which the German Federal Republic (FRG) decisively democratized not only its institutions, but its culture and habits, years in which, to borrow the title of Konrad Jarausch, Germans were recivilized.[1]

Ludlow recognizes that the EU's most significant bilateral relationship was perhaps with Germany itself: "The Federal Republic's self-image during the post-1949 period became inextricably linked with the idea of being the 'good European,' the willing participant in multilateral endeavors [...]." It was fitting that at the end of the process Jürgen Habermas could identify the values exemplified by the Bonn Republic as admirably democratic and the basis for what he described as "constitutional patriotism"—a commitment to liberal-democratic pluralism that his much younger reader, Jan-Werner Müller could urge as the civic glue of the EU.[2]

Ludlow asks why the EU as such did not have more to do with Cold War concerns, and he provides one unconvincing and one compelling answer. The less convincing is that there was too much else to do. Yes, the Commission and national leaders—grouped after 1974–1975 in the European Council—were busy with civilian business, above all when the Delors Commission re-energized integration with the signing of the Single European Act in 1986. But the Europeans played a major role when *détente* was on the agenda, during the protracted Conference on Security and Cooperation in

Europe (CSCE), or, admittedly, when vexed by the Americans under Nixon and Carter, who seemed ready to bypass them for direct dealings with Moscow. When geopolitical issues cascaded at the end of the 1980s, the EU was again able to lift its collective eyes from the quotidian matters of budget, structural funds, and other regulations. The real reason for the EU's pallid Cold War role was that across town from Berlaymont was the North Atlantic Treaty Organization (NATO) headquarters, and that was where serious Cold War issues would have to be thrashed out. What mattered, as Ludlow admits, is that the simultaneous existence of NATO (in which the United States played the outsize role) provided an alternative institution that possessed hard power. "Civilian power," as the EU took pride in claiming to embody, really depends upon having some potential source of hard power available. For France (which aspired to create an inner NATO directorate alongside the UK and United States), for Britain and potentially for the FRG (Federal Republic of Germany), NATO was where the big boys provided hard power. *Die große Politik*—"high politics," and the desire to cling to a great-power status that had been diminished by decolonization—remained too important for the major West European states to completely merge into the Community where they would have to answer to bit players. Efforts by the EC/EU to produce a convincing security mechanism have always been rather pitiful, as their relative fecklessness in the Yugoslav civil wars were to demonstrate anew in the 1990s.

Wilfried Loth's survey of the search for a foreign and security policy is usefully read in tandem with Ludlow's chapter. Despite Loth's habitual capacity to accentuate the positive, his solid account also discloses why the EC remained a marginal political actor. Over the era covered in this volume (and even afterward) national leaders and Brussels officials never succeeded in translating economic agreements—even when they provided for supranational sectoral policies—into political confederation. "Ever closer union" meant union forever out of reach.

The reasons can be grasped almost geometrically. For the French, and not only de Gaulle, the political integration of Europe would have to guarantee French ascendancy, whether by virtue of yoking Bonn to Paris, or by becoming the de facto patron over Mediterranean subordinates within the EU or association agreements. De Gaulle's "Europe of fatherlands" required standing up to the Americans on one hand and excluding the British, on the other—or at least compelling them to renounce imperial pretensions and any special relationship with the USA. For the Benelux countries, however, keeping Britain out would diminish their own leverage vis-à-vis Paris. And for the Germans, "dissing" the United States was not an option. A weak French deterrent umbrella could not replace the security that American provided, especially since Washington was not going to let Adenauer and Franz-Josef Strauß develop their own nuclear force.[3] That stalemate played itself out, as Loth documents, between the abortive Fouchet plan of late 1961 and the rather vacuous Elysée Treaty of 1963, with its teeth pulled by the FRG's insistence that the treaty had to be harmonized with NATO. The Elysée Treaty, like so many foundational acts associated with European integration, did not so much establish a new political order as it confirmed the only feasible arrangement that the wreckage of earlier political orders left as rational.

Loth offers a masterly narrative (as does his recent volume on EU history) but it works as a bit of a tease.[4] His protagonists continually renew the promise of a future union that never quite comes into being, though never devoid of some impact. Is the glass half full or half empty? De Gaulle's departure and the advent of Willy Brandt allowed the declaration "European Political Cooperation" in 1970, amplified by a "Document on European Political Identity" in December 1973, and filled out further by the inauguration of the European Council in 1974. This last institution, of course, has developed into a key component of EU governance, but it has led the EU as compellingly toward enhanced intergovernmentalism as political union. And in the very same years that the post-de Gaulle period and the influence of the Brandt government might seem to advance integration, Henry Kissinger reaffirmed America's ambition to keep the Europeans in line despite the German achievements of Ostpolitik and Washington's own abandonment of Bretton Woods. Kissinger's "Year of Europe" announced with fanfare in 1973 to take account of Western Europe's arrival as a factor in global politics (and also to recognize Japan's new influence in the Pacific) turned out be a way of exploiting the oil crisis to confirm Europe's safe alignment in conformity with NATO's Atlantic Declaration and to demonstrate that US leadership remained pre-eminent. The United States could ride out the 1973–1974 oil embargo and price-hike because Organization of Petroleum Exporting Countries (OPEC) set prices in dollars and the American oil "majors" preserved their status by serving, as critics pointed out, as tax farmers for the Middle East producers. Kissinger's version of Monnet's oft-cited dumbbell metaphor had a massive Washington at one end of the bar, and a hollow European sphere at the other.

In following the ambiguities of the European–American relationship, Kenneth Weisbrode's subtle and elegant analysis provides a judicious perspective. As Weisbrode asserts, even as Americans and Europeans worked out a relationship that did not challenge US leadership, the EU role "had to show itself, especially to critics, to be both viable and distinctive." This could be achieved in issues of trade and commerce, but not really in defense or culture. For all of America's ambivalences, Weisbrode insists that European integration remained a priority for Washington (granted, he was writing before the advent of the Trump Administration) and for the reasons publicly declared: peace, prosperity, and Western unity. "European integration was at the top of the list of transatlantic policy fads virtually from the moment the Second World War ended, if not earlier."

Weisbrode, however, separates the EU–US partnership from the Western alliance: the EU was too weak vis-à-vis its own national members and the United States too hegemonic to create a "proper duopoly." Instead, what resulted was an American patronage of West European integration that experienced continual vicissitudes.[5] Crises, such as the French rejection of the European Defense Community (EDC) in 1954, after the French and Americans had seemed to agree on integrated combat forces, prodded the Europeans to accept Anthony Eden's proposal for allowing a revived West German army to enter NATO. The move was made acceptable for the French by simultaneously enlarging the framework of the 1948 pre-NATO Brussels Pact, created when the threat of German military revival seemed a possibility, into a West European Union that included the FRG. The crisis, Weisbrode explains, also led to the breakthrough Messina conference and the Rome treaties, which despite John Foster Dulles' earlier talk of an "agonizing reappraisal," the United States strongly supported. Eisenhower's indignation at the Franco–British invasion of Suez, which contrasted with Adenauer's support for Guy Mollet, further strengthened the case for successful conclusion of the Rome Treaties. Europe paradoxically emerged the stronger as it stumbled from transatlantic crisis to transatlantic crisis. The Kennedy Round and negotiation of the General Agreement on Tariffs and Trade (GATT) in 1962 managed to advance trade liberalization even as the Europeans kept their Common Agricultural Policy (CAP), which antagonized US agrarian interests. Again, a "satisficing" result emerged at the end of the day. Sixteen years later the Europeans' concern at Henry Kissinger's pressure on the Soviets to desist from rescuing the Egyptian's impending disaster in the Yom Kippur War in 1973 similarly led to "a crisis and reaffirmation of both the EC and the partnership."

Nonetheless, the political design of Europe still took second place behind the agendas of its major national powers. The European rescue of the nation-state, to cite Milward's congenial concept, continued to have the cost of making it difficult for "Europe" to assume a more than aspirational role as an international actor—the always visible man who was not there. Its political elite, Weisbrode explains, continued to divide between those he terms Europeanists—who wanted to confront the United States with a strong and independent EC—and the Atlanticists—who dreamed of a harmonious collaboration. Atlanticists believed the Europeanists were pursuing an illusory *Weltpolitik* based on the EC; Europeanists reproached the Atlanticists for accepting a durable American hegemony or even empire. Weisbrode emerges from his long, dense chapter with a generous though paradoxical assessment of both the United States and Europe as historical actors, one with which I largely concur. Given the Cold War, the Atlantic Alliance remained, in Washington's eyes, the major structure within which to utilize Europe's wealth, loyalty, and energy. But granted that imperative, it was usually important to nudge European integration forward, although ironically it was the storms that blew East from across the Atlantic that accomplished the nudging.

Did the pattern of EC relations with Communist Europe in the years before 1990–1991 suggest a more independent and cohesive role than could be generated within the multiple intimate connections simultaneously cultivated with the United States? Angela Romano concludes that through the 1960s the Cold War ensured that "national governments were the most important actors involved, both individually and collectively." The state socialist regimes regarded the EU suspiciously as a wedge for Western influence and sought relations with its individual states. The era of *détente* and Ostpolitik and the creation of the CSCE framework (1969–1974) for a pan-European settlement began to change the approach from both West and East. Romano, however, emphasizes that the Nixon administration (less so the Ford presidency) and the EC really envisaged different purposes for the protracted discussions.

> For the Nine, the CSCE represented a terrific opportunity to assert the EC's international role and shape a new kind of relations in Europe, where they perceived and resented a superpower condominium over their heads. For the Nixon administration, the CSCE was merely a convenient little tool for strengthening the relationship with the Soviet Union.

The opportunity for the EC and the East bloc to knit closer ties waited until the advent of Mikhail Gorbachev and the Single European Act. The EC came into its own as the East European countries broke loose from communism. By that time the association agreements, based on the earlier compacts developed for the accession of recently democratized Greece, Spain, and Portugal from 1981 to 1986, offered a creative response that encouraged the countries to persevere in democratic reforms. Related initiatives provided for economic support.

Loth, too, argues that the EC gained collective negotiating presence because it rose to the opportunities of *détente*. The CSCE, sealed by the Helsinki Final Act and follow-up conferences, confirmed Soviet-bloc recognition of the EC and opportunities for trade with the East. Brezhnev believed that the *acquis communiste* in the East (above all in terms of securing the GDR from the wiles of the West) was now definitively secured; Bonn took satisfaction in the escape clause that allowed peaceful negotiation of national boundaries. Fast forward to Genscher's hope for a Treaty on European Union and Mitterand's renewed Gaullist-Lite proposal for German–French cooperation with Kohl's positive response, which yielded this time a Franco–German brigade in 1987 and agreement on a Joint Defense and Security Council on the 25th anniversary of the Elysée Treaty. Loth's positive narrative tends to converge with Weisbrode's for these final years of the Cold War order. By this time its fundamental stasis of the Cold War order was about to dissolve as Gorbachev and Reagan met at Reykjavik, the martial-law regime in Poland faced fundamental challenges, and the internal agenda of the EU was in the process of vigorous renewal. The collapse of the Soviets' European imperium and the advent of German unification seemed finally to equalize the two sides of the Atlantic and to offer the EU an opportunity to emerge as an equal security partner. The lesson is that the EC could come into its own when East–West relations could tend toward cooperation. Yet in both phases, I think, national motivations remained as powerful as EC allegiance: the French seeking policy autonomy from overriding American policy priorities, the Germans after 1966 pursuing an active Ostpolitik to edge toward accommodations with the GDR and its people. East Europeans by the end of the 1980s met a man who was there, but when they looked closely he seemed to look a lot like the actors they dealt with in the national capitals.

Perhaps Weisbrode, too, along with Loth and Romano, takes the formal rhetoric and analyses of this process too much at face value: citing thoughtful observers, he suggests that both the Soviets and the Americans were learning to deal with the Europeans as a unit. He valuably traces the growth of the formal institutions of the Union: the DG I and External Relations bureaucracy, and its interlocutors across the Atlantic. Still, from the perspective of all that has transpired in the quarter century since 1992, might not the process be more realistically described as the displacement of France (and even Britain) by Germany, now united and more populous by far than any other of the European states? Despite Loth's Whiggish history of EC/EU foreign and security policy, European security initiatives remained essentially gestures. When confronted with the major crisis in the wars of Yugoslav secession in 1991–1995, the EU powers failed to apply a coherent policy. Only under US and NATO leadership could the Dayton Accords and then the Kosovo agreement be achieved.

The Political Power of Enlargement

Perhaps, however, it can be objected that EC/EU expansion itself affirmed the Community's political vitality. "Brussels" achieved coherence as a unified political power by laying down rules for accession and attracting those who wanted to enter the framework it provided. Eirini Karamouzi cleverly interprets enlargement as foreign policy. Enlargement, spasmodic as it has been, has provided the leverage for civilizing the neighbors, or so it has appeared since the accession of Greece in 1981 and Spain and Portugal in 1986—each having emerged from authoritarian experiments. Britain, Ireland, and Denmark, admitted at the first enlargement in 1973, and later, Austria, Finland, and Sweden in 1995 hardly needed civilizing. It is still not certain that the Big Bang of 2004, when the EU admitted the formerly Communist states of Hungary, Poland, the Czech Republic, and Slovakia, as well as Slovenia, Malta, and the Baltic republics, or the follow-up of 2007, when Romania and Bulgaria entered, has durably succeeded.

To be sure, foreign-policy priorities can be described as capacious enough to account for Europe's motivation (Britain's clearly lay in the economic realm), but Karamouzi admits that as of 1969, enlargement was still "not seen as a foreign policy tool in and of itself," but designed rather to strengthen the rising commitment of the EC to widening external commercial relations and aid to developing countries. The Greek and Iberian accessions responded more explicitly to secure political goals; the applicant countries viewed the EC "as the only appropriate forum to support their countries' democraticization processes." The enlargement was supported by an American administration concerned with the political volatility—e.g. threats from the Left—in the region. Paradoxically "the Southern European countries became 'European' not because of what they could offer, but because of what they lacked: fragility and weaknesses constituted the countries' assets, creating a precedent of expectations and influencing their behavior and discourse once they became members of the EU." The Copenhagen conditions of eligibility, agreed on in 1993 to govern the future enlargement to the East,"echoed the processes that had taken place in the preceding years."

Granted, enlargement and reflection on the criteria for accession played an important function in defining the Community's identity. The process repeatedly forced the EC countries to reflect on their association as one of values and not merely economic advantages. Enlargement helped stabilize the neighborhood; and it enhanced what we might think of as the great power aspect of the Community by increasing its size—a classic index of prestige and power. It perforce set up the Community as a united political unit to which new countries adhered. But it enhanced the political role for the EU, in effect, as a non-competitive protagonist where the alternative to the EC/EU "order" was envisioned as the quasi-chaos of the periphery. Enlargement let the EU pose as a sort of Virgilian empire, called upon to raise the lowly and impose the rule of law. But enlargement did not serve as a foreign policy within the competitive world of states. Only when the early stages of enlargement approached the borders of Ukraine after 2012 did it become a stake in a game of power politics between the EU and a rival power, and the results of that competition have not been heartening.

The EC, the Far East and the Mediterranean

Perhaps the EC achieved more of a unified presence further away from Europe. The EC members established a foreign-policy coordination mechanism, the European Political Cooperation (EPC) at their Hague meeting in 1969. Giuliano Garavini writes that by the 1970s "for the first time it had begun to acquire its own international personality," and he cites François Duchêne's concept of a "civilian power." The expectation was that in a world where large-scale war seemed excluded, the EC's economic weight and democratic values would make it a major influence. Nonetheless—so I distill the lessons of this volume—the collective actor remained a shadowy presence in external politics, most effective when it could throw funding at problems, less so when it had to cope with conflicting priorities.

Not surprisingly it was the Chinese who talked most about Europe as a unit, for it increasingly seemed to offer a major partner against the Soviet ambitions for hegemony they felt were aimed at them. "We support Western Europe in its plan to unite in order to strengthen itself and in order to fight against hegemony," Fardella quotes Minister of Trade Affairs Li Qiang when he signed the keystone trade agreement of 1978. "The self-reliance of the Mao era was shifted from 1978 into an open cooperation that looked at the European Community members as the key partners in China's effort to modernize its economy and armed forces." The trade agreement of 1978 and that of 1985 allowed individual European countries to pursue their own bilateral deals. But the strategic goals of China, remained dominant: The path inaugurated by the EEC and the People's Republic of China (PRC) at the end of the 1970s allowed the two poles to survive the end of the Cold War and become leading actors alongside the United States. Both sides succesfully sought to increase their influence on the international stage. Clearly for China, the man who was not quite there closer to home seemed to be more materially present.

The contrast with China's stance toward Europe and Japan's is striking. Just as far away from the EC, the Japanese had no equivalent geostrategic aspirations. Europe was a market. "In a nutshell," Albrecht Rothacher argues, "it was the low politics of trade and economic competition that dominated the relationship, at the cost of hundreds of thousands of European industrial jobs." On the other hand Japanese relations "created the stress test of its [the EEC's] new common commercial policy" and brought Japan out of its economic preoccupation with Southeast Asia and the United States. Rothacher has brought to bear the perspectives of an EU official and a brilliant mastery of ironic English prose. He points out that Japan, too, maintained a protected agriculture (rice was a sacred product, not to be threatened from outside). The EC and Japan might have teamed up against the United States in the GATT, but failed to do so. What a difference a decade makes! The Japan that was a pillar of the Trilateral Commission from 1977 to 1981, and threatened to become "number one" economically and frightened both the United States and the Europeans in the 1980s became a normal trading partner by the 1990s, whereas China was to loom as a continental-sized rival. The Japanese customers who lined up in the Via Condotti to buy Gucci bags would be succeeded by Chinese clients. Nonetheless, Japanese cars replaced the home grown models in Europe (and the United States); their consumer electronics dominated the markets until the Koreans came along.

Closer to Europe than Asia, and far more problematic, lay the Mediterranean and sub-Saharan Africa. As Elena Calandri recognizes, the Mediterranean served as the sandbox where the EC might act as a great power, but granted that "national foreign policies and an intergovernmental dynamic continued to dominate." France played the key role as it sought to group the Mediterranean countries under its patronage, as it had already when it insisted in 1949 that NATO include an Italy that it expected to remain a de facto grateful dependency. For the Greeks and Turks, their applications, so Calandri details in her dense narrative, were accepted in 1979 to join the Community. President Pompidou launched the Global Mediterranean Policy in October 1972, designed to affirm the EC's role as a civilian power. As Calandri argues, the initiative was designed to magnify French pursuit of a role separate from the United States and separate as well from a coordinated German, Dutch and British approach for global development. Her chapter rather mercilessly exposes the contradictions that condemned the policy, especially once the Yom Kippur War and the oil embargo strengthened Washington's controlling voice anew. As the 1970s continued, the Palestinian issue intruded further. As the author notes, the intertwining of the Israeli–Palestinian conflict and other regional security issues—the politicization of Islam and the problem of terrorism (she does not specifically name the emergence of the Iranian Islamic Republic, which helped generate regional turmoil):

> expanded the political definition of the Mediterranean to permanently include the Middle East, a phenomenon that would peak with the 1990 Gulf War. In such a context, the EC's lack of military force and security resources, and the limits of a pure economic soft power [which in any case she shows was riddled with contradictory priorities and concern about import competition], were resounding.

By the 1980s, Community policy slipped into further disarray, while the United States assumed a greater role especially in the Eastern Mediterranean.

Reflections

Pause for a moment after these extraordinarily rich accounts to consider the paradoxes they raise. For Ludlow and Weisbrode, concerned with the Cold War and East–West relations, the United States emerges as a powerful but relatively benevolent sponsor of European integration. Lucia Coppolaro comes to a similar conclusion when it concerns the EC's role in the GATT framework for trade negotiations. As a customs union, the Europe of the Six operated as a united negotiating partner in the GATT negotiations, but other members were reluctant to accept the delicately achieved compromises brokered among the Six. Both the Treaties of Rome and subsequent trade agreements appeared too protectionist for most GATT members. Only an American-brokered compromise managed to let the EU continue. By the 1970s, however, US negotiators were themselves vexed by the Common Agricultural Policy, but gave way under the Carter administration. The EC accepted limitations on manufacturing duties, but the United States and EC together—the EC particularly responsive to

French priorities—resisted the demands from the developing world for freer trade in agriculture. Coppolaro follows the tough negotiations into the era of accelerating globalization of the 1990s and gives us the picture of a Community navigating from one round to another to sustain unity within its own ranks, which meant bowing to French demands to uphold the CAP. "From 1958 to the early 1990s, the EC's external trade policy evolved in a US-led GATT framework and was the result of defensive responses to the US initiative." As becomes clear in Garavini's chapter as well, the price of the Community was a demanding one in terms of global trade welfare.

For Calandri, focusing on the Community's role in Southern Europe and across the Mediterranean, US policy imperatives—Israeli security, the desire to preclude a revival of Europe's potentially neocolonial aspirations, the continuing irritations with French ambitions—Washington represented a far more unfriendly force. She does not really examine the diplomacy of arms sales or of individual firms, aside from mentioning Péchiney's involvement in Greece. But against the frustrations of Middle-Eastern efforts one can give more emphasis to the successes of confirming democracy in southern Europe. Greece, Spain, and Portugal have unquestionably remained democratic and have become wealthier and more normalized. That stabilization was a historic achievement. Perhaps in his reflective moments, Henry Kissinger asked himself: did the EU really need a Mediterranean foreign policy?

It did need a development policy: it was too rich, it had too many moral debts from the age of imperialism, and its leaders sensed that the pressures of migration would only increase. As Garavini argues, through the 1960s neocolonial aspirations governed European national policies, and the EC had largely to accept their existence. As of 1957 the European powers—Belgium, France, Britain, even Italy, later Spain and Portugal (up until entry)—had territories in Africa and remained deeply invested economically and emotionally. Fred Cooper, a leading historian of late colonial Africa, has argued that for a brief moment there were possibilities for "association" or "union" that might have offered a more creative or easier solution for the empires than the often violent path to independence and the civil strife afterward.[6] Whether this was realistic or not is hard to judge, but as Garavini says, Eurafrica was soon viewed as just a policy of exploitation. Indeed the term "Eurafrica," was one that Karl Haushofer's geopolitical tracts used to describe the global role he assigned to Germany. France made preservation of its colonial ties, still in force in Algeria and sub-Saharan territories, a *sina qua non* for ratifying the Treaties of Rome. Britain's empire, one might argue, kept Britain from accepting the EU into the 1950s, whereas France wagered that the EU would help preserve its empire. By 1960 the game was up. The rapid progress of Congo decolonization—with the intervention of the United States against Lumumba and the transparent Union Minière effort to prop up a secessionist Katanga—also doomed it. It certainly could not survive the Algerian War. The French rescued what could be rescued with the Yaoundé Association agreement of 1963. Garavini shows how central French leadership was to this effort although lodged in Brussels under DG VIII. Thereafter Europe cooperated more within the framework of the major international development-oriented organizations such as the World Bank.

Africa remained the main focus. The concepts of development and of modernization remained a major justification for foreign policies both East and West during the Cold

War.[7] Katja Seidel's related chapter on the external impact of the CAP, however, stresses how German opposition to the French efforts to shelter Senegal's peanut oil prices (the overwhelming source of national income) led to intransigent German opposition and ultimately a "raw deal" for former French colonies. What was at stake was a forerunner of the later disputes between neoliberal trade policies—now supported by the Germans—and a trade regime that had both neocolonial and social protection provisions for the African nations. The Germans won and the Senegalese paid the price. Reading the Seidel and Garavini chapters in parallel suggests how difficult it was to reconcile agricultural and industrial interests inside Europe and the deals finally struck in Brussels (often between different DGs) and the interests of the outer world. The EC was acting as a community but in the sense that any complex polity was—by hard bargains among different interest groups, supported by rival bureaucratic agencies.

By the Paris summit of 1972, imminent British adhesion to the EC widened the aspirations beyond Eurafrica, and the decade of the 1970s brought new complications—the so-called oil crisis, economic stagflation, and the emergence of a strong movement, centered in the United Nations Conference on Trade and Development (UNCTAD) and supported by political leaders on the Social Democratic Left for greater redistribution of resources to the less developed world, soon to be termed the Global South. Theoretical analyses associated with so-called "dependency theory" argued that the major commodity producers in the less industrialized countries were durably disadvantaged in terms of trade. As Garavini identifies, such pressures led the EC to agree on the Lomé Convention of 1975, which recognized the need to stabilize the prices of African exports, but also assure their flow. This brief convergence of a coherent EC policy vis-à-vis a coherent bloc of African states did not last, however. Just as the Brandt Report's consensus on global redistributive efforts was replaced by the critics of foreign aid, so general policy became imbued with the neoliberalism associated with Margaret Thatcher and Ronald Reagan. Europeans had to devote more aid to their own newly integrated South. Dependency theory and feelings of guilt for an imperial past fell out of fashion. The Soviet control of Eastern Europe represented the evils of empire; the path to development was privatization and foreign investment. Garavini brilliantly sketches in the triumph of the neoliberal Zeitgeist and its impact.

The critique complements Katja Seidel's discussion of the external ramifications of the CAP. Arguably the CAP has proved the major stabilization regime that the EC developed: farmers, whose distress in the 1930s helped account for the rise of fascist alternatives, were largely wound down as a major class of the population without tremendous protest. But Europe also became more self sufficient: Seidel's Table 9.1 (taken from a 1987 survey) shows that the Europeans who exported about one third of the amount they imported (in units of account ECU) in 1968 exported almost two thirds by 1985 even as both imports and exports massively increased. In general, the EC subsidized exporters and taxed imports, "raising the question to what extent the CAP obstructed the EC's quest to become a global civilian power." The Rome treaty envisaged that Europe's customs union would lead to reduced tariffs with the outside economies, but German and French farm organizations soon managed to have EC prices set above world-market levels, encouraging domestic producers to expand production. The first three tariff negotiation rounds under GATT auspices largely preserved the CAP because, according to Seidel, the United States had complementary interests in protecting its own farmers. The GATT Tokyo Round and the Uruguay Round saw tougher negotiations. A solution was found only by reforms, begun in 1990 and thereafter extended, to pay farmers directly while cutting the benchmark prices for EU producers. Seidel sums up the costs: supporting a sector of shrinking economic performance became a paramount objective for the Community despite glaring inconsistency with free-trade goals in industry and easy relations with the US, and since then at the cost of agricultural producers among the developing countries.

Toward a European Foreign Policy?

The contributions to this book narrate in rich detail the external relations of the EC. They summarize, interpret, and develop an accomplished monographic literature—filled with exhaustive studies but alas not epic history. Why, the reader wonders, has there been no gripping historical account of the EU, such as the late Tony Judt left us with *Postwar*? There are several possible reasons for this. Contemporary historical research is sponsored by Europe's ministries and foundations in the form of collective doctoral and post-doctoral projects. The literature cited in profusion by these chapters reflects the collective monography through which Europeans fund their younger scholars and produce their historiography. Beyond this organizational explanation, it can be maintained that the prevention of catastrophe is never as compelling a story as the descent into disaster. The EU has been an effort, an admirable effort, in getting beyond disaster. It has also had a history without a state that has offered no office with the potential for heroic leadership. Hallstein, Mansholt, and even Delors were admirable civil servants but had no stage to emerge as dramatic political protagonists. The EU thus had no Churchill, de Gaulle, nor Brandt. As Brecht wrote, happy the land that has no need for heroes. But sometimes a bit dull too. The EU as such has had a rich economic life. But this is not the same as having a foreign policy. Where it acts as a political unit most effectively and with most unity beyond its borders is precisely by welcoming in new neighbors, and it is not clear that it has always done so wisely.

Common Foreign and Security Policy has always been the major weakness of the EU. Money spent on development aid has not really made up for that lack. EU foreign policy has tended to be national foreign policies, in large agreement because of the adversarial pressures of the Soviet bloc during the period of this book, and by the tutelary efforts of the United States—anxious to assure the security of its star pupils but not to let them become an alternative to Washington. French political concerns have been central, in large part because the FRG was willing to defer to France (for the sake of demonstrating good citizenship) and to contribute to its foreign projects, just as the Federal Republic was willing to defer to France on the CAP, which served German domestic political interests as well. The EU has rested on a symbiosis of French ideas and German money: it was a good deal for both. But in recent years—at least until the elections of March 2017—French ideas seemed to be running out, and Germans were more reluctant to provide money, especially to the national economies they saw as spendthrift. Crucial too, the continuing efforts of the United States to wish the project well may also have come to an end. Perhaps as Donald Trump steers the United States away from Europe and toward rogue-state behavior, the EU will have to take on a collective power it never thought it must really assume. In that case its foreign policy still remains to be written.

Notes

1   Konrad H. Jarausch, *After Hitler: Recivilizing Germans, 1945–1995*, Brandon Hunziker trans. (New York: Oxford University Press, 2006).

2   Jan-Werner Müller, *Constitutional Patriotism* (Princeton: Princeton University Press, 2006). The concept originated with Dolf Sternberger in 1979 and was popularized by Habermas during the 1986 Historikerstreit.

3   Christian Tuschhoff, *Deutschland, Kernwaffen und die NATO 1949–1967: Zum Zusammenhalt von und friedlichem Wandel in Bündnissen* (Baden-Baden: Nomos, 2002).

4   Wilfried Loth, *Building Europe: A History of European Unification*, Robert F. Hogg (trans.) (Berlin: De Gruyter Oldenbourg, 2015).

5   Roy H. Ginsberg and Susan E. Penska, *The European Union in Global Security: The Politics of Impact* (New York: Palgrave Macmillan, 2012); Roy H. Ginsberg, *The European Union in International Politics: Baptism by Fire* (Lanham: Rowman & Littlefield, 2001).

6   Frederick Cooper, *Citizenship between Empire and Nation: Remaking France and French Africa* (Princeton: Princeton University Press, 2014).

7   See Sara Lorenzini's study of competitive German policies, *Due Germanie in Africa: la cooperazione allo sviluppo e la competizione per i mercati di materie prime e tecnologia* (Florence: Polistampa, 2003); David C. Engerman (ed.), *Staging Growth: Modernization, Development, and the Global Cold War* (Amherst: University of Massachusetts Press, 2003).

14

International History Meets International Relations

Ulrich Krotz

International history and International Relations (IR) would be natural bedfellows, one might think, and deeply engaged with each other's debates, discussions, and other developments. But, for a range of reasons, the evolution of these academic disciplines turned out differently, leaving them to largely develop in isolation from each other.

Although they have (or claim to have) a number of common ancestors dating back to Thucydides, and the modern discipline of IR has its roots in diplomatic and military history, the two fields often seem to exist in a state of mutual neglect and disregard.[1] The number of texts that international historians and IR or political science scholars read in common, or to which they regularly refer, has, if anything, decreased over the past several decades.[2]

This book was conceived to be primarily a work of historical analysis. First and foremost, we wanted to bring together in a single volume a range of historical accounts of the European Community's (EC's) external relations from the Treaties of Rome to the Treaty of Maastricht, across all major states and world regions and key policy domains. Collectively, the contributors to this volume seek to reconstruct the shape, form, and content of the EC's external relations from the mid-1950s to the early 1990s, and to take stock of the factors that propelled progress forward, constrained or limited its advance, or contributed to the varied and uneven trajectory of its development.

A second objective was to consider the Cold War, with all of its manifold and multifaceted implications, not simply as a backdrop to, or even as something entirely separate from, European integration and the EC, but rather as an important feature of the EC's external relations during its first formative decades. That is, we aspired to consider the European project and EC external relations as part of (and in light of) the international politics that shaped and defined the period, rather than dissociated from these global developments.

Yet, from the beginning, we also aspired to bridge the disciplinary chasm and forge connections between international history on the one hand and general IR theory and political science on the other when it comes to research on the European project and EC/EU politics and policies. To the extent possible, we wanted to enable this book's historical testimony to speak to IR and political science theorizing on European integration and vice versa.

The purpose of this concluding chapter is to explicitly relate the historical findings brought to light in this volume to some basic theoretical and conceptual thinking in IR and political science. To that end, this chapter outlines several different ways that we can view the volume's empirical findings from the vantage point of IR. The goal here is, however, somewhat modest: to elucidate how some of our key findings meet and fit with IR theory and theorizing (and vice versa), while making no pretense of systemically, let alone exhaustively, testing existing IR theories or building an overarching theoretical framework.

Section one examines this book's historical findings in light of "levels-of-analysis" thinking in IR theory, which locates the Cold War as a phenomenon operating at the level of the international system. The contributors to this volume uncover an interesting Cold War-induced "double logic," wherein the Cold War both permitted (or encouraged), but also hampered and limited the scope and influence of the EC's foreign relations from the late 1950s to the early 1990s. The chapters thus contribute insights on the double impact of important system-level catalysts to European politics during this period, which have often gone overlooked or underappreciated by IR theory and political science research on European integration.

However, our historical accounts do not present the Cold War's systemic impact on European affairs as a perpetually or unfailingly dominant or overriding factor, as some recent IR work in the structural realist vein argues. Instead, they provide a much more nuanced view of the Cold War's contingent and often indirect causal implications and historical relevance. Furthermore, the Cold War does not emerge as the sole or even the central force shaping EC external relations, but rather as an influence that mingles and intertwines with causes and factors found at other levels of analysis, including the national and even individual levels.

Section two seeks to make explicit the range of causal factors that affected, whether positively or negatively, the emergence and evolution of EC external relations, and link these to major debates in IR theory about the types of causal forces—material, institutional, or ideational—that shape and influence international relations.

Collectively, our authors find an interesting and intricate panoply of different factors from each of these three types of causes. Several of the chapters consider the basic Cold War configuration, with its US–Soviet superpower rivalry, materially conceived, as the key condition under which the EC and its external relations first took shape, or note the Community's material interests in trade, economic exchange, or agricultural protectionism as highly significant driving forces.

Others point to institutional factors and to institutionalization both at the intra-EC or the international level, such as the GATT framework, as cardinally important for shaping the development and evolution of EC external relations. Yet others detect the important role that was played by ideational factors, such as different national self-views, a sense of special links between EC member states and their former colonies, or the special meaning of agriculture for Europeans.

When insights from the diverse historical accounts are brought together, what clearly emerges is that different types of causes and causal forces of different sorts interlinked, interacted, and fed into each other in shaping the basic features and trajectory of EC external relations during this era.

Section three maps the book's historical investigation of the EC's external relations and the roots of the Community's emergence as an international actor, however fragmented or tenuous, onto debates within IR about which of the actors matter, and which matter most, in world politics.

The two main intellectual traditions in IR, realism and liberalism, disagree over the extent to which states are the main drivers and shapers of international processes and outcomes (as realists hold), or whether international affairs are best explained by considering the actions of a multiplicity of actors in addition to national governments, such as international organizations and other transnational and domestic actors (as liberals emphasize).

Evidence in support of both positions can be found in this volume. State actors—whether the two superpowers, the EC member states, or key EC interlocutors such as China and Japan—dominated the Cold War and influenced in important and lasting ways the EC's beginnings. Yet, the historical record also demonstrates that the EC, itself a non-state actor, began to assume its own agency among and amidst a multiplicity of actors that included not only states and national governments, but also international organizations, diverse domestic pressure groups, and states' "component parts," such as ministries and bureaucracies. The empirical findings, moreover, clearly show that the EC's emergent external agency sharply varied, not only over time, but also across policy domains and interlocutors (i.e. other states or groups of states).

Additionally, the EC itself did not evolve as a unitary actor, but as a polity with numerous units and bodies that spoke and acted for the Community as a whole, and continued to coexist with and function, without decisively weakening or replacing the authority of the member states that made up the Community.

The fourth section considers how the book's historical findings can help us evaluate claims that characterize the EC (or EU) with various (conceptual) *adjectives*, such as a "market," "normative," or "civilian" power, which is prevalent and popular in theorizing the nature, role, identity, self-image, and policies of the EC/EU.

This volume's wide-ranging examination of EC external relations from the end of World War II to Maastricht offers a rich source of evidence from which to draw when evaluating the various "adjective power Europe" claims, much of which has yet to be taken into account by those seeking to theorize the European project, which tends to focus exclusively on developments post-Maastricht.

A large number of findings from across diverse chapters in this book support recent work on "market power Europe," even though others hint at the limits or gaps of this perspective. By contrast, the empirical record gives little clear support for "normative power Europe" claims. Instead, the EC (and its member states) often appear to pursue their own interests in a manner and style closer to that of what was once called *Realpolitik*, or the preferences of domestic civil society and powerful domestic interest groups. Despite some pockets of evidence that the EC had at times acted "normatively," on the whole it is difficult to discern consistently "normative" or "ethical" behavior as characterizing the EC's emergence as an actor in global politics.

The record is more mixed with respect to claims of Europe as a "civilian power." Formally, the EC was largely "civilian" in the sense that it lacked a major security and defense component. What "civilian" exactly means, however, is unclear given that all

EC members except Ireland were members of the NATO alliance, and France and the United Kingdom were nuclear powers.

Furthermore, the EC's predominantly "civilian" nature came about hardly by choice or design, but was the result of political processes and historical outcomes most of which were not under its control. A number of the chapters illustrate that, despite many setbacks, the EC in fact never relinquished the desire ultimately to add competences for greater autonomy and capabilities in security and defense. A brief final section completes this concluding chapter.

Cold War (as Cause or Condition) and Levels of Analysis

The Cold War's strategic bipolarity, East–West confrontation, and superpower competition in various forms and manifestations defined the international system and its "logic" for over forty years. Because it structured the global conditions in which all states were operating, from the perspective of International Relations theory, the Cold War would be considered a causal factor at the "systemic level."

"Levels of analysis" has long been a central conceptual distinction in IR theory, and allows scholars to clarify and explain at what level (of analysis) a relevant causal factor or force (or, at times, outcome) is (or is not) located, and which causal forces at different levels do (or do not) drive political or historical outcomes, either by themselves or in combination with factors from other levels. IR scholars have conventionally identified three different levels of analysis: the international system, the domestic or "unit" level, and the individual level.[3]

Bringing this "levels-of-analysis" concept to bear on our thinking about the relationship between the Cold War and the European project can help us to identify which Cold War-related features affected the processes and outcomes of the EC's external relations between the Rome and Maastricht Treaties. It also allows us to understand how, and to what degree, the Cold War's systemic influence intertwined with other causal factors located at the other levels of analysis.[4]

Surprisingly, for a long time the Cold War did not figure prominently in (and was at times almost entirely absent from) political science and IR scholarship on European integration. In retrospect, many prominent accounts—no matter whether neofunctional/supranational, intergovernmental, sociological, or constructivist in orientation—appear inward-looking and detached from the broader forces that were shaping world politics that we could expect to affect the choices and behavior of European states.[5]

Ernst Haas's original neofunctionalist account, for example, focused on the dynamics of the integration process itself rather than the Cold War global context.[6] The Cold War figured mostly as an implicit background condition in Stanley Hoffmann's intergovernmentalist approach, which located key obstacles to integration in the domains of "high politics" at the nation-state level, including different historical experiences and various sorts of domestic-level influences.[7] Scholars working in the vein of Karl Deutsch's transactionalism and cybernetics perspective saw European integration as a response to the rise in the volume and density of transnational economic, societal, and informational interaction in Western Europe.[8] Andrew Moravcsik's "liberal intergovernmentalism" traced growing interdependence to domestic material interests, intergovernmental bargaining, and the creation of regional international institutions.[9] The "multi-level government" approach considered the different levels of decision-making authority of the EU polity (supranational, national, and subnational) without systematically taking into account the international context of the period.[10] The "embedded bilateralism" perspective on the history and politics of European integration considered the Cold War as a background condition and as a (mostly) permissive factor, yet did not systematically investigate the Cold War link.[11] "Post-functional" formulations emphasize the role of public opinion, political parties, and identity on preferences, strategies, and outcomes of regional integration rather than broader geopolitical features or circumstances.[12]

Only once the Soviet Union and bipolarity had begun to crumble or disappeared did international relations scholars begin to place prominent and explicit causal weight to the Cold War for the scope and direction of European integration. At this juncture, however, accounts veered in the opposite direction, with the Cold War pronounced to be the single most important causal force. John Mearsheimer deemed Cold War bipolarity as the key factor that had kept interstate rivalry and war at bay in Western Europe. With the end of the Cold War, he saw Europe reverting "back to the future"— an era defined by such levels of conflict and potential violence that we would, he claimed, "soon miss the Cold War."[13] More recently, Sebastian Rosato explained post-war European integration in terms of power balancing against the Soviet Union, and predicted that the European project would begin to crumble (or at best muddle along) in the absence of a threat on a par with the old Soviet Union.[14]

The historically grounded accounts comprising this volume both diverge from and add to the two perspectives of the Cold War that have dominated political science and IR. The contributors do not ignore or marginalize the Cold War and its manifold implications for European integration. But they also do not elevate it to the status of an all-important or omnipresent causal force shaping the European project across its many domains. Instead, this book's diverse accounts offer a wide-ranging view of the way in which the Cold War affected the emergence and evolution of the EC's external relations, laying bare not just its importance, but also its contingencies and limits.

Taken together, the analyses here demonstrate that the Cold War was an almost ever-present and pervasive system-level force that figured far more prominently in European integration than most political science theorizing has suggested. At the same time, the empirical findings and historical reconstructions within the volume offer a more careful and nuanced appreciation of the Cold War's effects, showing it to be a much more contingent and often indirect cause or condition rather than the all-powerful driving force that some IR works have depicted it to be.

The contributors to this volume uncover a complex web of causalities, many of which can be traced to the multifaceted implications of the Cold War and the dominant role of the United States within the Western camp. But they also reveal how the Cold War as a system-level factor intertwined and mingled with a wide range of causal impulses, pushes and pulls located at the member-state level or inside the domestic political arena.

A number of the findings showcased in several chapters strongly suggest that the Cold War exerted a fairly direct impact on the EC's external relations, whether in propelling or inhibiting its forward progress. Karamouzi, for example, shows that the EC's "Southern European enlargement" was motivated by the perceived need to tightly bind Greece, Spain, and Portugal to the Western camp while at the same time curbing Soviet expansion in the Mediterranean. By integrating these countries into the expanding Community, the Western alliance could address concerns about the instability of their internal order, thereby helping to stabilize the Cold War's southern flank against Soviet advances. Similar considerations, as Calandri documents, fueled the association agreements with Malta and Cyprus in 1970 and 1972, respectively.

And as Romano points out, the EC's relations with Yugoslavia were driven both by the goal to curb Soviet influence in the Balkans as well as Europe's unease with superpower duopoly and its desire to have more autonomy and independence for "Europe" itself in structuring interstate relations, at least on the European continent. The East–West confrontation, in Garavini's account, in the form of Europe's struggle against the political recognition of East Germany, likewise underpinned offers of development aid made by the Community or individual member states.

More often, however, the Cold War's causal impact is shown to be less linear and direct. Rather than directly bringing about historical outcomes, it functioned as a setting, environment, stage, or condition for the post-World War II European project, and affected the EC's evolving external relations through different, variegated, and contingent causal pathways.[15] In some cases, the conditions generated by the Cold War proved to be favorable, conducive, or at least permissive to the EC's attempts to lay the foundations for and subsequently foster its external relations. At other times, however, it inhibited, limited, or undermined the Community's ability to develop a more robust international personality.

Ludlow finds ample evidence for the Cold War's nuanced and variegated impact on European integration and EC foreign relations, yet also notes that the "interaction" between Cold War and European project "was nevertheless seldom straightforward or direct." Visible yet elusive, the Cold War, he says, "is present in most historical snapshots that could be taken of the EC or of collective European decision-making during the 1958 to 1990 period. But it is seldom in focus, rarely at the center of the picture."

A number of chapters lend credence to this image. Loth suggests that the intricate combination of Western Europe's fundamental dependence on the United States for security and lingering doubts over America's reliability not least because of credibility issues related to extended US nuclear deterrence ("risking New York for Berlin," as the saying went) on the one hand hindered the development of a more autonomous European role in security and defense, while, on the other, kept alive and even nourished Europe's desire to have a stronger hand in "high politics" and international security affairs more broadly.

Fardella and Rothacher, in their respective chapters, show that the Cold War underdogs EC and China—like the EC and Japan—could base their external relations almost exclusively on trade even in the shadow of the Cold War not least because all three were marginal players in world politics and the period's superpower competition.

For this reason, China's long-term objective of eventually escaping the Cold War strategic straitjacket and overcoming systemic bipolarity (its "anti-hegemonic struggle," as Fardella puts it), did not seriously alarm the superpowers or cause them to interfere. Thus, at least in terms of the development of these external relationships and in these policy domains, the Cold War can be viewed as a favorable and permissive underlying factor.

Furthermore, as seen throughout many of the chapters, the Cold War's systemic impact was not fixed across time. Rather, the kinds of opportunities and constraints that it generated waxed and waned. As Romano's and Loth's chapters illustrate in nicely complementary ways, in contrast to the decades that preceded it, the *détente* phase provided a conducive international environment for the development and consolidation of EC policies toward the Soviet bloc. *Détente* allowed for the Conference on Security and Cooperation in Europe (CSCE) process, which in turn provided the EC the opportunity (however embryonic) to venture in the (softer, to be sure) areas of security affairs.

Taken together, the historical accounts offered in this volume reveal an interesting double logic through which the Cold War both fueled and stymied the development of the EC's external relations (and West European integration at large) across four decades. On the one hand, not least through generally benign Cold War-driven or Cold War-compatible US support, the Cold War abetted the growth of the European project. Given the dueling US–Soviet plans (and management schemes) for the Old Continent, from 1947 onward American support for West European integration was directly tied to its more global Cold War strategies. Accordingly, as Ludlow underlines, Western European integration enjoyed strong financial, political, organizational, and ideational support from the United States from the late 1940s onwards.

Along similar lines, Weisbrode argues that US encouragement of European integration arose not simply for security reasons and the strategic goal of "keeping the Soviets out," but also from the desire to undermine the efforts of Communist parties or movements that sought to assume power or gain influence at the national level (especially in Italy, Greece, and France).

Both Seidel and Coppolaro, in their respective chapters, highlight the larger US Cold War strategic objectives for building up a West European continental "bulwark against communism" as well as strengthening the Atlantic alliance, which led the United States to take a relaxed stance on the EC's protectionist CAP policies. As Karamouzi shows, geopolitical motives also repeatedly surfaced in the domain of Community enlargement. For the United States, especially since the mid-1970s, (prospective) EC membership helped further additional strategic considerations, such as consolidating democracy, domestic stability, and securing a lasting NATO presence across the western half of the continent.

On the other hand, as several authors discuss, some of the ways in which the Cold War structured the international system or context, as well as the types of US foreign policies pursued during the era, also constrained or undermined the emergence of a more robust EC, especially in the realm of external relations. For example, Calandri demonstrates that in the Mediterranean and especially the Near East, US interests and its dominant role within the Western alliance significantly limited EC influence in the region. Loth and others also suggest that the United States wanted the EC and its member states as Cold War allies and supporters, but hardly on equal terms and certainly not as a separate and independent "pole" that could challenge American leadership or develop the potential for rivalry (as Chinese and French Gaullist goals had it). As a result, there were real limits to America's fostering of an independent EC, not least in the areas of security and defense, the traditional domains of "high politics."

Western Europe's basic dependence on the United States for security remained an enduring component of the Cold War. De Gaulle's attempt of a bilateral Franco–German answer to escape, at least partially, reliance on the United States fell prey to West Germany's "semi-sovereign" status and its dependence on the United States. When push came to shove, the transatlantic link and American guarantees tended to prevail in Bonn. Only late and grudgingly, as Loth reports, and only when West European dependence on American security guarantees had begun to decline, did the United States accept (and later in the 1990s begin to encourage) the development of a (tenuous) European defense identity.

But while laying emphasis on the myriad ways in which the Cold War affected or conditioned Europe's external relations, none of the authors argues that the Cold War's ramifications for the international system were the only, or even the dominant, causal factors. Rather, the chapters bring to the fore factors from all of the "levels" of analysis frequently invoked by IR scholars. Unsurprisingly given the political domains concerned, causal factors traceable to the individual EC member states or their domestic politics—"second-image" or "unit-level" factors as they are known in IR—loom large in many of the chapters.[16]

Romano shows that in dealing with the Soviet Union and its East European satellite states, EC member states were dominant until the 1970s, and remained key players even with and after the advent of the CSCE. As the Loth chapter makes clear, with the conclusive failure of the EDC in 1954, security and defense remained core areas of state sovereignty, with national politics heavily influencing Community affairs in these domains. And as Garavini highlights when discussing development aid and "Eurafrica," the former colonial powers, France and Britain in particular, continued to play major roles. They often proved to be the driving force behind many policies, even when the EC was formally involved in the process.

Rothacher, Seidel, and Coppolaro offer evidence that even in areas such as CAP, GATT, and trade more generally, in which the EC had developed a strong international personality, diverging national policy preferences mattered significantly, and at times led to the adoption of lowest-common-denominator positions in the EC's external relations. For example, conflicting member-state interests undermined the Commission's negotiations with and leverage over Japan. CAP frequently pitted France, the champion of agricultural protectionism, against more market-oriented EC members such as Germany or the Netherlands. And in international trade and GATT, individual EC member states remained vigilant about their own "relative gains" or losses.[17]

Bilateral relations, especially between Europe's major powers, also were influential. Ludlow, for instance, reveals the importance of Franco–German postwar reconciliation, and, subsequently, the highly influential role played by the pair's deeply institutionalized bilateralism within the European project at large.[18]

Alongside the relevance of the EC's member states conceived as "unitary" actors, the chapters also offer evidence for the impact of other "second-image" factors, such as the special interests groups that dominated domestic politics within the countries of Western Europe. Influential pressure groups and well-organized farm interests in France, Italy, or Germany, Seidel documents, did not simply shape CAP policies, but exerted an impact on the EC's international trade in agriculture more broadly. Business interests, including a wide variety of agricultural lobbies, often acting through national governments, also affected the EC's relations with Japan, Rothacher suggests.

Similarly, with respect to China, Fardella points out that domestic interest groups, especially in Britain, France, and West Germany, which had sought access to the Chinese market, served as an important base that helped to support and push ahead the evolving EC–China trade relationship. Domestic interests and lobbies complicated the development of a Community-wide policy for procurement and armament, a domain that remained largely in national hands and outside of the EC's control during the period covered here. Furthermore, in transatlantic affairs, Weisbrode demonstrates the importance of bureaucracies and the bureaucratic level in the United States, as well as particular Commission DGs or intergovernmental bodies such as Committee of Permanent Representatives (COREPER) at the Community-level.[19]

Finally, several of authors remind us that single political figures, especially during particular situations or critical junctures can have an impact, as IR theorizing on "first-image" or "individual-level" causality in international relations would have it.[20] Karamouzi notes de Gaulle's role in blocking of UK membership, while Calandri mentions his *souverainisme* and personal Arab diplomacy. Romano illustrates that top leadership changeover in France and Germany in the late 1960s opened the door for Community enlargement, and that, half a decade later, Schmidt and Giscard were key to establishing the European Council in 1974, boosting the EC's foreign relations options. Several authors likewise mention that European distrust or dissatisfaction with Nixon and Kissinger, Carter, or Reagan, in different ways fueled integration and aided the development of EC's incipient external relations.

Types of Causal Factors and Forces

The historical accounts and empirical findings featured in this volume also speak to important debates in IR theory about the basic types of factors and forces that shape international politics. Is it material factors and structures that drive state behavior and international outcomes, such as the desire for physical security or economic interests? Or, is it the rules and norms embedded in international institutions? Or could it be ideational variables, such as self-perceptions, perceptions of legitimacy, various types of collective identities, or other intersubjective meanings?[21]

Since these issues often remain implicit in many of this volume's chapters, this section seeks to make explicit the important causal factors uncovered by the contributors. In drawing connections across the chapters—as well as between these and the ideas underpinning international relations theory—it quickly becomes clear that no single type of causal factor can be said to have dominated in propelling or hampering the EC's external relations over the period covered in this volume. Instead, factors and forces of different types were at work, often simultaneously, and seemed to reinforce and interact with each other. The authors document a wide and varied set of material, institutional, and ideational factors that shaped the EC external relations from the late 1950s to the early 1990s.

Material conditions such as the Berlin Wall and Iron Curtain that physically divided Europe, the superpowers' economic and military confrontation, and the specter of nuclear or conventional war come out strongly in many of the chapters. These structural features could not but set strong incentives for the EC, as well as its individual member states, to seek to at least partially mitigate the continent's inherent divisions and reduce the likelihood of military confrontation through external engagements of various kinds, including trade and the CSCE.

However, we also see that an array of material economic motives and incentives instigated certain choices and decisions, and propelled particular outcomes. Mutually beneficial trade interests, as Fardella underscores, fueled the emerging EC–China relationship and the remarkable growth in trade between them between 1970 and 1990. Calandri points out how the EC and EC member states' economic interests also permeated European involvement in the Mediterranean, while the absence of "hard" material power resources, including a military component, limited the EC's role in the Near East.

Trading states such as Germany or the Netherlands, seeking greater access to foreign markets, pushed the EC to deploy its weight and power accordingly, which, as Coppolaro records, resulted in the EC's contributions to trade liberalization and the setting of GATT rules. And as Karamouzi mentions, the urge to enhance the size, weight, reach, influence and power of the EC was at least one of the key motivations behind enlargement.

CAP's agricultural protectionism, and the exclusion of agricultural products from trade liberalization—to the benefit of producers not least in Italy's *mezzogiorno* and France's south—are classic examples of economic policy being driven by interest group pressure and domestic materialist considerations. However, material interests (and materialist factors generally) need not always, as Coppolaro and Rothacher remind us, causally pull in the same direction. Coppolaro reports that through GATT, EC member states often tended to privilege short-term economic gains over geopolitical or strategic interests, such as strengthening the cohesion of the Atlantic alliance (or the EC as an emergent foreign policy actor). Rothacher, for his part, emphasizes the difficulties caused by divergent member state interests with respect to finding common EC positions vis-à-vis Japan.

Several authors speak to the importance of institutional opportunities or constraints in shaping EC external relations, at least in some domains and with respect to particular states or regions of the world. The empirical record hints at the interplay of the institutional context at two levels simultaneously for EC external relations: At the international level, most notably the GATT regime in trade, and the "domestic" Community level via intra-EC institutionalization.[22]

At the international institutional context, Coppolaro shows that the 1947 GATT framework, the central trade component of the post-World War II American-made liberal international order, not only provided the institutional forum in which the EC developed its trade policies, but also served as the cradle in which the EC could develop its international personality and become an actor in trade altogether.[23] "The GATT Kennedy Round (1964–1967) marked the emergence," Coppolaro notes, "of the EC as a single and powerful unit in world trade, with the capacity to inscribe its preferences in the final outcome and, consequently, to shape the trade regime." Seidel, in turn, shows how GATT rules, based as they were on American preferences and power, provided institutionalized exemptions for farming, including import quotas under some circumstances and export subsidies for primary goods, and thus at least partially abetted the EC's staunch defense of the CAP within the world trade regime.

In the spirit of historical institutionalism, Seidel also points to the CAP's lock-in effects and the path-dependent persistence of some of its basic features, which proved difficult to reform or redefine all the way up to the Uruguay Round (1986–1994). And indeed, CAP consumed the lion's share of EC (and EU) spending for decades, despite its problematic consequences for Third World trade and development, and international trade in agriculture more broadly, as the Seidel, Garavini, and Coppolaro chapters vividly illustrate.

Institutionalization internal to the EC also contributed to a consolidation and expansion of the Community's ability to conduct and grow its external relations. Romano shows how the 1974-instituted European Council, an intergovernmental institutional set-up that regularly brought together the leaders of the EC member states, strengthened the EC's capacity to voice common international positions and to act diplomatically.[24] Romano's, Fardella's, Rothacher's, and Coppolaro's chapters also underscore that the 1986 adoption and subsequent completion of the SEA further invigorated the EC as an actor in areas related to its market, customs, and commercial policy, and reinforced the EC's coherence and standing vis-à-vis China and Japan.

Karamouzi shows that the use of enlargement as a genuine EC foreign policy tool— which had emerged slowly through discovery, practice, and demand for Community membership—became fully institutionalized only late with the 1993 "Copenhagen criteria," but had by then already become highly effective based as it was on rather strict conditionality and "a sophisticated and ever-growing list of demands" that served to make accession candidates compatible with the Community club. More generally, Calandri links institutional and formal changes within the EC-frame and the Community's emergence as an international actor in its own right.

However, a number of chapters also identify the reverse effect of formal institutionalization, showing how the difficult, often cumbersome, and frequently slow EC decision-making machinery put a break on some of the EC's external relations. The stumbling blocks arose not only from the difficulty of translating and reconciling divergent national interests and positions into and with Community stances (with the unanimity requirement often being a particularly consequential institutional ingredient), but, in some cases, also from the need to bring in line various voices from the EC itself, such as the Commission, the European Council, the Parliament, or even frictions or jealousies between different Commission Directorate Generals (DGs).

This intricate and complex institutional set-up shaped or affected EC policies across numerous externally relevant policy domains, and perhaps even more dramatically, as Ludlow's, Weisbrode's, and Romano's chapters detail, the Community's dealings with several key interlocutors such as the United States and the Soviet Union. Such institutional hindrances also help explain the EC's protracted inability to design a robust, or at least satisfactory, common position to answer the "Japan threat" in trade, and gain greater access to the Japanese market for the Community's exports.

Ideational (or "idea-ist") factors likewise affected the EC and its external relations and European integration during the Cold War period, as a number of chapters show.[25] Ludlow points to the importance of Germany's self-perception, and, more specifically, of its goal to be a "good European" deeply committed to multilateralism. While this striving was certainly related to the Federal Republic's physical vulnerability as a divided country on the Cold War's front line, and to the country's physical destruction during the war, West Germany's self-perception is not reducible to strictly materialist conditions.[26] Instead, the idea of "Europe" or "European" beckoned because it offered a welcome counterpoint and escape from the country's nationalist socialist past, and its physical and moral devastations.[27]

Ideational factors also include what Weisbrode labels as "historical" (rather than geopolitical) drivers, such as the international legitimacy emanating from American liberal internationalism, which radiated through America's West European allies in the form of the EC. French and British ideas of a special connection with or allegiance to their former colonies, detailed by Garavini and Calandri, also seem to have been based on more than just material interests or institutional drivers. This was the case even in instances where such ideational inclinations bred organizational and material consequences, such as when Moroccan and Tunisian (from the 1957 Rome Treaties) and then Algerian (from the 1962 Evian agreements) goods were granted duty-free access to the Common Market. Along similar lines, one could argue that *détente* is best viewed through "constructivist-interactionist" conceptual lenses as a non-material temporary feature at the level of the international system that offered an opportunity for the EC to assume additional external functions through CSCE, as Romano and Loth suggest.[28]

Alongside material stakes and powerful domestic pressures, Seidel also stresses the CAP's ideological nature, showing that the ideational importance of agriculture enabled farmers' lobbies and agricultural ministers in France, Italy, Germany, and elsewhere to exert wide and powerful influence. The resulting "specific nature" of agriculture fueled the very possibility of keeping the agricultural chapter in GATT separate from negotiations that liberalized trade in industrial goods.

Emergent External Agency

This book's historical investigation of the EC's external relations and the roots of the Community's emergence as an international actor in its own right also pair well with and map onto debates within IR about which actors matter, and which matter most, in world politics. For IR realists, states are the key wielders of power and authority and the most important "conflict group" in international affairs.[29] IR Liberals, in contrast, tend to stress the multiplicity of international, transnational, and domestic actors. States (or national governments), while important, are accorded a less exclusive or prominent role on the world stage.[30] Constructivists, for their part, focus on the intersubjective meanings among and between states as well as domestic and transnational actors, and frequently fall somewhere between realists and liberals when it comes to arguments about the central actors in international affairs, drawing closer to one or the other depending on the issue.[31]

This book's chapters suggest that both realism and liberalism may be right, or, at least, that neither can be rejected outright. During the Cold War, the United States, the Soviet Union, and other EC interlocutors, such as China and Japan, as well as the EC members states themselves, were state-based international actors that clearly shaped the beginnings of the EC. At the same time, the EC and its external relations emerged among and amidst a variety of domestic, international, and transnational actors. International institutions such as GATT, domestic agricultural pressure groups, most notably in France and Italy, various organized industrial interests, as well as the component parts that make up states themselves, such as particular ministries and bureaucracies, all had a role to play in the formation and trajectory of EC external affairs.

While the EC started out as a more or less run-of-the-mill international organization, it soon developed, however piecemeal at first, into an international organization with its own agency and reach that went beyond its constitutive parts (that is, the member states that comprised it).[32] And as the EC expanded its role and relevance during the Cold War period, it did so as an external "personality" of a distinct and particular kind.

First, the pace and decisiveness with which the EC came to acquire its own international personality varied widely not only over time, but, as importantly, across political domains and with respect to different interlocutors. In the economic sphere, as seen with respect to trade and GATT, the EC assumed agency not only fairly early on but also to a reasonably high degree. "[T]he [EC's] role in world trade," Coppolaro says, "is fundamental to its external activities and that trade policy has been the linchpin of the [Community's] engagement and relations with the rest of the world."

Foreign relations standing related to enlargement followed next. The growth and robustness of EC agency in the domain of development policy and "Eurafrica" falls in the middle, not least because the larger parts of development aid went through national channels. During the Cold War period, security and defense lagged far behind and remained weakly developed, especially compared to autonomous EC defense capabilities.

The EC's capacity to effectively conduct its external affairs also varied across states and regions. The EC's position in the developing world, underpinned as it was by agriculture and trade within the GATT framework, was fairly strong, and increasingly so from the 1970s onward. The Community's ability to define and carry out its relations with China and Japan remained weak and tied mostly to issues of trade and economic exchange. A similar conclusion applies to the Mediterranean and the Middle East, except where issues of enlargement (or association) were concerned. The EC's capacity to act autonomously with respect to either of the superpowers remained limited, especially in the areas of traditional "high politics," even as it began to assert some agency in other spheres, most clearly trade. Still, the CSCE process provided an opening for the EC to engage more independently, and it seized the opportunity.

Second, the EC assumed aspects of agency in a highly uneven and fragmented way. For quite some time, it acted as one might expect as an evolving polity rather than a unitary actor (that would be equipped with a clear head of government or single center of authority) to behave. As many authors discuss, a variety of units, representative bodies, or component parts acted as and for the EC, including the Commission, Commission Directorate Generals (DGs, in external affairs especially DG I, External Relations and III, Industry), Commissioners, particular DGs' heads of division; as well as special representatives (such as in trade, "puzzling to Japanese negotiators," as Rothacher puts it), all of whom represented the Community alongside senior national officials, trade and economic ministers, and, at times, foreign ministers or heads of national governments. To this panoply, we also should add the European Council (from 1974), the Council of Ministers, the European Parliament, as well as groups of member states on occasion.

Third, and contrary to the expectations of some early post-War integration theories, the EC grew as an actor without decisively weakening, eradicating, or systematically replacing the authority of the member states that made up the Community or their national foreign policies, all of which continued to coexist with and function in parallel to the evolving new polity. Critically, such a polity's "external relations" are not the same as the "foreign policy" of a unitary modern nation-state, let alone anything like a "grand strategy" that ties and integrates the EC's capabilities into a set of well-ordered and overarching strategic goals and ambitions.[33] In fact, to judge the EC's evolving external relations (either its achievements or its shortcomings), especially during the Cold War decades, against the benchmark of nation-state foreign policy seems too demanding, unrealistic, and, even unfair. Measured against such a standard, the Community's progress in this area would always fall short.

As several of the chapters illustrate, the EC developed agency and became a subject or actor by doing. That is, it slowly grew its own agency through incremental action, whether by participating in the consecutive rounds of GATT, in seizing the opportunities that the CSCE negotiations offered with respect to the socialist world and the Soviet Union, or by developing trade relations with China or Japan. Moreover, it did so for a long time on terms unfavorable for the Europeans or in ways that made the EC look like an apprentice in international affairs, even in its prime area of trade and economic exchange.

As Karamouzi's chapter on the (as with EC external relations) often under- or unappreciated domain of enlargement argues, "becoming by doing" entailed the discovery of relevance and agency. The EC "learned agency," and often learned it by accident.[34] As Karamouzi notes, "There was no strategic plan within European circles, and the historical analysis of enlargement's earlier rounds unearths an almost accidental use and appreciation of its value for the Community's foreign policy machinery." Because the applicant states experienced (potential) "accession" as a central goal of its foreign policy, the Community started to see it as a key EC policy area, and consequently began to develop a more institutional and instrumental approach.

We can, however, discern some critical milestones along the EC's meandering and at times intermittent path toward the assumption of partial international agency. For instance, as Coppolaro discusses, "the initial appearance of the EEC [at the GATT negotiating table] in Geneva marked the first sign of EEC actorness." At this juncture, however, "the EC was informally accepted as a player." Also, as Garavini points out, early on, the Community had taken on some (perhaps inchoate) aspects of actorhood in dealing with the colonies and former colonies that the EC had inherited through its member states. Formal recognition also was critical. For example, Weisbrode mentions how the United States appointed a permanent ambassador to the EC in 1961, and the EC's representative assumed the rank of an ambassador to Washington in 1971. The GATT Kennedy Round (1964–1967), as Coppolaro suggests, "marked the emergence of the EEC as a single and powerful unit in world trade, with the capacity to inscribe its preferences in the final outcome and, consequently, to shape the trade regime."

For political economy reasons, starting in the 1960s the socialist regimes of Eastern and Central European "fertilized" (to use Romano's term) the ground for direct relations with the EC, which led to the development of EPC guidelines for an "embryonic collective Eastern policy" in the early 1970s. In November 1974, Romano reports, the EC Commission informed all eastern European socialist governments that the Commission had assumed the competence in trade and that bilateral trade agreements with EC member states had become a matter of the past. From the second half of the 1970s, the Soviet Union and its satellites began to have "regular contacts with the Commission. Although unofficial, these interactions came very close to classic diplomacy in their substance." The year 1975 also saw the official establishment of EC/EEC relations with China, which followed on the heels of the recognition of China by the individual EC member states over the first half of the decade.

The EC's "international personality" in the areas of development and "Eurafrica," Garavini points out, further strengthened during the 1970s with the signing of the Lomé Convention (Lomé II was negotiated and signed the following decade), the "North–South Dialogue," and the cooperation agreements between the EC and Mediterranean and Arab states. By the mid-1980s, he reports that the EC's development aid stood at some 15 percent of the EC member states' total development aid. In 1983, Weisbrode notes, the United States and the EC initiated regular ministerial meetings focusing on economic matters, with the Commission representing the EC as a whole.[35] With the adoption and implementation of the SEA in 1986, the EC completed the single market, further boosting its external agency in the economic domain.

While it remained far from a full-fledged international actor that could make its own mark on the Cold War as a whole, by the time the Berlin Wall fell and the powerful desire on the part of the former socialist states to "join Europe" or "return to Europe" became overwhelming, the EC had grown enough to take an important international role in post-Cold War settlements almost by default.

"Adjective Power" Europe

The tendency to use particular adjectives in order to characterize the nature, role, identity, self-image, or policies of the EC and EU dates back to the 1970s and 1980s, with the publication of influential essays by François Duchêne and Hedley Bull.[36] In recent years, a minor cottage industry has sprung up around the question of what kind of "adjective" power Europe has become in the twenty-first century. The most widely circulated and debated accounts make the case for (or against) Europe being a "market," "normative," and/or a "civilian" power.[37]

The accuracy or theoretical, conceptual, or empirical usefulness of these characterizations are generally debated based on evidence taken from more recent years, and the past one or two decades in particular. The longer-term view of the EC's external relations from the end of World War II to Maastricht that can be gleaned from this volume offers a rich and generally untapped source of evidence from which to draw when considering the various "adjective" power Europe claims. What do this volume's accounts of the history of external relations tell us about the various depictions of "adjective" power Europe? In what ways does the historical record support or contradict existing depictions?

Given that trade issues and other aspects of Europe's political economy figured prominently in the development of EC's external relations during the decades covered in this book, it is unsurprising that a number of the chapters can speak directly to arguments about "market power" Europe and its various claims.[38] Chad Damro identifies three core pillars of "market power Europe": the size of the EU market; institutional features, such as the EU's regulatory powers; and interest contestation, or societal pressures and interest group coalitions that promote and externalize their preferences.[39] Thus conceived, the EC/EU "is fundamentally a large single market with significant institutional features and competing interest groups."[40] It matters because the EC/EU has the capacity to externalize "its internal market-related policies and regulatory measures."[41]

Within GATT, Coppolaro reports, the EC contributed to trade liberalization and the setting of GATT rules—thus shaping the world trade regime in some ways—by deploying its "trade power." Despite frequent member state differences on trade and related matters, the EC often managed to speak with one voice. With the 1973 enlargement, which added Denmark, Ireland, and the United Kingdom to the "original Six," the EC's common market became the world's largest trading bloc (measured in terms of share of world trade). The increase in the attractiveness of its market and the ability to either grant or deny market access to others countries further enhanced the EC's bargaining power and leverage vis-à-vis other actors.

Moreover, access to the Community's common market was a strong incentive for candidates to pursue accession, a formidable carrot that the EC could hold out to possible applicant states. For example, according to Karamouzi, Denmark relinquished its neutrality policy not least in order to gain access to the Community's market for its agricultural produce and to boost trade. Weisbrode likewise shows that the EC being a very major market with agency had important consequences even for its relations with the United States, while Calandri reminds us that the EC's role in the Mediterranean rested largely on the Community's economic power.

The significant market power and potential of the Six, and, even more the Nine, made the EC an attractive interlocutor for China, with trade and economic exchange forming the core of the EC–China relationship. China's long-term vision of a multipolar world that could replace the Cold War's strategic bipolarity fueled the expansion of trade relations between the Community and China. Furthermore, several of the chapters illustrate that interest group politics figured prominently in the expansion of external trade, or, as in the case of agriculture and CAP, in the EC's adherence to market protectionism.

These "market power" aspects, however, are not always visible in other policy domains or with respect to the EC's other interlocutors, particularly in Eurasia and East Asia. Several of the book's chapters leave us wondering why the EC did not take more advantage of its "market power" and the potential leverage that derived from it when dealing with, for example, Japan or the Soviet Union.

The record that emerges from this volume with respect to the EC being a "normative power" is at best mixed. Many of the findings do not sit well with claims that the EC's actions were particularly "normative" in its formative years. The normative power perspective depicts the EC/EU with or through its member states, either adhering to or promoting a set of universally applicable principles, values, and shared beliefs. Ian Manners identifies nine "substantive normative principles" which, in his view, both constitute and are promoted by the EC/EU: "sustainable peace, freedom, democracy, human rights, rule of law, equality, social solidarity, sustainable development and good governance."[42] Viewed through this lens, the Community's normative power is the power of example.

With respect to enlargement, "the Six," and later "the Nine," all of which were democratic, market-oriented, and members of NATO, insisted that others adopt similar political, legal, economic principles and standards before accepting new arrivals into the club. In keeping the Community an exclusive circle of like-minded modern liberal democratic states, the EC broadly acted as a "normative power." Democracy promotion, Karamouzi also shows, was a key objective behind enlargement, even if it went alongside other motives, including Cold War strategic considerations and what Wolfers might call "possession" and "milieu" goals.[43] And as Garavini documents in his chapter, the EC became the second largest (with France being the largest) donor of development aid to Africa's Francophone countries, and that an acceptable human-rights record became a condition for receiving aid through the Lomé II framework.

Other findings, however, sit uncomfortably with the "normative power" characterization. As seen in the Seidel and Coppolaro chapters, as well as the Calandri and Garavini contributions, the EC's CAP, with its agricultural protectionism through internal purchase and price guarantees, import levies, and export subsidies cannot be easily reconciled with the idea that the Community sought to act in particularly "normative" ways.

The CAP's market-distorting implications came at the expense of Third World producers and export prospects (as well as European taxpayers and consumers). Although, as Seidel points out, the CAP's exact impact is difficult to quantify because it affected developing countries differently and to different degrees, the CAP undermined and partially crowded out developing countries' agricultural products from world markets, hindering their ability to benefit from international trade even in areas where they would otherwise have been competitive. As in other domains of world trade, Seidel notes the paradox that the EC "expected African states to liberalize their agricultural sectors while at the same time the Community was setting up a highly protectionist agricultural policy."

Coppolaro notes that developing countries frequently felt excluded from important or decisive trade negotiations. Calandri reports that the EC's persistent protectionism led to a drop in agricultural activity in countries like Morocco and Tunisia, which, in turn bred a number of ills in these countries, including desertification, environmental problems, and, due to swift population growth and a concomitant rise in domestic consumption, food shortages.

The Community clung to the sharply discriminating CAP all through the period covered here. As both Seidel and Coppolaro show, rather modest, at least according to some, CAP reforms came only with the Uruguay Round (1986–1994) and the 1992 MacSharry Reforms—and these were brought about through strong external pressures and tremendous internal costs, rather than because of any "normative" insights or "ethical" considerations.

Moreover, it is not just the CAP that goes against claims of a "normative power Europe." Developing nations, Coppolaro reminds us, similarly encountered staunch EC (and US) antagonism when they tried to liberalize international trade in textiles in which many Third World countries had become or were becoming competitive. EC trade with China in military, dual use, and space technology, Fardella notes, never fully evolved. Not because of any "normative" concerns on Europe's part, however, but rather because of strong American opposition.

The EC was hardly a champion of the powerless when it came to "Eurafrica." As Garavini writes, "Western European powers clung to their colonies with all their strength, tried to revitalize them with new development efforts, and exerted extreme violence in the process." And even after the empires had fallen and the former colonies became associated with the young Community, the "'associated' countries had no role and no voice in the shape or the management of the association."

Notwithstanding what Garavini calls the "process of 'mental decolonization'" that, according to him, started in the late 1960s, and similar to CAP reforms in the Uruguay Round, adjustments to the EC's development policy in the 1970s and 80s resulted from external and internal political pressures rather than normative impulses. Finally, Rothacher's reports of EC and European leaders' stereotypes of Japan and the Japanese appear to contradict the Community's self-image as a "normative" or "ethical" actor in world politics. Even without relying on contemporary standards of political correctness, an EC Commissioner calling Japan a country of "workaholics living in rabbit hutches" and a French prime minister comparing Japanese workers to yellow ants, seem retrograde.

A similarly mixed, though perhaps less grim, record emerges with respect to the idea of the EC acting as a mainly "civilian power" during the decades covered by this book.[44] The "civilian power Europe" perspective sees the EC/EU as pursuing its interests mainly through non-military (i.e. civilian) instruments, such as trade, development aid, and humanitarian assistance, and through negotiation, persuasion, or attraction, rather than coercion, threats, or the application of military force. This approach lays emphasis on the EU's soft power reserves rather than its military capabilities and willingness to use them.[45] Despite some four or five decades of writing about Europe as a "civilian" power, proponents of this view have yet to generate a straightforward, testable, or widely accepted definition of what exactly a "civilian power Europe" would look like and how we would expect it to behave.

In purely formalistic terms, the EC's external relations from 1955 to 1992 were by and large "civilian" in the sense that the EC as an organization neither engaged in military action nor took any significant steps in that direction. EC initiatives such as the Global Mediterranean Policy (GMP) and the Euro–Arab Dialogue (EAD) of the 1970s, which Calandri discusses, thus were "civilian" in nature. However, given the EC's actual capabilities at the time, how could they have been anything else?

It thus remains problematic to characterize the EC (and its external relations) as "civilian." Five of the EC's "original Six" were founding members of NATO (West Germany joined the alliance in 1955) and, protected by the American nuclear umbrella, soon integrated into NATO's forward defense. Two of the EC "Nine," France and the United Kingdom, were nuclear powers. And though France exited NATO's integrated military command in 1966, it hardly made it less of a military power (or, as part of the EC, more "civilian"). Moreover, the EC and its member states aspired to and attempted to acquire capabilities and options for at least some autonomous action in the distinctly non- or un-civilian areas of security and defense, even if they did not succeed in doing so for a long time. In other words, "they would have if they could have, but they couldn't so they didn't."

As Loth shows, the Community's exclusion from the domains of traditional "high politics" was an outcome neither of design nor intention. Instead, the EC's un- or under-developed potential in security and defense during the Cold War period was the result of history and politics, induced by Cold War necessity rather than any kind of conscious European choice to remain a "civilian power." With the conclusive failure of the EDC in 1954, NATO became the supreme security organization for Western Europe (with the WEU no more than a token institution), and ultimate decision-making in security and defense remained at the level of the nation-state.

Furthermore, the desire to enhance the Community's foreign, security, and defense capabilities—what Loth calls "the striving for common policies"—never disappeared, even in the face of setbacks and failures. Instead, it displayed remarkable tenacity throughout all phases of the Cold War, and the ups and downs of superpower relations. Moreover, as soon as the Cold War straightjacket had fallen off, and the shock of a violently disintegrating Yugoslavia had appeared, the EU began to develop capabilities in foreign policy, security, and defense, even if slowly and in a distinctly non-linear fashion.[46]

Thus it remains unclear what further insights the "civilian" designation adds to our understanding of the EC's external relations with the Soviet Union and the Socialist world, in the Mediterranean or the Middle East, and of its actions across domains such as trade, enlargement, or development policy that the "market power" perspective does not already provide.

Conclusion

The first three sections of this chapter provided several different theoretical and conceptual lenses to view this volume's empirical findings, and examined how these findings fit with some of the core theoretical, conceptual, and empirical debates in IR theory and the theorizing of European integration. Considerations of (1) the level of analysis at which causal variables operate (system, state, or individual); (2) the type of causal factor at work (material, institutional, or ideational); and (3) the key actor or actors in world politics (the nation-state, domestic interest groups, transnational entities, international organizations, and so forth), underpins much IR theorizing about what at bottom drives international affairs and the behavior of states, international organizations, and other actors.

While these conceptual and theoretical considerations often remain implicit in the accounts offered by international historians, they define and distinguish the main intellectual traditions or schools of thought in IR (the "isms" or "paradigms," as some call them), as well as major disciplinary and interdisciplinary debates.

Structural realism (or "neorealism") focuses on the systemic level (and often what is referred to as the material structure of the international system, or the distribution of material capabilities) and views states as the main actors in international affairs.[47] "Neoclassical realism" also gives central causal importance to the material structure of the international system. While maintaining the central role and importance of states in world politics, this strand of realism augments its analysis by incorporating various factors within states as "intervening" causal variables, such as leader images (i.e., the calculations or misperceptions of individual leaders), strategic culture, state–society relations, and domestic institutions.[48] For classical realists, on the other hand, the implications of the international system are more variegated, and may remain partially in the background. Scholars in this vein also prioritize the state as a key in world politics, but tend to combine various structural, institutional, and ideational variables—as well as elements from the international system, domestic politics, and the impact of individual leaders—into their narratives to create a more "holistic" perspective of international relations and foreign policy behavior.[49]

Liberal institutionalists (or "neoliberals") emphasize the role of international institutions and organizations in world politics. There are different varieties of institutionalism in IR (as there are in the social sciences more broadly): rational choice institutionalism, historical institutionalism, and sociological institutionalism. Neoliberalism belongs to the first category, and in addition to its rationalist micro-foundations, it provides a materialist approach that may or may not integrate aspects of domestic politics.[50] Other IR scholars in the liberal vein commonly (though not exclusively) adopt materialist assumptions and premises. Next to and alongside states (or "national governments," as many liberals prefer), IR liberals accord analytical importance to a multiplicity of domestic, international, and transnational actors across different levels of analysis.[51]

Like the various types of realism, Wendt's seminal constructivist account also focuses predominantly on states as the key actors in world politics. Yet when probing the significance and implications of formal international anarchy, constructivists emphasize intersubjective structures of meaning created by state interaction.[52] Other constructivists, however, focus on the causal or constitutive impact of ideational structures and processes such as culture, norms, social learning, the socialization of actors' identities and interests, discourse, and "practices."[53]

What comes out clearly when this volume's chapters are viewed together is that there is no single theoretical logic that fully explains the origins or evolution of the EC's external relations across various policy domains and over the four decades of Cold War history. As the chapters illustrate, the Cold War mattered for the nature and development of EC external relations in a number of direct and indirect ways, and more so than many of the studies of European integration during this period in IR and political science concede. Yet the Cold War's impact mixed with factors from other levels of analysis so that the constraints and opportunities produced by the structure of the international system combined with factors or impulses from the domestic and intergovernmental levels of EC member states. A wide range of domestic, transnational, and individual actors thus served to encourage, limit, undermine, or otherwise shape the outcomes and decisions examined in this volume. This volume's findings thus show the fruitfulness of taking an eclectic approach when seeking to understand and explain the EC's external relations over time, toward individual states or world regions, and across policy domains.[54]

Finally, section four connects our volume's key findings to debates on the nature and role of the EC/EU as an international actor, which by now have spawned a small cottage industry of various adjectival modifiers. Surprisingly, however, current debates about whether Europe is a "market," "normative," "civilian" or other "adjective" power, leave largely untapped an important source of empirical evidence—the four decades of the EC's external relations that are covered here. This volume's empirical judgments and conclusions lend uneven support to some of the most common "adjective" power Europe positions. Europe's role and influence as a "market" power comes out strongest while its status as a "normative" power appears to be weakest. Europe's capacity as a "civilian" power falls somewhere in between.

Collectively, therefore, the volume's contributions not only offer a nuanced, comprehensive, and empirically rich "pre-history" to the contemporary political and scholarly debates on Europe's role and place in the world, but also contribute valuable historical and empirical evidence for theorizing what drives international affairs and how best to grasp Europe's nature, role, and its pursuit of specific policies.

And this volume demonstrates that international history and international relations speak to each other in a variety of ways, and offer important insights for each other. There is significant potential for mutual learning, enrichment, and even reconsiderations of disciplinary conventional wisdoms. The current divide did not always exist. But in recent decades specialization and idiosyncratic developments in each discipline have pulled the two further apart. Bridging the current divide and initiating a disciplinary *rapprochement* holds potential benefits for both international history and international relations.

Whereas "change is certain," E. H. Carr—one of the few figures who still seem to be read by both historians and IR scholars—is reputed to have said, "progress is not." With respect to creating more dialogue between the academic tribes of international history and international relations, however, things seem to be the other way around: change is anything but certain, but if it were to happen, it could surely reveal possibilities and opportunities for scholarly progress.

Notes

1   On the history of international relations as an academic discipline, see Stanley Hoffmann, "An American Social Science: International Relations," *Daedalus*, 106:3 (1977), 41–60; Brian C. Schmidt, "On the History and Historiography of International Relations," in Walter Carlsnaes, Thomas Risse and Beth A. Simmons (eds.), *Handbook of International Relations* (London: SAGE, 2002), 3–22.

2   Collaborations between international historians and IR scholars are surprisingly rare. Some notable instances include the *Journal of Cold War Studies*, 2:3 (2000), 69–116; Colin Elman and Miriam Fendius Elman (eds.), *Bridges and Boundaries: Historians, Political Scientists, and the Study of International Relations* (Cambridge: The MIT Press, 2001); Ernest R. May, Richard Rosecrance and Zara Steiner (eds.), *History and Neorealism* (Cambridge: Cambridge University Press, 2010).

3   Classically, see Kenneth N. Waltz, *Man, the State, and War: A Theoretical Analysis* (New York: Columbia University Press, 1959); J. David Singer, "The Level-of-Analysis Problem in International Relations," *World Politics*, 14:1 (1961), 77–92; Robert Jervis, *Perception and Misperception in International Politics* (Princeton: Princeton University Press, 1976); Nicholas Onuf, "Levels," *European Journal of International Relations*, 1:1 (1995), 35–58; James D. Fearon, "Domestic Politics, Foreign Policy, and Theories of International Relations," *Annual Review of Political Science*, 1 (1998), 289–313.

4   What all system-level perspectives have in common, no matter their theoretical or conceptual differences, is that the international system as a whole is different from the sum of its parts. For a structural-materialist formulation, see Kenneth N. Waltz, *Theory of International Politics* (Reading: Addison-Wesley, 1979); John J. Mearsheimer, *The Tragedy of Great Power Politics* (New York: Norton, 2001). For a systemic-constructivist idea-ist take, note Alexander Wendt, *Social Theory of International Politics* (Cambridge: Cambridge University Press, 1999). For a formulation of international systems in the historical-sociological tradition, see Raymond Aron, *Paix et guerre entre les nations* (Paris: Calmann-Lévy, 1962), Part I.

5   For overviews of theorizing on European integration, see Ben Rosamond, *Theories of European Integration* (Basingstoke: Palgrave Macmillan, 1999); Brent F. Nelsen and Alexander Stubb (eds.), *The European Union: Readings on the Theory and Practice of European Integration*, 4th Edition (Boulder: Lynne Rienner, 2014); Mark A. Pollack, "International Relations Theory and European Integration," *Journal of Common Market Studies*, 39:2 (2001), 221–244; Ulrich Krotz and Joachim Schild, *Shaping Europe: France, Germany, and Embedded Bilateralism from the Elysée Treaty to Twenty-First Century Politics* (Oxford: Oxford University Press, 2013), 11–16.

6   Ernst Haas, *The Uniting of Europe: Political, Social, and Economic Forces, 1950–1957* (Stanford: Stanford University Press, 1958). In a similar neofunctional vein that soon followed Haas, see Leon N. Lindberg, *The Political Dynamics of European Economic Integration* (Stanford: Stanford University Press, 1963); Philippe Schmitter, "Three Neo-Functional Hypotheses about International Integration," *International Organization*, 23:1 (1969), 161–166; Leon N. Lindberg and Stuart A. Scheingold (eds.), *Regional Integration: Theory and Research* (Cambridge: Harvard University Press, 1971); Joseph S. Nye, *Peace in Parts: Integration and Conflict in Regional Organization* (Boston: Little, Brown and Co., 1971).

7   Stanley Hoffmann, "Obstinate or Obsolete? The Fate of the Nation-State and the Case of Western Europe," *Daedalus*, 95:3 (1966), 862–915.

8   See Karl W. Deutsch, Sidney A. Burrell, Robert A. Kann, Maurice Lee Jr., Martin Lichterman, Raymond E. Lindgren, Francis L. Loewenheim and Richard W. Van Wagenen, *Political Community and the North Atlantic Area: International Organization in the Light of Historical Experience* (Princeton: Princeton University Press, 1957); Wayne Sandholtz and Alec Stone Sweet (eds.), *European Integration and Supranational Governance* (Oxford: Oxford University Press, 1998); Alec Stone Sweet, Wayne Sandholtz and Neil Fligstein (eds.), *The Institutionalization of Europe* (Oxford: Oxford University Press, 2001); Wayne Sandholtz and Alec Stone Sweet, "Neo-Functionalism and Supranational Governance," in Erik Jones, Anand Menon and Stephen Weatherill (eds.), *The Oxford Handbook of the European Union* (Oxford: Oxford University Press, 2012), 18–33.

9   Andrew Moravcsik, "Preferences and Power in the European Community: A Liberal Intergovernmentalist Approach," *Journal of Common Market Studies*, 31:4 (1993), 473–524; Andrew Moravcsik, *The Choice for Europe: Social Purpose and State Power from Messina to Maastricht* (Ithaca: Cornell University Press, 1998).

10   Markus Jachtenfuchs, "The Governance Approach to European Integration," *Journal of Common Market Studies*, 39:2 (2001), 245–264; Beate Kohler-Koch and Berthold Rittberger, "'The Governance Turn' in EU Studies," *Journal of Common Market Studies*, 44:1 (2006), 27–49.

11   Krotz and Schild, *Shaping Europe*.

12   Liesbet Hooghe and Gary Marks, "A Postfunctionalist Theory of European Integration: From Permissive Consensus to Constraining Dissensus," *British Journal of Political Science*, 39:1 (2009), 1–23.

13   John J. Mearsheimer, "Back to the Future: Instability in Europe After the Cold War," *International Security*, 15:1 (1990), 5–56; John J. Mearsheimer, "Why We Will Soon Miss the Cold War," *The Atlantic Monthly*, 266:2 (1990), 35–50.

14   Sebastian Rosato, *Europe United: Power Politics and the Making of the European Community* (Ithaca: Cornell University Press, 2011); Sebastian Rosato, "Europe's Troubles: Power Politics and the State of the European Project," *International Security*, 35:4 (2011), 45–86. For discussions and criticisms of Rosato's argument, see Ulrich Krotz, Richard Maher, David M. McCourt, Andrew Glencross, Norrin M. Ripsman, Mark S. Sheetz, Jean-Yves Haine and Sebastian Rosato, "Correspondence: Debating the Sources and Prospects of European Integration," *International Security*, 37:1 (2012), 178–199.

15   On causes and causality in IR, see, for example, Milija Kurki, *Causation in International Relations: Reclaiming Causal Analysis* (Cambridge: Cambridge University Press, 2008); and Ulrich Krotz, *History and Foreign Policy in France and Germany* (Basingstoke: Palgrave Macmillan, 2015), 17–21.

16   On "second-image" or "unit-level" explanations and theorizing in IR, see, for example, Andrew Moravcsik, "Taking Preferences Seriously: A Liberal Theory of International Politics," *International Organization*, 51:4 (1997), 513–553; Helen V. Milner, *Interests, Institutions, and Information: Domestic Politics and International Relations* (Princeton: Princeton University Press, 1997); Kenneth Schultz, "Domestic Politics and International Relations," in Carlsnaes, Risse and Simmons (eds.), *Handbook of International Relations*, 478–502.

17   Thus echoing the "relative" versus "absolute" gains debate that featured prominently in IR theory during this period. Theories that emphasize relative gains assume that

international cooperation is or tends to be zero-sum. While absolute gains reveal the possibility of international cooperation, relative gains underscore the propensity for conflict. See Joseph M. Grieco, "Anarchy and the Limits of Cooperation: A Realist Critique of the Newest Liberal Institutionalism," *International Organization*, 42:3 (1988), 485–507; Joseph M. Grieco, *Cooperation among Nations: Europe, America, and Non-tariff Barriers to Trade* (Ithaca: Cornell University Press, 1990); Robert Powell, "Absolute and Relative Gains in International Relations Theory," *American Political Science Review*, 85:4 (1991), 1303–1320; David A. Baldwin (ed.), *Neorealism and Neoliberalism: The Contemporary Debate* (New York: Columbia University Press, 1993).

18   For the basic importance of France–Germany, and Franco–German embedded bilateralism as a distinct level of political analysis, note Douglas Webber (ed.), *The Franco-German Relationship in the European Union* (London: Routledge, 1999); Krotz and Schild, *Shaping Europe*; Ulrich Krotz and Joachim Schild, "Back to the Future?," *Journal of European Public Policy*, 25:8 (2018), 1174–1193. For a long-term perspective of France–Germany in Europe, see Ulrich Krotz, "Three Eras and Possible Futures: A Long-term View on the Franco-German Relationship a Century after the First World War," *International Affairs*, 90:2 (2014), 337–350.

19   On bureaucracies and the "bureaucratic level" in international relations and foreign policy, classic statements include Graham T. Allison, *The Essence of Decision: Explaining the Cuban Missile Crisis* (Boston: Little, Brown and Co., 1971); Graham T. Allison and Morton H. Halperin, "Bureaucratic Politics: A Paradigm and Some Policy Implications," *World Politics*, 24:1 (1972), 40–79.

20   On such "first-image" scholarship, note, for example, Daniel L. Byman and Kenneth M. Pollack, "Let Us Now Praise Great Men: Bringing the Statesman Back In," *International Security*, 25:4 (2001), 107–146; Giacomo Chiozza and H. E. Goemans, *Leaders and International Conflict* (Cambridge: Cambridge University Press, 2011); Michael C. Horowitz, Allan C. Stam and Cali M. Ellis, *Why Leaders Fight* (Cambridge: Cambridge University Press, 2015); Robert Jervis, *How Statesmen Think: The Psychology of International Politics* (Princeton: Princeton University Press, 2017).

21   For a similar breakdown, see Craig Parsons, *How to Map Arguments in Political Science* (Oxford: Oxford University Press, 2007). Parson includes "psychological" factors as a fourth type of explanation in social science. These would fall under "first image" explanations above. However, the authors in this volume do not emphasize psychological explanations, even if mentioning the impact or importance of individual leaders at certain moments. On materialism versus idea-ism, see James Fearon and Alexander Wendt, "Rationalism v. Constructivism: A Skeptical View," in Carlsnaes, Risse and Simmons (eds.), *Handbook of International Relations*, 52–72.

22   "Institutionalism" in international relations and political science comes in three main types or versions, rationalist or rational choice institutionalism, historical institutionalism, and sociological institutionalism. Classically, see Peter A. Hall and Rosemary C. R. Taylor, "Political Science and the Three New Institutionalisms," *Political Studies*, 44:5 (1996), 936–957. On the various versions, see Barbara Koremenos, Charles Lipson, and Duncan Snidal (eds.), "Rational Choice of International Institutions," *International Organization* 55:4 (2001), special issue; Thomas Rixen, Lora Anne Viola, and Michael Zürn (eds.), *Historical Institutionalism and International Relations: Explaining Institutional Development in World Politics* (Oxford: Oxford University Press, 2016); Jeffrey T. Checkel, "The Constructivist Turn in International Relations Theory," *World Politics*, 50:2 (1998), 324–348. Given the

purposes of this concluding chapter (and space constraints), I will not further break down the differences here.

23 On GATT within the larger institutional context of the American-made world order post-World War II, see, for example, G. John Ikenberry, *After Victory: Institutions, Strategic Restraint, and the Rebuilding of Order After Major Wars* (Princeton: Princeton University Press, 2000); G. John Ikenberry, *Liberal Leviathan: The Origins, Crisis, and Transformation of the American World Order* (Princeton: Princeton University Press, 2011); John Gerard Ruggie, "International Regimes, Transactions, and Change: Embedded Liberalism in the Postwar Economic Order," *International Organization*, 36:2 (1982), 379–415.

24 On "regularized intergovernmentalism," see Ulrich Krotz, "Regularized Intergovernmentalism: France–Germany and Beyond (1963–2009)," *Foreign Policy Analysis*, 6:2 (2010), 147–185. Intergovernmentalist theories of European integration include Moravcsik, *The Choice for Europe*; Christopher J. Bickerton, Dermot Hodson and Uwe Puetter (eds.), *The New Intergovernmentalism: States and Supranational Actors in the Post-Maastricht Era* (Oxford: Oxford University Press, 2015).

25 For basic work on non-material factors in international relations, see Emanuel Adler, "Seizing the Middle Ground: Constructivism in World Politics," *European Journal of International Relations*, 3:3 (1997), 319–363; Friedrich V. Kratochwil, *Rules, Norms, and Decisions: On the Conditions of Practical and Legal Reasoning in International Relations and Domestic Affairs* (Cambridge: Cambridge University Press, 1989); John Gerard Ruggie, "What Makes the World Hang Together? Neo-Utilitarianism and the Social Constructivist Challenge," *International Organization*, 52:4 (1998), 855–885.

26 On such historically rooted domestic construction, not least for the period covered here, see Krotz, *History and Foreign Policy*; along similar lines, Ulrich Krotz and James Sperling, "The European Security Order between American Hegemony and French Independence," *European Security*, 20:3 (2011), 305–335.

27 Similarly, Franco–German reconciliation and cooperation was appealing for instrumental reasons, yet is hardly reducible to just these. For the main building block of Franco–German bilateralilsm, see Krotz and Schild, *Shaping Europe*.

28 On social structures generated through interaction thus understood, see Wendt, *Social Theory of International Politics*; Alexander Wendt, "Anarchy Is What States Make of It: The Social Construction of Power Politics," *International Organization*, 46:2, 391–425; Alexander Wendt, "Collective Identity Formation and the International State," *American Political Science Review*, 88:2 (1994), 384–396; Anthony Giddens, *The Constitution of Society: Outline of the Theory of Structuration* (Cambridge: Polity, 1984); Peter J. Katzenstein (ed.), *The Culture of National Security: Norms and Identity in World Politics* (New York: Columbia University Press, 1996).

29 Hans J. Morgenthau, *Politics Among Nations: The Struggle for Power and Peace* (New York: Knopf, 1948); Waltz, *Theory of International Politics*; William C. Wohlforth, "Realism," in Chris Reus-Smit and Duncan Snidal (eds.), *The Oxford Handbook of International Relations* (Oxford: Oxford University Press, 2008), 131–149; Colin Elman and Michael A. Jensen (eds.), *The Realism Reader* (New York: Routledge).

30 Richard A. Matthew and Mark W. Zacher, "Liberal International Theory: Common Threads, Divergent Strands," in Charles Kegley (ed.), *Controversies in International Relations Theory: Realism and the Neo-Liberal Challenge* (New York: St. Martin's Press, 1995), 107–150; Moravcsik, "Taking Preferences Seriously."

31 More indirectly perhaps, the historical findings of the chapters in this volume also connect to IR writings on the emergence (and consolidation or decay) of

international actors. Generally see Lars-Erik Cederman, *Emergent Actors in World Politics: How States and Nations Develop and Dissolve* (Princeton: Princeton University Press, 1997). On the historical rise and consolidation of the nation-state among other actors and units, see Karl W. Deutsch, *Nationalism and its Alternatives* (New York: Alfred A. Knopf, 1969); Hendrik Spruyt, *The Sovereign State and Its Competitors: An Analysis of Systems Change* (Princeton: Princeton University Press, 1994). On the rise of international organizations and transnational actors, see, for example, Thomas Risse-Kappen (ed.), *Bringing Transnational Relations Back In: Non-State Actors, Domestic Structures and International Institutions* (Cambridge: Cambridge University Press, 1995). On the EU specifically, see Ulrich Krotz, "Momentum and Impediments: Why Europe Won't Emerge as a Full Political Actor on the World Stage Soon," *Journal of Common Market Studies*, 47:3 (2009), 555–578.

32   The terms in the literature denoting the EC taking on aspects of its own agency include "actorness," "actorhood," "actorship," and "international personality." In this volume we use all of them interchangeably.

33   On different perspectives of EU grand strategy, see Pascal Vennesson, "Competing Visions for the European Union Grand Strategy," *European Foreign Affairs Review*, 15:1 (2010), 57–75.

34   For learning in international organizations and international affairs more generally, see Karl W. Deutsch, *The Nerves of Government: Models of Political Communication and Control* (New York: Free Press, 1966); Ernst B. Haas, *When Knowledge Is Power: Three Models of Change in International Organizations* (Berkeley: University of California Press, 1990).

35   On "regularized intergovernmentalism" generally, see Krotz, "Regularized Intergovernmentalism."

36   François Duchêne, "Europe's Role in World Peace," in Richard Mayne (ed.), *Europe Tomorrow: Sixteen Europeans Look Ahead* (London: Fontana, 1972), 32–47; François Duchêne, "The European Community and the Uncertainties of Interdependence," in Max Kohnstamm and Wolfgang Hager (eds.), *A Nation Writ Large? Foreign Policy Problems before the European Community* (Basingstoke: Palgrave Macmillan, 1973), 1–21; Hedley Bull, "Civilian Power Europe: A Contradiction in Terms?," *Journal of Common Market Studies*, 21:2 (1982), 149–170.

37   The number of adjectives describing the EU's role in world politics has proliferated. In addition to the three mentioned here, the list also includes "ethical" and "small" power Europe, "peace power" (*Friedensmacht*), "quiet" (super)power, "ambiguous" power, "good" international citizen, and "silent global player". Lisbeth Aggestam, "Introduction: Ethical Power Europe?" *International Affairs*, 84:1 (2008), 1–11; Tim Dunne, "Good Citizen Europe," *International Affairs*, 84:1 (2008), 13–28; Michèle Knodt and Sebastiaan Princen, "Introduction: Puzzles and Prospects in Theorizing the EU's External Relations," in Michèle Knodt and Sebastiaan Princen (eds.), *Understanding the European Union's External Relations* (London: Routledge, 2003), 1–16; Hanns W. Maull, "Europe and the New Balance of Global Power," *International Affairs*, 81:4 (2005), 775–799; Andrew Moravcsik, "Europe: The Quiet Superpower," *French Politics*, 7:3/4 (2009), 403–422; Asle Toje, *The European Union as a Small Power: After the Post-Cold War* (Basingstoke: Palgrave Macmillan, 2010); Asle Toje, "The European Union as a Small Power," *Journal of Common Market Studies*, 49:1 (2011), 43–60.

38   On "market power Europe," see Chad Damro, "Market Power Europe," *Journal of European Public Policy*, 19:5 (2012), 682–699; Chad Damro, "Market Power Europe:

Exploring a Dynamic Conceptual Framework," *Journal of European Public Policy*, 22:9 (2015), 1336–1354.

39 See, for example Damro "Market Power Europe," 686; Damro "Market Power Europe: Exploring a Dynamic Conceptual Framework," 1339.

40 Damro, "Market Power Europe," 682.

41 Damro, "Market Power Europe: Exploring a Dynamic Conceptual Framework," 1336.

42 Ian Manners, "The Normative Ethics of the European Union," *International Affairs*, 84:1 (2008), 45–60, here 66. For basic formulations and discussions, also see Ian Manners, "Normative Power Europe: A Contradiction in Terms?" *Journal of Common Market Studies*, 40:2 (2002), 235–258; Richard Whitman (ed.), *Normative Power Europe: Empirical and Theoretical Perspectives* (Basingstoke: Palgrave Macmillan, 2011); Helene Sjursen, "The EU as a 'Normative' Power: How Can This Be?" *Journal of European Public Policy*, 13:2 (2006), 235–251. For critiques of the notion of normative power Europe, see Adrian Hyde-Price, "'Normative' Power Europe: A Realist Critique," *Journal of European Public Policy*, 13:2 (2006), 217–234; Adrian Hyde-Price, "A 'Tragic Actor'? A Realist Perspective on 'Ethical Power Europe'," *International Affairs*, 84:1 (2008), 29–44.

43 Arnold Wolfers, *Discord and Collaboration: Essays on International Politics* (Baltimore: Johns Hopkins University Press, 1962), 67–80.

44 On "civilian" or "civilizing" power Europe, note Duchêne, "Europe's Role in World Peace"; Duchêne, "The European Community and the Uncertainties of Interdependence"; Richard Whitman, *From Civilian Power to Superpower? The International Identity of the European Union* (Basingstoke: Palgrave Macmillan, 1998). For more recent overviews and reviews, see Karen E. Smith, "The End of Civilian Power EU: A Welcome Demise or Cause for Concern?" *International Spectator*, 35:2 (2000), 11–28; Jan Orbie, "Civilian Power Europe: Review of the Original and Current Debates (Review Essay)," *Cooperation and Conflict*, 41:1 (2006), 123–128. Maull calls the EU a civilian "force" rather than a civilian "power." Maull, "Europe and the New Balance of Global Power". For critiques of the notion, see Bull, "Civilian Power Europe"; Mark A. Pollack, "Living in a Material World: A Critique of 'Normative Power Europe'," in Hubert Zimmermann and Andreas Dür (eds.), *Key Controversies in European Integration* (Basingstoke: Palgrave Macmillan, 2012), 199–204.

45 For more detailed discussions than possible here, note especially Whitman, *From Civilian Power to Superpower?*; Smith, "The End of Civilian Power EU"; Orbie, "Civilian Power Europe"; Mario Telò, *Europe: A Civilian Power?* (Basingstoke: Palgrave Macmillan, 2005).

46 On the rise of a European foreign and security policy from various theoretical perspectives, see Ulrich Krotz and Richard Maher, "International Relations Theory and the Rise of European Foreign and Security Policy," *World Politics*, 63:3 (2011), 548–579; for a skeptical view on the prospects for Europe swiftly developing into a fully developed international political actor, see Krotz, "Momentum and Impediments."

47 Waltz, *Theory of International Politics*; Mearsheimer, *The Tragedy of Great Power Politics*.

48 Steven E. Lobell, Norrin M. Ripsman and Jeffrey W. Taliaferro (eds.), *Neoclassical Realism, the State, and Foreign Policy* (Cambridge: Cambridge University Press, 2009); Norrin M. Ripsman, Jeffrey W. Taliaferro and Steven E. Lobell, *Neoclassical Realist Theory of International Politics* (Oxford: Oxford University Press, 2016).

49   Morgenthau, *Politics Among Nations*; Aron, *Paix et guerre*; Hoffmann, "Obstinate or Obsolete?"; Jonathan Kirshner, "The Tragedy of Offensive Realism: Classical Realism and the Rise of China," *European Journal of International Relations*, 18:1 (2012), 53–75.

50   Robert O. Keohane, *After Hegemony: Cooperation and Discord in the World Political Economy* (Princeton: Princeton University Press, 1984); Koremenos, Lipson and Snidal (eds.), "Rational Choice of International Institutions"; Lisa L. Martin and Beth A. Simmons (eds.), *International Institutions* (Cambridge: MIT Press, 2001).

51   Zacher and Matthew, "Liberal International Theory"; Haas, *The Uniting of Europe*; Moravcsik, *The Choice for Europe*; Daniel H. Deudney, *Bounding Power: Republican Security Theory from the Polis to the Global Village* (Princeton: Princeton University Press, 2006).

52   Wendt, *Social Theory of International Politics*.

53   Katzenstein (ed.), *The Culture of National Security*; Jeffrey T. Checkel (ed.), *International Institutions and Socialization in Europe* (Cambridge: Cambridge University Press, 2007); Emanuel Adler and Vincent Pouliot (eds.), *International Practices* (Cambridge: Cambridge University Press, 2011).

54   Rudra Sil and Peter J. Katzenstein, *Beyond Paradigms: Analytic Eclecticism in the Study of World Politics* (Basingstoke: Palgrave Macmillan, 2010).

Index

Please note the acronym EC is used for European Community and EU for European Union in subheadings.